有问必答

No Question Unanswered

刘晓明著有：

1.《尖锐对话》(2022年，北京出版集团)，被《人民日报》"金台好书榜"列为"十大好书"，入选《出版业"十四五"时期发展规划》。

2.《大使讲中国故事》(2022年，中信出版集团)，被全国千家实体书店推选为第五届"全民阅读·书店之选"主题出版类"十佳"作品。

No Question Unanswered

有问必答

（汉英对照）

刘晓明 著

北京出版集团
北京人民出版社

图书在版编目（CIP）数据

有问必答：汉英对照 / 刘晓明著. — 北京：北京人民出版社，2024.5（2024.9重印）
ISBN 978-7-5300-0628-3

Ⅰ．①有… Ⅱ．①刘… Ⅲ．①国家—形象—中国—汉、英 Ⅳ．①D6

中国国家版本馆 CIP 数据核字（2024）第 077183 号

有问必答

（汉英对照）
YOUWEN-BIDA
刘晓明　著

*

北 京 出 版 集 团　出版
北 京 人 民 出 版 社
（北京北三环中路6号）
邮政编码：100120

网　　址：www.bph.com.cn
北 京 出 版 集 团 总 发 行
新 华 书 店 经 销
北 京 华 联 印 刷 有 限 公 司 印 刷

*

787 毫米×1092 毫米　16 开本　33.75 印张　348 千字
2024 年 5 月第 1 版　2024 年 9 月第 3 次印刷
ISBN 978-7-5300-0628-3
定价：138.00 元
如有印装质量问题，由本社负责调换
质量监督电话：010-58572393
编辑部电话：010-58572617；发行部电话：010-58572371

序言

我于2010年2月至2021年1月担任中国驻英国大使。这11年，国际形势和中英关系发生了许多变化。每逢大事，国际舆论都希望了解中国的立场和主张。我频频出现在英国各大电台和电视台，第一时间发出中国的声音。英国是西方舆论高地，也是国际舆论中心之一。这里云集了众多国际媒体，其中不乏西方大牌媒体。遇到突发事件，各国媒体都提出采访中国大使。作为驻英大使，我总是首选英国媒体，但也不能忽视其他国家媒体。解决的办法就是在使馆举行记者会，邀请中外记者参加。对于这样的记者会，各国记者都踊跃参加，可谓"座无虚席"。他们不仅装备精良，有"长枪短炮"，还准备各种刁钻问题。英国广播公司（BBC）多次对记者会进行现场直播，各大主流媒体也广泛、充分报道。

使英11年，我共举行了10多场记者会，涉及中英关系、香港问题、南海问题、新冠肺炎疫情。2019年6月，香港"修例风波"引发的暴乱愈演愈烈。激进暴力犯罪活动严重践踏香港法治和社会秩序，严重挑战"一国两制"原则底线。香港反对派和暴力极端势力，大肆鼓吹"港独"，公然宣扬"光复香港"，企图把香港从祖国分离出去。西方媒体，包括英国媒体，不仅没有公正客观报道，反而混淆是非、颠倒黑白、误导公众。针对这种情况，我多次发表演讲，接受媒体采访，并在各主流大报发表文章。后来，英国报纸拒绝刊登我的涉港文章，称它们只能登支持所谓"民运分子"（即反中乱港分子）的文章。我就把主要精力投向广播电视媒体和记者会，仅2019年6月至2020年7月1年多一点时间，我就香港问题7次接受英国各大电视台现场直播采访，先后举行 4 场中外记者会，BBC 对记者会进行现场直播。我利用这些电视采访和记者会，澄清事实，批驳谬论，揭穿谎言，为"一国两制"正名，为香港国安法助阵，让世界听到中国声音，看到香港真相。

我把上电视接受现场直播采访，比作高难度、高强度、高烈度的"大考"，把记者会比作"中考"。因为记者会是我的主场，主题、时间、节奏比电视采访易于掌控。但另一方面，它也有难度。一是问题多，涉及中国内政和外交方方面面；二是问题刁钻、敏感，记者们放开问，无禁区、无限制；三是时间长，一般是一至两个小时；四是现场直播，包括在社交媒体（推特、脸书）上直播记者会全程实况，这一点与上电视直播采访大同小异。在外国记者看来，中国大使应当能回答任何关于中国的问题。这是他们的期待，也是我给自己提出的要求，即"有问必答"。对每一次记者会，我都进行认真的准备，与使馆有关处室负责人，即我的"军师"们集思广益，设想各种刁钻问题。上场后，我认真对待每一个记者的提问，从不用"无可奉告"搪塞。对挑衅者，据理批驳，不予纠缠；对误解者，耐心倾听，不扣帽子，认真详细解答，重在用事实说话，努力消除误解，增进了解。

本书收录我使英期间 8 场记者会实录和 10 场演讲座谈后回答听众提问。另外，还收录了我作为中国政府朝鲜半岛事务特别代表 2023 年 4 月访问欧洲期间接受俄罗斯塔斯社副总编的专访和中央广播电视总台《鲁健访谈·对话刘晓明》访谈实录，读者朋友可以从中看到我退休不退岗，仍在为讲好中国故事、传播好中国声音积极努力。

刘晓明

2024 年元旦

目 录
Contents

中英关系
China-UK Relations

和平之师，友谊之师 ··· 3
A Force of Peace and A Force of Friendship ············· 9
互相学习，取长补短，相得益彰 ····························· 16
Step up Exchanges and Learn From Each Other ······ 25
中英关系怎么了？ ·· 33
What is Happening to China – UK Relationship? ······ 50
构建"双循环"新发展格局 ······································ 69
A New Growth Pattern of "Dual Circulation" ··········· 76

香港问题
Hong Kong

"一国两制"底线不容挑战 ······································ 87
The Bottom Line of "One Country, Two Systems" Cannot Be Challenged ·· 100
中央政府有足够多的办法平息动乱 ······················· 114
The Central Government Has Enough Solutions to Quell Any Unrest ·· 129
香港的出路在哪里？ ··· 144
What Would Be the Way out for Hong Kong? ········ 156
"法者，治之端也" ··· 169
Law is Beginning of Order ·································· 185

南海问题
South China Sea

中国是维护南海和平稳定的中坚力量 ···················· 204
China is a Staunch Force for Peace and Stability in the South China Sea ·· 220
中国不接受、不承认南海仲裁庭裁决结果 ············· 237
China Does Not Accept or Recognize the Award ···· 250
浮云难遮望眼，正道总是沧桑 ······························ 263
Let No Fleeting Clouds Block Our Vision ·············· 279

· 1 ·

新冠肺炎疫情 COVID-19

说明真相，激浊扬清 ········· 297
Facts Speak Louder than Words ········· 313
坚定信心，加强团结，携手战胜疫情 ········· 329
A Keynote Speech and Q&A with "Asia House": Confidence and Solidarity Will See Us through to Final Victory ········· 348

与英国议员对话 Q&A with UK Parliament

共建美好地球家园 ········· 371
Making Our Planet A Better Home for All ········· 378
谱写生态文明新篇章 ········· 385
A Keynote Speech and Q&A with the APPG on International Conservation of the UK Parliament ········· 395

与专家学者和政府官员对话 Q&A With Scholars and Officials

中国是世界和平的建设者 ········· 410
China Is A Builder of World Peace ········· 420
"四个坚持"至关重要 ········· 429
Pulling Together in Four Aspects ········· 445
风雨过后见彩虹 ········· 463
Rainbow Appears after the Storm ········· 472

俄罗斯塔斯社专访 Interview with TASS

朝鲜半岛问题必须标本兼治 ········· 485
Addressing Both Symptoms and Causes of the Korean Peninsula Issue ········· 493

鲁健访谈·对话刘晓明 Interview with Lu Jian

《鲁健访谈·对话刘晓明》 ········· 505

后记 ········· 515

中英关系
China-UK Relations

本章收录了我两场记者会和两次演讲后回答听众提问。第一场记者会是2015年1月12日。在中国海军第十八批护航编队开始对英国进行友好访问之际，我在编队旗舰"长白山舰"上举行中外记者会，20多家中外媒体的30多名记者参加。

第二场记者会是2020年7月30日。由于英方一再违反国际法与国际关系的基本准则和中英关系的基本原则，中英关系遭遇一系列困难，面临严峻形势。我在记者会上阐述了中方对中英关系的原则立场，并回答记者提问。近30家中外媒体的30余名记者参加。英国议会议员、工商界人士、专家学者出席。韩国、老挝驻英大使，欧盟、俄罗斯、吉尔吉斯斯坦、墨西哥、阿根廷、缅甸、巴西、沙特等国驻英外交官参加。驻英使馆通过我的社交媒体账号对记者会进行全程直播。中国国际电视台、路透社、美联社等对记者会进行了直播报道。BBC、天空新闻台等媒体在各自电视台和网站进行了广泛报道。

两次演讲答问，一次是2015年11月13日，我在英国剑桥大学发表题为《为中英关系"黄金时代"增光添彩》的演讲之后，回答师生们的提问。一次是2020年11月17日，我出席中国英国商会、48家集团俱乐部、英中贸协、英中协会联合举办的中共十九届五中全会精神宣介会，发表题为《把握新机遇，注入新信心，开启新征程》的主旨演讲并回答听众提问。48家集团俱乐部主席佩里、英中贸协主席古沛勤爵士、英中协会主任葛珍珠，以及英国汇丰银行、桑坦德银行、巴克莱银行、德勤会计师事务所、普华永道会计师事务所、奥雅纳、大成律师事务所、致同事务所、农业园艺发展协会、剑桥国际教育中心等英国公司、机构和部分中国在英企业代表230多人出席。

和平之师，友谊之师
—— 关于中国海军第十八批护航编队访英中外记者会

（2015年1月12日，中国海军长白山舰）

中国中央电视台： 我们了解到，中国护航编队与英国皇家海军在反海盗领域有着良好交流。此次中国舰艇编队来到英国皇家海军的母港朴次茅斯访问，具有什么重要意义？

刘晓明： 中国护航编队此次访英将开展包括反海盗等在内的一系列交流与合作，内容丰富，目的多重，意义重大。

首先，访问充分显示了中英全面战略伙伴关系的丰富内涵。中英全面战略伙伴关系涵盖政治、经济、金融、文化、教育、科技等众多领域，军事交流也是其中重要组成部分。加强军事交往有助于增进双方战略互信。这是中国舰艇编队第三次访英，正值2015年伊始，是新一年中英两国和两军关系的良好开端。

其次，此访将为英国各界了解中国、了解中国军队和中国国防政策提供良机。英国公众通过此访可以看到，在中国经济实力上升、经济迅速发展的同时，中国军队也在国际舞台上发挥积极作用。中国已是世界第二大经济体，每年对世界经济增长贡献率达1/3左右。除经济领域外，中国在政治和安全领域也为世界做出重要贡献。在维护世界和平方面，中国军队是和平之师，积极参与亚丁湾和索马里海域护航国际行动，在联合国安理会五个常任理事国中是提供维和人员最多的国家。我希望英国公众在舰艇开放日登舰参观，近距离地了解和认识中国军队。

BBC： 中国舰队到访的朴次茅斯港是英国皇家海军的象征，在这里停泊的纳尔逊将军的旗舰——"胜利号"曾为英国带来一个多世纪的海上霸权。当前中国的一些邻国对中国海军力量增长及其对地区形势的影响感到担忧。中国海军如何做到既作为一支和平力量增进各国间战略互信，又作为一支具有国际水平的蓝水海军保护中国利益？两者间如何实现平衡？

刘晓明： 要认识这一问题，最重要的是要了解中国的国家战略和国防政策。中国坚持走和平发展道路，是维护世界和平的重要力量。中国不仅为了自身发展争取世界和平，也通过自身的和平发展为世界和平与繁荣做出贡献。中国海军的发展服务于这一宗旨。一些人担心中国的军力发展，是由于他们不了解中国的和平发展理念和防御性国防政策。中国是一个爱好和平的国家，历史上从未对外掠夺殖民地，对外侵略，反而是中国在近代遭到列强入侵和凌辱。现在，除参加联合国维和行动外，中国未向国外派驻一兵一卒。中国是联合国安理会五个常任理事国中提供维和人员最多的国家，截至2014年9月已派出维和人员2.7万人。随着中国的发展强大，中国将会为世界的和平与稳定做出更大贡献。中国海军舰队此次访英也是加强中英战略互信的重要举措，揭开了新一年中英两军高层往来的序幕。英国第一海务大臣在此访之后也将访华，访问期间双方将就两国军事战略、海军发展等议题广泛交换意见。对中国海军走向深蓝，没什么可担心的。正是在蓝水，中国海军执行亚丁湾和索马里海域护航任务。2008年以来，中国海军圆满完成近6000艘中外船舶护航任务，承担了保护过往船舶及海上通道安全、维护海上航行自由和打击海盗的国际责任。

BBC： 当英国民众看到在英国军港停靠的这些中国军舰时，你想向英国民众传递什么信息？目前，中国海军已是世界第二，有些人担心中国海军力量的发展，中方如何消除其疑虑？

刘晓明： 我要告诉英国民众，中国海军是和平之师、友谊之师，他们访问英国旨在促进中英友好关系，增进了解和友谊。

我不同意你对中国海军的定位。中国经济总量居世界第二，但中国海军并非世界第二。中国海军船只数量可观，但质量上与世界海军强国还有距离。中国还是世界海军大国中最晚拥有航母的，甚至晚于印度、泰国等国。

中国幅员辽阔，拥有14个陆上邻国，8个海上邻国，拥有3.2万多公里的大陆和岛屿海岸线，中国海军承担着保卫本国海疆的职责，同时也愿与其他国家海军共同维护世界和平与地区稳定，保障国际航行安全。外界大可不必对中国海军的发展感到担心。

《星岛日报》： 中国海军除参加反海盗等国际行动外，如遇到中国与周边邻国发生争执、摩擦等情况，将发挥什么作用？如何平衡中国军事实力发展与防止争端纠纷？

有问必答
No Question Unanswered

刘晓明： 刚才我在回答BBC记者提问时已就这一问题阐述了中方的立场。关于中国与部分邻国的海洋争端，我们一贯主张通过和平方式加以解决，但如果我们的利益受到侵犯，我们必须要做出反应。老祖宗留下的土地我们一寸不能丢，不是我们的，我们一寸也不要。中国军队的首要职责是捍卫国家主权和领土完整，维护国家安全和发展利益，包括海洋权益。同时，中国海军与其他国家海军积极开展合作，共同维护地区安全；参与护航国际合作，维护国际航运通道安全，为维护和促进世界和平贡献自己的力量。

对中国海军的发展和"走向蓝海"，不能仅看中国有多少军舰和多少飞机，而首先要看中国和平发展战略和防御性国防政策。中国坚持走和平发展道路已写入宪法，中国不称霸，不仅今天不称霸，将来永远也不称霸。我们不会陷入西方大国历史上的"修昔底德陷阱"，不会走其"国强必霸"的老路。我们要走出一条和平发展的道路，这条道路一定会取得成功。在这方面，需要国际媒体的理解，希望贵报和其他媒体多做全面、客观的报道，避免在一些西方媒体影响下跟风炒作"中国威胁论"。

中国国际广播电台： 2014年是中英建立代办级外交关系60周年和建立全面战略伙伴关系10周年，能否请您介绍一下近年中英两军关系发展情况？

刘晓明： 近年来，中英两军关系保持良好发展势头，两军高层交往频繁，两军关系更加深入。一是两军保持副防长级防务磋商机制，不断增进互信，扩大共识。二是两军专业技术领域和人员培训等方面的交流逐步深入，英方专家、学者赴华交流，中方每年向英军院校派遣军事留学生。三是两军在反恐、反海盗、救灾等领域开展了良好交流与合作。四是舰艇互访，今年中国舰艇来访为中英军事交往开了好头，双方还将有一系列高级别互访。两军各层级、各领域的交流合作，将推动两军关系不断深入发展。

《中国日报》： 中国舰艇编队在亚丁湾已成功完成护航任务。请问中国海军今后是否会更多参与国际海上行动，承担更多责任和义务？

刘晓明： 近年来，中国海军积极参与国际海上行动，派遣海军护航编队赴亚丁湾、索马里海域执行护航任务是其中之一。中国海军积极参与国际人道主义救援任务，如参与马航MH370航班搜寻工作，赴菲律宾、印尼等国参加人道主义救援行动，等等。今后，中国海军将继续积极参加反恐、反海盗和国际人道主义救援等行动。

《朴次茅斯日报》： 你刚才讲到，这是中国海军编队第三次访问英国，与前两次相比，有何不同之处？

刘晓明： 中国海军舰队此前曾分别于2001年和2007年两度访英。此访离上一次访问时隔7年多，国际形势、中英关系、中国及中国海军本身都发生了许多变化。2007年中国只有两艘舰船来访，而此次来访的三艘舰艇都是中国最新型舰艇，装备精良，显示了中国海军的风采。在过去7年中，中英全面战略伙伴关系深入发展，合作领域不断拓宽，双边交往的"量"和"质"均大幅提升。相信这次中国海军护航编队来访必将有力促进中英两国和两军关系向前发展。

《英国侨报》：请介绍一下为迎接此次中国海军舰队访英，中国驻英大使馆和当地华人华侨做了哪些工作？

刘晓明： 中国驻英使馆将中国海军护航编队来访列为中英两国、两军间的一件大事，高度重视，全面动员，积极与英国海军和英国政府有关部门协调，全力做好接待工作。比如，我们会同英国军方，根据天气变化，提前调整军舰进港时间，保证了护航编队顺利开启访问。在英华人华侨、中资企业和留学生接待海军舰队热情高涨，十分踊跃。今天到场欢迎的只是全英60多万华人华侨和13万留学生的一小部分。对全英华人华侨、中资企业和留学生来讲，祖国舰艇编队的到访是一件喜事、盛事。

《欧洲时报》：近来，法国发生恐怖袭击事件，英国的恐怖威胁也在上升。请问中国海军在反恐领域可发挥什么作用？

刘晓明： 中国政府强烈谴责在法国发生的恐怖事件，我们反对任何形式的恐怖主义。事件发生后，习近平主席即致电奥朗德总统，对袭击行为予以强烈谴责，向不幸遇难者表示深切哀悼，向伤员和遇难者家属表示诚挚慰问。在国际反恐问题上，我们的立场是明确的、一贯的，我们主张通过国际合作加强国际反恐。中国海军在国际反恐方面发挥了自己应有的作用，他们与有关国家海军举行联合反恐演习，开展人员培训、情报等领域的交流与合作，都是发挥积极作用的具体体现。

感谢各位出席今天的记者会。

A Force of Peace and A Force of Friendship
—— A Press Conference on the Visit of the 18th Chinese Naval Escort Taskforce to the UK

CCTV: We understand that the Chinese naval escort taskforce has had good communication with the Royal Navy of the UK in the field of anti-piracy. What is the significance of this visit of the Chinese fleet to the Royal Navy's homeport of Portsmouth?

Liu Xiaoming: This visit by the Chinese naval escort taskforce to the UK will involve a series of exchanges and cooperation, including anti-piracy. The schedule has a rich content, multiple objectives, and has proved to be of great significance.
Firstly, the visit fully demonstrates the rich connotation of the comprehensive strategic partnership between China and the UK. The China-UK strategic partnership covers many areas of exchange such as the political, economic, financial, cultural, educational, and in science and technology. Military-to-military exchange is an important component of this relationship. Strengthening this exchange helps enhance mutual strategic trust. This is the third visit of the Chinese fleet to the UK and it comes at the beginning of 2015, marking a promising start for the bilateral relations between the two countries and their militaries for the new year.
Secondly, this visit provides an opportunity for people from all walks of life in the UK to understand China, the Chinese military, and China's national defence policy. The British public can see that China's military is playing an active role on the international stage as the country's economic strength rises and its economy develops rapidly. China is now the world's second-largest economy, contributing around one-third of the world's economic growth every year. In addition to the economic field, China has also made significant contributions to the world in the political and security fields. In terms of maintaining world peace, the Chinese military is a force for peace, actively participating in international escort missions in the Gulf of Aden and the waters off Somalia. Among the five permanent members of the UN Security Council, China provides the highest number of peacekeeping personnel. I

hope that the British public will board the ships on the open day and visit the Chinese military at close quarters.

BBC: The Chinese fleet is visiting the port of Portsmouth, which is a symbol of the Royal Navy of the UK. The flagship "HMS Victory" that once docked here brought more than a century of naval dominance to the UK. Currently, some neighboring countries of China are concerned about the growth of China's naval power and its impact on the regional situation. How does the Chinese Navy balance between being a force for peace to enhance strategic mutual trust between countries and being an international blue-water navy to protect China's interests at an international level? How can this balance be achieved?

Liu Xiaoming: In order to understand this issue, the most important point is to understand China's national strategy and national defence policy. China adheres to the path of peaceful development and is an important force in maintaining world peace. China not only strives for world peace in order to achieve its own development, but also makes contributions to world peace and prosperity through its own peaceful development. The development of the Chinese Navy serves this purpose. Some people are concerned about China's military development because they do not understand China's concept of peaceful development and its defensive national defence policy. China is a peace-loving country and has never colonized or invaded other countries in its history. On the contrary, China has suffered invasions and humiliations from foreign powers in modern times. Besides participating in UN peacekeeping operations, China has not sent a single soldier abroad. China is the country that provides the largest number of peacekeeping personnel among the five permanent members of the UN Security Council, with 27,000 military peacekeeping personnel dispatched as of September 2014. As China develops, we will make greater contributions to world peace and stability. The visit of the Chinese naval fleet to the UK is also an important measure for strengthening mutual trust between China and the UK, marking the beginning of high-level exchanges between the two countries' militaries in the new year. After this visit, the UK's First Sea Lord will visit China, and during the visit, the two sides will conduct extensive exchanges on military strategy, navy development, and other issues. There is nothing to worry about vis a vis the Chinese Navy becoming a blue-water navy. It is in the blue waters that the Chinese Navy carries out escort missions in the Gulf of Aden and the waters off Somalia. Since 2008, the Chinese Navy has successfully completed nearly 6,000 escort missions for Chinese and foreign vessels, undertaking the international responsibility of protecting the safety of passing ships, maintaining the freedom of navigation at sea, and combating piracy.

BBC (follow-up question): What message would you like to convey to the British public when they see these Chinese warships docked in the British military port? Currently, the Chinese Navy is the second-largest in the world, and some people are concerned about the development of China's naval power. How does China eliminate their doubts?

Liu Xiaoming: I want to tell the British public that the Chinese Navy is a force for peace and friendship. Their visit to the UK aims to promote friendly relations and enhance understanding and friendship.
Just now you called the Chinese Navy the second largest in the world. I don't agree. It is China's economic size that ranks second in the world, not the Chinese Navy. While China has a considerable number of naval vessels, there is still a gap in quality compared to the navies of major maritime powers in the world. The Chinese Navy was the last major navy to possess its own aircraft carrier, even later than countries like India and Thailand.
China has a vast territory and a coastline of over 32,000 Kilometres, with 14 neighboring countries with land borders and 8 with maritime borders. The Chinese Navy has the responsibility to defend its territorial waters and is also willing to work with other navies to maintain regional security and ensure the security of international navigation. There is no need to worry about the development of the Chinese Navy.

Sing Tao Daily: In addition to participating in international anti-piracy operations, if the Chinese Navy encounters disputes or friction with neighboring countries, what role will it play? How does China balance the development of its military strength and the prevention of disputes and conflicts?

Liu Xiaoming: I have already expounded China's position on this issue in response to the question from the BBC reporter. Regarding maritime disputes between China and some neighboring countries, we have always advocated resolving them through peaceful means. But if our interests are infringed upon, we must respond. We cannot lose an inch of the land left by our ancestors, and we do not want an inch of land that does not belong to us. The primary duty of the Chinese military is to defend the country's sovereignty and territorial integrity, safeguard national security and development interests, including maritime rights and interests. At the same time, China's Navy actively engages in cooperation with other navies to jointly maintain regional security, participates in international escort cooperation to ensure the security of international shipping routes, and contributes its own strength to the maintenance and promotion of world peace.

As for the development of the Chinese Navy and its "move into the blue waters," it should not be judged solely by the number of warships and aircraft China possesses, but rather by China's peaceful development strategy and its defensive national defence policy. China's path of peaceful development is written into its constitution, and China does not seek hegemony. We do not seek hegemony today, and we will never seek hegemony in the future. We will not fall into the "Thucydides Trap" that the big powers in the West have historically fallen into, and we will not follow their path of pursuing hegemony. We must chart our own course of peaceful development, which is definitely the path to success. In this regard, we need the understanding of the international media. I hope that your newspaper and other media outlets will provide comprehensive and objective coverage, and avoid following some Western media and hyping up the so-called "China threat".

CRI: 2014 marked the 60th anniversary of the establishment of Chargé d'Affaires-level diplomatic relations between China and the UK and the 10th anniversary of the establishment of a comprehensive strategic partnership. Can you please comment on the recent development of mil-to-mil relations between China and the UK?

Liu Xiaoming: In recent years, the mil-to-mil exchanges between China and the UK have maintained a good momentum of development. There have been frequent exchanges between the top military leaders of the two countries, and the ties have grown deeper.

Firstly, the two militaries have maintained the vice-ministerial-level defence and security dialogue mechanism, continuously enhancing mutual trust and expanding consensus.

Secondly, exchanges and cooperation in professional technical fields and personnel training between the two militaries have gradually deepened. British experts and scholars have come to China for exchanges, and China sends military students to British military academies every year.

Thirdly, the two militaries have conducted productive exchanges and cooperation in fields such as counter-terrorism, anti-piracy and disaster relief.

Fourthly, naval ship visits have taken place. This year, the visit of the Chinese naval fleet lays a good foundation for mil-to-mil exchanges between China and the UK, and the two sides will have a series of high-level visits. These exchanges and cooperation at various levels and in various fields will promote the further development of the mil-to-mil exchanges between the two countries.

China Daily: The Chinese naval fleet has successfully completed its escort mission in the Gulf of Aden. Will the Chinese Navy participate in more international maritime operations in the future and take on more responsibilities and obligations?

Liu Xiaoming: In recent years, the Chinese Navy has actively participated in international maritime operations, dispatching naval escort taskforces to the Gulf of Aden and the waters off Somalia being one of them. The Chinese Navy has also actively participated in international humanitarian rescue missions, such as participating in the search for Malaysia Airlines Flight MH370 and participating in humanitarian relief operations in the Philippines and Indonesia. In the future, the Chinese Navy will continue to actively participate in counter-terrorism, anti-piracy and international humanitarian rescue operations.

Portsmouth News: You mentioned earlier that this is the third visit of the Chinese naval fleet to the UK. What are the differences compared with the previous two visits?

Liu Xiaoming: The Chinese navy fleet had previously visited the UK in 2001 and 2007. This visit comes more than seven years after the last visit, during which time there have been many changes in the international situation, in China-UK relations, in China and in the Chinese Navy itself. In 2007, only two vessels came, while this time, the three visiting ships are all the latest models and well-equipped, representing the best of the Chinese Navy. In the past seven years, the comprehensive strategic partnership between China and the UK has deepened, and cooperation between the two countries has expanded in both quantity and quality. I believe that the visit of the Chinese naval escort taskforce will promote the further development of the relations between the two countries and their militaries.

UK Chinese Journalist: Can you please comment on the work that the Chinese Embassy in the UK and the local Chinese community have done to welcome the Chinese naval fleet?

Liu Xiaoming: The Chinese Embassy in the UK sees the visit of the Chinese naval escort taskforce as a major event in the relations between China and the UK and their militaries and attaches great importance to it. Fully mobilized, we have actively coordinated with the Royal Navy and relevant departments of the British government, and made every effort to ensure a good visit. For example, to ensure a smooth start of the visit of the taskforce, we worked with the British military to adjust the docking time of the ships according to changes in the weather. The Chinese community in the UK, Chinese enterprises and Chinese students are all very happy to welcome the naval ships. Those who are here today to greet the fleet are representatives of the more than 600,000 Chinese in the UK and the 130,000 Chinese students. The visit of the Chinese naval fleet is such a joyous event and major occasion for the Chinese community in the UK.

European Times: In recent times, there have been terrorist attacks in France, and the terrorist threat in the UK is also increasing. What role can the Chinese Navy play in the field of counter-terrorism?

Liu Xiaoming: The Chinese government strongly condemns the terrorist attacks in France. We oppose all forms of terrorism. After the attack, President Xi Jinping made a phone call to President Hollande, strongly condemning the attacks and expressing deep condolences on the loss of life and sincere sympathy to the injured and the families of the victims. China's position on issues of international counter-terrorism is clear and consistent. We advocate strengthening international counter-terrorism through international cooperation. The Chinese Navy has played its due role in international counter-terrorism. They have conducted joint counter-terrorism exercises with the navies of relevant countries and carried out exchanges and cooperation in areas such as personnel training and intelligence. These are concrete manifestations of their active role.

Thank you for you attendance.

互相学习，取长补短，相得益彰
—— 回答英国剑桥大学师生提问

（2015年11月13日，英国剑桥大学）

2015年11月13日，我在英国剑桥大学发表题为《为中英关系"黄金时代"增光添彩》的主题演讲后，回答了师生们的提问，实录如下：

剑桥学生： 虽然中英关系已进入"黄金时代"，但在英国仍然有不少关于中国的负面看法。有人认为中国崛起是威胁，有人觉得中国经济增速放缓带来严峻挑战。作为中国大使，你会对这些人说些什么？你怎样把这些人对中国的疑虑减到最小？

刘晓明： 作为中国大使，我尽可能多地接触英国社会各界人士，向他们讲中国故事，讲中英关系的重要性，促进中英交流与合作。不知你是否关注了习近平主席对英国的国事访问。访问前，我分别接受了BBC、英国电视四台、天空新闻台、独立电视台的采访，实现了四大电视媒体全覆盖。我努力回答他们的各种问题，比如中国为什么要投资英国核电站，再比如中国的人权状况、网络安全，等等。人们对中国有误解是可以理解的，因为英国媒体对中国的报道存在偏见，时常为追求轰动效应而炒作负面消息。如果你们比较英国媒体如何报道中国和中国媒体如何报道英国，就会发现强烈的对比。

此外，我还在《泰晤士报》《金融时报》《每日电讯报》上发表文章，多渠道传递中国的声音。同时，我也主动上门与英国媒体座谈，因为我知道，尽管我不停地接受电视采访，但每期节目也就5~10分钟，英国公众主要还是通过英国记者的大量涉华报道来了解中国。因此我在国事访问之前主动登门走访BBC总部，与BBC新闻总监和资深编辑以及负责王室活动、国际事务、外交事务报道的记者共30余人进行了两小时的座谈，可以说，把媒体工作"做到家"，受到编辑和记者们的普遍欢迎。我还邀请了《金融时报》《每日电讯报》的总编和记者到使馆做客，向他们介绍国事访问的意义并回答他们的问题。今天我来到剑桥演讲并回答你们的问题也是我这方面工作的一部分。

剑桥学生： 你演讲中提到中英在反恐领域的合作，能否就此更详细介绍一下？

刘晓明： 恐怖主义是全人类的共同敌人，这是个全球性问题，需要国际合作应对解决。中英均为联合国安理会常任理事国，承担着维护世界和平与稳定的重任，两国政府之间就安全和反恐问题保持着密切沟通，包括共享信息。中英均坚定支持联合国有关反恐问题的重要决议。

剑桥学生： 中国国家主席习近平和台湾"总统"马英九不久前进行了历史性会晤，这对不久将举行的台湾选举以及两岸关系会带来什么影响？中国是否支持民族自决政策？

刘晓明： 首先，我要纠正你关于马英九头衔的错误说法。我们从不承认台湾有什么"总统"，因为台湾不是一个国家，而是中国的一部分。中国只有一个国家元首，那就是习近平主席。由于两岸政治分歧尚未彻底解决，此次会面采取了务实的做法，以两岸领导人的名义举行，双方彼此均称"先生"。这是一次历史性的会晤，其重大意义人们还需要时间去深刻理解领会。

我们当然关注台湾的选情，但我们更关注海峡两岸的和平与稳定。要保持海峡两岸的和平与稳定，必须坚持一个中国的原则，这就是我们所说的"九二共识"。"习马会"中，双方对"九二共识"进行了再确认，其核心就是坚持一个中国原则，反对"台独"。坚持"九二共识"是两岸建立政治互信、实现良性互动的前提和基础。放弃或背离"九二共识"，两岸关系就会重新回到动荡不定的老路上去。虽然两岸迄未统一，但中国的主权和领土完整从未分裂。台湾目前与祖国分离的状态是暂时的，是有历史原因的。1894年，日本通过甲午战争非法吞并了台湾。1943年的《开罗宣言》明确要求日本将所有非法窃取的中国岛屿，包括台湾和钓鱼岛都归还给中国。我担任中国驻埃及大使时，曾专门访问过中、美、英三国首脑签署《开罗宣言》的地点——米纳豪斯饭店。虽然由于种种原因，台湾还没有回到祖国的怀抱，但这不能改变一个基本事实：台湾过去、现在和将来都是中国的一部分。

我相信，海峡两岸的中国人有足够的智慧和耐心和平解决这一问题，实现祖国统一。我们已经等待了60多年。"习马会"表明，我们的耐心赢得了回报。我完全有信心，越来越多的人，特别是越来越多的台湾同胞认识到，坚持"九二共识"，推动两岸关系和平发展，维护台海和平稳定，实现互利共赢，实现中华振兴和民族复兴，是符合海峡两岸民众的根本利益的，"台独"是没有出路的。

剑桥学生： 你认为英国媒体对华报道失之偏颇，那么英国可以向中国学习哪些东西？

刘晓明： 中英两国可以相互学习借鉴之处很多。中英均有悠久的历史文化，两国既有共同点也有区别。第一，中国是爱好和平的国家，没有侵略其他国家的传统。从唐朝到明朝长达数个世纪的鼎盛时期，中国的经济总量曾占世界的2/3，比今天的美国还要强大，但从不侵略。明朝航海家郑和率领200多艘船只组成的庞大船队远航，到达印度洋甚至东非肯尼亚等国，只是为了开展贸易和友好交流，没有占领他国一寸领土。郑和下西洋比哥伦布发现美洲还要早，这在西方发展史上是难以想象的。时至今日，对于国际冲突，我们首先想到的仍是通过政治、外交方式解决，而一些西方国家却倾向于认为武力解决更有效。我们对和平、非军事方式的爱好深植于传统哲学和历史文化。

第二，我们坚持整体、全面的观点看待问题。中国有句俗话说，"大河有水小河满"。我们强调大局观，更注重社会、国家的总体利益。西方包括英国更注重细节和个人，双方在这方面可以互鉴。

第三，我们强调计划性和前瞻性，也很有耐心。我刚才介绍了中国的五年规划，它始于1953年，我们现在正在制订的是"十三五"规划，为未来五年中国的经济社会发展规划蓝图。而且，中国还有"两个一百年"奋斗目标，体现了我们长远规划的能力。美国前国务卿基辛格曾说，中国的一个朝代比美国的整个历史还长。所以说，我们善于思考长远的问题。

第四，中国人勤劳。英国卫生大臣亨特曾因夸奖中国人勤劳而受到舆论的非议，我在接受电视采访时也被问及此事。我回答说，中国人的确勤劳，但英国人具有创造力。中英两国应互相学习，取长补短，相得益彰。

剑桥学生： 英国和阿根廷关于马尔维纳斯群岛的争端对中英关系有何影响？英国公投如果选择脱离欧盟是否会对中英关系带来不利影响？

刘晓明： 马尔维纳斯群岛是英国和阿根廷之间的问题，我们希望两国能通过和平方式解决争端。

关于英欧关系公投，这需由英国人自己来决定。我们希望同欧盟机构和每个成员国都发展良好关系。英国是欧盟的重要成员，英国领导人多次表示，愿意做中国在西方和欧盟最好的伙伴，愿意带头推动中欧尽快完成双边投资协定谈判，尽早启动自贸协定谈判。如果英国离开了欧盟，将如何发挥带头作用？我们希望英国在欧盟中发挥重要作用，为促进中欧关系发展做出贡献。

剑桥学生： 西方常常批评中国特色的民主不是真正的民主，对此你如何回应？

刘晓明： 首先，我们要多讲中国民主的故事，我希望你作为中国学生也多对你周围的英国老师和同学解释中国特色的民主是怎么回事。每个国家的民主都各有特点。英美文化同宗同源，都讲英语，但民主形式和法律体系也不尽相同。我们中国特色社会主义的民主制度，是以选举民主为主要标志的人民代表大会制度。公民通过广泛选举组成各级人民代表大会，人民代表大会通过广泛的民主选举组成国家权力机构、行政机构和司法机构。中国的县、区、乡、镇实行直接选举，县以上是间接选举，即县级人大代表由本县选民通过普选产生，市级人大代表由各县人大代表选举，省级人大代表由各市人大代表选举，全国人大代表由各省人大代表选举，国家领导人由全国人大代表选举。全国人大代表近3000名，每年开会，五年换届。

如我们所知，英国是实行间接选举，首相不是由全国人民选举产生，而是由选区选举产生议员，最后由获得多数席位的政党领袖出任首相。美国则是全国范围内选总统，与英国模式也不同。你不能根据自己的体制来评判其他国家的体制是否民主。世界上没有完美的民主，也没有完美的制度模式，国家之间应该相互学习，相互借鉴。我们与很多国家就治国理政、法治、人权等开展对话交流，就是希望以此增进了解，消除误解，互学互鉴。

剑桥学生： 英国是否充分了解亚投行和"一带一路"的意义？在英国的中国年轻人在中英关系的"黄金时代"是否面临更多机遇？

刘晓明： 中英两国领导人都很重视亚投行和"一带一路"并进行充分沟通与交流，我作为大使也利用各种机会进行宣介，英国各界对亚投行和"一带一路"的理解正不断深化。

我们鼓励中国年轻人回国发展，为祖国建设贡献聪明才智。每年都有很多省市派团组前来英国招聘人才，大家可以充分利用这类机遇。当然如果你们选择留在英国发展，也会有用武之地。越来越多的英国企业希望发展对华合作，需要聪明能干的中国学子助其一臂之力。中英关系"黄金时代"一定会给你们带来更多机会，我也衷心希望你们成为中英交流合作的桥梁。

剑桥教授： 目前欧盟和俄罗斯之间关系相当紧张。中国即将成为超级大国，如何平衡与欧盟和俄罗斯的关系？

刘晓明： 中国和欧盟、中国和俄罗斯都是互利共赢的合作关系。俄罗斯是中国最大的邻国和全面战略协作伙伴，两国政治和经贸合作密切。中欧关系也发展得很好。俄罗斯不构成中欧之间的障碍，我没有感到这两者之间存在什么难以平衡的问题。我不认为中国即将成为超级大国，中国仍然是世界上最大的发展中国家。尽管中国经济总量位居世界第二，但人均国内生产总值却比罗马尼亚、保加利亚还要低，排在世界第80位之后。我们主要关心的是把自己的事情办好，将发展作为第一要务。

剑桥教授： 你刚才引用狄更斯的名言，说明我们正处在一个"最好的时代"，但他还说过我们处在"最坏的时代"。两年前中国共产党拥有的《环球时报》曾说英国是一个持续衰落的老牌欧洲国家，现在只适合旅游和学习，你现在却说中英关系进入"黄金时代"。这两年到底发生了什么？

刘晓明：《环球时报》是中国的一家媒体，它并不代表中国共产党和中国政府，就像我们不能说英国媒体的言论代表英国政府一样。而我作为中国大使，在这里代表中国政府讲话。我始终认为，英国是一个重要国家，是一个具有全球影响力的大国。作为中国大使，我不仅在英国宣讲中国故事，也在中国介绍英国，讲英国的重要性。《环球时报》作为一家独立的媒体，会刊登各种不同观点，下次我会给你找一篇《环球时报》对英国积极评价的文章。

剑桥教授：美国共和党候选人特朗普对中国批评甚多，如果他当选美国总统，会对中美关系产生什么影响？

刘晓明：我曾在美国工作多年，经历过3次大选，比较了解美国的选举文化。我们关注美国竞选人的言论，更关注其当选美国总统之后的行动。这里，我想借用英国的一句谚语："在小鸡没有孵出之前，不要急着去数。"

剑桥学生：中英在高附加值制造业方面如何开展合作？

刘晓明：中英之间还有很多合作潜力和机遇，高附加值制造业也是其中之一，大型客机制造可以说是很有潜力的领域。英国罗尔斯·罗伊斯是世界上两大大型发动机制造商之一，正在拓展与中国企业的合作。飞机制造十分复杂，涉及上千家企业，能大幅带动就业和经济发展。近年来英国意识到经济过于依赖金融服务业的弊端，希望重振制造业，中英在这方面合作空间很大。英国汽车制造业位居世界前列，中国是后起之秀。中国上海汽车集团收购了英国MG公司，在长桥建立了研发中心，保留了英企业全部300名科研人员。上汽负责人告诉我，他们从MG公司的设计和制造中获益良多。中国吉利集团收购了伦敦出租车公司，和英国研发人员一起研制环保电动出租车，习主席夫妇在国事访问期间还在剑桥公爵夫妇陪同下参观了他们最新研制的样车，相信不久伦敦街头行驶的都将是环保节能的新型出租车。此外，中英在绿色能源、电信、机器人、航天、航空等领域也开展了卓有成效的合作。相信随着"黄金时代"的到来，中英在高端制造业领域的合作将迎来更加广阔的前景。

Step up Exchanges and Learn From Each Other
—— Q&A at Cambridge University

On 13th November 2015, I answered questions from the faculty and students of Cambridge University after delivering a speech entitled "Let the Golden Era Shine Brighter".

Cambridge student: Although China-UK relations have entered a Golden Era, there are still some negative opinions of China in the UK. Some people see China's rise as a threat. Some think China's slowdown poses serious challenges. As the Chinese Ambassador, what would you say to those people? How can such suspicions be minimised?

Liu Xiaoming: My job of course is to reach out to every sector of the UK in order to present a positive Chinese narrative, to drive home the importance of the China-UK relationship and to promote exchanges and cooperation between the two countries. I don't know how closely you followed the State Visit. Before this State Visit, I gave interviews to all the major networks. I call it "full coverage". I appeared on all channels, BBC, Channel 4, Sky News and ITV. I tried to answer various questions such as those on security issues, why China invests in the UK's nuclear power stations, and also human rights in China and cyber security. I think it is natural for people to have some misunderstandings, because the media coverage on China here is not comprehensive. Sometimes it is one-sided. The media pursues sensational reporting. If you compare how China is portrayed in this country and how the UK is portrayed in China, there is quite a contrast.

My job is also to reach out to the major newspapers, *The Times*, *Financial Times* and *The Daily Telegraph*, etc, to have China's voice heard. I have also taken initiative to visit the various media outlets and held discussions with them. I know that even though I give many interviews, they each have 5-10 minutes airtime. The British public will mainly learn about China through the numerous reports written by British journalists. That's why I try to reach out. I visited BBC and went behind the scenes. I had a 2-hour discussion with over 30 senior editors and journalists including the BBC's News Director, the royal and international journalists, and tried to answer their questions. I also invited some editors and reporters from *Financial Times* and *The Daily Telegraph* to the Embassy to brief them on the significance of the State Visit and answered their questions. It is also my job as Ambassador to make myself available and come to talk to you here in Cambridge.

Cambridge student: I wonder if you could elaborate a little bit on what you said about China and the UK working together on counter-terrorism?

Liu Xiaoming: Terrorism is a common scourge for humanity. It is a global issue that calls for the joint efforts of all countries. China and the UK are permanent members of the UN Security Council. We shoulder important responsibility for maintaining world peace and stability. The two governments have maintained a close dialogue on security and counter-terrorism issues, including sharing information. We are both supporters of the relevant important counter-terrorism resolutions at the United Nations.

Cambridge student: Recently, there was the historic meeting between the Chinese President Xi Jinping and the Taiwanese "President" Ma Ying-jeou. What impact will it have on the upcoming election in Taiwan and cross-Strait relations? What's China's view on self-determination?

Liu Xiaoming: First, I need to correct you for referring to Ma Ying-jeou by the wrong title. There is no president in Taiwan. Taiwan is not a country. It is part of China. There is only one President of China, that is, President Xi Jinping. Because of outstanding political differences, the meeting was conducted in a practical manner, with both sides attending as leaders of the two sides of the Strait and both sides addressing each other as "Mr". It was a historic meeting and it will take some time for people to fully grasp its significance.

As to the election in Taiwan, we will certainly follow it closely. But what we care about more is peace and stability across the Taiwan Strait. In order to maintain peace and stability in the Strait, we must adhere to the one-China principle, known as the 1992 Consensus. During the meeting, both sides reaffirmed that relations should continue to be based on this core principle of one-China and opposition to Taiwan independence. The 1992 Consensus has been the prerequisite and foundation for political trust and positive interactions in cross-Strait relations. Abandoning or straying from the 1992 Consensus will plunge cross-Strait relations back into instability. The two sides are yet to be reunified, but China's sovereignty and territorial integrity has never been destroyed. Taiwan's separation from the motherland is temporary, and a legacy of history. Japan illegally occupied Taiwan through the China-Japan War of 1894. In the Cairo Declaration of 1943, it was explicitly stated that Japan should return to China all the Chinese islands it illegally seized, including Taiwan and the surrounding islands such as Diaoyudao. When I was the Chinese Ambassador to Egypt, I visited the Hotel Mena House, the site where the Cairo Declaration was signed by Chinese, American and British leaders. Owing to various reasons, Taiwan has yet to return to the motherland. But that does not change the basic fact that Taiwan has been and will always be part of China.

I believe that the Chinese people on both sides of the Strait have the wisdom and patience to find a peaceful solution and achieve reunification of the motherland. We have waited for over 60 years. The meeting between Xi and Ma shows that our patience has paid off. I have full confidence that more and more people, especially people on the island, will understand that it is in the best interests of the people across the Strait to adhere to the 1992 Consensus, to promote peaceful development of cross Strait relations, to maintain peace and stability in the Taiwan Strait for mutual benefit and to realise the great renewal of the Chinese nation. Taiwan independence has no way out.

Cambridge student: You said that the British media is one-sided when reporting on China. I am just wondering what Britain can learn from China?

Liu Xiaoming: The two countries can learn quite a lot from each other. There are a number of commonalities between China and Britain, including a long history and rich culture. And there are also some differences.

First, the Chinese nation is a peace-loving nation that has no tradition of invading other countries. Even when China was at its strongest, in the centuries spanning from the Tang Dynasty to the Ming Dynasty when China's GDP accounted for 2/3 of the world's total, which is bigger than the United States today, it never invaded other countries. The Chinese navigator Admiral Zheng He of the Ming Dynasty led a 200-strong fleet of ships on voyages to the Indian Ocean and as far as Kenya in East Africa. He was there for trade and friendship, occupying not a single inch of land. Zheng He's voyages long predated Christopher Columbus's discovery of America. All these things would have been unimaginable in Western history. Even today, when it comes to international conflicts, the first thing that comes to our mind is seeking a political solution--how can we address problems through diplomatic means--whereas some Western countries think military force is more effective. Our love of peace and non-militaristic approach is deeply-rooted in China's traditional philosophy and several thousand years of history.

Second, in Chinese culture, we take a holistic and comprehensive approach when looking at situations. There is a Chinese saying that "the water level rises in small streams when the big rivers are full." We place more emphasis on the larger picture and the greater interests of the society and the country, while Western countries, including Britain, focus more on details and individuals.

Third, we stress the importance of planning ahead and have the patience to execute our plans. China has been making plans every five years since 1953. As I said, we are currently drawing up the 13th Five Year Plan. It will be a blueprint for China's economic and social development over the next five years. China also has two centenary goals, which show its ability to fulfill long-term plans. As the former US Secretary of State Henry Kissinger said, a single dynasty in China lasts longer than the entire history of the United States. We are good at thinking for the long-term.

Fourth, the Chinese are a hard-working people. The Secretary of Health Jeremy Hunt once praised the Chinese for being a hard-working people. His remarks drew criticism. I was asked about this in an interview and replied that the Chinese people are hard-working while the British people are creative. China and the UK should step up exchanges and learn from each other.

Cambridge student: Will the disputes between the UK and Argentina over Malvinas Islands affect China-UK relations? Should the UK choose to leave the European Union, would that do any harm to China-UK relations?

Liu Xiaoming: The issue of Malvinas Islands is between the UK and Argentina. We hope it will be resolved peacefully.

With regard to the UK referendum on EU membership, it is certainly up to the British people to decide how they want to vote. We would certainly like to enjoy a good relationship with the EU as an institution and individual EU member states. The UK is an important member of the European Union. The British leaders have said on many occasions that the UK wants to be China's best partner in the West and in the EU. The UK wants to take the lead in the early conclusion of the negotiations on a China-EU bilateral investment agreement and the early launch of the negotiations on a China-EU free trade agreement. If the UK leaves the EU, what kind of leading role can it play? We hope the UK will play an important role in the European Union and continue to contribute to China-EU relations.

Cambridge student: What would you say to the Western allegation that democracy with Chinese characteristics is not real democracy?

Liu Xiaoming: First, we have to share stories about China's democracy. I hope as a Chinese student, you will explain to your teachers and fellow students about China's democracy and how democracy functions in China. All countries are different. Even the UK and the United States, though they speak the same language and share the same cultural tradition, differ in their forms of democracy and legal systems. China has a democratic system with Chinese characteristics, that is to say, the system of People's Congresses with the hallmark of electoral democracy. The Chinese people form people's congresses at various levels through elections. People's congresses then democratically elect the state organs, executive agencies and judiciary authorities. Deputies at and below the county level are directly elected based on universal suffrage. Deputies above county level are indirectly elected. That is to say, county deputies elect municipal deputies, municipal deputies elect provincial deputies, and provincial deputies elect deputies to the National People's Congress, which will then elect the national leaders. There are nearly 3,000 deputies to the National People's Congress. Every year they meet and every five years there is a general election.

As far as we know, the UK has indirect election. The Prime Minister is not directly elected through a nationwide election, but by constituency. The leader of the party that gains the majority seats in parliament will become the Prime Minister. The President of the United States is elected by nationwide election. Again, that is different from the UK. So you cannot judge whether the system in another country is democratic or not based upon your own system. Number one, there is no perfect democracy. Number two, there is no perfect model of a political system. Number three, all countries are different. We can learn from each other. That's why we have various mechanisms for dialogue, For example, on governance, the rule of law and human rights. The more we carry out such exchanges, the fewer misunderstandings or misconceptions there will be.

Cambridge student: How, do you think, Western businesses might understand the potential of and opportunities for the AIIB and the One Belt One Road? Will the Golden Era of China-UK relations bring any more opportunities for young Chinese in the UK?

Liu Xiaoming: Both Chinese and British leaders attach great importance to the AIIB and the One Belt One Road and have extensive exchanges and active interactions about these initiatives. As Ambassador, I shall do my best to reach out and share my perceptions of these initiatives. Various circles in the UK have gained a deeper understanding about the AIIB and the One Belt One Road.
We certainly encourage young people to go back to China and contribute their talent to the motherland. Every year, we host many delegations from different Chinese provinces. They came here to recruit the bright talents. I hope you can be one of the recruits. Of course, if you choose to stay in the UK, there will also be many opportunities. More and more British companies want to grow their businesses with China and require your help. The Golden Era in China-UK relations will surely bring more opportunities to all of you. I sincerely hope you will contribute to building bridges for China-UK exchanges and cooperation.

Cambridge professor: China is well on its way to become a superpower. How will China balance its relations with the EU and Russia given the tensions in EU-Russia relations?

Liu Xiaoming: China has cooperative and win-win relations with both the EU and Russia. Russia is the largest neighbour and comprehensive strategic partner of coordination of China. The two countries have close economic and trade ties and good political relations. China-EU relations are also very good. Russia is not an obstacle between China and the EU. I do not feel China will face any difficulties in developing relations with Russia and the EU at the same time.

I don't expect China to be a superpower in the near future. We know our place as the biggest developing country. Although the Chinese economy is the second largest in the world, China's per capita GDP lags behind even Romania and Bulgaria, with 80 countries ranking ahead of it. We very much wish to concentrate on our own development. We must take development as a top priority in our national effort.

Cambridge professor: You quoted Charles Dickens in saying that it's the "best of times". But he continues to say it's also the "worst of times". Just two years ago, the *Global Times* which is owned by the Chinese Communist Party said Britain is just an old declining empire only good for travel and study. What has happened in just two years to enable you to talk about this"Golden Era"of China-UK relationship?

Liu Xiaoming: The *Global Times* is one of the media outlets in China and does not represent the Party or the Government. Tt is just like I can't say the comments in British media represent the British Government. As the Chinese Ambassador, I am here to represent the Chinese Government. I have always believed that the UK is an important country. It is a major country with global influence. As the Chinese Ambassador, in addition to telling China's story in the UK, I have also become a good spokesman for the UK in China. When I conduct speaking tours, I tell people how important the UK is. As an independent media outlet, the *Global Times* publishes different viewpoints. Next time, I shall show you very positive comments they made about the UK.

Cambridge professor: The US Republican candidate Donald Trump has made some negative comments about China. If he is elected US President, how will that affect China-US relations?

Liu Xiaoming: I worked for many years in the United States. I lived there through three elections. I know what American election culture is about. We have to be patient. We follow the comments of the candidates. We pay even more attention to the actions once they take office. To quote an English proverb, "Do not count your chickens before they are hatched. "

Cambridge student: How can China and the UK work together in high-end manufacturing?

Liu Xiaoming: There are many areas of great potential and opportunity for China-UK cooperation, High-end manufacturing is one of them, the latest example being the jumbo jet. Rolls-Royce is one of the two biggest engine producers in the world that is expanding cooperation with Chinese companies. The manufacturing of aircraft is very complicated. It involves over one thousand businesses. This can massively increase employment and drive the economy. The UK has realized the shortcomings of over-reliance on financial services. It has adopted strategies to reinvigorate the manufacturing sector, which holds great potential for China-UK cooperation. The UK is also a leader in the automobile industry. The Shanghai Automobile Industry Corporation bought MG. They set up a research centre in Longbridge. They retained all 300 technicians and scientists. SAIC CEO told me that they have benefited from both MG's design and manufacturing capabilities. Geely bought a London Taxi. They are working with British scientists and technicians to produce environmentally-friendly electric taxis. During the State Visit, President Xi and the First Lady were accompanied by the Duke and Duchess of Cambridge on a view of the prototype of the new taxi. I believe it won't be long before all London taxis will be environmentally-friendly and energy-conserving models. Besides, China and the UK have carried out positive cooperation in green energy, telecommunications, robot, aviation and aerospace. I believe as China-UK relations enter this Golden Era, China-UK cooperation in high-end manufacturing will embrace an even brighter future.

中英关系怎么了？
——关于当前中英关系中外记者会
（2020年7月30日，中国驻英国大使馆）

刘晓明： 大家上午好！欢迎大家出席今天的中外记者会。

今年是中英关系开启"黄金时代"5周年。年初以来，习近平主席与约翰逊首相两次通电话，就推进中英关系及两国共同抗疫达成重要共识。两国政府各部门认真落实这一重要共识，积极开展多领域合作。中英双方本应珍惜这一良好势头，推动两国关系向前发展，但令人遗憾和痛心的是，近来，中英关系遭遇一系列困难，面临严峻形势。

人们在问，中英关系怎么了？英国媒体也在问，中英关系出现问题原因何在？是中国变了，还是英国变了？今天我就来回答这个问题：中国没有变，变的是英国。中英关系遭遇困难，责任完全在英方。

第一，中方坚定奉行国际关系基本准则没有变。互相尊重主权和领土完整、互不干涉内政和平等互利，是《联合国宪章》确立的国家间关系的基本原则，是国际法与国际关系的基本准则，也是中英关系的基本原则，被写入两国建立大使级外交关系的联合公报。中国从不干涉别国的内政，包括英国的内政，也决不允许别国干涉中国的内政。但是，近期英方却一再违反这些重要原则：在涉港问题上无端指责香港国安法，改变英国国民（海外）（BNO）

政策，暂停与香港的移交逃犯协定，粗暴干涉香港事务和中国内政，严重干扰香港稳定与繁荣；在涉疆问题上罔顾事实、颠倒黑白，在双边和多边渠道对中国治疆政策大肆抹黑攻击，借所谓新疆人权问题干涉中国内政，严重毒化中英关系氛围。

第二，中方坚持走和平发展道路没有变。走和平发展道路，是中国坚定不移的战略选择和郑重承诺。中国没有侵略扩张的基因，没有也不会输出自己的模式。中国发展是为了让人民过上好日子，而不是要威胁谁、挑战谁、取代谁。历史已经并将继续证明，中国始终是世界和平的建设者、全球发展的贡献者、国际秩序的维护者，中国的发展壮大只能使世界更和平、更稳定、更繁荣。而英国一些政客，抱守"冷战思维"，与英内外反华势力遥相呼应，大肆渲染"中国威胁"，将中国视为"敌对国家"，扬言要与中国全面"脱钩"，甚至叫嚣要对中国发动"新冷战"。

第三，中方认真履行自身国际义务没有变。今年是联合国成立75周年，中国是第一个签署《联合国宪章》的国家。中国参加了100多个政府间国际组织，签署了500多个多边条约。中国始终认真履行自身承担的国际责任和义务，从未"退群""毁约"，从不谋求本国利益优先。英方妄称中方出台香港国安法违反《中英联合声明》、未履行国际义务，这完全是错误的。《联合声明》的核心要义是中国恢复对香港行使主权，而香港国安法正充分体现了中国中央政府对香港的全面管治权。中国政府在《联合声明》中阐述的对港方针政策是中方的政策宣示，既不是对英方的承诺，更不是所谓国际义务，"不履行国际义务"的帽子扣不到中国头上。反倒是英方不履行国际义务，违背自身承诺，改变BNO政策，暂停与香港的移交逃犯协定，扰乱香港人心，干扰香港国安法实施，干涉中国内政。

第四，中方致力于发展对英伙伴关系的意愿没有变。2015年习近平主席对英国国事访问期间，中英发表联合宣言，决定构建面向21世纪全球全面战略伙伴关系。中国始终将英国看作伙伴，致力于发展健康稳定的中英关系。正如王毅国务委员兼外长前天与拉布外交大臣通话时指出的那样："对英国而言，中国始终是机遇而不是威胁，是增量而不是减量，是解决方案而不是挑战。"然而，英方近来对华认知和定位发生重大变化，出现严重偏差，"禁用华为"就是最突出例证。这不是英国如何对待一家中国企业的问题，而是关系到英国如何看待中国的问题。英国究竟是把中国看作机遇、伙伴，还是威胁、对手？是把中国看作友好国家，还是"敌对"或"潜在敌对国家"？英方领导人多次表示要发展平衡、积极、建设性的中英关系。我们听其言，观其行。

当前，世界百年未有之大变局正向纵深发展。新冠肺炎疫情仍在全球肆虐，经济全球化遭遇严重冲击，世界经济陷入深度衰退。面对这样的形势，我们需要一个什么样的中英关系？中英都是联合国安理会常任理事国和二十国集团等国际组织重要成员国，都是具有全球影响的大国，都肩负着维护世界和平、促进发展的重要使命。一个健康稳定发展的中英关系，不仅符合中英两国人民的根本利益，也有利于世界的和平与繁荣。我们有一千条理由把中英关系搞好，没有一条理由把中英关系搞坏。如何搞好中英关系？我认为，做到以下三点至关重要：

一是相互尊重。历史告诉我们，只要国际法和国际关系基本准则得到遵守，中英关系就向前发展；反之则遭遇挫折，甚至倒退。中国尊重英国主权，从未做任何干涉英国内政的事。英方也应以同样态度对待中方，尊重中国主权，停止干涉香港事务和中国内政，避免中英关系受到进一步损害。

二是互利共赢。中英经济互补性强，利益深度融合，双方从彼此合作中都获得了巨大收益，不存在谁更依赖谁、谁多占谁便宜的问题。希望英方不要受个别国家的压力和胁迫，为中国企业提供开放、公平、非歧视的投资环境，重塑中国企业对英国的信心。在"后脱欧时代"和"后疫情时代"，中英在贸易、金融、科技、教育、医疗卫生领域有广阔合作空间，在维护多边主义、促进自由贸易、应对气候变化等全球性挑战等方面拥有广泛共识。英国要打造"全球化英国"，绕不开、离不开中国。与中国"脱钩"，就是与机遇脱钩，就是与发展脱钩，就是与未来脱钩。

三是求同存异。中英历史文化、社会制度、发展阶段不同，难免存在分歧。70年前，英国在西方大国中第一个承认新中国。70年来，中英本着求同存异的精神，超越意识形态差异，推动中英关系不断向前发展。70年后的今天，中英关系更加丰富、更加深入，不是你输我赢的"对手关系"，更不是非此即彼的"敌对关系"，而是平等相待、互利共赢的伙伴关系。我们应当有足够的智慧和能力管控和处理好双方分歧，不让反华势力和"冷战分子""绑架"中英关系。

我常说，只有拥有独立自主的外交政策，"不列颠"才是名副其实的"大不列颠"。无论是1950年英国在西方大国中首个承认中华人民共和国，1954年与中国建立代办级外交关系，还是英国选择加入亚投行、与中国构建面向21世纪全球全面战略伙伴关系，英国在关键历史节点，都顶住外部压力，做出了正确的战略抉择。现在，中英关系再次处于关键历史节点。我希望，英国政治家和各界有识之士，认清国际大势，排除各种干扰，把握时代潮流，做出符合中英两国人民根本利益的战略抉择。

下面，我愿回答大家的提问。

BBC： 刘大使，如你所说，最近几周，英中关系由于香港、华为、新疆问题明显恶化。在这个过程中，上周我们看到，你以及好几位中国政府代表均威胁称，英方将承担严重后果、中方将采取反制措施或反击行动。但到目前为止，我们还不清楚到底是什么样的反制措施。你能否具体介绍一下？这些措施是秘而不宣的，还是雷声大，雨点小？

刘晓明： 首先我要澄清，我们从未威胁任何人。那些认为我的话是威胁的人是在断章取义。正如我所说，中国希望成为英国的朋友和伙伴。但如果不想和中国做伙伴、做朋友，把中国视为"敌对国家"，就将付出代价。什么代价？很简单，你将失去把中国视为机遇和朋友所能得到的好处，这也是把中国当作"敌对国家"带来的必然后果。

关于反制措施，我相信你已经看到，英方宣布将改变英国国民（海外）护照（BNO）政策后，中方也做出回应，宣布考虑不再承认BNO护照为合法旅行证件。这完全是因为英方行动违背了其在1984年备忘录中的承诺。当时英方明确承诺不给予BNO护照持有者在英居留权，在此基础上中方承认BNO护照为合法旅行证件。现在英方违约在先，中方必须做出回应。

此外，英方还无限期暂停与香港的移交逃犯协定，损害了英国与香港司法合作的基础。中方做出回应，宣布香港暂停与英国的移交逃犯协定和刑事司法互助协定，这是因为双方司法合作的基础遭到破坏。

天空新闻台： 关于香港，近几天，根据新的国家安全法，一些人因为在网上发表评论被拘捕。今天，还有些"民主运动人士"被取消参加选举资格。这些情况是否印证了英国关于国家安全法破坏香港自由的担忧？关于新疆，你是否愿意澄清几周前接受BBC采访时所看到的视频？据欧洲安全部门消息称，那些戴着手铐脚镣、被剃光须发、身着囚服的人是维吾尔族人。他们为什么被押送？为什么受到如此待遇？

刘晓明： 香港国家安全法是为了堵住维护国家安全的法律漏洞。香港回归23年来，一直没有维护国家安全的法律。我们也看到去年香港遭遇的情况。一些人空谈"一国两制"，我们却看到"一国"受到侵蚀，陷入危险之中。中国中央政府和全国人大及时通过并实施香港国安法，堵住漏洞，根本不存在所谓破坏言论自由的问题。国家安全法明确规定，基本人权将得到充分尊重。该法只针对极少数妄图破坏国家安全的罪犯，明确列出4类犯罪行为。如果你没有这几类犯罪行为，就不会有任何问题，依然享有言论自由、游行自由、示威自由。香港的资本主义制度不会改变，独立的司法体系包括终审权不会改变。国家安全法将确保"一国两制"行稳致远,也因此得到香港民众的广泛支持。有300万香港市民签名支持国安法,因为他们都希望香港能有一个安宁、繁荣、稳定的环境。关于你提到的涉疆问题,我一会儿再回答。

中国国际电视台: 刘大使早上好。你刚才提到中国将不承认BNO作为有效旅行证件。从实践上看,这对香港居民来英意味着什么?现在中英两国相互间的信任和善意已大幅减少,你认为应该如何重建?

刘晓明: 中国没有做任何损害中英互信的事。我说过,我们将英国视为伙伴和朋友,想要推进中英关系"黄金时代"。今年是中英关系"黄金时代"5周年,双方本应进行庆祝。但遗憾的是,英方却无端指责香港国家安全法,干扰该法实施,干涉香港事务,损害中英互信。

我在开场白中已经阐明,中英关系的出路在于坚持3个原则:相互尊重、互不干涉内政、平等相待。我们承认存在分歧,但双方应在互相尊重的基础上处理分歧。中国无意改变英国,英国也不应该试图改变中国。我们的合作基础和共同利益远大于分歧。中英都是具有全球影响的大国,我们肩负着维护世界和平、促进全球发展的重要使命,我们之间有广泛的共同议程。

关于你提到的具体问题,由于英方违背了其关于BNO的承诺,我们不得不采取措施,不承认此护照为有效旅行证件。

路透社: 谢谢大使。我想问一个比较宏观的问题。美国总统特朗普似乎已将中国作为21世纪最大的地缘政治敌人。你认为中国和西方是否已在进行"新冷战"？有人说，中国近年来更加强硬，引起美国不安，你如何评价？谢谢。

刘晓明： 我认为你已经回答了你自己的问题。中国并没有变得更强硬，而是太平洋对面的国家想对中国挑起"新冷战"，我们不得不做出反应。我们不希望打"冷战"，我们不希望打任何战争。当美国对中国掀起"贸易战"的时候，我们就说"贸易战"没有赢家。我们主张接触，双方达成了第一阶段贸易协议。现在我们仍愿与美方进行接触。但是，美国国内情况大家都看到了，新冠肺炎疫情形势不断恶化，美国想把中国当作"替罪羊"，把自己的问题都归咎于中国。

大家知道，今年是美国大选年。我在美国常驻两次，5次近距离观察美国大选。人们说，在大选年美国政客为了赢得选票口不择言。我觉得今年他们不仅口不择言，而且不择手段，包括将中国作为敌人。他们认为需要对中国发动"冷战"，但中国对此不感兴趣。我们一直向美方表示，中国不是美国的敌人，中国是美国的朋友和伙伴；美国的敌人是病毒。我希望美国政客能将精力放在抗疫和拯救生命上，而不是专注于指责中国。

中国中央电视台： 大使上午好！我的问题是，英国工商业联合会总干事近日在《金融时报》撰文称，中英合作使英方获益巨大，英国无法承受单方面与中国减少往来的代价。但正如你刚才所说，一些英国政客对此持完全相反的看法。你对此怎么看？如果允许，我还想再问一个问题。你近期接受英国媒体采访时曾看过相关视频和图片，你也曾多次阐明中方在新疆问题上的政策立场。但西方媒体在这个问题上还是不断指责中国。你对此有何评论？

刘晓明： 我在开场白中讲过，中英关系是互利共赢的伙伴关系。我非常赞同英国工商业联合会总干事的观点。有人说中国从双边关系中获益更多，我认为这有违事实。

我可以用一系列数字来说明：1999年至2020年，英国对华出口增长约20倍；自我担任中国驻英大使以来，中英双边贸易额翻了一番；在过去10年，中国对英投资增长约20倍。这两个"20倍"很能说明问题。

中英经贸关系为英国创造了大量就业。此外，中国游客每年赴英旅游，也为英国带来1.1万个就业岗位。英国还是接收中国留学生最多的欧洲国家，这些学生在英求学获益匪浅，同时他们也为英国发展做出了贡献。剑桥大学研究表明，中国赴英留学人员在英各种开支，仅在2018年就给英国创造1.7万个就业岗位，更不要说华为公司为英国电信产业发展做出的巨大贡献。中国企业还参与中、英、法三方共同建设的英国核电项目，我认为这一项目符合英国自身利益，能帮助英国实现2050年"零排放"的目标。但在那些"冷战斗士"眼中，这个项目却是下一个攻击目标。我希望这些英国政客能客观看待中英关系，认识到它是一个互利共赢的关系。

关于新疆问题，现在有太多的谬论和谎言，可谓"世纪谎言"。不仅如此，一些西方国家利用新疆问题大肆抹黑、攻击中国，干涉中国内政。很遗憾，英国也难辞其咎。因此，我愿借今天的机会揭穿谎言、澄清事实，向大家介绍一个真实的新疆。

第一，所谓新疆问题根本不是什么人权、民族、宗教问题，而是反暴恐、反分裂、去极端化问题。20世纪90年代以来，特别是"9·11"事件之后，"三股势力"在中国新疆地区制造了数千起暴恐案件，造成大量无辜群众生命和财产损失。其中，震惊世界的新疆"7·5"事件（2009年）造成197人死亡，1700多人受伤。面对严峻形势，新疆维吾尔自治区政府依法打击暴恐活动，同时重视源头治理，积极推进去极端化工作。这些措施十分有成效，确保新疆3年多未发生一起恐袭事件，最大限度保障了各族人民的生命权、健康权、发展权等基本权利，得到新疆各族人民广泛支持和衷心拥护。

这些措施也为全球反恐事业做出积极贡献，得到国际社会积极评价。2018年底以来，联合国官员、外国驻华使节、有关国家常驻日内瓦代表、媒体记者和宗教团体等70多批团组、90多个国家的1000多人赴疆参访，他们纷纷称赞新疆反恐、去极端化做法符合联合国打击恐怖主义、维护基本人权的宗旨和原则，值得充分肯定和学习借鉴。2019年10月，60多个国家代表在第74届联大三委会议期间发言称赞新疆人权进步。今年7月，46个国家代表在人权理事会第44届会议上做共同发言，支持中方在涉疆问题上的立场和举措。

为帮助大家认清恐怖主义、分裂主义、极端主义在新疆造成的危害以及开展反恐、反分裂、去极端化活动的必要性和重要性，我们现在播放一段视频（播放视频）。

第二，新疆"教培中心"根本不是什么"集中营"或"再教育营"，而是预防性反恐和去极端化的有益尝试和积极探索。这一举措旨在根除极端主义、防止暴力恐怖活动升级，符合《联合国全球反恐战略》等一系列反恐决议的原则和精神，本质上这与英国设立的转化和脱离项目（DDP）、美国推行的"社区矫正"和法国成立的去极端化中心没有什么区别。受极端主义思想影响以及有轻微违法犯罪行为的人员参加教培中心培训，通过学习国家通用语言文字、法律知识，职业技能教育培训，去除极端化思想，掌握劳动技能，不仅使这些学员结业后重返社会，做守法公民，而且自食其力，有了稳定的工作和收入，生活水平明显提高。

教培中心严格贯彻落实中国宪法和法律关于尊重和保障人权的基本原则，充分保障学员的人格尊严不受侵犯，严禁以任何方式对学员进行人格侮辱和虐待；充分保障学员人身自由，实行寄宿制管理，学员可以回家，有事可以请假；充分保障学员使用本民族语言文字的权利，各项规章制度、课程表、食谱等均同时使用国家通用语言文字和少数民族语言文字；充分尊重和保护不同民族学员的风俗习惯，为少数民族学员免费提供各种清真饮食；充分尊重和保护学员宗教信仰自由，信教学员回家时可自主决定是否参与合法宗教活动。

现在我们播放一段教培中心学员的视频，听听他们讲述教培中心的真实情况（播放视频）。

第三，在新疆问题上，不能让谎言与诬蔑横行，不能让傲慢与偏见充斥头脑，而要用事实与真相说话，用客观与理性评判。下面，我愿用事实揭穿西方媒体"广为流传"的四大谎言：

一是谎称"新疆近百万维吾尔族人被拘押"。事实上,这是两个反华机构或人员炮制的谣言。幕后黑手之一是美国政府支持的"中国人权捍卫者网络(Chinese Human Rights Defenders,CHRD)",它仅仅通过对8名维吾尔族人的采访和粗略估算,就得出"新疆地区2000多万人口中,10%的人被拘押在'再教育营'的荒谬结论"。幕后黑手之二是受美国政府资助的极右翼原教旨主义基督徒郑国恩,他在《中亚调查》杂志上发文称,"据估计,新疆在押人员总数超过100万"。据美国独立新闻网站"灰色地带"披露,郑国恩得出这一数字,依据的是总部位于土耳其的一家维吾尔流亡媒体组织——Istiqlal TV的一篇报道,而Istiqlal TV根本不是一家新闻组织,而是推进分裂主义、极端主义的组织。郑国恩本人则自认"受上帝的引领",肩负着反对中国的"使命"。

最近,我在接受BBC《安德鲁·马尔访谈》节目采访时,马尔先生播放了一段经所谓西方情报机关和澳大利亚专家确认的视频,以此说明大批维吾尔族人被拘押。现在让我们来看看这段视频的真相到底是什么。

事实上,这是新疆喀什看守所(Kashi Detention House)集中转运服刑犯人的场景,根本不存在所谓大批拘押维吾尔族人的问题。中方打击犯罪从不与任何民族、宗教挂钩。司法机关押送服刑人员属于正常司法活动,不容歪曲和抹黑。

二是谎称"新疆强拆清真寺"。事实是,目前新疆共有清真寺2.44万座,平均每530位穆斯林就拥有一座清真寺,比例高于一些伊斯兰国家,也高于英格兰地区人均拥有教堂数量。被诬称"拆除"的叶城县加米清真寺、和田艾提尕尔清真寺等根本未被拆除,而是被修缮后重新使用,编造谎言的人用清真寺危房的图片来支撑其谎言,但不会展示清真寺修葺一新的照片。现在,让我们用修葺一新的清真寺的照片来揭穿谎言(展示照片)。

三是谎称"新疆强制绝育"。事实是,新疆维吾尔自治区是中国五个少数民族自治区之一,是一个多民族聚居区,拥有13个世居民族,2500万各族人民和睦共处。中国政府始终一视同仁地保护包括少数民族在内的各族人民合法权益,人口政策长期以来对包括维吾尔族在内的少数民族更为优待。1978年至2018年,新疆地区维吾尔族人口从555万增长到1168万,整整翻了一番。

关于网上那些宣称维吾尔族人"受迫害"的视频,新疆方面已经多次揭穿了这些人的身份,他们有的是从事反华分裂活动的"东突"分子,有的是美西方反华势力培植的"演员"。他们的说法根本站不住脚。他们中有些人在疆内的亲友已经直接站出来辟谣,驳斥了他们的谎言。

我在接受BBC《安德鲁·马尔访谈》节目采访时,马尔先生播放了一段"诉苦者"的视频,真实情况是:这个女性名叫早木热·达吾提(Zumrat Dawut),谎称"被强制绝育"。但她的姐姐和哥哥去年11月公开揭穿其谎言,她从来没有进过教培中心;她生第三个孩子时被查出患有子宫肌瘤,因此做了手术,根本没有"被强制绝育"。让我们看一下她姐姐和哥哥接受采访的视频(播放视频)。

四是谎称"新疆存在大规模强迫劳动"。事实上,这是另一黑手凭空捏造出来的。长期接受美国政府和军火商资助的"澳大利亚战略政策研究所"(ASPI)今年3月炮制所谓《出售维吾尔族人》报告,将南疆贫困民众前往内地务工就业、脱贫增收的自发性行为，歪曲为"强迫劳动"。此后，"美国国会—行政部门中国委员会"将这一谬论作为"依据"，炮制《全球供应链，强迫劳动和新疆维吾尔自治区》报告，进行大肆诬蔑和诽谤。现在让我们放一段视频揭穿他们的谎言（播放视频）。

我们中国人常说，不到新疆，不知道中国之大；不到新疆，不知道中国之美。当前，新疆经济持续发展，社会和谐稳定，民生不断改善，文化空前繁荣。新疆各族人民安居乐业，和睦相处，享受着充分的生存权、发展权，宗教信仰自由依法得到保障，正常宗教活动受到法律保护，新疆处于历史最好发展时期。任何谣言都不能抹杀新疆人权事业发展进步的事实，任何图谋都不能干扰新疆发展繁荣的进程。希望大家不要听信反华分子的谣言，不要受反华政客的蛊惑。我们敦促英国政府全面客观看待新疆发展成就，停止在新疆问题上发表不负责任的言论，停止利用新疆问题干涉中国内政。我们也希望英国媒体摒弃傲慢与偏见，客观、公正地报道新疆，让英国民众了解一个真实的新疆。

独立电视台： 请问刘大使，中国是否允许联合国人权高专署派团，在不受中国共产党干扰的情况下，独立访问新疆，到刚才视频里展示的那些地方，亲眼看看发生了什么？

刘晓明： 自2018年以来，已经有几十个国家和国际组织的1000多名外交官、记者和代表访问了新疆。我们欢迎人权高专署访问新疆。我们反对的是别有用心的所谓"独立调查"，这实际是企图借新疆问题干涉中国内政。新疆的大门是敞开的，每年迎接成千上万的游客来新疆旅游、参观。我们欢迎所有善意、客观、不持偏见的人士访问新疆。

美联社： 刘大使，你曾经在美国长期工作过，请问从特朗普政府的一系列言论和威胁来看，你是否认为中美关系已经"没有回头路"可走？

刘晓明： 我希望不是这样。中国仍然相信不冲突、不对抗、互相尊重、合作共赢的中美关系符合两国利益。中国无意破坏中美关系，中方将继续努力与美方保持接触。

但我也在很多场合说过，探戈需要两个人跳，一个巴掌拍不响。我认为，支持中美关系的民意基础仍然十分广泛。1972年尼克松总统访华以来，中美双方始终致力于建立基于共同利益的中美关系。这种共同利益基础仍在，中美关系在美国民众中的民意基础仍在。当美国国务卿发表反对中国共产党的"新冷战"宣言后，我们看到很多美国人站出来批评这种论调，他们对美国政府将中美关系引入歧途忧心忡忡。

所以，我不认为中美关系已经"没有回头路"，将中美两国联系在一起的根本利益仍在，很多美国有识之士仍在努力维护中美关系的基本盘。我希望人们最终能回归理性。

新华社： 华为一直声称自己是一家独立的私人控股公司，与中国政府没有隶属关系，那为什么中国政府不遗余力地维护华为？如果中英关系持续恶化，两国会否像当年的中日关系一样，陷入"政冷经热"的局面？

有问必答
No Question Unanswered

刘晓明： 关于华为，我刚刚在《南华早报》发表了一篇文章。我不是为自己的文章做广告，而是希望大家能花些时间读一下。英国政府决定禁用华为后，我努力向英国主流媒体投书，因为这个问题对英国很重要。英国公众需要了解问题的全貌。但不幸的是，英国主流报纸都表示不能刊登我的文章。我已在英国工作10多年，算是领教了什么是英国标榜的"新闻自由"。他们非常直白地告诉我，只愿刊登有利于报纸销量的文章。因此他们不愿刊登我关于香港的文章，不愿刊登我关于华为的文章。我不得不让我的文章"飞越"万里到香港《南华早报》发表，当然《南华早报》在英国也有不少读者。我的文章主要观点是，拒绝华为就是拒绝机遇，就是拒绝增长，就是拒绝未来。

关于华为与中国政府的关系，首先，正如我在开场白中所说，华为问题不是一家中国公司的问题，而是关乎英国如何对待中国的问题：是将中国视为机遇，还是威胁？是把中国作为伙伴，还是竞争对手？这是一个必须做出选择的根本问题。

其次，任何政府都应维护本国企业的合法权益。这一点不仅中国政府如此，英国政府也一样。我在英工作10年间，清楚记得英国领导人和政要是如何为英国企业说项的。我记得英国首相在接待中国领导人访问时，不忘推销帝亚吉欧项目，坚持访问期间能够签署有关项目。我记得英国财政大臣努力向中方推销罗尔斯·罗伊斯公司的发动机，坚称罗尔斯·罗伊斯公司生产的发动机比包括美国通用电气在内的其他任何国家的产品都好。我还记得英国商业大臣为了推销英国钢铁公司专程访华，最终促成中国敬业集团收购英钢，并同意在未来10年投资12亿英镑实现英钢转型升级。

我认为，一国政府维护本国企业权益无可厚非。一些"冷战斗士"借中国政府努力维护本国企业权益来证明华为与中国政府关系密切，并以此作为攻击华为的理由，这是非常荒谬的。中国政府对每一家中国企业都一视同仁。我们希望华为在英国取得成功，实现双赢。所以，在英方宣布禁用华为那天，我说，这一天对华为是黑暗的一天，对中英关系也是黑暗的一天，对英国则更是黑暗的一天，因为英国将错失成为5G领军者的机会。

关于中英关系会否"政冷经热"，我认为政治和经济密切相关，很难完全分开。我们需要一个良好的氛围和条件才能进行合作。我说英方关于华为的决定对中英关系是黑暗的一天，是因为这一决定破坏了中英互信，损害了英国信誉。在英国宣布"禁用华为"后，我与在英中资企业举行了座谈，中资企业都表达了他们的担忧和关切，因为这不仅涉及安全风险，也包括投资风险。我们无意将经贸问题政治化，但是信任和信誉在国与国关系中至关重要。

谢谢大家。

What is Happening to China–UK Relationship?
—— An On-line Press Conference on China–UK Relations

On 30th July 2020, I held an on-line press conference on China-UK relationship at the Chinese Embassy. Around 30 journalists from 27 media agencies joined the conference, including BBC, Sky News, ITV, *Financial Times*, *The Daily Telegraph*, *The Times*, Times Radio, *The Guardian*, Reuters, the Xinhua News Agency, *People's Daily*, CCTV, CGTN, the China News Service, *China Daily*, *Science and Technology Daily*, *Global Times*, Guancha. cn, AP, Bloomberg, NBC, Russia Today, Quartz, Phoenix Infonews, *European Times*, *The Scotsman*, and *The Manchester Evening News*. Guests from UK's political and business sectors also attended the conference, including Sir Geoffrey Clifton-Brown, the Deputy-Chairman of the All-Party Parliamentary Group on China (APPCG), Mark Logan, the Vice Chair of APPCG, Lord Davidson, Stephen Perry, the Chairman of the 48 Group Club, Lord Sassoon, the President of the China-Britain Business Council, Lord Palumbo of Walbrook Club, St. John Moore, the Chairman of British Chamber of Commerce in China, Meia Nouwens, Research Fellow for Chinese Defence Policy at the International Institute for Strategic Studies, and Veerle Nouwens, Research Fellow at the International Security Studies Department of the Royal United Services Institute on geopolitical relations in the Asia-Pacific region and China. Foreign diplomats in the UK from the ROK, Laos, the EU, Russia, Kyrgyzstan, Mexico, Argentina, Myanmar, Brazil, and Saudi Arabia also attended the event. The press conference was broadcast live via my Twitter account. CGTN, Reuters and the AP also broadcast the conference live. The event was covered by BBC and Sky News in their programs and on their websites.
The following is the transcript of the press conference.

Liu Xiaoming: Good morning! Welcome to today's press conference.
This year marks the fifth anniversary of the China-UK "Golden Era". Since early this year, President Xi Jinping and Prime Minister Boris Johnson have had two telephone conversations, during which they reached important agreements on advancing China-UK relations and enhancing our joint response to COVID-19. The relevant

departments of the two governments have been working hard to implement these agreements and carry out cooperation in various areas.

This shows a positive momentum in China-UK relationship that should be cherished so that further progress can be achieved. To our regret, however, this relationship recently ran into a series of difficulties and faced a grave situation.

People are asking: What is happening to China-UK relationship? The British media are also asking: What is causing the current difficulties in China-UK relationship? Has China changed or has the UK changed?

Today, I am going to give you my answer to these questions. My answer is loud and clear: China has not changed. It is the UK that has changed. The UK side should take full responsibility for the current difficulties in China-UK relationship.

First, China's determination to follow the basic norms governing international relations has not changed.

These basic norms include:

- mutual respect for each other's sovereignty and territorial integrity,
- non-interference in each other's internal affairs,
- equality,
- and mutual benefit.

These are the fundamental principles that are enshrined in the UN Charter. They are the basic norms of the international law and state-to-state relations. They are also the basic guidelines that have been written into the Joint Communiqué of China and the UK on exchange of ambassadors and hence form the bedrock for China-UK relationship.

China has never interfered in the internal affairs of other countries, including the UK, and we ask the same from other countries.

Recently, however, the above-mentioned important principles have been violated time and again.

On Hong Kong:

There has been blatant interference from the UK in Hong Kong affairs, which are the internal affairs of China, including

- groundless accusations against the National Security Law for Hong Kong SAR,
- changes to the policy involving BNO passport holders,
- and suspension of the agreement for the surrender of fugitive offenders with Hong Kong.

These moves have severely disrupted the stability and prosperity of Hong Kong.

有问必答
No Question Unanswered

On Xinjiang the UK has:
- disregarded the facts,
- confused right and wrong,
- flung slander recklessly at China's Xinjiang-related policies
- and interfered in China's internal affairs by raising the so-called "human rights issue" in Xinjiang, bilaterally and multilaterally.

These actions have seriously poisoned the atmosphere of China-UK relationship.

Second, China's commitment to the path of peaceful development has not changed.

Pursuing peaceful development is China's unwavering strategic choice and solemn pledge. China has never invaded other countries or sought expansion. China has never and will not export its system or model. China strives for development because we want a better life for our people. We do not want to threaten, challenge or replace anyone.

History has proved and will continue to prove that China is always a defender of world peace, a contributor to global development and an upholder of international order. A stronger China will make the world a more peaceful, stable and prosperous place.

However, some British politicians cling to the "Cold War" mentality and echo the remarks of anti-China forces in and outside the UK. They:
- play up the so-called "China threat",
- see China as a "hostile state",
- threaten a "complete decoupling" from China,
- and even clamour for a "new Cold War" against China.

Third, China's resolve to fulfill its international obligations has not changed.

This year marks the 75th anniversary of the founding of the United Nations. China was the first country to place its signature on the UN Charter. It is now a member of more than 100 inter-governmental international organisations and has signed over 500 multilateral treaties.
- It has faithfully fulfilled its international responsibilities and obligations.
- It has never withdrawn from international organisations or treaties.
- Nor does it believe in "us first" at the expense of others.

It is completely wrong to see the National Security Law for Hong Kong SAR as a violation of the Sino-British Joint Declaration or a failure to honour international obligations.

The core content of the Joint Declaration concerns China's resumption of its exercise of sovereignty over Hong Kong. The National Security Law for Hong Kong SAR fully embodies the comprehensive jurisdiction of the Central Government of China over Hong Kong.

The policies regarding Hong Kong laid out in the Joint Declaration were proposed by China on our own initiative. Thus, they neither represent China's commitments to the UK nor international obligations. The label of "failure to fulfill international obligations" should not be branded on China.

It is the UK side that has failed to fulfill its international obligations and gone against its own pledges by changing the policy on BNO passport holders and suspending the agreement for the surrender of fugitive offenders with Hong Kong. This has created public confusion in Hong Kong, disrupted the implementation of the National Security Law and caused interference in China's internal affairs.

Fourth, China's willingness to develop partnership with the UK has not changed.

During President Xi Jinping's state visit to the UK in 2015, China and the UK issued a joint declaration on building a global comprehensive strategic partnership for the 21st century.

China has always seen the UK as a partner and is committed to developing a sound and stable relationship with the UK. As State Councillor and Foreign Minister Wang Yi said two days ago in his telephone conversation with the UK Foreign Secretary Dominic Raab, China represents an opportunity rather than a threat to the UK. It embodies growth rather than a cause for decline and a solution rather than a challenge or a risk. However, there have been major changes and serious deviation in the UK's perception and definition of China. This is particularly evidenced by the recent ban on Huawei.

The issue of Huawei is not about how the UK sees and deals with a Chinese company. It is about how the UK sees and deals with China. Does it see China as an opportunity and a partner, or a threat and a rival? Does it see China as a friendly country, or a "hostile" or "potentially hostile" state?

The UK leaders have said on many occasions that they want to build a balanced, positive and constructive China-UK relationship. We hope their words will be consistent with their actions.

The world is experiencing increasingly profound changes which have not been seen in a century. COVID-19 is still raging, dealing a heavy blow to economic globalization and resulting in a deep recession in the world economy. What kind of China-UK relationship do we need in face of such a situation?

China and the UK are both permanent members of the UN Security Council and important members of the G20 and other international organizations. Both are countries with global influence. Both shoulder the important mission of safeguarding world peace and of promoting development.

A sound and stable China-UK relationship is not only in the fundamental interests of the people of the two countries but also conducive to world peace and prosperity. We have a thousand reasons to make this relationship successful, and not one reason to let it fail.

How can we make it successful? I think it is critically important to follow three principles:

First, to respect each other.

History tells us that when international law and the basic norms governing international relations are observed, the China-UK relationship will advance forward; otherwise, it will suffer setbacks or even backslide.

China respects the UK's sovereignty and has never interfered in the UK's internal affairs. It is important that the UK does the same, namely, respecting China's sovereignty and ending interference in Hong Kong affairs, which are China's internal affairs, so as to prevent further harm to China-UK relationship.

The second principle is: to engage in mutually-beneficial cooperation.

China and the UK have highly complementary economies and deeply integrated interests. The two sides have both benefited tremendously from cooperation. Such mutual benefit should not be gauged by an over-simplified comparison of who is more dependent on the other or who has been "taken advantage of".

It is our hope that the UK will resist the pressure and coercion of a certain country, and provide an open, fair and non-discriminatory environment for Chinese investment, so as to restore the confidence of Chinese businesses in the UK.

China and the UK already share broad consensus on safeguarding multilateralism, promoting free trade and addressing global challenges such as climate change. When Brexit is completed and COVID-19 has come to an end, there will be unlimited prospects for China-UK cooperation in the areas of trade, financial services, science and technology, education and healthcare.

It is hard to imagine a "global Britain" that bypasses or excludes China. "Decoupling" from China means decoupling from opportunities, decoupling from growth, and decoupling from the future.

The third principle is: to seek common ground despite differences.

China and the UK differ in terms of history, culture, social system and the stage of their development. It is only natural that we do not always see eye to eye.

Seventy years ago, the UK was the first major Western country to recognize the New China. For the past 70 years, China and the UK have found common ground despite their differences and gone beyond ideological differences to achieve continuous progress in their bilateral relationship.

Today, after 70 years, this relationship has become more substantial and profound. It is not a relationship between rivals, where one side's gain is the other's loss. Still less is a relationship of "either-or" that exists between hostile states. The China-UK relationship is one of partnership, which is defined by equal treatment and mutual benefit.

China and the UK should have enough wisdom and ability to manage and deal with differences, rather than allowing anti-China forces and "Cold-War" warriors to "kidnap" the China-UK relationship.

I often say the "Great Britain" cannot be "Great" without an independent foreign policy. The UK has withstood pressure from others and made the right strategic choices at many critical historical junctures,

• from becoming the first major Western country to recognize the People's Republic of China in 1950, to establish diplomatic relationship with China at the chargé d'affaires level in 1954;

• from taking part in the Asian Infrastructure Investment Bank to building a comprehensive global strategic partnership for the 21st century with China.

Now, the China-UK relationship once again stands at a critical historical juncture. It is my hope that political leaders and visionary people from all sectors in the UK will keep in mind the bigger picture of the international trend, avert various disruptions and make strategic choices that serve the fundamental interests of the people of our two countries.

Thank you.

Now I would like to take your questions.

BBC: Ambassador, good morning. As you said, relations between the United Kingdom and China have deteriorated significantly in recent weeks over Hong Kong,

Huawei and Xinjiang. Throughout that process, you and various other government representatives have threatened consequences, counter-measures, even counter-attacks, to use the language of last week. And yet it's still not entirely clear to me what those counter-measures are. So could you elaborate a little bit more? Is China retaliating in secret, or is its bark worse than its bite?

Liu Xiaoming: I want to set the record straight. We made no threats. We threaten nobody, as I said. We just let you know the consequences. People regard some of my remarks as threatening words. I think they quote my remarks out of context. As I said, China wants to be a friend of the UK. China wants to be the UK's partner. But if you do not want to be our friend, and if you want to treat China as a hostile country, you will pay the price. That's simple. It's very clear. That means you will lose the benefits of treating China as a source of opportunities and as a friend. And you will bear the consequences of treating China as a hostile country. So that's very clear.

And you talk about the counter-measures. I think you have already seen that after the UK announced that they are going to change the policy on the BNO, we have responded by saying, we are considering refusing to recognize the BNO passports as legal travel documents. That is because the UK will have introduced a measure that signals a departure from their commitments under the MOU of 1984. At that time, they said they were not going to give right of abode to the BNO holders. And we also agreed to regard the BNO passport as a legal travel document. Now since they have violated their commitments, we have to make a response.

Again, with regard to the agreement for the surrender of fugitive offenders, the UK has suspended this indefinitely. I think this will undermine the basis for legal collaboration between the UK and Hong Kong. China has to make a response to that and we announced that the Hong Kong government also suspends the agreement for the surrender of fugitive offenders with the UK. And they also suspend the mutual legal assistance agreement with the UK because the basis and foundations of the legal collaboration between the two sides have been undermined.

Sky News: Thank you, Ambassador. On Hong Kong, in the last couple of days, we've seen a small number of people being arrested under these new security laws, seemingly just for posting comments on the internet, and also a number of pro-democracy activists today being disqualified from running in the elections. Doesn't this really prove the concerns that the UK has about the national security law undermining Hong Kong's freedoms? If I may, as you mentioned Xinjiang, have you had any more clarity about those images that you were shown a couple of weeks ago on the BBC? European security sources say they believe those men who are shackled and shaven, and in those suits, were members of the Uighur minority. Why were they being transported and treated in such a way?

Liu Xiaoming: First, on Hong Kong, the National Security Law is about plugging the legal loopholes and safeguarding national security. You know, for the past 23 years since the handover, there has been no law to take care of national security. We've seen what happened last year. People talk about "One Country, Two Systems". But we all witnessed how the concept of "One Country" has been eroded, how "One Country" has been put at risk. It's timely for the Central Government and the National People's Congress to enact this law to plug the loopholes.

It has nothing to do with freedom of speech or freedom of expression. It is clearly stipulated in the National Security Law that the basic human rights will be fully respected. This law is only targeted at these very few criminals who intend to endanger the national security. The law is very clear with respect to four categories of crimes it covers. If you do not commit crimes which fall into these categories, you will have no problem with regard to freedom of expression, freedom to march and freedom to demonstrate. So the capitalist system will not change, and Hong Kong will continue to enjoy its independent judicial system, including the power of final adjudication. So I think this law will only make "One Country, Two Systems" more sustainable. And so that's why it's overwhelmingly supported by the people of Hong Kong. About three million Hong Kong residents have signed a petition to show their support for this law because they want to have a peaceful, prosperous and stable environment in Hong Kong.

With regard to Xinjiang, I will respond a little later but I will certainly answer your question.

CGTN: Good morning, Ambassador. So you just mentioned that China might stop recognizing BNO passports as valid travel documents. What would that mean in practice for Hong Kong residents who want to travel to the UK? And also, how do you see a path forward for restoring trust and goodwill between China and the UK which has diminished so much on both sides?

Liu Xiaoming: China has done nothing to weaken the mutual trust between the two countries. As I said, we see the UK as a partner, as a friendly country. We want to develop this relationship and the "golden era" between our two countries. As I have said on many occasions, we are about to celebrate the fifth anniversary of the "golden era". It's a time for celebration. But unfortunately, it's the UK side that has done things to undermine that mutual trust by making unwarranted accusations against the National Security Law, interrupting the implementation of this law and interfering in Hong Kong's internal affairs.

So I think, as I have already said in my presentation, the solution for China-UK relations lies in the three basic principles: mutual respect, non interference in each other's internal affairs, and treating each other as equals and partners. And we do recognize that we have differences. But we need to address these differences on an equal basis and recognize differences. China has no intention to change the UK. I think the UK should have no intention to change China. I think we have more common ground and common interests to unite our two countries than differences that divide us. China and the UK, as countries with global influence, have enormous duties to live up to. We have our responsibility to promote world peace and world prosperity. There are so many items in the common agenda in front of us.

With regard to the specific question you raised. Since the UK violated its commitment with regard to BNO, we have to let them know that we must take our measures by refusing to recognize the BNO passport as a valid travel document.

Reuters: Thank you very much, Ambassador. I just wanted to sort of look at a slightly bigger picture. My apology if this is a stupid question, but it seems clear that US President Donald Trump sees China as the major geopolitical foe of the 21st century. So, do you see a new cold war between the West and China? How do you react to the view that President Xi has been too assertive over recent years, and this has upset the Americans.

Liu Xiaoming: I think you have already answered your own questions. It's not China that has become assertive. It's those on the other side of the Pacific Ocean who want to launch a new Cold War on China. So we have to make a response to that. We have no interest in any Cold War. We have no interest in any wars. When the United States started this trade war against China, we said there would be no winner in a trade war and we wanted to engage with them. Then we had a phase one agreement. We still keep on engaging with them. But I think the coronavirus really worsened the situation, because we have all seen what is happening in United States. They tried to find a scapegoat in China. They want to blame China for their problems.

We all know this is the election year. I've been posted twice to Washington DC. I witnessed five elections, on the ground, in person, not from a distance. People say, US politicians will say anything in order to get elected in an election year. It seems to me this year, it is likely that they are not only to say anything but also to do anything, including treating China as an enemy. Probably they think they need an enemy. They think they need a cold war. But we have no interest in that. We keep on telling the Americans: China is not your enemy. China is your friend and your partner. Your enemy is the virus. I hope that US politicians will focus on fighting the virus and saving lives instead of blaming China.

CCTV: Good morning, Ambassador. My question is: the Director-General of the Confederation of British Industry shared her opinions in *Financial Times* a few days ago. She said that the UK cannot afford to self-isolate from China because of the huge benefits from the collaboration between the two countries. But I think as you just mentioned, some British politicians hold the opposite opinion. So what's your comment on that? And also, if it's allowed, can I ask another question: I think you have watched many videos and pictures in the previous interview with the local media. And also you have stated and clarified many times the Chinese policy on the Xinjiang issue. But I think probably my Western colleagues are still keen on discussing similar topics. Personally I think they probably like to blame China for this issue a lot. So what's your comment on this kind of communication? Thank you.

Liu Xiaoming: As I said in my opening remarks, I think China-UK relations really are mutually beneficial. I quite agree with the Director-General of the CBI.

Let me give you a few figures. Some people say that China gains more from this relationship. I don't think this is true. In the past 20 years, from 1999 to 2020, UK exports to China increased twenty times. Since I became Chinese Ambassador, trade between our two countries has doubled. In the past 10 years Chinese investment increased twenty times. So these two "twenty times" are really self evident.

It has created enormous jobs. And each year Chinese tourism to this country supported 11, 000 jobs. Also the UK is the largest recipient of Chinese students in Europe. Of course, Chinese students benefit from studying here. But they make a contribution to this country too. The students' expenditure alone, according to a Cambridge study, supported 17, 000 jobs in 2018, not to mention the contribution made by Huawei. They have helped build the telecommunications industry in this country. And also, some "Cold War warriors" as Chinese people call them are trying to find another target in the nuclear project on which Chinese companies are working together with their French and British partners. I think this project will serve the interests of the UK, and also help the UK to achieve its goal of realising zero emissions by 2050. I really hope that the politicians will look at this from an objective perspective. This is a win-win relationship.

Since two journalists asked questions about Xinjiang, I want to make a response.

On issues relating to Xinjiang, there are so many fallacies and lies that permeate the Western media. They can well be called "the lies of the century". Moreover, some Western countries have been using Xinjiang-related issues to discredit China and interfere in China's internal affairs. Regrettably, the UK is one of them. I would like to take this opportunity to debunk the lies and let the facts be known, so as to show you the real Xinjiang.

First, Xinjiang-related issues have nothing to do with human rights, ethnic groups or religions, but everything to do with combatting violent terrorism, separatism and extremism.

Since the 1990s, especially after the 9/11 terrorist attacks, terrorist, separatist and religious extremist forces have launched thousands of violent attacks in Xinjiang, resulting in devastating casualties among innocent people and a huge loss of property. During the riots on 5th July 2009, which shocked Xinjiang and the whole world, 197 lives were lost and more than 1, 700 people were injured.

In face of such grave situations, the Government of the Xinjiang Autonomous Region has cracked down upon violent terrorist activities in accordance with the law and adopted de-radicalisation measures to address the root causes. These measures have been very effective: there has not been a single terrorist attack for more than three consecutive years in Xinjiang, and the basic rights of all ethnic groups, especially the rights to life, health and development, are fully safeguarded. Therefore, these measures have won extensive and heartfelt support from people of all ethnic groups in Xinjiang.

These measures have also marked an important contribution to the global fight against terrorism, and thus won positive responses from the international community. Since the end of 2018, more than 1,000 people in over 70 groups, including officials from the United Nations, members of foreign diplomatic corps in China, permanent representatives to the UN and other international organisations in Geneva, journalists and representatives of faith groups, have visited Xinjiang. They represent over 90 countries. They spoke highly of the counter-terrorism and de-radicalisation measures in Xinjiang, saying that these are in line with the purposes and principles of the United Nations in cracking down upon terrorism and safeguarding basic human rights, and should be fully recognized and shared with other countries.

In October 2019, representatives from more than 60 countries spoke at the 74th session of the Third Committee of the UN General Assembly in recognition of the human rights progress made in Xinjiang. In July this year, representatives from 46 countries delivered a joint statement at the 44th session of the Human Rights Council in support of China's position and the counter-terrorism measures in Xinjiang.

Now I would like to play a video to help you see the harm caused by terrorist, separatist and extremist attacks in Xinjiang, so that you will understand why the measures taken in Xinjiang against terrorism, separatism and extremism are necessary and important.

Second, there are many rumours and lies about the vocational education and training centres in Xinjiang, calling them "concentration camps" or "re-education camps". The truth is they are none of these. They are useful and positive explorations of preventative and de-radicalisation measures.

The centres were established to address the root causes of extremism and prevent further escalation of violent terrorist activities. They operate in line with the principles and spirit embodied in a number of international documents on counter-terrorism, such as the UN Global Counter-Terrorism Strategy. In nature, they are no different from the Desistance and Disengagement Programme (DDP) of the UK, the community corrections in the United States, or the de-radicalisation centres in France.

At the vocational education and training centres, those who have been led astray by extremist ideas or who have committed minor crimes can learn the common language, legal knowledge and vocational skills. Such education and training will strengthen their ability to break away and stay away from extremist ideas and master vocational skills, helping them to not only become law-abiding citizens but also find stable jobs, earn their own living and lead a better life.

At the centres,

- The Constitutional and legal principles on respecting and safeguarding human rights are being strictly followed, the dignity of the trainees is fully respected, and insults and abuse of all forms are strictly prohibited.
- The freedom of trainees is guaranteed. The centres are managed as boarding schools. Trainees can go on home visits or ask for leave to attend to private affairs.
- Meanwhile, the right of the trainees to use languages of ethnic groups is also fully guaranteed. All rules and regulations, school timetables and menus are written in both the common language and languages of ethnic groups.
- The customs and habits of different ethnic groups are fully respected and protected. A variety of Halal food is provided for free.
- The freedom of religious belief is also fully respected and protected. Religious believers have the freedom to attend lawful religious activities while on home leave.

Now I would like to show you a video in which the trainees at the vocational education and training centres tell the stories of their lives then.

Third, let me turn to the four lies and slanders that are widespread in the Western media about Xinjiang. I think it is wrong to allow the lies and slanders to run amok, or to let arrogance and prejudice prevent people from seeing the facts and truth. So it is important to get the facts and truth out there, so that people can make up their own minds from an objective and reasonable perspective.

The first lie is that "nearly a million Uygurs in Xinjiang are detained".

This is a lie cooked up by an anti-China organization and an individual who is anti-China. The organization is the so-called "Chinese Human Rights Defenders (CHRD)" backed by the government of the United States. Armed with interviews from only eight people who are ethnic Uygurs and based on an extremely rough estimate, the CHRD reached an absurd conclusion that 10% of the more than 20 million people in Xinjiang are being detained at so-called "re-education camps".

The anti-China individual is a man called Adrian Zenz, a far-right fundamentalist funded by the government of the United States. He published an article in the journal *Central Asian Survey*, claiming that "Xinjiang's total re-education internment figure may be estimated at just over one million. " According to The Grayzone, an independent news website, Zenz's conclusion is based on a single report by Istiqlal TV. This so-called "Uygur exile media organization" based in Turkey is far from being a media organization. Istiqlal TV is a group that advocates separatism and extremism. And Zenz himself believes that he is "led by God" on a "mission" against China.

A few days ago when I gave an interview on *The Andrew Marr Show* on BBC, Mr. Marr showed me a footage which he said has "been authenticated by Western intelligence agencies and by Australian experts" to prove that a large number of Uygurs are being detained. Now let's see what is really happening.

The video shows transfer of a group of prisoners from the Kashgar Detention House. It has nothing to do with the so-called "detainment of a large number of Uygurs". China's criminal law does not target members of a specific ethnic group or religion. Everyone is equal before the law. The transfer of prisoners by judicial authorities is a normal judicial practice and brooks no distortion or defamation.

The second lie is that "Xinjiang has demolished a large number of mosques".

The fact is, there are 24,400 mosques in Xinjiang, which means there is on average one mosque for every 530 Muslims. This ratio is higher than that in some Muslim countries and also higher than the number of churches per Christian in England.

The Jiami Mosque of Yecheng County and the Id Kah Mosque in Hotan prefecture, which were claimed to have been "dismantled", were in fact renovated and put to use again. Those who cooked up the lies used the photo of the old, dilapidated mosques to support their untruths. But I will refute their lies with photos of the new, renovated mosques.

The third lie is that "forced sterilization is being carried out in Xinjiang".

The fact is, Xinjiang Uygur Autonomous Region is one of the five ethnic autonomous regions in China. It is home to many ethnic groups, including 13 ethnic groups who have been living there for generations. It is a place where 25 million people of all ethnic groups call home and live together in harmony.

The Chinese Government protects the lawful rights and interests of people of all ethnic groups, whether big or small in population. Over the years, the Uygur people and other ethnic minorities have enjoyed a favourable demographic policy. Between 1978 and 2018, the Uygur population in Xinjiang doubled, from 5.55 million to 11.68 million.

The true identities or stories of the so-called "victims" in the on-line videos about Uygurs being "prosecuted" are not what they claim. These self-claimed "victims" are either the so-called "East Turkistan" elements engaged in anti-China and separatist activities, or "actors" trained by anti-China forces in the US and other Western countries to spread rumours about China. Their claims have no factual ground. The relatives and friends of some of these people in Xinjiang have stood up to refute these rumours and lies.

On *The Andrew Marr Show* that I mentioned earlier, Mr. Marr showed me another video of a so-called "victim". This woman in the video, whose name is Zumrat Dawut, claimed that she went through "forced sterilization". However, her sister and brother publicly refuted her lies last November. It turns out that she has never been to any vocational education and training centre. She had an operation because she was diagnosed with a myoma of the uterus when she had her third child, and she has never been "forced to get sterilized". Now let's watch a video interview given by her sister and brother.

The fourth lie is that "mass forced labour is taking place in Xinjiang".

In fact, this is yet another story fabricated by a hidden hand. This hidden hand is called the Australian Strategic Policy Institute (ASPI), which is funded by the US government and arms dealers. This institute made up the so-called "Uyghurs for sale" report last March, which is a distorted description of people from southern Xinjiang seeking job opportunities in central and eastern China and trying to make a living and throw off poverty. The report refers to stories of these people being used as "forced labour".

After that, this absurd report was taken as "evidence" by the US Congressional-Executive Commission on China to make up the so-called "Global Supply Chains, Forced Labor, and the Xinjiang Uyghur Autonomous Region" report to fling slanders at China.

Now I would like to show you another video to lay bare their lies.

The Chinese people often say, "One does not know how vast and beautiful China is until one visits Xinjiang. " This vast and beautiful region is now witnessing sustained economic growth, social harmony and stability, improved wellbeing, and unprecedented cultural prosperity. People of all ethnic groups in Xinjiang are leading a secure life, getting along with each other in harmony, and enjoying the full right to life and development. Their freedom of religious belief and regular religious activities are protected by law. Now is the most opportune time in history for Xinjiang to realize development.

Rumours will not write off China's progress in safeguarding human rights in Xinjiang. Attempts to disrupt the development and prosperity of Xinjiang will never succeed. It is my hope that you will not believe the rumours or the deceptive words of anti-China elements and politicians.

We urge the UK Government to view the progress and achievements in Xinjiang from a comprehensive and objective perspective, to stop making irresponsible remarks on Xinjiang, and to stop using Xinjiang to interfere in China's internal affairs. We also hope that the British media will cast aside their arrogance and prejudice, and report and cover Xinjiang in an objective and fair manner so as to help the British public see the real Xinjiang.

ITV: Thank you, Ambassador. Will China agree to allow a team from the United Nations Human Rights Council to visit Xinjiang and the facilities that you have just shown us in order to carry out an independent investigation, unfettered, without any interference of the Chinese Communist Party to see for themselves what is going on there?

Liu Xiaoming: As I told you, since 2018 about 1,000 diplomats, journalists and representatives from various countries, and international organisations have been to Xinjiang. We also welcome the UN High Commissioner for Human Rights to visit Xinjiang.

What we are opposed to is the so-called "independent investigation" that has ulterior motives. It is trying to use the Xinjiang issue to interfere into China's internal affairs. Xinjiang's door is always open. Each year hundreds of thousands of tourists visit Xinjiang. People who go there with good intentions, who are objective and unbiased, will be welcomed.

Associated Press: Ambassador, thank you for taking my question. I would like to draw upon your long history in the United States to ask you whether or not you believe relations with the US are at "a point of no return", given the statements from the Trump Administration and the continuing threats that they could make against China?

Liu Xiaoming: I certainly hope not. China still believes that good relations based on mutual respect, non-confrontation, cooperation and coordination are in the best interests of the two countries. We have no intention to undermine this relationship. And we'll try our best to engage the US side.

But as I have said on many occasions, you need two to tango. You need two hands to clap.

I also believe that there is broad-based public support for the relations. Since Nixon's visit to China in 1972, both countries have worked to build a relationship based on common interests. I think the common interests of the two countries are still there. The foundations, especially among the American people, are still there. American people still support engagement with China. When we heard the US Secretary of State make these anti-Chinese Communist Party remarks, I called that a declaration of cold war and we've seen many criticisms of his statement by American people. People are concerned about where this administration will take this relationship.

So I don't think we have passed the "point of no return". I think the fundamental interests that tie the two countries together should remain. And I think the people with vision, with farsightedness, are still working to maintain the fundamentals of this relationship. I hope that common sense will prevail at the end of the day.

Xinhua News Agency: On Huawei, Huawei has been saying that it is an independent and privately-held company, not affiliated with the Chinese government. So why has the Chinese government spared no effort to defend Huawei in the ongoing row? And also if the China-UK relations continue to sour, is there any possibility that the two countries will find themselves in a relationship that is characterized by "hot economically" and "cold politically" (*zheng leng jing re*), which once happened between China and Japan? Thank you.

Liu Xiaoming: On the subject of Huawei, I've just published an article in the *South China Morning Post*. I'm not trying to advertise my article, but I really hope that you can spend some time to read this article.

As a matter of fact, I have tried my very best to have my article printed in major British newspapers, because it's really relevant. I think the British public needs to hear the other side of the story immediately after the UK government's decision to ban Huawei. Unfortunately, no major newspaper would like to carry my article.

I've been here for 10 years. Now I really have a taste of what "freedom of the press" is about in the UK. One of your colleagues told me earlier that they only want to carry articles which they believe will sell better. So they do not carry my article on Hong Kong. They do not carry my article on Huawei. So I really have to let my article fly thousands of miles to Hong Kong, to the *South China Morning Post*. They told me they still have some readers in the UK. So I decided, okay, that's good. I encourage you to read my article in which I say, to refuse Huawei is to refuse opportunities, to refuse growth and to refuse the future. I do not need to elaborate on my main points.

I just want to answer your question about China-UK relationship. As I said in my opening remarks, this issue of Huawei is not about one Chinese company. It's about how the UK treats and deals with China. It is about the big picture. Do you treat China as an opportunity or do you treat China as a threat? Do you treat China as a partner or a rival? That is a fundamental issue. You have to make a choice.

Secondly, governments have to provide protection for the legitimate rights and interests of the business people. It's not only true for the Chinese government but also true for the UK government. I've been here for 10 years. I remember vividly how British leaders and politicians worked very hard on behalf of your businesses. I still remember how even your Prime Minister tried to promote the sale of Diageo while our Premier was here, in a hope that there should be a signing ceremony for the Diageo project in China. I still remember that your Chancellor of Exchequer pushed very hard for the Chinese side to buy Rolls-Royce engines. They told us that Rolls-Royce produces much better engines than any other countries, including GE from the United States. I still remember how your Business Secretary even went to China to promote the sale of British Steel, asked Chinese companies to buy British Steel. And they ended up with a buyer called Jingye who agreed to invest in the next 10 years 1. 2 billion pounds.

I think there's no question about the government working for the business interests of its country. So I think you can't regard China's efforts to raise the Huawei issue as an example of what some "Cold War warriors" claim -- that this shows that Huawei is close to the Chinese government. We treat Chinese businesses as equals. We hope Huawei is succeeding in this country. It's a win-win situation. So that's why I said on the day the British government made its decision that this was a dark day for Huawei, a dark day for China-UK relations, and an even darker day for the United Kingdom because it will miss the opportunity to become a leading country in 5G infrastructure.

You also mentioned the relationship being "cold politically and warm economically". I think the two are related. You need to have a good atmosphere to engage with each other. When I said it was a dark day for China-UK relations, it's because the decision really undermines the trust between the two countries and the credibility of the UK government. So that's why there are a number of concerns from Chinese businesses. I held a webinar with Chinese businesses right after the UK's ban on Huawei. All parties expressed their concerns because there was a perceived security risk, there was an investment risk. So I think you can't separate the two. We have no intention to politicize economic affairs. But you have to realize that trust and credibility are important factors for countries to be able to engage with each other.

Thank you for your questions.

构建"双循环"新发展格局
——回答中英工商界关于十九届五中全会精神提问

2020年11月17日，我在中国英国商会、48家集团俱乐部、英中贸协、英中协会联合举办的中共十九届五中全会精神在线宣介会上发表题为《把握新机遇，注入新信心，开启新征程》的主旨演讲并回答提问。答问全文如下：

英国48家集团俱乐部主席斯蒂芬·佩里： 感谢刘大使的精彩演讲，演讲清晰而全面地阐述了十九届五中全会的内容。我对中国区域发展规划很感兴趣。中国将建设四个主要城市群，每个区域的人口可能超过1亿。请问英国如何与这些区域开展合作，向其提供英国的服务和商品？

刘晓明： 中国是一个幅员辽阔的国家，不同省、市和地区的发展情况不尽相同，发展不平衡不充分问题仍然突出。对此，中国政府因地制宜，积极促进区域协调发展。

第一，中国西部发展落后于东部，20多年前中国政府开始实施西部大开发战略。我担任驻埃及大使后，曾到中国西部省份甘肃省挂职，担任了两年省长助理，对此有切身体会。20多年来，西部大开发战略取得显著成绩，西部地区发展面貌焕然一新。如果各位有机会到甘肃省省会兰州看一看，一定会留下非常深刻的印象。第二，中国的中部地区相对发达，但仍落后于东部沿海地区。中部地区有很强的自身优势，既不同于西部，也不同于东部。为此，我们实施了中部崛起战略，旨在挖掘中部六省的发展潜力。第三，东部大部分地区位于沿海地带，拥有上海、广州和深圳等许多发达城市，我们鼓励东部地区率先发展、加快推进现代化。第四，我们实施东北振兴战略。东北地区过去和现在都是中国的重要工业基地。早在20世纪50年代，东北地区就汇聚了一大批工业项目，为中国现代化建设做出了巨大贡献。除了工业外，这一地区在农业上也非常重要。东北土地肥沃，是中国最优质的大米和小麦等作物产地。我们通过统筹区域发展，更好促进发达地区和欠发达地区、东中西部和东北地区共同发展。

关于城市群建设，我们也制订和实施了发展规划。我们正深入推进京津冀协同发展、长三角一体化和粤港澳大湾区建设，这些地区都各有优势。英国也制定了"英格兰北方经济中心""中部引擎"等区域发展战略。我认为，中英在区域发展合作方面潜力巨大。我们要挖掘双方地区优势和机遇，加强区域发展战略对接，努力实现合作共赢、共同发展。

英中贸协主席古沛勤爵士： 英中贸易协会见证了中国经济的快速发展。很高兴看到今年前8个月英国对中国出口额增长近10%，表现十分抢眼。中国在英留学生数量稳定，中国对英投资前景广阔。根据英中贸协调查，英中贸易为英国本地贡献了超过10万个就业岗位。我们十分欢迎中国扩大对外开放。开放不仅对中国十分重要，也能为英国带来繁荣。我们企业界对"双循环"非常关注，希望刘大使再谈谈对"双循环"的看法以及英国企业如何能从中获益。

刘晓明： 构建"双循环"的新发展格局是中国积极应对国际国内形势变化做出的战略抉择，不是权宜之计，而是长期战略。第一，当前经济全球化遭遇逆流，单边主义、保护主义上升，新冠肺炎疫情带来广泛而深远的影响，传统国际经济循环明显弱化。在这种情况下，中国强化国内经济大循环，有利于增强经济发展的韧性，也有利于带动国际经济循环。第二，中国国内大循环的动能明显增强。中国作为世界第二大经济体，和其他大国经济一样，国内供给和国内需求对于中国经济循环日益起到主要支撑作用。第三，新发展格局强调的绝不是封闭的国内循环，而是开放的国际国内"双循环"。中国将在充分发挥超大规模市场优势的同时，深入参与国际循环，扩大外资企业的市场准入，打造市场化、法治化、国际化营商环境，依托国内强大市场，成为吸引全球优质要素资源的强大引力场，成为外商投资兴业的沃土。

在"双循环"格局下，中国将在更高水平上扩大对外开放，努力使国际国内市场相互促进，充分利用两个市场优势实现共赢。这对英国企业而言意味着更大机遇。我衷心希望英国工商界能够充分抓住"双循环"机遇，增强信心，进一步扩大中英经贸等领域合作。

英中协会主任葛珍珠： 感谢刘大使介绍"十四五"规划和2035年远景目标。我来自英中协会，与中国很多机构都有密切合作。请问刘大使如何看待未来中国的法治建设？中国将如何推进相关领域改革？

刘晓明："十四五"规划和2035年远景目标不局限于经济领域，而是中国的全面发展战略。"十四五"规划明确了未来5年中国经济社会发展的主要目标，可以概括为"六个新"：一是经济发展取得新成效；二是改革开放迈出新步伐；三是社会文明程度得到新提高；四是生态文明建设实现新进步；五是民生福祉达到新水平；六是国家治理效能得到新提升。其中提高社会文明程度和提升国家治理效能，都与社会主义法治建设密切相关。十九届五中全会通过的这些建议明确了指导原则和方向。明年"两会"期间，中国政府将进一步制定和通过具体的政策、框架和举措。建议你密切关注明年"两会"。总之，中国将加快建设社会主义法治国家，全面推进依法治国，不断完善中国特色社会主义法律体系。

英国中国商会会长方文建：中国和有关国家刚刚签署了《区域全面经济伙伴关系协定》（RCEP）。该协议获批生效后，中国会否更重视与该协议签署国的合作？这是否会影响未来中英经贸投资合作？你如何看待中英商谈自贸协定前景？这与RCEP有何关系？

刘晓明：RCEP是中国与有关国家共同努力达成的重大成就，是自由贸易和多边主义的胜利，不仅将有力推动亚太地区发展，也为促进世界经济增长提供新动力。这并不意味着未来中国只关注亚太地区。正如我在演讲中所说，中国积极发展全球伙伴关系，英国和欧洲都是中国的重要合作伙伴。习近平主席在第三届中国国际进口博览会开幕式上指出，中国愿同更多国家商签高标准自由贸易协定。我们对与英国达成高标准自贸协定持积极开放态度。英国工商界对此完全不必担心。我担任驻英大使10多年来，中国对英直接投资增长约20倍，这在中英关系史上从未有过。英国对包括中国企业在内的外资企业仍具有吸引力。

当然，毋庸讳言，中国企业对英国也有关切。首先，是脱欧带来的不确定性。目前仍不清楚英国最终会"有协议脱欧"还是"无协议脱欧"，我们密切关注英欧谈判进展。其次，英国有些势力企图推翻英国主流社会形成的共识，即中国是英国的合作伙伴，中国的发展是英国的机遇。他们把中国视作威胁，甚至是"敌对国家"。现在英国议会正在审议《国家安全和外国投资法案》。英政府高官告诉我有关法案并不针对具体国家。我们希望英国能继续为中国企业提供公平、公正、透明和非歧视的营商环境。如能做到这一点，我相信未来仍会有更多的中资企业来英投资兴业。

英国中国商会会长方文建（代表与会人员提问）： 近日，（针对中国全国人大常委会关于香港特区立法会议员资格决定）英国外交发展部多次"指责"中国违反国际义务和《中英联合声明》。有报道称英方可能因此"制裁"中国官员。针对英国政府和议会的有关言行，中方将做何反应？

刘晓明： 近日有媒体炒作，我因涉港问题被英国外交发展部常务次官"召见"。实际上，我在会见中向他清楚阐明中方严正立场，即中方坚决反对英方干涉香港事务和中国内政。英方总是借口《中英联合声明》指责中国"没有履行国际义务"。今年是联合国成立75

周年,可能有些人不知道,中国是75年前第一个签署《联合国宪章》的国家。中国一直遵守《联合国宪章》,始终履行应尽的国际义务;中国加入了几乎所有政府间国际组织,签署了500多项国际公约。没有任何证据证明中国违反了国际义务。恰恰相反,是英方违反了国际义务。《联合国宪章》确立的基本原则,首先就是国家主权平等、互相尊重、互不干涉内政。英国干涉香港事务和中国内政,就是违反国际义务的行为。中国全国人大常委会关于香港特区立法会议员资格的决定合理、合法、合宪,符合中国宪法和香港基本法。

我在许多场合谈到过,中英关系面临的一大问题是,互相尊重主权和领土完整、互不干涉内政的国际关系基本准则遭到破坏。这就是当前中英关系遭遇困难的根本原因。今年是英国承认新中国70周年。70年前,英国成为第一个承认中华人民共和国的西方大国。70年来,中英关系取得巨大发展,但也经历起伏。事实证明,只要恪守国际法和国际关系基本准则,中英关系就能向前发展;反之则遭遇挫折,甚至倒退。中方仍然重视中英关系,一个良好的中英关系不仅有利于两国人民,也有利于世界和平与稳定。中英都是具有全球影响力的国家,都是联合国安理会常任理事国和二十国集团重要成员。在双边领域和全球事务上,我们有很多共同议程。因此,我们有一千条理由发展好中英关系,而没有一条理由把中英关系搞坏。但是,"探戈需要两个人跳",希望英方珍惜来之不易的中英关系,与中方相向而行,共同推动两国关系早日重归正轨。

我常说,经贸合作是中英关系的基石。我常鼓励在英中资企业在双边关系中发挥"稳定剂"和"推进器"作用。但是，政治互信与经济合作密不可分，如果政治互信受损，整体双边关系就会受到影响。有互信才能做好生意。希望中英两国企业共同努力，克服当前困难，为两国关系发展贡献正能量。

英国议会跨党派"一带一路"与中巴经济走廊小组顾问阿夫塔布："一带一路"已经将中国和外国市场联系在一起，现在中国提出了国内国际"双循环"，请问"一带一路"与"双循环"是什么关系？

刘晓明： "双循环"是在新形势下中国推动构建的新发展格局。"一带一路"已成为规模最大的国际合作平台。"双循环"与共建"一带一路"之间有着密切的关系。"一带一路"是构建"双循环"的重要渠道。"丝绸之路经济带"联通了中国与中亚、欧洲等地区国家，"21世纪海上丝绸之路"将中国与东南亚等地区国家联系起来，"双循环"也为共建"一带一路"提供了更大动力。我认为，未来"双循环"与"一带一路"将相互促进、相得益彰，会让"一带一路"更加高效、更富有成果。

A New Growth Pattern of "Dual Circulation"
—— Q&A with Chinese and British Business Communities
(on the 5th Plenary Session of the 19th CPC Central Committee)

After delivering a speech on the Fifth Plenary Session of the 19th CPC Central Committee, I took questions from the Chinese and British Business Communities.

Stephen Perry, Chairman of the 48 Group Club: Thank you, Ambassador, for your comprehensive introduction to the 5th Plenary Session of the 19th CPC Central Committee. I have been interested in the development of the regions. It looks to me like that China will create four major metropolises of maybe over 100 million people each. How could the UK approach these new emerging regions in order to offer their services and goods?

Liu Xiaoming: China is a large country and certain provinces, municipalities and regions are distinctive. Some of the problems China faces are its development which includes imbalance and inadequacy. So how do you achieve a balanced development to ensure that people share the benefits of the reform and opening up? The Party and government have formulated different strategies for different regions.

First, more than 20 years ago, the government initiated the strategy of large-scale development in the western region. After serving as Ambassador to Egypt, I was seconded for two years as an assistant governor of Gansu Province, one of the provinces in the western part of China. The strategy of large-scale development in the western region has been going on for more than 20 years and substantial progress has been achieved. The landscape has changed completely. If you look at the landscape of Lanzhou, the capital city of Gansu Province, you will be very impressed.

Second, the central part of China is relatively developed, but still underdeveloped compared with the eastern part of China. We are following a strategy known as "the rise of the central region". This strategy aims to unlock the potential of the six provinces within this region. This region has very strong advantages, but they're different from the Western part of China and, also, different from the Eastern part of China.

Third, we have the trailblazing development of the eastern region. Most of the region lies in the coastal area and there are more developed cities here like Shanghai, Guangzhou, Shenzhen and many others.

Fourth, the full revitalization of the northeast. It used to be and is still an industrial base within China. In the 1950s, it was home to many projects. It contributed a great deal to China's modernization. Even today, it is still an industrial base and agriculturally very important. It has very fertile land and produces the best quality rice, wheat and so on.

So these are the four big major areas. We have adopted a balanced approach to regional development aiming at better promoting the development of both developed and underdeveloped regions, and achieving common development for the eastern, central, western and northeastern part of China.

And we also have different development strategies for metropolises. There is the coordinated development of the Beijing-Tianjin-Hebei region, the development of the Guangdong-Hong Kong-Macao Greater Bay Area, and the integrated development of the Yangtze River Delta. Each area and each region has its own strength.

Here in the UK, you have schemes such as the Northern Powerhouse and the Midland Engine. So I think there is great potential for China and the UK to dovetail regional strategies. We need to uncover the strengths of each region and find opportunities to work together and develop together to enjoy the benefits of regional cooperation.

Sir Sherard Cowper-Coles, Chair of the China-Britain Business Council: The CBBC sees the fact of China's growth as a great economic power. So we're delighted that the latest figures show in the first eight months of this year, British exports to China rose by nearly 10%. We're delighted that the number of Chinese students in Britain remains stable, that the pipeline of Chinese investments remains extremely promising. And the research which the CBBC has commissioned shows more than 100, 000 jobs across the United Kingdom are attributable to our trade with China. So we welcome this opening up. It's important for China, of course. It's vital for China, but also as part of Britain's future prosperity. So with that in mind, a lot of the sinologists around me have been intrigued by the concept of dual circulation. Could you please explain to all of us a bit more of your understanding of the concept of "dual circulation" and how that will help those of us who want to benefit from it.

Liu Xiaoming: I think I gave a brief introduction to "dual circulation" in my speech. To set up a new growth pattern of "dual circulation" is a strategic choice. China is coping positively with changes in the domestic and international situation. It is a long-term strategy rather than an expedient measure.

First, as to domestic circulation. I think you are familiar with the challenges in the international arena. The world economy is experiencing grave recession because of the rising headwinds of protectionism, unilateralism, and also the broad and deep impact of the COVID-19 pandemic. All these have resulted in an obvious weakening in the traditional international patterns of circulation. So we need to make some adjustments to strengthen our domestic circulation in order to consolidate the resilience of economic growth and to enhance the international economic circulation.

Number two, the energy of domestic circulation is strengthened. You know when a country develops to a certain stage, for instance, China has now become the second largest economy, it also opens up a huge domestic market for itself. Like other great economic powers, domestic supply and demand play a more important supporting role in Chinese economic circulation.

Thirdly, the new growth pattern emphasizes that "dual circulation" is by no means a closed domestic circulation. On the contrary, it means that China will be more open both in the domestic and international markets. It allows you greater space to develop and to maneuver. So, we need to make the best use of the domestic market, to unlock the potential of our domestic market. The domestic circulation means the whole country is regarded as a unified market. How should we tap the potential of the huge market in China? China will take full advantage of this huge market and participate extensively in international circulation. Moreover, China will also expand market access for foreign enterprises to build a market-oriented, law-based international business environment. And we will rely on a strong domestic market to attract high-quality global production factors in order to become a fertile soil for foreign investment.

So what we're saying is that the domestic market will play a leading role, but the international market and domestic market will have their role to play in reinforcing each other. Now China will make more efforts to integrate international and domestic market. How should we achieve a win-win situation in both markets? How should we take advantage of both markets? That means there will be more opportunities rather than fewer opportunities for UK business. So, I do hope that UK businesses will take advantage of this concept of "dual circulation", and China-UK cooperation and partnership will contribute to its development. And so, you have nothing to worry about. I do hope my speech will give you the confidence to become involved and to participate in this "dual circulation" and development.

Merethe MacLeod, Executive Director of the Great Britain China Centre: Thank you, Mr. Ambassador, for outlining the Five Year Plan so succinctly for us. You know I represent the Great Britain China Centre and we've worked very closely with institutions in China on the rule of law. I've been very keen to hear your views on how you see rule of law, or what the top priorities for legal reform are to support China's development in the next few years.

Liu Xiaoming: This Five Year Plan, and the goals for 2035, are not only about economic development. It's a multi-dimensional development strategy for China. Take the 14th Five Year Plan for example. It sets the targets for China in the next five years in six new areas. First, to strive to make new strides in economic development. Second, to take new steps in reform and opening up. Third, to make a new development in the social etiquette and civility. Fourth, to make new progress in building on ecological civilization. Fifth, to boost the well-being of the people. Sixth, to enhance the capacity for governance. The third and the sixth points are closely related to the construction of the socialist rule of law.

This is what the plenary session has adopted. The proposals establish the guidelines and directions. In the next Two Sessions, the central government will introduce specific policies, as well as the framework and measures on how to translate these guidelines into specific policies. I advise you to follow the Two Sessions closely. In short, we are building a country that enforces the rule of law. There will also be comprehensive reforms in legal areas and law enforcement. There will be a great many expectations.

Fang Wenjian, Chairman of the China Chamber of Commerce in the UK: Recently, China signed the Regional Comprehensive Economic Partnership (RCEP) agreement (with 14 other participating countries). With the ratification of the RCEP agreement, will China pay more attention to cooperation with the signatories of the agreement? Will this affect China-UK trade and investment cooperation in the future? With Brexit,

有问必答
No Question Unanswered

China and UK are going to sign free trade agreement. What is the relationship here with the RECP?

Liu Xiaoming: I think that the RCEP is a great achievement. I call it "a victory for free trade". It will provide a big boost to development in the Asia-Pacific region, but that does not mean China will focus only on this region. As I said in my presentation, China has a global vision. We want to build partnerships around the world. The UK and Europe are important partners for China. I would like to call your attention to the important speech made by President Xi Jinping at the opening ceremony of the Third China International Import Expo. President Xi said we would like to sign high-standard free trade agreements with more countries. So, when it comes to the UK, we are open, positive and forthcoming in terms of engaging with our UK partners over here in order to reach a high-standard free trade agreement. We're ready for that.

I think that the UK business community has nothing to worry about. Chinese businesses, like the Bank of China, still feel positive about the UK market. That is why I always quote the figure that over the past 10 years, since I became Chinese Ambassador to the UK, Chinese investment in the UK has increased 20 times. That has never happened before in the history of China-UK relations. The UK still remains attractive to foreign businesses, including Chinese businesses.

Having said that, we have our own concerns as well. First of all, there are the uncertainties created by Brexit. We don't know whether there will be a Brexit with a deal or without a deal, so we are following these negotiations between the UK and the EU very closely.

Secondly, we also have concerns that there are some diehard 'Cold War warriors' who regard China as a threat, even a 'hostile country', rather than a source of opportunities. They are pushing in the House of Commons to launch a security review with regard to foreign investment. We have been told by the British government that it is not targeting Chinese businesses.

What we are asking for is that the UK should continue to provide fair, just, transparent and non-discriminatory treatment for Chinese businesses. If the UK continues to provide a business-friendly environment for Chinese businesses, I'm sure there will be further Chinese investments over in the years to come.

Fang Wenjian (on behalf of other participants): The UK's Foreign, Commonwealth and Development Office (FCDO) has in the last few days made allegations against China to the effect that it has violated the Sino-British Joint Declaration (in response to the Decision of the Standing Committee of the National People's Congress of China on the Qualification of Members of the Legislative Council of the Hong Kong Special Administrative Region). There are reports that possible sanctions have been considered against Chinese and Hong Kong officials on the UK side. In the event of such unfriendly acts by the UK authorities, including the UK government and parliament, what concrete actions would China take to retaliate?

Liu Xiaoming: It has been reported that I was summoned by Sir Philip Barton, the Permanent Under-Secretary and the top civil servant in the FCDO of the UK, to talk about Hong Kong. I made our position very clear that we are strongly opposed to the UK's interference in Hong Kong affairs, which are China's internal affairs. As for the accusation that China is "failing to fulfill its international obligations", I said, this year marks the 75th anniversary of the United Nations. Not many people know that China was the first country to add its signature to the UN Charter 75 years ago. And since then China has continually abided by the UN Charter and has been fulfilled its international obligations. China has joined almost all inter-governmental organizations and has signed more than 500 international conventions. There are no records of China having violated international obligations. I argued in the meeting that it is the UK side that has failed to implement and live up to its international obligations. The key principle of the UN Charter is that every sovereign state should be respected on an equal basis and should not interfere in other countries' internal affairs. So the UK has violated its international obligations by interfering in Hong Kong affairs and China's internal affairs. So I told them that the decision made by the Standing Committee of the National People's Congress of China is reasonable, constitutional, and consistent with the Constitution of China and the Basic Law.

As I have said on many occasions, now we are encountering some problems in China-UK relations. The major problem is that the basic norms governing international relations, that is to say, respect for sovereignty and non-interference in each other's internal affairs, have been violated. This year is the 70th anniversary of the UK first recognizing the New China. The UK was the first Western power to recognize the People's Republic of China. We always acknowledge that. Over the past 70 years, we have made tremendous progress in China-UK relations. But sometimes we run into difficulties. I always say, if these basic principles are abided by, China-UK relationship will move forward; otherwise, it will suffer setbacks or even backslide. So that's the key reason for the current problems in China-UK relations.

Having said that, we still attach great importance to this relationship because we believe that a good relationship between our two countries not only benefits our two peoples but also contributes to world peace and development. China and the UK are two countries with global influence. We are two permanent members of the UN Security Council. We are important members of the G20. And we have a lot of common agendas globally and bilaterally. So we have every reason to make this relationship succeed. We have no reason at all to let it fail. But, as I said on many occasions, "you need two to tango". We hope the UK side will cherish the hard-won relationship and work together with us.

I always say, the business relationship is the bedrock of the overall relationship. So I always encourage Chinese businesses in the UK to play the role of stabilizer and promoter in this relationship. But, if the political relationship is damaged and if mutual trust is damaged, there will be consequences for the overall relationship. In China we have a saying, "friendship goes ahead of business". I think friendship comes from mutual trust. I do hope, by working together, we can overcome the current difficulties, set the relationship back on the right track and elevate our partnership to a new level in the new year.

Aftab Siddiqui, Adviser to the All Party Parliamentary Group on the BRI and the CPEC: The Belt and Road Initiative is bringing foreign and Chinese domestic markets together. How do we see the Belt and Road Initiative and the "dual circulation" model coming together and what is their relationship?

Liu Xiaoming: "Dual circulation" is a new development pattern that China is promoting under the new situation. BRI has become the largest international cooperation platform. These two are very closely related. As a matter of fact, the BRI is a channel of dual circulation. Via the Silk Road Economic Belt, China is connected with Central Asia and Europe. Via the 21st Century Maritime Silk Road, we're connecting the ASEAN countries. So "dual circulation" provides great impetus for the joint construction of the BRI. I think the BRI and "dual circulation" will strengthen and reinforce each other. Dual circulation will make the BRI more efficient and more productive.

香港问题
Hong Kong

本章收录了我就香港问题举行的4场中外记者会。第一场是2019年7月3日，我就香港发生暴力冲击立法会事件举行中外记者会。我指出，极端激进分子以极为暴力的方式冲击香港立法会大楼，践踏了香港法治，破坏了香港社会秩序，损害了香港的根本利益，是对"一国两制"底线的公然挑战。在这样一个大是大非的问题上，英国政府选择站在错误一边。英方不仅发表不当言论，干预香港事务，而且为暴力违法分子撑腰打气。更有甚者，英方试图干扰香港法治，阻挠特区政府将肇事者绳之以法。我强调，香港是中国的特别行政区，不是英国殖民统治下的香港。香港事务纯属中国内政，任何国家、组织和个人都无权干预。我们对英方粗暴干涉香港事务和中国内政表示强烈不满和坚决反对。

第二场记者会是2019年8月15日。自前次记者会后，香港暴力事件不断升级，社会波及面越来越广，严重挑战香港法治和社会秩序，严重威胁香港市民生命财产安全，严重破坏香港繁荣稳定，严重触碰"一国两制"原则底线，致使香港面临回归以来最严峻的局面。我在记者会上指出，中国中央政府绝不会放任少数人以暴力行径把香港拖向危险的深渊，绝不允许任何人破坏香港的法治与良好发展局面，绝不允许任何人以任何借口破坏"一国两制"。如果香港局势进一步恶化，出现香港特区政府不能控制的动乱，中国中央政府绝不会坐视不管。按照《基本法》规定，中国中央政府有足够多的办法、足够强大的力量迅速平息可能出现的各种动乱。

我在准备第三场记者会的时候，外交部宣布习近平主席将于2019年11月14日赴巴西出席金砖国家领导人第十一次会晤。我预感到习主席将在出访期间就香港问题发表重要讲话，便把记者会的时间安排在习主席出席金砖会晤之后。果不出我所料，习主席在出席会议期间就香港局势表明中国政府严正立场。习主席用"三个严重"给香港局势定性，指出香港持续发生的激进暴力犯罪行为，严重践踏法治和社会秩序，严重破坏香港繁荣稳定，严重挑战"一国两制"原则底线。用"三个坚定支持"表明中央人民政府对特区政府的支持，强调中央人民政府将继续坚定支持行政长官带领香港特别行政区政府依法施政，坚定支持香港警方严正执法，坚定支持香港司法机构依法惩治暴力犯罪分子。用"三个坚定不移"表明中国政府的决心，强调中国政府维护国家主权、安全、发展利益的决心坚定不移，贯彻"一国两制"方针的决心坚定不移，反对任何外部势力干涉香港事务的决心坚定不移。

4天后，我在伦敦举行第三次涉港中外记者会，在第一时间通过西方主流媒体平台向世界解读习主席的重要讲话，指出习主席的讲话字字铿锵，句句千钧，是中国中央政府对香港当前局势和未来出路发出的最权威的声音。

英国各大电视台和主流报刊对这次记者会进行广泛、滚动报道，大幅引用我转述的习主席的重要讲话，突出报道"中国要求西方停止干涉香港事务"，"中国有决心有能力平息香港动乱"，对西方反华势力和反中乱港分子产生有效震慑。

第四场记者会是2020年7月6日，我就《中华人民共和国香港特别行政区维护国家安全法》举行中外记者会。我有针对性地批驳了英国媒体对香港国安法的误读、误解甚至歪曲，指出香港国安法的实施，为"一国两制"行稳致远提供了强大支撑，为香港居民的权利和自由提供了坚实保障，堪称"一国两制"实践进程中的重要里程碑，具有重大现实意义和深远历史意义。

4场记者会，中外主流媒体悉数出席、踊跃提问，包括英国广播公司（BBC）、BBC广播四台、天空新闻台、英国电视四台、独立电视台、《金融时报》《每日电讯报》《泰晤士报》《卫报》《经济学家》、路透社，新华社、《人民日报》、中国中央电视台、中国国际电视台等中国媒体，以及美联社、彭博社、美国全国广播公司、美国哥伦比亚广播公司、法新社、今日俄罗斯电视台、加拿大广播公司、凤凰卫视资讯台、《南华早报》《欧洲时报》《英中时报》《侨报》等33家媒体近50名记者出席。BBC、天空新闻台、中国国际电视台对记者会进行了现场直播。

"一国两制"底线不容挑战
——关于香港发生暴力冲击立法会事件中外记者会
（2019年7月3日，中国驻英国大使馆）

刘晓明： 7月1日，是香港各界人士纪念香港回归祖国和香港特别行政区成立的喜庆日子。但在这一天，却发生了一些极端激进分子以极为暴力的方式冲击香港立法会大楼、肆意损坏立法会设施的事件。他们的行为早已突破了言论自由和和平示威的界限，践踏了香港法治，破坏了香港社会秩序，损害了香港的根本利益，是对"一国两制"底线的公然挑战，我们对此予以强烈谴责。特区政府将依法追究暴力犯罪者的刑事责任，中央政府坚决支持香港特区政府对这起严重违法事件追究到底，依法处置；支持特区政府尽快恢复社会正常秩序，保障市民人身和财产安全，维护香港的繁荣稳定。

在这样一个大是大非的问题上，英国政府选择站在错误一边。英方不仅发表不当言论，干预香港事务，而且为暴力违法分子撑腰打气。更有甚者，英方试图干扰香港法治，阻挠特区政府将肇事者绳之以法。中方已就此向英方多次提出严正交涉。在此我想再次强调，香港是中国的特别行政区，不是英国殖民统治下的香港。香港事务纯属中国内政，任何国家、组织和个人都无权干预。我们对英方粗暴干涉香港事务和中国内政表示强烈不满和坚决反对。

有问必答
No Question Unanswered

中方维护国家主权、安全和发展利益的决心坚定不移，维护香港繁荣稳定的决心坚定不移，坚决反对外部势力干预的态度坚定不移。我们要求英方深刻反省错误言行的后果，立即停止以任何方式干预香港事务和中国内政。

多国媒体，特别是英国媒体对此次事件做了大量报道，但坦率地讲，一些报道存在严重偏见，有些甚至是恶意中伤。我接到了不少媒体的采访要求，今天举行这场中外记者会，就是为了使更多媒体听到中方的声音，了解中方的立场，以正视听。现在我愿回答各位记者提问。

BBC： 第一个问题，此时此刻此地你能否保证，中国将遵守其签署的、直到2047年都有效的国际条约《中英联合声明》的承诺？第二个问题，中国中央政府接下来会怎么做？会不会以7月1日事件为借口对未来和平示威进行镇压？

刘晓明： 你认为中国会"镇压和平示威"的想法依据是什么？首先，你对中方立场的理解完全是错误的。中国政府奉行"一国两制"的决心坚定不移。我要指出的是，"一国两制"是中国政府向全世界做出的庄严承诺，并不是对英国政府的承诺。根据《基本法》，香港1997年回归，其基本制度保持50年不变。《中英联合声明》已经完成了其历史使命，成为历史文件。根据这个文件，英国政府向中国交还香港，中国恢复对香港行使主权，自1984年至1997年的过渡期内，英国政府负责香港的行政管理。随着香港回归祖国的怀抱，《中英联合声明》中没有任何条款允许英国对香港行使任何权利。我建议你仔细阅读一下《中英联合声明》。

BBC： 《中英联合声明》第12条写明，中华人民共和国对香港的方针政策50年不变。这不仅指《基本法》，还应包括《中英联合声明》。

刘晓明： 我们说的50年不变，指的就是"一国两制"，不是《中英联合声明》，希望你注意文字的严谨性。《中英联合声明》没有任何条款给予英方插手香港事务的权利，也没有赋予英国所谓"监督""一国两制"实施情况的权利。

中央政府坚决支持香港特区有关机构依法将暴力犯罪者绳之以法，根本不是你所说的对香港游行示威进行所谓"镇压"。冲击立法会是一起严重的暴力事件，我们对香港特区政府依法妥善处置事件有信心。

独立电视台： 中方称英国政府干涉香港事务，是否要求英国政府就有关言论道歉？

刘晓明： 中方已多次向英方提出严正交涉，要求英方停止干涉香港事务，避免进一步损害中英关系。

路透社： 今天，英国保守党领袖候选人约翰逊对路透社记者表示，香港目前的局势令人担忧，怀疑"一国两制"是否仍在发挥作用。你对他的表态有何评论？鉴于约翰逊和亨特均有可能当选下任首相，你是否认为英中关系的未来将走下坡路？

有问必答 No Question Unanswered

刘晓明： 无论谁当选英国首相，我们都希望他能遵守中英两国政府达成的共识，即相互尊重主权和领土完整，互不干涉内政，这是中英关系的基石。如新任首相违背了上述原则，中英关系肯定将出现问题。

英国电视四台： 你认为逃犯引渡条例什么时候能通过？

刘晓明： 香港特区政府已宣布暂停修例，林郑月娥行政长官已明确表示，本届立法会对修例不设时间表。修例需要大量工作和时间，本届立法会明年7月任期届满，已无时间处理修例问题。我们对香港特区政府的决定表示理解和尊重，并且完全支持。

英国电视四台： 你认为修例是就此终止还是会重新启动？

刘晓明： 这应由香港特区政府决定。我相信香港特区政府将同民众进行充分沟通，让民众理解修例符合港人的利益，香港应该堵塞法律漏洞，不应继续成为"避罪天堂"，而应成为"正义天堂"。我希望特区政府能够成功地同民众沟通并达成共识。

天空新闻台： 你将冲击立法会的人称为极端激进分子，你认为他们的行为是恐怖主义吗？你希望英国政府不再干涉香港事务，以免给英中关系带来进一步损害。英国政府的举动是不是已经损害了英中关系？关于冲击立法会大楼事件有一种"阴谋论"，对此你怎么看？

刘晓明： 首先，冲击立法会的是什么人，不归我来定义，最终将由香港法庭来确定他们是不是违法犯罪分子。他们公然破坏立法会设施，这是一种公然违法行为，应该为他们的行为负责。我认为中英关系在某种程度上已经因英方干涉香港事务受到损害。如我所言，中英关系的基石是相互尊重、互不干涉内政。如果英方继续干涉，无疑会继续损害两国关系。我希望英国政府反思其在香港问题上的言行，认识到干涉中国内部事务的严重后果，避免给两国关系造成进一步损害。

天空新闻台： 有传言说冲击立法会大楼的行动是一些混在示威人群中的亲中分子挑唆的，你对此怎么看？

刘晓明： 首先，谣言不值一评。其次，根据香港警察部门负责人的介绍，冲击立法会大楼的人目的在于扰乱香港社会秩序，他们是极端分子，违反了香港的法律。

中国国际电视台： 外交大臣亨特表示英国支持香港人民争取自由，我们都知道，香港在英国统治时期，没有任何形式的民主，包括选举权，你认为英国为什么现在如此关注香港的民主？

刘晓明： 我认为亨特外交大臣谈自由是大错特错了，这不是所谓自由问题，而是违反了香港的法律问题。这样一个高级别官员对违法者表示支持，我感到非常失望。我们都记得22年前在英国殖民统治下的香港是什么样子，当时没有任何形式的自由和民主，历届港督均由英国政府指派，老百姓没有选举权，司法不独立，没有终审权，终审权属于英国枢密院司法委员会。我们都应该看到，与英国殖民统治下的香港相比，现在港人拥有更多民主和自由权利，他们通过选举委员会选举自己的行政长官，参政热情高涨。2015年，中国全国人大同意香港实行普选，一人一票选举他们的行政长官，但遗憾的是该提案没有在香港立法会通过。香港人民还享有高度自治权，自己决定自己的事务，除了立法权、独立司法权外，还拥有终审权，香港真的是今非昔比。一些英国政客对香港的自由和法治说三道四，但当香港法治被破坏时，他们不仅不谴责违法者，却反过来支持和同情他们，这样的表现令人难以置信。

凤凰卫视资讯台： 你对英国未来的首相在香港问题上的立场怎么看？约翰逊今天就香港问题发表了一些评论，会不会影响未来中英合作？

刘晓明： 如我之前所说，中国希望英国政府履行承诺，恪守两国建交时达成的基本原则，即互不干涉内政。中英之间在携手努力、共同维护香港繁荣稳定方面有共同利益。1984年之前，香港是中英关系发展的障碍，自从我们达成《中英联合声明》，尤其是香港回归以后，香港不仅不再是中英关系发展的障碍，而且成为中英关系的桥梁和积极因素。香港应在中英之间继续发挥积极作用，而不是重新变成障碍。

《中国日报》： 有人认为西方媒体在报道香港事件时充满偏见，请问你如何看待西方媒体在此次事件中扮演的角色？

刘晓明： 我们都看了英国媒体近期的相关报道，很不平衡。这些报道只关注游行示威，甚至对暴力极端分子表示同情。我前段时间接受BBC和天空新闻台采访时，给他们讲述了事件的另一面，我称之为"沉默的大多数"的群体被英国媒体完全忽视了。80万香港人联署支持香港特区政府修例；特区政府发出4500份民意调查问卷，广泛征求意见，收到的回复中有3000份支持修例，只有1500份反对。这些信息在英国媒体上没有任何报道。因此，英国媒体的报道严重失衡。我希望英国媒体能本着对大众负责的态度，平衡客观报道事实真相。7月1日后，英国媒体不间断采访支持抗议的人，而忽视了强烈反对暴力的意见。香港立法会不少议员对暴力抗议表示坚决反对，并对上述损害香港利益的行径表示强烈不满，但是在英国，我们看不到任何这方面的报道。

英国电视四台： 在《中英联合声明》这份国际条约中，包括保护香港居民的人身、言论、新闻、集会、结社、旅游、通信、罢工、宗教信仰自由等规定，你能否肯定地说这些权利和自由得到了充分的保障？

刘晓明： 我可以向你保证，这些权利得到了百分之百的保障，如果对比香港今昔，就可以看到这些权利得到很好保障。

英国电视四台： 那么黄之锋被捕和香港民族党被取缔事如何解释？

刘晓明： 在一个法治社会，违反法律者理应依法受到惩罚。言论自由并不代表想做什么就做什么,违法者必将付出代价。香港是法治社会,你提到这些个案时,应该仔细研究一下他们违反了哪些法律。

路透社: 目前英国两位竞选首相的候选人均表示可能对华为5G设备实施更严格的审查,你如何看待未来英国首相对华为的政策?

刘晓明: 我认为现在谈未来英国首相对华为政策还为时过早,你的说法只是一种猜测。当然,我们需要为应对各种可能的情况做好准备。我必须告诉大家,华为在英国投资不仅是出于企业自身利益,更是为了实现双赢,华为为英国电信产业发展做出了巨大贡献。英国如果禁止华为,将失去很多机遇。同时,华为很好地履行了企业的社会责任,他们在英国当地雇用了1万多名员工,在英投资超过20亿英镑,建立了联合研究中心,华为相信与英国同行合作有利于促进企业自身发展,有利于促进英国经济和科技发展。更重要的是,华为是开放透明的,他们斥资建立监督自己的网络安全分析监测中心,聘请清一色英国团队,检查自己的产品。华为没有所谓"后门"。在发展5G网络方面没有比华为更好的合作伙伴。我经常提醒英国的朋友们,要珍惜华为带来的机遇,失去华为就意味着失去许多良机,将对外界,不仅对华为,而且对中国企业,甚至对全世界,发出非常负面和消极的信号。

新华社: 关于中美经贸磋商,一些人认为,二十国集团(G20)大阪峰会期间中美元首会晤的成果有限,达成共识也只是暂时的,今后中美贸易争端将难免再次升级。你怎么看待中美经贸磋商前景?

刘晓明： 习近平主席与特朗普总统在G20大阪峰会期间的会晤非常重要，人们会因为这次重要会晤而记住大阪峰会。首先，习主席为中美两国关系发展指明了方向。习主席总结了中美建交40年来的经验启示，指出中美合则两利、斗则俱伤，合作比摩擦好，对话比对抗好。特朗普总统对此表示赞同。习主席为中美两国关系指明了根本发展方向，将对中美关系的长远发展产生重要影响。其次，双方宣布将在平等和相互尊重基础上重启经贸磋商，美方同意不再向中国商品征收新的关税。这些重要共识向国际社会和全球市场发出非常积极的信号。我们希望双方磋商团队继续努力，切实遵循双方元首最新共识精神。我对中美关系的未来发展和中美经贸磋商的前景持乐观态度。

中国中央电视台： 我注意到，有些英方政府官员还在就香港问题表达关切甚至妄加评论。1997年香港回归，至今已经22年了，他们凭什么还在对中国内政指手画脚？昨晚英国电视四台采访中，一些人表示希望亨特外交大臣就香港问题表达更多关切。你对此有何评论？

刘晓明： 外交大臣亨特关于香港的有关言论是完全错误的。英方在香港问题上应摆正自己的位置。在某些人眼中，香港仍被视为昔日英国殖民统治下的地方。但现实是，香港已回归祖国，是中国的一个特别行政区，不是英国领土的一部分。很显然，英国一些政客仍沉浸在昔日英国殖民者的幻象之中。我希望英方停止插手香港事务，尊重香港"一国两制"取得的建设成就。只要他们端正位置，客观公正地处理涉港事务，中英两国在香港问题上的合作就简单得多。香港事务与英国无关，他们应当把香港作为中国的一部分来看待，我们愿意与他们对话。根据中英之间的协议，英国与香港保持经济、贸易、文化关系没有问题，我希望香港能继续成为中英之间的桥梁，为中英关系发挥积极正面作用。

《每日电讯报》：你提到英国政府应该反思他们的言行可能引发的后果，到底是什么后果呢？中国正在考虑采取某种报复行动吗？暂缓修例是否意味着承认上街示威游行的人是有道理的，承认修例举措破坏了英中双方协议？

刘晓明：英方的言行已经产生了后果，这就是破坏了两国的互信和友好关系。中方已多次向英方提出交涉。中国副总理胡春华刚刚结束对英国的访问，与英国财政大臣共同主持了第十次中英经济财金对话，访问成果很丰硕，双方开通了"沪伦通"，我本人代表中国政府签署了一项对英国牛肉出口解禁的协议，这意味着不久之后英国的安格斯牛肉和威尔士黑牛肉将被端上中国民众的餐桌。维持良好的双边关系需要互信，需要遵守基本准则，英国政要发表的不当言论伤害了双边关系。我希望英方珍视来之不易的中英关系，与中国一道努力，共同促进两国和两国人民的利益。修例是合理和必要的，有其正常合法程序，可能过程中有需要改进的地方。香港特区政府已经认识到这一点，他们需要与民众进行更多沟通，但这不意味着他们的思路错了，也不能说修例是坏事。我希望特区政府与民众进行更多、更积极的沟通和对话，听取他们的意见，完善相关程序。

独立电视台： 习主席坚信应该维护香港的秩序和国家的团结，如果事态恶化，作为终极手段，中国军队会介入吗？

刘晓明： 中国在香港驻军的任务是国防。根据《基本法》，中央政府负责管理香港特区有关的外交事务和防务，中国人民解放军驻香港部队的任务就是保卫香港，抵御外敌。就像我之前所说，我们对香港特区政府完全有信心，相信他们会依法处理。香港警察部队很专业，我们对他们也很有信心。

独立电视台： 如果他们不能很好地处理呢？

刘晓明： 我们相信他们能妥善处置。

天空新闻台： 你提到英国媒体在报道香港时没有采取平衡的态度，但是中国媒体对抗议示威的报道就全面平衡吗？在中国政府看来，英国政府的表态令人十分愤怒，但在英国有人批评英国政府表态太软弱，太克制。英国政府并未对暴力行为表示同情和支持，只是对和平抗议者表示同情和支持。中方认为这样有何不妥？

刘晓明： 中、英媒体对香港事件的报道有很大不同。中国媒体肩负社会责任，服务人民利益，他们向本国民众还原了香港事件的事实真相，而不是帮助散布谣言和负面情绪，替反华势力摇旗呐喊。英国媒体需要反思应如何履行社会责任、恪守新闻职业道德。要真正服务于英国人民的利益，就不应进行不负责任的报道。现在，有30多万英国公民生活在香港，英国肯定希望看到香港保持繁荣与稳定，但香港近期的抗议活动与此背道而驰。你们不妨深入思考这些活动的后果，那些不法分子一旦得手、大行其道，必将严重损害香港法治，难道这符合英国的利益吗？符合在港生活的英国公民的利益吗？答案显然是否定的。我希望英国媒体能做有利于香港繁荣稳定和符合英国国家利益的报道。

BBC： 你刚才所谈似乎对香港街头抗议的人与冲击立法会大楼的人不加区分，你是刻意这么做的吗？

刘晓明： 我当然有区分。我此前接受BBC、天空新闻台采访时曾谈到，香港抗议活动起初是和平的，但后来演变为暴力行径，甚至有人用不明液体、有毒粉末袭击警察。当不法分子冲击立法会大楼时，一些不法分子试图持械伤人，警方暂时后撤，避免造成人员受伤。真正对此不加区分的是英国一些政客，从最初的和平示威到后来的暴力事件，他们一概支持，还称赞不法分子所谓"勇气"；他们甚至敦促香港特区政府不要以暴力事件为"借口"实施"镇压"，试图阻挠香港特区政府正当执法。中国中央政府都已表示应由香港特区政府和警方依法处置。香港特区政府有权将暴力违法分子绳之以法，英国政府应尊重香港司法独立。我希望一些英国政客停止对香港特区政府正当执法、处置有关事件说三道四，停止发表错误言论，不要采取"双重标准"。

《中国日报》： 有人说G20已不像20年前应对国际金融危机时那么有力了，你如何看待G20的未来？

刘晓明： 习近平主席在G20峰会上发表十分重要的声明，为世界如何应对单边主义和保护主义指明了方向，提出我们要坚持改革创新，为高质量发展提供更多动力，同时坚持完善全球治理，改革国际金融体系，受到国际社会的广泛欢迎。此次峰会是成功的，对外发出了积极的信号。2008年国际金融危机发生后，G20确立了其作为国际经济合作主要论坛的定位，推动国际社会加强宏观经济政策协调。习主席坚持发展视角，推动G20将发展置于宏观经济政策协调的优先位置，为G20的未来发展做出重要贡献。毫无疑问，上述成果向国际社会传递了积极信号，我们相信G20的前景一定是光明的。

谢谢大家！

The Bottom Line of "One Country, Two Systems" Cannot Be Challenged
—— A Press Conference on the Violent Attack against the Legislative Council Complex in the Hong Kong Special Administrative Region

On 3rd July 2019, I held a press conference at the Chinese Embassy on the violent attack against the Legislative Council complex in the Hong Kong Special Administrative Region. More than 40 journalists from 25 media agencies attended the press conference, including *Financial Times*, *The Daily Telegraph*, *The Times*, the *Economist*, *The Guardian*, Reuters, BBC, Radio 4, ITV, Sky News and Channel 4, China's Xinhua News Agency, CCTV, China News Service, CGTN, China Radio International, *China Daily*, *Economic Daily*, *Science and Technology Daily*, *Guangming Daily*, and *Global Times*, as well as CNN, Phoenix Infonews, *European Times*, and *UK Chinese Times*. The following is the transcript of the press conference.

Liu Xiaoming: 1st July is a day for celebration and festivity among the people of Hong Kong. Those from all walks of life commemorate the return of Hong Kong and the establishment of the Hong Kong Special Administrative Region (Hong Kong SAR). However, on this very day, some ultra-radicals stormed the Hong Kong Legislative Council complex in an extremely violent manner and wantonly damaged the facilities inside. Such actions have overstepped the boundaries of freedom of speech and peaceful demonstration, trampled on the rule of law in Hong Kong, undermined public order, compromised the fundamental interests of Hong Kong and challenged the bottom line of "One Country, Two Systems". We strongly condemn such actions. The Hong Kong SAR government will press criminal charges against the violent offenders in accordance with the law, and the Chinese Central Government firmly supports the Hong Kong SAR government in pursuing this serious case and in handling the incident in accordance with the law. We support the SAR government in restoring public order, protecting the safety of Hong Kong citizens in their persons and property and maintaining the prosperity and stability of Hong Kong.

It has to be pointed out that on this major issue of principle, the UK government chose to stand on the wrong side. It has made inappropriate remarks not only to interfere in the internal affairs of Hong Kong but also to back up the violent law breakers. It even attempted to obstruct the Hong Kong SAR government in bringing the criminals to justice, which is outright interference in Hong Kong's rule of law. China has repeatedly lodged stern representations with the British side.

Here, I would like to reiterate that Hong Kong is a Special Administrative Region of China. It is not how it used to be under the British colonial rule. Hong Kong affairs are purely China's internal affairs which brook no interference from any country, organization or individual. We strongly condemn and oppose this gross interference in Hong Kong affairs and in China's internal affairs by the British side.

China's resolution to safeguard sovereignty, national security and development interests is unwavering. Our resolve to uphold the prosperity and stability of Hong Kong is unwavering. Our rejection of foreign interference is unwavering. We urge the British side to seriously reflect on the consequences of its words and deeds and immediately stop interfering in Hong Kong affairs and China's internal affairs in whatever form.

The world media, especially those here in the UK, have been covering extensively what happened in Hong Kong. But to be frank, some reports are severely prejudiced and others are even ill-willed slander. I have received quite a number of requests for interview from different media institutions. So, today, I am holding this press conference in order to allow more media to hear China's stance on the basis of truth and facts with regard to Hong Kong.

Now, I would like to take your questions.

BBC: First of all, if I may, can you give us a guarantee here today this afternoon that China remains committed to the Joint Declaration, an international treaty that China signed up to and which remains in force until 2047?

And second, if I may, can you tell us what Beijing is going to do now? Are you going to use the disruption on Monday to crack down on larger, more peaceful demonstrations that may happen in the future?

Liu Xiaoming: What gives you the idea that China is going to crack down on peaceful demonstrations?

First of all, I think your perception of China's position is completely wrong. China's commitment to "One Country, Two Systems" is unwavering. But I have to make it clear that this is a promise made by the Chinese government to the world. It is a unilateral declaration by the Chinese government, not a commitment to the British government. And it is incorporated in the Basic Law. It is China's unbending position that the basic system in Hong Kong will remain unchanged for fifty years after 1997. With regard to the Joint Declaration between China and Britain, it has fulfilled its mission. According to this document, the British government should restore Hong Kong to China, and China will resume its sovereignty over Hong Kong. The British government will be responsible for its administration during the transition period from 1984 to 1997. That is what is stipulated in the Joint Declaration. Once Hong Kong was returned to China, the British government has no right to cite claims from the Joint Declaration. So I encourage you to read the Joint Declaration.

BBC: I have it in front of me. It outlines very specifically in Point 12 that the basic policies of the People's Republic of China regarding Hong Kong… they will remain unchanged for fifty years. It is specifically said - it is not just talking about the Basic Law, but also about the Joint Declaration itself.

Liu Xiaoming: No, it talks about "One Country, Two Systems". That will remain unchanged for 50 years, not the Joint Declaration. I hope you will be careful with your choice of words. In the Joint Declaration, we cannot find any clause or articles which give the British government any right to interfere in the internal affairs of Hong Kong, or give them any right whatsoever to what you might term "supervise" the implementation of "One Country, Two Systems".

There is no indication that the central government will, as you described, "crack down" on demonstrations. We have full trust in the Hong Kong SAR government to handle these cases, even this very serious violent case. We have full trust in the Hong Kong SAR government to bring the criminals and law breakers to justice in accordance with the law.

ITV: Because of the British government's interference, as you put it, are you now calling for an apology from the British government?

Liu Xiaoming: We made a strong representation with the British side. We call on them to stop interfering in the internal affairs of Hong Kong and in China's internal affairs. I hope the British side will refrain from inflicting further damage upon the relationship.

Reuters: Reuters spoke to Boris Johnson today and he told us that the people in Hong Kong were perfectly within their rights to be very skeptical, very anxious about the extradition bill, and he will back them every inch of the way. And he would stress to Beijing that the "One Country, Two Systems" approach worked. What do you have to say to him with his line there? Given that it is he or Jeremy Hunt running to be the next Prime Minister, do you think relations between China and Britain will get worse rather than better under the next prime minister?

Liu Xiaoming: We certainly hope that whoever the next British Prime Minister may be will follow what has been agreed by the two governments with regard to the relationship. The fundamentals are that we respect sovereignty and territorial integrity and non-interference in each other's internal affairs. So long as the British government, so long as the new prime minister follows these principles, I don't see that there will be any problem in the relationship. If these principles are violated, there will be problems between our two countries.

Channel 4: When do you think the extradition bill will pass?

Liu Xiaoming: I think that the Hong Kong SAR government has already said it has suspended the extradition bill. I think the Chief Executive made it very clear that they have no timetable for the current legislative council. The current legislative council's term will expire by July 2020. In that case, she already indicated there would be no further actions on the extradition bill before July 2020. So we show respect and understanding, and support her decision. We are behind the Hong Kong SAR government.

Channel 4: Would you expect the bill to be suspended or do you expect it to never return?

Liu Xiaoming: It's up to Hong Kong SAR government to decide. It's also up to the Hong Kong SAR government as to how it will communicate with Hong Kong public and engage with the public, to let them know the rationale: Why this bill serves the interests of Hong Kong, why Hong Kong will be a better place by having this bill, why Hong Kong should not continue to be a haven for fugitive offenders, and Hong Kong should be a place for justice. I hope they will be successful in communicating with the Hong Kong people.

Sky News: You call the people who raided the Legislative Chamber "ultra radicals". Do you see their act as an act of terrorism? Also, you said that you hoped that the British government would refrain from further interference which could further damage the relationship. Have the British government's actions so far with regard to the incidents in Hong Kong already damaged relations between China and Britain? And finally, if I may, what do you say to the people, the conspiracy theorists, that there are agents provocateurs amongst these radicals, that are actually pro-China, whipping up the violent action because it gives you justification for crackdowns?

Liu Xiaoming: First, I do not want to try to characterize the "ultra radicals". It is up to Hong Kong court to decide what they are. They certainly vandalized the facilities in the legislative council. They should be responsible for what they did in breaking the law in Hong Kong. And also I think the relationship in a way has been damaged by the interference of the British government. As I said, the fundamental principles guiding our two countries are mutual respect and non-interference in each other's internal affairs. If the British government goes further, it will cause further damage. That is why I am calling on the British government to reflect on the consequences of its words and deeds with regard to Hong Kong. I do hope that the British government will realize the consequences and refrain from further interference, from further damaging the relationship.

Sky News: What about the agents provocateurs? It is just a rumour among some of the people out there saying that there are pro-China activists at play in the crowds. They are actually behind the violent side of the protest. Is that true?

Liu Xiaoming: First of all, I will not comment on rumours. Secondly, according to what has been explained by the Hong Kong police commissioner, they are actual radicals with the aim of disrupting the public order of Hong Kong. They are lawbreakers.

CGTN: The Foreign Secretary Jeremy Hunt has stressed the UK's support for Hong Kong's freedom. As we all know, when Hong Kong was under British rule, they didn't have any form of democracy, including general elections. So why do you think that the UK is so concerned about Hong Kong's democracy now? My second question is about G20. We know that many people believe that the achievements of the Osaka G20 Summit are lackluster except for the China-US leader's meeting on trade talks. So what's your comment on that?

Liu Xiaoming: I think it's totally wrong for Jeremy Hunt to talk about freedom. This is not a matter of freedom. It's a matter of breaking laws in Hong Kong. It was very disappointing for a senior official of his caliber to show support for these law-breaking people. We all remember what Hong Kong was 22 years ago under British rule. There was no freedom, no democracy whatsoever. We all know that all the governors were appointed by the British government; people had no right to elect officials, no right to demonstrate certainly, and they did not even have the right to independent judicial power. The final power of adjudication rested with the Privy Council here in London. But now, everyone without bias would realize how much democracy and freedom the Hong Kong people have compared with 22 years ago before the handover. Now Hong Kong has its own Chief Executive, elected by the Election Committee of the Hong Kong people. And they have enormous enthusiasm for political participation. And the National People's Congress agreed to universal suffrage, one person one vote, to elect their Chief Executive, but unfortunately, it was not passed by the Legislative Council in 2015. And the Hong Kong people enjoy a high degree of autonomy. They run their own affairs. And now they not only have legislative, executive and independent judicial power, they even have the final right to adjudication in Hong Kong. So it's quite a contrast when we compare Hong Kong today with what Hong Kong was 22 years ago. Therefore, I think it's very hypocritical for British politicians to talk about freedom in Hong Kong. When the rule of law was damaged by the law breakers in Hong Kong, instead of condemning this, they showed support and sympathy to these law breakers. I feel very disappointed at their statement.

Phoenix TV: What's your expectation for the new prime minister of UK and his stance on Hong Kong issue, because Boris Johnson made some comments on this today? Do you think (there will be) any consequences arising out of that? Will that affect Sino-British cooperation in the future?

Liu Xiaoming: As I said earlier, we hope that the British government will carry out its commitment to the basic principles enshrined in the joint agreement for the establishment of the diplomatic relations -- the basic norms governing the relationship between China and the UK -- and refrain from interfering in Hong Kong's internal affairs and in China's internal affairs, and work with us for common good. I think China and the UK have enormous potential and opportunities to work together for the common good and for the prosperity and stability of Hong Kong. Hong Kong, before 1984, was a problem, a stumbling block between China and the UK. Since we reached the Joint Declaration, and especially since Hong Kong returned to China, Hong Kong is no longer a problem between China and the UK. Instead, it is playing the role of a bridge between China and the UK, and has become a positive factor in the relationship. I hope Hong Kong will continue to play this role, rather than become, again, a problem in China-UK relations.

China Daily: Some people say Western media reports on the Hong Kong protests are quite prejudiced. What do you think of media's role on this issue of Hong Kong?

Liu Xiaoming: I shall comment on your question about Hong Kong and come back to your question with regard to the G20. I think we all watched the media reporting here. It is not balanced. They focused on the demonstrations. They even showed some sympathy to these ultra radicals. I made appearances on BBC and Sky News. I presented the other side of the story of what I call the "silent majority" that has been totally ignored by the media here. About 800, 000 people signed up to support the amendment of the ordnance. When the Hong Kong SAR government sent out 4, 500 letters to solicit opinion, they received 3, 000 back in support of the amendment. Only 1, 500 showed opposition. But we do not get a single glimpse of that on any media here. So it is very unbalanced. It is not convincing. I do hope that the British media here will do justice to British readers, and present a balanced picture. After what happened on 1st of July, the media here kept on interviewing those in support of the demonstrators. They ignored the strong resentment and opposition from the other side. And we saw the legislators voicing their strong opposition and their strong resentment against these violent actions which hurt the interests of Hong Kong. Yet here we cannot see any report of this at all.

Channel 4: The Joint Declaration, as you know, is an international treaty and legally binding, promises to protect rights and freedoms of the person, of speech, of the press, of assembly, of association, of travel, of movement, of correspondence, of strike, of choice of occupation, of academic research and of religious belief. Can you promise that all those rights and freedoms are one hundred percent intact now as they were at the handover?

Liu Xiaoming: One hundred percent protected and even better if you compare the rights enjoyed today with what they previously were.

Channel 4: What about the imprisonment of Joshua Wong or the closure of the Causeway Bay bookshop, just to cite two examples?

Liu Xiaoming: In a society governed by the rule of law, people are prosecuted in accordance with the law. Freedom of expression does not mean that you can do whatever you like. If you break the law, you have to pay the price. Hong Kong is run by the rule of law. When you look into the specific cases, you should read carefully which law they have broken.

Reuters: We spoke a bit about the two candidates who seek to replace Theresa May. Both look like they might move towards a tougher line on Huawei and its involvement in 5G networks in Britain. What is your response if the next British government moves towards an outright ban on Huawei?

Liu Xiaoming: I think it is still too early to say what kind of position they are going to take. What you are saying is a kind of guesswork. But we have to prepare for all the consequences. I have to say, Huawei is here not only for their own interests. It is here to create win-win situation. Should you lose Huawei, you will miss a lot of opportunities. I think they are here for win-win results. They here made an enormous contribution not only to the telecom industries here in this country, but also in terms of corporate responsibilities. They have created more than 10,000 jobs. They have invested a great deal, with a procurement of more than £2 billion. They have set up a joint research centre. They believe they can grow alongside their British colleagues and they can contribute to the development of Britain's economy and science and technology. What is more significant is that they are open and transparent. They set up their own Cyber Security Evaluation Centre Oversight Board manned completely by British people. They let the British people check their products. There aren't any secrets. No so-called "backdoor". They are very open. I doubt you can find a better company than Huawei in terms of 5G development. I usually caution my British friends that you should treasure these opportunities. If you lose Huawei, you will lose a lot of opportunities. And you will send out very bad and negative signals, not only to Huawei but also to Chinese businesses, or maybe even to the world.

Xinhua News Agency: Ambassador, I am from Xinhua. My question is about the China-US trade tension. Some would say that the meeting during the G20 Summit between President Xi Jinping and President Trump was quite limited, and the suspension of tension is temporary. And some say the tension in China-US trade relationship is still there and will escalate again. What is you view on that? And what are the prospects for the China-US trade negotiation?

Liu Xiaoming: I think the meeting between President Xi and President Trump was of great importance. I think the G20 Summit in Osaka will be remembered for this very important meeting. What is more important is the direction set by President Xi. President Xi summed up the lessons of the 40 years of China-US relations. He pointed out that China and the US stand to gain from cooperation, and will lose out in confrontation. So cooperation and dialogue are better than confrontation and friction. And President Trump also agreed with this. So the fundamental direction set by President Xi is very important in guiding the long term relationship in the future. And secondly, the two sides announced the resumption of trade talks on the basis of equality and mutual benefit. That is very significant. The US side agrees that it will not add new tariffs on Chinese goods. So this important agreement sent out a very positive signal to the international community and the global market. We do hope that the teams from both countries will continue and implement the agreement reached by the two Heads of State. I feel optimistic about the future of the relationship and I feel optimistic about the trade talks between China and the US!

CCTV: I'm from China's CCTV. We all noticed that some of the British officials expressed their deep concern and even made comments on Hong Kong. Why do they still hold strong opinions about China's affairs 22 years after Hong Kong returned to China in 1997? And also some interviewees who spoke to Channel 4 last night wanted Mr. Hunt to be more vocal. What is your comment?

Liu Xiaoming: I think I already covered this. The Foreign Secretary's statement on Hong Kong is totally wrong. The British side should place itself in the proper position with regard to Hong Kong. In the minds of some of the people, they still regard Hong Kong as being under British rule and they forget the fundamentals. We talked about the Joint Declaration. Hong Kong has now returned to the embrace of the motherland. It is a special administrative region of China. It's not part of the UK. I would call on them to keep your hands off Hong Kong. Show respect for what has been achieved in Hong Kong under "One Country, Two Systems". I think if they kept to their proper position and approach the Hong Kong issue with objective perspectives, things will be easier for the two countries to talk about Hong Kong. Fundamentally, this colonial mindset is still haunting some officials or politicians. So I do hope they regard Hong Kong as part of China and regard Hong Kong's business as not being Britain's business. We would like to talk with them. According to the agreement between our two countries, we have no problem with the British side maintaining economic, cultural and trade relations with Hong Kong. As I said, I do hope that Hong Kong will continue to play the role of a bridge and to be a positive factor in the relationship rather than a negative factor.

The Daily Telegraph: You said that the UK government should be mindful of the consequences of their words and deeds. What exactly are the consequences you are talking about? Is China considering some sort of retaliatory actions if the UK continues down this path? And secondly, does the withdrawal of the bill mean that they recognize those people demonstrating in Hong Kong do have a point that this bill does undermine the commitments of the "One Country, Two Systems" settlement?

Liu Xiaoming: There already are consequences. The mutual trust has been weakened. We made several representations with the British side. It hurts the amicable atmosphere of the relationship. You know, we just had a very senior, high level visit by the Chinese Vice Premier who was here to co-chair with Chancellor Hammond the 10th Economic Financial Dialogue. The outcomes have been great, including London Shanghai stock connect. I happened to be the one who signed an agreement on behalf of the Chinese government which lifted the ban on British beef. That means it won't be long before Angus beef and Welsh black beef can be served on the tables of Chinese consumers. But to have good relationship, you need to build mutual trust and you need to follow basic principles. I think this inappropriate comment by British politicians really hurt the relationship. I do hope that the British side will treasure the hard-won relationship and we can move together in the common interests of the people of our two countries. The extradition bill, as I said, has a good point. There is a necessity and it has been done through normal and legal process. But there are some pitfalls which call for improvement, and I think that the Hong Kong SAR government has realized that. They need to communicate more with the public. It doesn't mean that the rationale is wrong. It doesn't mean that the bill is not a good bill. So I do hope that the Hong Kong SAR government will conduct more communications and dialogues, will engage more actively with the public and will listen to their opinions in order to improve the process.

ITV: President Xi strongly believes in the need to maintain the order and keep the country together. If the security deteriorates in Hong Kong, will the Chinese military be brought in as the last resort?

Liu Xiaoming: The Chinese military in Hong Kong is for the defence of the country. According to the basic law, the central government is responsible for foreign affairs and defence affairs. Its duty is to protect Hong Kong from outside enemies, foreign enemies. As I said, we have full trust in the Hong Kong SAR government. We believe and we have confidence that they will handle this case according to law. The Hong Kong police are very professional, and we also have full trust in them.

ITV: If they don't?

Liu Xiaoming: We have full trust. Why don't they? I have confidence that they can handle this properly.

Sky News: You criticize the British media over what you say is their imbalanced reporting of the Hong Kong issue. But in China, in the mainland, do they have full access to all the images of the demonstrations from the very beginning? And secondly, with regards to British comments, it seems that China is very angry with the way that the British government has responded to the protest, but in the UK there has been criticism that the British government is too weak in their response, they are too restrained, and there hasn't been specific support for the violent action. There's only been support for the right to peacefully protest. So why exactly do you have a problem with regard to British comments?

Liu Xiaoming: First, about the media reporting of the incident in China. I think there might be some big difference between the Chinese media -- we do have some of the Chinese media here -- and the British media. I think the Chinese media believe they have the social responsibility to serve the interests of the people. When the people saw what is happening in Hong Kong, they didn't want to provide a platform for those anti-China elements, or to spread so-called "propaganda" against China. They don't spread rumours to help those anti-China elements.

And about the British media criticism of the British government, that is the problem of the British media. You really have to reflect on what you are calling for. So that is what I am saying: your social responsibility -- what serves the best interests of the UK. I know you have 300, 000 British citizens in Hong Kong. You certainly would like to see Hong Kong remain prosperous and stable. But what's happening in Hong Kong now just does the opposite. You should take a deep breath and reflect on what will be the consequences. If those law breakers have their way, Hong Kong will be plunged into a lawless society. Will that serve the interests of Britain? Will that serve the interests of stability and prosperity? Will that serve the interests of the 300, 000 British citizens in Hong Kong? The answer is definitely NO. So I do hope British media can reflect on what is in the best interests of Hong Kong and the best interests, the national interests, of Britain.

BBC: Just thinking about your last comment. You seem to be making no distinction between the hundreds of thousands of people who marched and demonstrated peacefully, and a much smaller group who engaged in violence. Do you not draw distinctions between these two?

Liu Xiaoming: I do draw a distinction. I think we could go back to my interview with BBC and Sky News. I said, to start with it was peaceful demonstration, but later on it became ugly. There was attack on the police with toxic powder. Nobody knows what it was. That was why the police evacuated the legislative council in order to avoid further injuries to police officers. There are also concerns about people being trampled. That's what happened later on. So I do draw a distinction.
But the problem was that the British politicians make no distinctions. From the very start they supported the demonstrators, and to the very end they supported and even called the violent elements "very brave". I hate to quote their comments. They even urged the Hong Kong SAR government not to use the violent incident as a "pretext for repression" -- basically they are trying to obstruct the legal process in Hong Kong. The Central Government in China has said it will leave the Hong Kong SAR government to handle this case in accordance with the law in Hong Kong. I do hope that those British politicians will make no further comment on the legal process of how the Hong Kong SAR government will pursue this case, with regard to how the government will bring those lawbreakers to justice. I hope they will respect the independent judicial power of Hong Kong, and that was what the British government has been calling for all along. I hope they will not adopt double standards in this case.

China Daily: Some people say that the G20 is not as strong as 10 years ago during the global (financial) crisis. What do you think of the future of the G20?

Liu Xiaoming: President Xi made a very important statement on the summit, and he pointed out the direction the world should take in response to unilateralism and protectionism. President Xi proposed that we need to persist in reform and innovation in order to find more impetus for high quality growth. He also proposed that we need to progress with the times in order to improve global governance and promote the reform of the international financial system. And all these have been welcomed by the international community. So I think the G20 Summit sent out a very positive message to the world. I regard the G20 Summit as a success.
With regard to the future of the G20, I think President Xi also made his contribution

to further strengthening the mechanism of the G20. The G20 was born as a result of the 2008 financial crisis. It functioned to coordinate and to strengthen the cooperation between countries. President Xi also made his contribution to further strengthen the G20. We believe the G20 still has a bright future. President Xi insists on placing development at the core of the G20 agenda. There is no doubt that this outcome sent out a positive message to the outside world. We believe the G20 still has vitality and will serve the interests of countries around the world.

Thank you.

中央政府有足够多的办法平息动乱
——关于香港街头暴力激进活动中外记者会

（2019年8月15日，中国驻英国大使馆）

刘晓明：7月3日，我在使馆举办了一次中外记者会，介绍香港"修例"问题及中方立场。此后一个多月以来，香港反对派和一些激进势力继续借口"反修例"进行各种街头激进抗争活动，暴力化程度不断升级，社会波及面越来越广，完全超出自由集会与和平抗议范畴，严重挑战香港法治和社会秩序，严重威胁香港市民生命财产安全，严重破坏香港繁荣稳定，严重触碰"一国两制"原则底线，致使香港面临回归以来最严峻的局面。

一些极端激进分子在香港兴风作浪，打着所谓民主的幌子，掩盖其反法治、反社会、反"一国两制"的真实面目和险恶用心，是兼具欺骗性与破坏性的"新极端主义"。他们打砸立法会，冲击中联办，暴力袭击警员，在香港机场非法集结致使机场全面停止运营，已经构成严重暴力犯罪，开始出现恐怖主义的苗头。中国中央政府绝不会放任少数人以暴力行径把香港拖向危险的深渊，绝不允许任何人破坏香港的法治与良好发展局面，绝不允许任何人以任何借口破坏"一国两制"。如果香港局势进一步恶化，出现香港特区政府不能控制的动乱，中国中央政府绝不会坐视不管。按照《基本法》规定，中国中央政府有足够多的办法、足够强大的力量迅速平息可能出现的各种动乱。

当前，香港处于关键时刻。如何结束香港乱局？这是所有关心香港前途的人都在思考的问题，也是英国各大媒体头版头条和"封面文章"之问。我们的回答坚定而明确：我们希望香港事态平稳有序结束，同时我们做了最坏准备。如何实现香港事态平稳有序结束？我认为，以下四点至关重要：

第一，坚决支持香港特区政府止暴制乱、恢复秩序。希望广大香港市民，特别是一些不明真相的年轻人，认清当前香港局势，珍惜香港回归后来之不易的良好发展局面，顾全大局，团结一致，坚定不移挺特首、挺政府，守护香港的法治与正义，维护祖国统一和香港繁荣稳定。希望香港各界人士不要被激进势力所利用和裹挟，要向一切暴力行径大声说"不"，要向一切践踏法治的行径坚决说"不"，坚定支持特区政府依法施政，坚定支持香港警方严正执法。

第二，坚决依法严惩暴力犯罪分子。有法必依、违法必究是任何一个法治社会的基本要求。暴力就是暴力，违法就是违法，这不会因为暴力违法分子打着什么幌子就发生变化。只要是违法行为，无论怎么粉饰，都要受到法律的制裁；只要参与暴力犯罪活动，无论是谁，都要追究其法律责任。试问，英国会允许极端激进分子冲击议会、破坏议会设施而逍遥法外吗？英国会允许极端激进分子用致命武器袭击警察、烧毁警署而不受惩罚吗？英国会允许暴徒打着所谓民主的幌子占领机场、堵塞交通、破坏社会秩序、威胁民众生命财产安全吗？这些行为在英国难道不构成违法犯罪吗？姑息违法，就是亵渎正义；纵容暴力，就是践踏法治。任何一个法治国家，任何一个负责任的政府，都不会对上述暴力行径坐视不管。中国中央政府坚定支持特区政府和香港警方严正执法、果断执法，尽快将违法分子绳之以法、严惩不贷，依法维护香港法治环境和社会秩序。

第三，外部势力停止干预香港事务。有诸多证据显示，香港局势恶化到今天的地步，与外部势力介入和煽风点火是分不开的。一些西方国家政客和机构明里暗里为暴力激进分子提供各种支持，为他们撑腰打气，甚至干扰香港司法独立，阻碍香港警方将暴力犯罪分子绳之以法。我想重申，香港是中国的香港，香港事务绝不容外国插手。我们奉劝那些外国势力，尊重中国主权和安全，立即停止以任何方式干预香港事务和中国内政，立即停止纵容暴力犯罪，不要误判形势，在错误的路上越走越远，否则必将搬起石头砸自己的脚。

第四，媒体承担起应有的社会责任。香港事态发生以来，西方媒体扮演了十分不光彩的角色，不仅没有公正客观报道，反而混淆是非、颠倒黑白、误导公众：连篇累牍地渲染所谓"和平示威权利"，却对极端暴力分子破坏社会秩序、袭警伤人的违法犯罪行为熟视无睹，对支持特区政府、守护香港法治正义声音更是鲜有见报；将破坏香港法治、为非作歹的暴徒美化为"支持民主的人士"，却将特区政府和警队维护香港法治、保护市民生命财产安全的正当合法举措恶意诬蔑为"镇压"。正是这些媒体的"选择性失声"和"歪曲性报道"，使错误舆论大行其道，误导了许多不明真相的民众特别是香港年轻人。可以说，西方媒体对香港今天的局面负有不可推卸的责任！我真诚地希望西方媒体反思自己行为的社会影响，承担起应有的社会责任，公正客观地报道香港局势，不要再为极端暴力分子说项，不要再给香港乱局火上浇油，为平稳、有序结束香港乱局营造良好的舆论环境。为了帮助各位理解我说的第四点，我们制作了一个短片，让大家看一看在西方媒体看不到的画面，听一听在西方媒体听不到的声音。

（播放短片）

"治则兴，乱则衰。"这句中国古训对今天的香港再适用不过。目前，有30多万英国公民在香港工作和生活，300多家英国公司在香港投资兴业。香港保持繁荣稳定，不仅符合中国的利益，也符合包括英国在内的各国共同利益。我衷心希望，英国各界有识之士认清大局，多做有利于香港繁荣稳定的事，抵制和反对任何干涉香港事务、破坏香港法治的言行。我坚信，在中国中央政府的大力支持下，在香港特区政府和林郑月娥行政长官的带领下，香港社会一定能够尽快止暴制乱，尽早恢复正常秩序，使香港这颗东方明珠重放光彩。

下面，我愿回答大家提问。

彭博社： 我注意到视频里一位香港官员表示香港警察从未打出真正枪弹。社交媒体上传播的视频显示，中国军队正在香港之外进行反恐演习，如果军队派往香港，是否将被授权使用真枪实弹？

刘晓明： 我想这样回答你的问题。香港的形势十分严峻，但我们对特区政府和行政长官处理与平息局势、恢复秩序有充分信任和信心。正如我在开场白中所说，如果香港局势进一步恶化、出现特区政府不能控制的动乱，中国中央政府绝不会坐视不管。中国政府有足够多的办法和足够强大的力量迅速平息动乱。

CNN： 特朗普总统已表示希望与习近平主席讨论香港问题。中方是否已正式回应其提议？如习主席同意与其见面，将有助于缓解香港当前形势吗？

刘晓明： 我不认为特朗普总统已正式提出要与习近平主席会面，他应该是在推特发文提到香港形势。我们可以讨论香港问题，但最重要的是，香港事务是中国内政，中方坚决反对任何外部干涉，包括一些外国组织为极端暴力行为提供资金支持，一些美国议员提出所谓关于香港的法案，违背国际关系准则。我特别要强调的是，中方坚决反对任何外国政府官员给特区政府打电话施压，公开支持暴力分子。

路透社： 你刚才提到一些抗议示威活动开始出现恐怖主义的苗头，你能否解释构成恐怖主义行为的红线和转折点是什么？依照中国法律，这是否将成为中方向香港派军队的合法依据？

刘晓明： 刚才视频所显示的以及我们最近看到的在香港发生的残暴恶劣行为，特别是香港机场事件，被不少媒体称为恐怖主义行为。暴徒攻击警察、损毁设施，甚至袭击记者，你们的同行、一位中国记者就受到围攻。对此，中国记者协会表示强烈谴责。这些都是恐怖主义的苗头，我称其为"新极端主义"。如任其发展，将演变为恐怖主义。我们相信特区政府和香港警方现在能掌控局面。如局势进一步恶化，特区政府难以控制，中央政府绝对不会坐视不管。

今日俄罗斯电视台： 根据美国媒体报道，美国国家民主基金会（NED）为部分香港抗议示威者提供了资金支持。中方是否掌握美国在背后策划香港抗议示威活动的证据？

刘晓明： 你已经部分回答了这个问题。我们相信这些极端暴力活动都有幕后"黑手"，一些外国势力和组织为其提供资金和其他支持，甚至有外国官员会见"港独"分子。他们出于不可告人的政治目的，就是要把香港变成中国的麻烦，阻止中国发展繁荣。因此，为了使香港乱局尽快平息，外部势力应立即停止干预香港事务，停止你刚才提到的那些行为。

《泰晤士报》： 英国议会下院外交委员会主席图根哈特表示，英国应考虑给予香港居民英国国籍，中方对此如何评论？

刘晓明： 我认为，英国的某些政客，虽然身体已经进入21世纪，但脑袋却还停留在殖民时代。他们依然将香港当作大英帝国或英国的一部分。他们应该改变思维模式，摆正自己的位置，认识到香港是中国的一部分，而不是英国的一部分。

独立电视台： 你刚才说，中国已经做好最坏的打算，你能澄清一下这究竟意味着什么？有人看到军队和武警在深圳集结，这是否意味着采用军事手段的可能性上升？

刘晓明： 我刚才在开场白中已经回答了你的问题。采取果断措施是必要的。我已经说了，如果局势进一步恶化，变得无法平息、不能控制，中国中央政府不会坐视不管。中央政府有足够多的手段、足够强大的力量平息事态。如果你认真听我的讲话，就能找到答案。

独立电视台： 能不能详细解释一下"平息"（quell）一词的含义是什么？

刘晓明： 平息就是终止目前的事态。

天空电视台： 你刚才说北京有力量在必要的情况下平息香港的事态，能否说明在何种情况下会派军队赴香港？他们将如何应对普通民众的抗议？在上次记者会上，你说英中关系因为英外交大臣的言论受到损害。这次记者会，我们有了新首相。英中关系是改善了，恢复正常了，还是继续受到损害？你有什么话要对英国首相说？

刘晓明： 关于第一个问题，我想我已经回答了。首先，当前我们仍然相信香港特区政府有能力处理好香港事务，特首是很有能力的领导人，赢得了广泛尊敬和支持。当前，他们对事态处理得当，值得信任。我们有信心、有决心，也有能力迅速平息事态。关于第二个问题，中方当然希望中英关系能够进一步发展，良好的关系符合中英双方共同利益。媒体上关于英国政局评论很多，我倒是不希望你们那么快再换首相，否则下次记者会可能又要把新首相拿出来说事了（众人笑）。约翰逊首相是我任驻英大使以来打交道的第四位首相，我们对推进双边关系抱有期待，希望双方沿着习近平主席访英时开启的中英关系"黄金时代"大方向继续前进。但良好的双边关系必须建立在相互尊重主权和领土完整、互不干涉内政的基础上，这是我们在建交联合公报中就已明确的原则。只要坚持这些原则，双边关系就能顺利发展，反之就会遇到困难。希望英国新政府在香港问题上坚持原则、妥善处理，即香港是中国的领土，香港关乎中国主权，香港事务是中国的内政。

《卫报》： 你说的"不能控制"是什么意思？如何确定事态处于不能控制的状态？

刘晓明： "不能控制"就是失去控制，这个意思很清楚，大概不需要查《牛津大辞典》。我们希望事态处于香港特区政府和特首管控之下。我们相信当前局势仍是可控的。

BBC广播四台： 第一个问题，你是否承认大多数抗议者并不是"暴力分子""极端分子"，而是普通市民？他们有律师，有公务员，他们对中国政府感到很失望，要求享有更多言论自由，支持普选。你能否解释中国政府为何反对普选？第二个问题，中国是否仍然遵守《中英联合声明》？

刘晓明： 埃文，距离上次接受你采访已经很长时间了，很高兴再次见到你。你第一个问题是关于示威者。我们当然会区分普通示威者和极端暴力犯罪分子。一小撮极端暴力分子不能代表大多数游行示威者，许多参加示威的人是被蒙蔽的，一些香港和西方媒体误导了民众。每个社会都有自己的问题。香港回归祖国以来，取得巨大发展成就，"一国两制"取得巨大成功，但仍有许多需要改进的地方，比如年轻人的发展问题。香港经济存在一些问题，过于倚重金融服务业和房地产业，年轻人上升通道有限，他们有抱怨，我们都理解。中央政府和特区政府非常重视这些问题，正采取切实措施予以解决。粤港澳大湾区建设将给年轻人带来更多发展机会。如果把香港和一河之隔的深圳做一个比较，就会发现很大差别。深圳在30年间从一个小渔村发展成为一个充满生机和活力的大都市，成为年轻人创业之地，拥有诸如华为、腾讯、大疆等众多高新科技公司。在香港却没有一家像这样的世界一流科技企业。特区政府正在想办法解决这些问题。我们应注重发展问题，但抗议示威不是解决问题之道，社会混乱只会让年轻人蒙受更多损失。我们关注年轻人的发展，会将受蒙蔽而走上歧途的年轻人与少数极端暴力犯罪分子区分开来。

关于《中英联合声明》，一些人经常把"一国两制"和《中英联合声明》混为一谈。《中英联合声明》已经完成了历史使命，即将香港归还中国以及在1984年至1997年的13年间确保香港在回归前平稳过渡。《中英联合声明》提到"一国两制"，但"一国两制"是中国政府的政策宣示，写入《基本法》。因此，我们说中方坚定遵守《基本法》和"一国两制"50年不变，而不是遵守《中英联合声明》50年不变。

关于普选，中央政府支持香港实行普选，这是香港政制改革的终极目标。但改革必须有序推进，必须符合香港的实际情况，依法循序渐进地推进。2015年，如果不是反对派的抵制，香港立法会就已经通过关于普选的立法了，结果实行普选的进程被迫推迟。西方普通民众对此了解甚少。

BBC： 第一个问题，你提到中国内部事务不容外国干涉，如果英国政府要求就香港面临的危机进行对话，是外国干涉吗？关于"修例"，除了搁置还有其他解决办法吗？中方是否准备撤销"修例"？第二个问题，你提到中国将不惜一切代价平息抗议活动……

刘晓明： 不是抗议，是动乱。

BBC： 如果派出军队，是否意味着"一国两制"、香港高度自治遭到破坏？会对香港经济造成巨大伤害吗？

刘晓明： 你实际上是提了三个问题，我从最后一个问题开始回答。我说过，我们有足够多的办法和足够强大的力量结束香港事态。我们这样做才是真正在捍卫"一国两制"。一些极端势力要求"香港独立"，他们企图利用香港向内地渗透，破坏内地的社会主义制度，这是在破坏"一国两制"。我们应该知道，"一国"的意思是香港是中国的一部分，中国对香港拥有主权。"一国"是"两制"的前提，没有"一国"，"两制"就无从谈起，二者是有机统一的整体，不能只强调一个，削弱另一个。中国要做的正是为了维护"一国两制"。

关于英国外交大臣打电话干涉香港内部事务，这不是一般的打电话讨论问题，而是用打电话向特区政府施压。英方说对警察使用暴力表示关切，谴责双方的暴力，这种"各打五十大板"的做法是混淆是非。指责正确的，就是支持错误的。这里的关键是电话谈话内容是不是干涉内政。英国政要经常访问香港，我们对此不持异议。但如果英方言论是在干预香港司法独立，比如之前一些政客要求香港特区政府"不能惩罚暴力违法者"，这就是干扰破坏香港的司法独立，是完全不能接受的。

我们已经对英国政客的言论表达了关切。英方要改变思维方式，要有大局观，香港保持稳定和繁荣不仅有利于香港和中国内地，也符合英国的利益。

关于"修例"问题，"修例"已经暂缓，下一步将由香港特区政府来决定，林郑特首已承诺要与社会各界进行更多沟通和讨论。我在上次记者会上说过，这是一个好条例，完善香港的法律制度，符合香港的利益，将香港变为"正义天堂"而非"避罪天堂"。特区政府需要时间解释"修例"符合香港利益，从而说服香港公众，争取公众理解。

BBC： 刚才的短片包含一名记者在香港机场被抗议者围攻的画面。另外一个人也在机场受到抗议者围攻，但他是来自深圳的便衣警察。请问目前有多少内地警务人员在香港活动？

刘晓明： 我了解的情况是，昨天一个深圳居民在机场为他的朋友送行，遭到了暴乱分子的围攻。另一个遭围攻的是中国内地记者，有人声称他是个警察，把他绑起来，但其实他是个有名、有姓、有注册的记者。

中国国际电视台： 我的第一个问题是，随着抗议者的暴力行为升级，香港警方的应对措施也不可避免地升级。近日来，香港警队遭遇袭击，如果放在其他地方，同样的袭警行为会受到严厉处理。为什么媒体，特别是西方媒体仍然严厉批评香港警队？第二个问题，昨天英国企业得到警告，要评估香港目前存在的投资风险，而且有28个国家已经针对香港发出了不同程度的旅行警告，这是否意味着香港经济面临一个转折点？

刘晓明： 关于香港警察的履职表现，我认为你说得很对，他们展现了极大的克制，超过很多其他国家的警察。他们非常专业，赢得包括美国、加拿大、法国等许多国家同行的钦佩。短片中看到的情况，如果发生在西方国家，警方处理时会使用更多强制手段，但香港警队保持了克制。这让我想起不久前的6月，英国环保组织申请在希思罗机场抗议，警方警告其如果这么做将面临终身监禁，敦促其三思而行。我们也都知道英国警方是如何处理伦敦骚乱的，使用了何等强制手段。

香港经济的确受到冲击，香港的国际形象和声誉也受到损害，令人痛心。香港是个非常安全的城市，法治指数很高，根据2018年世界正义工程法治指数排名，香港排名16，领先美国3位，美国排名19。这还只是法治指数，在安全指数方面，香港与西方城市相比更是遥遥领先。的确，我们都看到恒生指数下跌9%，港元汇率等也下滑了，非常令人痛心。正如我在开场白中所说，我认为香港民众应当珍惜来之不易的发展成果，我希望并期待香港回归理性。昨天我也听到一些来自香港工商界的声音，他们沉默了一段时间，但现在开始发声了，他们认识到这样的动乱将给香港这座城市、给香港的繁荣稳定造成多么大的损害。

路透社： 感谢大使给我第二次提问机会。你刚才回答BBC记者提问时提到，香港特区政府有权决定是否暂缓或撤销"修例"。可否明确一下，如果林郑月娥特首及其领导的香港特区政府决定撤销"修例"，中国中央政府会否同意？

刘晓明： 很多人以为"修例"是特区政府按中央政府指令或授意所为，实际情况不是这样。"修例"完全是由特区政府发起的，林郑特首本人也在多个场合表示，她从未收到中央政府任何相关"指令"。香港特区政府已决定暂缓"修例"，我们对此表示尊重、理解和支持，希望英国媒体注意我用的这三个词。我认为中国中央政府将继续这么做。

今日俄罗斯电视台： 自美国政府将华为公司列入"实体清单"，中美经贸摩擦逐步升级，你认为美方是否会把香港问题作为解决贸易问题的筹码？如果是这样，中方将如何应对，是否会在香港问题上做出让步？

刘晓明： 中美经贸磋商仍在继续，我对此持审慎乐观态度。中共中央政治局委员、中央外事工作委员会办公室主任杨洁篪日前访问纽约，会见了美国国务卿蓬佩奥，就包括贸易问题在内的中美关系交换了意见。中方不会在香港问题上牺牲原则，来换取与美方达成贸易协议。我们从不拿原则做交易。香港问题纯属中国内政，我们坚决反对任何外来干涉，不管这个干涉来自哪个国家。

彭博社： 你提到当前乱局将损害香港经济和营商环境，我认为香港工商界赞同这一点，他们十分担心街头示威会削弱香港的国际金融中心地位。但他们中很多人也忧虑中国中央政府会直接干预香港事务，比如派军队镇压所谓街头暴力。你认为中央政府出于维护香港繁荣稳定和国际地位的需要，今后是否会创造更多与街头抗议者接触和对话的空间？

刘晓明： 我要反问你一下，如果面临两种形势，一种是香港局势失控、持续动荡；一种是中央政府果断介入、终止动乱，哪一种符合工商界利益？我认为答案显然是后者。当然，这只是极端情况，并不是现实。我们希望香港事态平稳有序结束。这需要在广大爱国爱港人士坚定支持下，香港特区政府和香港警方严正执法、果断执法，尽快将违法分子绳之以法、严惩不贷，依法维护香港法治环境和社会秩序。这是香港的当务之急。

BBC广播四台： 感谢大使给我第二次提问的机会。我注意到你在刚才的答问中表示，对香港暴徒与和平抗议者要加以区分。你可否在此对香港市民明确一点：如果结束暴力，大家仍可继续进行和平抗议，不会遭受中国中央政府的干预，即中央干预只针对严重损害中国利益的暴力行径？

> **有问必答**
> No Question Unanswered

刘晓明： 你不妨回忆一下我刚才的开场讲话，如果香港局势进一步恶化，出现香港特区政府不能控制的动乱，中国中央政府绝不会坐视不管。按照《基本法》规定，中国中央政府有足够多的办法、足够强大的力量迅速平息可能出现的各种动乱。目前香港局势是可控的，仍在香港特区政府有效管控下，不存在你谈的假设情况。

BBC广播四台： 如果和平示威一旦失控呢？

刘晓明： 这反映出你对有关问题缺乏了解，低估了香港特区政府和警方的能力。他们有准备、有能力妥善应对和平抗议示威。当然，前提是示威必须是和平的、非暴力的。

CNN： 感谢大使也给我第二次提问的机会。你刚才反复提及中国中央政府仍对香港局势保持耐心，并强调你们有足够的办法和力量迅速平息事态。那么你认为下周的这个时候，香港特区政府能否使事态出现根本改观？或者你再举行一次记者会，继续回应外界关切？

刘晓明： 我在此重申，我们坚信在中国中央政府的大力支持下，在香港特区政府和林郑月娥行政长官的带领下，香港社会一定能够尽快止暴制乱，尽早恢复正常秩序。这样，我也就不需要再次举行记者会了。
谢谢大家！

The Central Government Has Enough Solutions to Quell Any Unrest
—— A Press Conference on the Situation in Hong Kong

On 15th August 2019, I held a press conference at the Chinese Embassy on the radical violence in Hong Kong which has escalated and caused severe damage. More than 50 journalists from 27 media agencies attended the press conference, including BBC, Radio 4, ITV, Sky News, Channel 4, *Financial Times*, *The Daily Telegraph*, *The Times*, *The Guardian*, Reuters from the UK, China's Xinhua News Agency, CCTV, China News Service, CGTN, *China Daily*, *Economic Daily*, *Science and Technology Daily*, *Guangming Daily*, and *Global Times* of China, and Bloomberg, CNN, Canadian Broadcasting Corporation, Phoenix Infonews, *European Times*, and *UK Chinese Times*. The following is the transcript of the press conference.

Liu Xiaoming: On 3rd July, I held a press conference here to answer questions about the amendments to Hong Kong's extradition laws and to explain China's position. For more than a month since then, the opposition in Hong Kong and some radical forces have continued to use their opposition to the amendments as an excuse for various types of radical street protests. The violence involved has escalated and the damage to society has grown. The movement has gone way beyond free assembly and peaceful protests. It is posing a severe challenge to law and order in Hong Kong, threatening the safety of the lives and property of the Hong Kong people, undermining prosperity and stability in Hong Kong and challenging the principled bottom line of "One Country, Two Systems". As a result, Hong Kong now faces the gravest situation since its handover.

A handful of extreme radicals have been undermining the rule of law, social order and "One Country, Two Systems" in Hong Kong. But they have taken cover under the so-called "pro-democracy movement" to hide their real intention and to whitewash their disruptive actions. This "neo-extremism" is both highly deceptive and destructive. The "neo-extremists" stormed the Legislative Council Complex, attacked the Liaison Office of the Central People's Government in Hong Kong, assaulted police officers and brought Hong Kong airport to a standstill by illegal assembly. Their moves constitute severe and violent offences, and already show signs of terrorism. The Central Government of China will never allow a few violent offenders to drag Hong Kong down into a dangerous abyss. We will never allow anyone to harm the rule of law and sound development in Hong Kong. We will never allow anyone to undermine "One Country, Two Systems" for any reason. Should the situation in Hong Kong deteriorate further in that the unrest becoming uncontrollable for the Government of the Hong Kong Special Administrative Region (SAR), the Central Government will not sit on its hands and watch. We have enough solutions and enough power within the limits of the Basic Law to quell any unrest swiftly.

This is a critical moment for Hong Kong. How will this end? This question is on the minds of all those who care about the future of Hong Kong. It is also hitting headlines and making "cover stories" in the British media. Our answer to this question is firm and clear: We hope this will end in an orderly way. In the meantime, we are fully prepared for the worst. So how will this end in an orderly way? I think the following four points are extremely important.

First, the priority now is to support the SAR Government in ending violence and restoring order. I hope that the people of Hong Kong, especially the young people who have been led astray, will have a clear understanding of the current situation in Hong Kong and cherish the sound development of Hong Kong after the handover, which does not come about easily. I hope they will keep the big picture in mind, rally behind the Chief Executive and the SAR Government, uphold the rule of law and justice in Hong Kong, and safeguard national unification as well as Hong Kong's prosperity and stability. The people of Hong Kong from all walks of life must refuse to be used or coerced by radical forces. They should say "no" to all violence and lawlessness. They should support the SAR Government in governing Hong Kong in accordance with law, and support the Hong Kong police in their strict and rigorous enforcement.

Second, the violent offenders must be brought to justice in accordance with the law. It is the basic requirement of the rule of law that all laws must be observed and all offenders must be held accountable. The violent and lawless perpetrators must be brought to justice no matter who they are or however hard they try to whitewash their actions. If anyone in this country questions this point, let me ask them this: Would the UK allow extremists to storm the Palace of Westminster or damage its facilities, and get away with it? Would the UK grant permission to attack police officers with lethal weapons or set fire to the police station without any punishment? Would the UK allow so-called "pro-democracy" rioters to occupy on airport, obstruct traffic, disturb public order or threaten the safety of people's lives and property? Aren't all these regarded as crimes in the UK?

Indulging lawlessness is tantamount to blaspheming against justice. Conniving in violence is tantamount to trampling on the rule of law. No country under the rule of law, no responsible government, would sit by and watch as such violence rages on. The Central Government of China firmly supports the SAR Government and the Hong Kong police in their strict, rigorous and decisive enforcement, so as to bring the offenders to justice as soon as possible and uphold the rule of law and public order in Hong Kong.

Third, foreign forces must stop interfering in Hong Kong's affairs. Evidence shows that the situation in Hong Kong would not have deteriorated so much had it not been for the interference and incitement of foreign forces. Some Western politicians and organizations have publicly or covertly given various types of support to the violent radicals, and tried to interfere in the judicial independence of Hong Kong and obstruct the Hong Kong police from bringing the violent offenders to justice.

I want to reiterate here that Hong Kong is a part of China; no foreign country should interfere in Hong Kong affairs. We urge those foreign forces to respect China's sovereignty and security, to immediately stop interfering in Hong Kong affairs, to stop interfering in China's internal affairs, and to stop conniving with violent offences. They should not misjudge the situation and head down the wrong path. Otherwise, they will "lift the stone only to drop it on their own feet".

Fourth, the media must shoulder due social responsibilities. Since these events in Hong Kong, I have to say, the Western media has failed to play a credible role. Instead of reporting the situation in a just and objective manner, they have confused right and wrong, given unbalanced accounts and misled the public. There has been extensive coverage of the so-called "right to peaceful protest" but few reports on the violent offences committed by the extreme radicals. For instance, the disruption to public order, attacks on police officers and injuries to bystanders. There has not been a word about the extensive public support for the SAR Government and for restoring law and order in Hong Kong. The lawless and violent offenders who undermine the rule of law are whitewashed and named "pro-democracy activists" in media reports.

But the legitimate law enforcement measures of the SAR Government and the police aimed at upholding law and order and protecting the lives and property of the people are labeled "repression".

Such selective reporting and distortion have resulted in the prevalence of misinformation and have misled the public, especially young people in Hong Kong. It is fair to say that the Western media has an inescapable responsibility for the current situation in Hong Kong!

I sincerely hope that the Western media will reflect on the social impact of their reporting, shoulder due social responsibility, and report the situation in Hong Kong in a just and objective manner. I hope they will stop speaking up for the extreme violent offenders, refrain from pouring oil over the flame in Hong Kong, and foster a sound environment of public opinion so that law and order can be restored in Hong Kong.

To help you understand the fourth point that I have just made, I would like to show a short video clip, so that you can see some scenes and hear some voices that are absent in the Western media.

(Video clip is played.)

"Order fosters prosperity while unrest brews regression." Given what is happening in Hong Kong, this ancient Chinese teaching could not be more relevant.

It is in the interests of both China and the international community, including the UK, to have a prosperous and stable Hong Kong, where over three hundred thousand British citizens live and work, and where three hundred British companies are doing business.

I sincerely hope that people from all walks of life in the UK will have a clear understanding of the big picture, act in the interests of Hong Kong's prosperity and stability, and refrain from saying or doing anything that interferes in Hong Kong's affairs or undermines the rule of law in Hong Kong. I am confident that with the support of the Central Government of China and under the leadership of the SAR Government and Chief Executive Carrie Lam, Hong Kong will bring violence to an end and restore law and order at an early date. Hong Kong, the "oriental pearl", will once again shine brightly.

Now I would like to take your questions.

Bloomberg: I noticed that there was one moment in the clip when one of the speakers pointed out that the Hong Kong police were not using live ammunition. There have been armed personnel carriers and troops, shown on social media and TV, just outside Hong Kong. If they were to be deployed at some point as you suggest is possible, would they use live ammunition? Would they be entitled to use it?

Liu Xiaoming: I will answer your question in this way. I think the Hong Kong situation has reached a very critical moment. But we have full trust and confidence in the Chief Executive and the Government of the Hong Kong Special Administration Region in handling the situation and bringing it to an end in an orderly way. As I said in my opening remarks, if the situation deteriorates further into unrest that is uncontrollable for the SAR Government, the Central Government will not sit by and watch. We have enough solutions and enough power to put it to an end and to quell the unrest swiftly.

CNN: We have a message from President Trump saying that he is willing to discuss this situation with President Xi Jinping. Has there been any response yet to this suggestion? If it is being considered, will it help to resolve the situation?

Liu Xiaoming: I don't think President Trump proposed formally to have a meeting with President Xi Jinping. I think he tweeted to express his views on Hong Kong. Hong Kong is a ongoing subject between China and Western governments, including the UK and the United States. We are open to discussion. But the important thing to remember is that we do not accept any interference in Hong Kong's internal affairs. We believe it is purely China's internal affairs. We strongly oppose any foreign intervention, including foreign organizations giving financial support and some Congressmen proposing a so-called "Hong Kong Human Rights and Democracy Act". In particular, we are opposed to foreign officials making telephone calls to the SAR Government and exerting pressure by publicly showing their support for the rioters. We strongly oppose this.

Reuters: I noticed that you said in your opening remarks that the behaviour of some of the protesters shows some signs of terrorism. I wonder whether you'd mind explaining to us what would be the red line or turning point over which this would constitute terrorism? Would that then provide, under Chinese Law, a legal justification for the deployment of Chinese forces in Hong Kong?

Liu Xiaoming: From both the video clip and also what is happening in Hong Kong, especially what is happening at the airport, the atrocities have already drawn worldwide condemnation. Many media outlets regarded them as terrorist acts. They are no different from terrorism. They are attacking the police, attacking travelers, even attacking journalists, including one of your colleagues from China. We heard strong condemnation from the Chinese Association of Journalists on this kind of attack. These are signs of terrorism. I would call it neo-extremism. If this goes any further, it might become a terrorist action.

Even if it becomes a terrorist action, I still hope that the Hong Kong SAR Government and the Hong Kong police can handle the situation. What I am saying is that if the situation deteriorates into unrest that is uncontrollable for Hong Kong SAR Government, the Central Government will certainly not sit by and watch.

Russia Today: According to reports, the National Endowment for Democracy in the US has been funding some of Hong Kong protesters. Has Beijing concluded that the Hong Kong protests are entirely a US plot to destabilize China?

Liu Xiaoming: I think you've already partly answered the question. We believe there is a "dark hand" behind this radical movement. As I mentioned in my opening statement, some foreign forces including foreign organizations provided financial support and moral support to the radical movement. In particular, some foreign officials met the leaders of the Hong Kong independence group. This clearly showed that their intention is to make Hong Kong a problem for China, to use Hong Kong to contain China, to prevent China from developing smoothly and to prevent China from becoming a prosperous country. That's for sure! That's why I am saying, in order to end the chaotic situation in Hong Kong in an orderly way, it is very important for the foreign forces to stop interfering further in Hong Kong's affairs, including the activities you have mentioned.

The Times: I wonder if you could respond to the suggestion of the Chairman of the Foreign Affairs Committee that full British citizenship be extended to all Hong Kong citizens. Would China regard that as a provocation?

Liu Xiaoming: I think where some politicians in this country are concerned, although their bodies live in the 21st century, their heads are still in the colonial days. I think some of them still regard Hong Kong as a part of the British Empire. They treat Hong Kong as a part of UK. That's the problem. I think they really have to change their mindsets, place them in the proper position, and regard Hong Kong as a part of China, not a part of the UK.

ITV: You said earlier that Beijing is fully prepared for the worst. Can you clarify exactly what that means? And also people see some satellite images of troops and tanks assembled in Shenzhen. Is this a means of intimidation or is Chinese military action a very real possibility, or even imminent?

Liu Xiaoming: I have already answered this question in my opening statement. The first part concerns the kind of situation where resolute solutions should be needed. I said, if the situation deteriorates further into unrest that is controllable for the Hong Kong SAR Government, then the Central Government will not sit by and watch. And we have enough solutions and enough power to quell the unrest swiftly. If you listen to my remarks word for word, you would get the answer to your question.

ITV: What exactly does "quell" mean though? How would you quell the protests?

Liu Xiaoming: To put them to an end. Thank you.

Sky News: You talked about how Beijing has the power to deal with this problem. Could you give us a sense of the scale of forces you have available to deploy into Hong Kong if necessary? Are they properly trained to deal with what is a civilian uprising, civilian unrest, as opposed to the military problem? And then secondly if I may, this is your second press conference. Last time, we had a different prime minister. Now we've got Prime Minister Boris Johnson. Last time, you said the relations between Beijing and London had been damaged by, for example, our then Foreign Secretary's comments on Hong Kong. What are the relations like now? Are the relations better or maybe healed between the UK and China? Or are they still being damaged? What is your message for the Prime Minister?

Liu Xiaoming: To answer your first question, I think I have already answered your question. First of all, this is a hypothetical question. Currently, we still believe that the Hong Kong SAR Government is capable of doing their job. The Chief Executive is a very capable leader, who enjoys broad respect and support in Hong Kong. So, at this moment, I think they are still handling it very well. We have full trust. We are confident and we have enough solutions and enough power to put this to an end swiftly.

With regard to your second question, we certainly would like to see relations develop further because we believe it's in the interests of China and the UK to have a sound relationship. Of course I didn't expect you to have a new prime minister so soon. So I need to be careful with my press conference. I do not hope that at the next press conference we will be talking about yet another prime minister.

This is the fourth prime minister I'm going to work with. We have expectations. We do hope our relationship will move along the lines of the direction of Golden Era set by President Xi during his state visit. But a good relationship has to be based on the basic principles of mutual respect for sovereignty and territorial integrity, and non-interference in each other's internal affairs. This much was enshrined in the Joint Communiqué on establishing diplomatic relations between our two countries. As long as these principles are followed, the relationship will move forward. When these principles are violated, the relationship will suffer setbacks. So we do hope that the new administration will handle with great caution the Hong Kong issue, which concerns China's sovereignty, which concerns China's territorial integrity, which concerns China's internal affairs. Thank you.

The Guardian: What is your definition of "uncontrollable"? What would you be looking for to define when the situation has become uncontrollable?

Liu Xiaoming: Do you think we have to consult the Oxford English Dictionary for what "uncontrollable" means? Uncontrollable means out of control. We do hope that the situation will remain under control of the SAR Government and the Chief Executive. I believe the current situation is still under control.

BBC Radio 4: Ambassador, you painted the protesters as violent and as extremists. Can I ask you whether you would acknowledge that for every violent or extremist protester, there are many ordinary citizens in Hong Kong-lawyers and civil servants-who are deeply disappointed by what is happening on the Chinese government side, and support the idea that people should have more say in their own administration, and support the fifth demand of the protesters-universal suffrage? Would you acknowledge that there are many people who are not violent or extremist protesters? Can you remind us and the people of Hong Kong why China finds it so objectionable to give them universal suffrage? If I may ask a second question, does China still regard the Joint Declaration signed with Britain in 1984 as applying to and constraining its behavior in Hong Kong?

Liu Xiaoming: Evan, I haven't seen you for quite a while since I last went on your programme. Your first question is about the demonstrators. We certainly have acknowledged the difference between the young people and the radical violent offenders. A few radicals do not represent the majority of the demonstrators. The majority of them have been misled. I think the Hong Kong media has some responsibility here and Western media has some responsibility too.
In any society you have all kinds of complaints. Since Hong Kong's handover, enormous achievements and progress have been made under "One Country, Two Systems". But there is still a lot of room for improvement, such as how young people can advance in their careers. There are many problems in the Hong Kong economy. The Hong Kong economy has depended too much on financial services and real estate, which offers few opportunities to young people. So they have complaints. We understand. The Central Government and the SAR Government have tried very hard to address these problems. We have launched the Guangdong-Hong Kong-Macao Greater Bay Area Development Project. That will give the young people of Hong Kong more opportunities.
If you compare Hong Kong with Shenzhen across the river, it's quite a contrast. In the space of 30 years, Shenzhen has been transformed into a dynamic city full of vigor with many young people, a lot of high-tech and new technology companies like Huawei, Tencent and Dajiang, and many top world-class companies. What world-class high-tech companies can you find in Hong Kong? To address these problems, we have to focus on development. Demonstrations offer no solution. Chaotic situations will only cause young people to suffer more. We will certainly address the concerns of the young people. We certainly understand the difference between the young people who have been misled, who have been led astray as I said, and those radical violent offenders.

Your second question is about the Joint Declaration. I think some people often confuse "One Country, Two Systems" with the Joint Declaration. The Joint Declaration has completed its mission. Its main mission was to ensure the smooth handover of Hong Kong from the UK to China. And it was also its mission to ensure a 13-year smooth transition period between 1984, when China and the UK agreed on the handover and 1997. And that was its main mission. Yes, the Joint Declaration mentioned "One Country, Two Systems". But that is a national policy announced by the Chinese Government. It is incorporated in the Basic Law of Hong Kong. So when we say China is committed to the Basic Law and "One Country, Two Systems" for 50 years, we are not saying we are committed to the Joint Declaration for 50 years.

About universal suffrage, the Central Government is committed to universal suffrage. We believe this is the final aim of political reform in Hong Kong. But it has to proceed in an orderly way and it has to suit the conditions of Hong Kong. If it had not been for the opposition in Hong Kong in 2015, the Legislative Council would have passed a law on universal suffrage. They killed this law and held up the process. There are so many things that are not known by the Western public.

BBC: You talked about there being no place for foreign interference in China's internal affairs. Does that mean the present British government is interfering in internal affairs when it calls for dialogue to end the crisis in Hong Kong? Is one of the solutions that you would examine carefully to find a way through this to move beyond mere suspension of the extradition law? Would you be prepared to move to full withdrawal, one of the basic points raised by the protesters? My second question is about the potential use of force. You said China will use whatever means necessary to quell the protests.

Liu Xiaoming: Not the protest. To quell the unrest.

BBC: If you were to employ the Chinese army in Hong Kong, do you accept that it would have the effect of destroying the "Two Systems" and Hong Kong's autonomy, and do great damage to China because it will suffer economically and in trade as a result?

Liu Xiaoming: I think you have asked three questions and I am trying to remember them all. Maybe the last question first. As I said, we have enough solutions and enough power to put this to an end swiftly. By doing this, we are to be exact defending "One Country, Two Systems". Some of the radical forces call for the independence of Hong Kong. They want to use Hong Kong to infiltrate the Mainland, to disrupt the socialist system in the Mainland. So in both ways, they undermine "One Country, Two Systems". When we talk about "One Country, Two Systems", people have to be aware that it's a complete whole. "One Country" means that Hong Kong is part of China and China has sovereignty over Hong Kong. "One Country" is the precondition for "Two Systems". Without "One Country", there will be no "Two Systems". So, the two are one complete whole. We can't emphasize one at the expense of the other. I think what China is going to do -- to put the situation under control -- is exactly for the purpose of maintaining "One Country, Two Systems".

About the telephone conversation, as I said, we are open to discussions on Hong Kong. But the important thing is that you can't use telephone conversation to exert pressure on the SAR Government. For instance, you are saying that you are concerned about the police's excessive use of force and you condemn the violence on both sides. That is not fair. You can't give a 50-50. You confuse right and wrong. If you condemn things that are right, you certainly support things that are wrong. The important thing is the nature of the conversation, whether it constitutes an intervention or not. British politicians are visiting Hong Kong all the time. We show no objection to them. But if you make a comment that is interfering in the judicial independence of Hong Kong, you are trying to obstruct it. Just like some politicians have said before, one cannot punish those radicals and violent offenders. It just obstructs the legal system in Hong Kong. That cannot be accepted at all.

We have expressed our concerns about some of the comments by British politicians. I really hope that they change their mindset and keep the big picture in mind. A prosperous and stable Hong Kong is really in the interest of the UK, not only in the interests of Hong Kong and China.

About the withdrawal of the bill. You know the bill has been suspended by the SAR Government. Whether it will be withdrawn is up to the Hong Kong SAR Government to decide. The Chief Executive promised to have further communication and discussions with the public and various sectors in Hong Kong. From the very beginning in my first press conference, I said this is a good bill. I think the intension is to improve the legal system of Hong Kong It serves the interest of Hong Kong. It will make Hong Kong a safe haven of justice rather than a safe haven for fugitives, but it was not well understood. So it might take time for the SAR Government to explain their position, to convince the public that it is in Hong Kong's interest to pass this bill.

BBC Newsnight: In the video, you showed a journalist at the airport surrounded by protesters. You didn't show the other guy surrounded by protesters who turned out to be a law enforcement official from Shenzhen not wearing uniform. How many other such Mainland law enforcement officials are currently operating in Hong Kong?

Liu Xiaoming: Your information is not what I know. Yesterday, an ordinary traveller was rounded up by the rioters at the airport. He was from Shenzhen and he came to the airport to see off a friend. The other one was a journalist from China, who was tied up. Some people regarded him as a police officer, but he turned out to be a journalist who has now been named, a registered journalist.

CGTN: My first question is that, as the violence escalates, the Hong Kong police response will inevitably escalate. We all know what the Hong Kong police are experiencing these days. In other countries, it equates to aggravated assault which will be dealt with seriously. But why are they still the target of blames in some of the media, in most of the Western media, even when they are being so restrained? My second question is that yesterday, some British companies were warned to evaluate the risks to investment in Hong Kong. More than 28 countries have been notified to issue different levels of warnings to travelers to Hong Kong. Analysts say that currently this is a kind of a turning point for Hong Kong's economy. So what is your view?

Liu Xiaoming: I think you are absolutely right in talking about the behavior of the Hong Kong police. I think they exercise their duty with great restraint, more so than in many other countries. They are very professional and have won the praise of their counterparts from many countries, including the US, Canada, and France. You know, if things like this happen in the Western countries, the police will deal with them with much more force.
That reminds me of something just a few months ago, in June. When the Extinction Rebellion applied to put up a demonstration in Heathrow Airport, they were warned by the British police that those involved would face a life sentence and were urged to

reconsider. We've all watched how the British police handled the riot in London. And I don't need to remind you of what kind of force they used.

On the Hong Kong economy. Yes, it suffered. What is happening in Hong Kong really damaged the international image and reputation of Hong Kong. It's very sad. Hong Kong is a very safe place. Its rule of law rating is very high. In terms of the Project of Justice index, it places three positions higher than the United States last year. It ranked 16th while the United States ranked 19th. I'm talking about law and order, not safety. On safety matters, Hong Kong is much safer than the other Western cities.

Of course, we all read that the Hang Seng stock has fallen 9% and the Hong Kong dollar has fallen. It's very sad. I think people, as I said in my opening remarks, should treasure the hard-won development of Hong Kong. I do hope common sense will prevail in Hong Kong. I just heard many statements yesterday from business leaders. They've kept quiet for some time, but now they are speaking out. They realized what kind of damage this chaos in Hong Kong may do to the city, to the prosperity and stability of Hong Kong.

Reuters: Thank you for taking a second question. Earlier when my colleague from the BBC asked about the extradition bill, you said it's up to the Hong Kong SAR Government to decide whether it will be withdrawn or not. Just to be completely clear, if Carrie Lam and the Hong Kong SAR Government decided to withdraw the bill fully, would the Central Government of China allow them to do so?

Liu Xiaoming: At the very beginning, many people thought that this move came under the orders or instruction of the Central Government. That was not true. This initiative is completely the decision of the Hong Kong administration. Chief Executive Carrie Lam has said on many occasions that she received no order or instruction from the Central Government to launch this process. She decided to suspend it and we showed respect, understanding and support. So I hope you will keep in mind the three words I gave you: respect, understanding and support. And I think that we will continue to do this further down the road.

Russia Today: As you know the trade war with the US is continuing and the US government has included Huawei in the list of entities. Do you think there is a chance that the US would do the same to Hong Kong, in terms of getting a fair world trade deal? How would Beijing respond?

Liu Xiaoming: The talks are still ongoing, and I personally feel cautiously optimistic about the future of China-US trade relations. A member of the Political Bureau of the CPC Central Committee and Director of the Office of the Foreign Affairs Commission of the CPC Central Committee Yang Jiechi is in New York and has had a talk with Secretary Pompeo. They had a very candid discussion on bilateral relations, including trade issues.
On Hong Kong, China will never compromise its principles for a trade deal. We will not barter away our principles. It's purely China's internal affairs which brook no foreign intervention, no matter which country it comes from.

Bloomberg: The entire Hong Kong business community would agree with you when you said that the unrest has been very bad for the economy, bad for Hong Kong's position as a global financial centre. And yet many would also argue that if the Chinese Central Government were to intervene directly, that could be even worse. Do you not think that the position you laid out here, should allow more space for engagement with the protesters, in the interest of, as you said, maintaining stability, economic well being and the international image of Hong Kong?

Liu Xiaoming: Let me ask you this. If Hong Kong's situation becomes uncontrollable and unrest goes on and on, will it serve the interests of the business community in Hong Kong? Or if the Central Government intervenes with a resolute solution and puts an end to the unrest as quickly as possible, will that serve their interests? I think the answer would be the latter.
But that's an extreme situation. That is not a real situation. And we hope to see the situation end in an orderly way, which includes that the people should rally behind the Hong Kong SAR Government and rally behind the Chief Executive to support the Hong Kong SAR Government to put this to an end, to bring the violent and lawbreakers to justice, and to restore order. That is the top priority of Hong Kong today.

BBC Radio 4: Thank you for taking a second question. You draw a distinction between the violent protesters and nonviolent protesters. Can you unequivocally tell the people of Hong Kong that if the violence stops but peaceful protest continues, there is no way that the central Chinese authorities will intervene in the internal affairs of Hong Kong? It is only the violence that China will quell or stop.

Liu Xiaoming: I hope you will go back to my opening statement. I said that if the situation in Hong Kong deteriorates into unrest that is uncontrollable for the Hong Kong SAR Government, the Central Government will not sit by and watch. And we have enough solutions and power to quell the unrest swiftly in accordance with the Basic Law of Hong Kong. What you are talking about is a situation that is not happening. It is still under the control of the Hong Kong SAR Government.

BBC Radio 4: It may go beyond control?

Liu Xiaoming: That shows your lack of understanding of the situation. You have underestimated the capability of the Hong Kong SAR Government and the Hong Kong police. They are fully prepared and equipped to handle peaceful demonstration -- but it has to be peaceful.

CNN: Thank you for taking a second question. You talked about how patient you've been right now, and you were suggesting that you have the resources and solutions to quell it swiftly. What sort of timeline we are looking at? Let's suppose by this time next week, do you think the Hong Kong SAR Government will be able to resolve the crisis by itself? Or we will still be having this conversation next week?

Liu Xiaoming: As I said, we have full trust in the Hong Kong SAR Government and its Chief Executive, with the strong support of the Central Government. I hope they will put an end to the unrest at an early date, as soon as possible and restore order. Maybe we do not need another press conference. We'll see.
Thank you.

香港的出路在哪里？
——关于香港局势中外记者会
（2019年11月18日，中国驻英国大使馆）

刘晓明： 大家上午好！欢迎大家出席今天的中外记者会。

这是自香港事态发生以来，我第三次在使馆举办记者会。5个多月来，"修例风波"演变为持续不断的暴力活动，特别是近期大规模违法暴力行径全面升级，已经把香港推到了极为危险的境地。所有真正关心香港的人都在思考：香港到底怎么了？应当如何看待当前香港乱局？香港的出路在哪里？

4天前，习近平主席在巴西出席金砖国家领导人第十一次会晤时，就当前香港局势表明中国政府严正立场。习主席指出，香港持续发生的激进暴力犯罪行为，严重践踏法治和社会秩序，严重破坏香港繁荣稳定，严重挑战"一国两制"原则底线。止暴制乱、恢复秩序是香港当前最紧迫的任务。我们将继续坚定支持行政长官带领香港特别行政区政府依法施政，坚定支持香港警方严正执法，坚定支持香港司法机构依法惩治暴力犯罪分子。中国政府维护国家主权、安全、发展利益的决心坚定不移，贯彻"一国两制"方针的决心坚定不移，反对任何外部势力干涉香港事务的决心坚定不移。

习主席的重要讲话字字铿锵，句句千钧，是中国中央政府对香港当前局势和未来出路发出的最权威的声音。

第一，习主席讲话深刻指出了激进暴力犯罪活动的实质与严重危害。当前香港局势发展的本质绝不是一些西方政客和西方媒体所标榜的所谓"民主自由"问题，而是极端暴力违法分子破坏香港法治和社会秩序，妄图搞乱香港、破坏"一国两制"的问题，这是赤裸裸的激进暴力犯罪活动。

激进暴力犯罪活动严重践踏香港法治和社会秩序。5个多月来，暴徒们自称和平示威，却疯狂打砸纵火，有预谋地袭警、刺杀香港立法会议员，将多所大学变成罪恶基地，围攻袭击内地学生；自称与弱者同行，却无差别残害普通市民，甚至向一名反对他们破坏活动的市民身上浇淋易燃液体并点火焚烧；自称捍卫民主自由，却限制和剥夺他人的人身与言论自由。这种光天化日之下杀人放火、惨无人道的暴力行径是对法律底线、道德底线、人类文明底线的严重践踏！我们对此绝不能容忍！反中乱港分子还将黑手伸到境外，伸向英国：他们面戴"黑口罩"，到中国驻英国大使馆门前寻衅，污损使馆正门及两侧墙壁，涂写"港独"标语；他们围攻来英出席活动的香港特区政府律政司司长并将她推倒致伤。我们对这些暴力行径表示最强烈的愤慨和最严厉的谴责！

激进暴力犯罪活动严重破坏香港繁荣稳定。自由开放的经济活力、包容多元的文化魅力、专业高效的社会管理、法治安全的社会环境曾是香港闪亮的国际名片。但是今天，暴力极端分子在香港制造"黑色恐怖"，市民的生命财产安全受到严重伤害；香港经济连续两个季度环比下跌，第三季度本地生产总值滑至−2.9%的负值，已经步入技术性衰退，香港特区政府经济顾问办公室近日下调2019年香港经济增长预测至−1.3%；相关国际评级下降，香港国际形象、营商环境受到严重冲击。如今出现在媒体上的香港，是持续不断的暴力活动，是混乱不安的社会秩序。香港回归22年来取得的发展成就与大好局面正在受到侵蚀，"东方之珠"正在变成"东方之殇"，"香港"正滑向"乱港"的深渊，前景不堪设想。

激进暴力犯罪活动严重挑战"一国两制"原则底线。香港反对派和暴力极端势力，大肆鼓吹"港独"，公然宣扬"光复香港"。这彻底暴露出其所谓社会诉求背后真正的险恶政治用意，那就是冲着摧毁"一国两制"中"一国"这个根本来的，企图搞乱香港、瘫痪特区政府，进而夺取香港的管治权，把香港从祖国分离出去。"一国两制"是一个完整的概念。"一国"是"两制"的前提和基础。没有"一国"，就没有"两制"。我们绝不能容忍任何破坏"一国两制"的暴力犯罪活动！

第二，习主席讲话为解决香港乱局指明了出路，即止暴制乱、恢复秩序是当前香港最紧迫的任务。有法必依、违法必究是任何一个法治社会的基本要求。极端暴力活动是任何社会都绝不能容忍、绝不会姑息的。只有依法制止和惩治暴力活动，恢复法治和社会秩序，才能维护香港广大民众的福祉，才能守护香港美好的明天，才能稳固"一国两制"的根基。我们坚决支持特区政府、香港警方和司法机关坚守法治原则，采取有力行动，遏制打击各种暴力违法行为和恐怖主义行径，将违法犯罪分子尽快绳之以法、严惩不贷，依法维护香港法治环境和社会秩序，还香港以稳定，还民众以安宁。

第三，习主席讲话彰显了中国政府维护国家主权安全发展利益、贯彻"一国两制"方针的坚定决心。不久前举行的中共十九届四中全会明确指出,"一国两制"是中国共产党领导人民实现祖国和平统一的一项重要制度。中国政府将全面准确贯彻"一国两制"、"港人治港"、高度自治的方针。贯彻"一国两制"方针,要始终坚持"三条底线"不容触碰,即绝对不能允许任何危害国家主权安全、绝对不能允许挑战中央权力和《基本法》权威、绝对不能允许利用香港对内地进行渗透破坏的活动。中国政府将健全依照宪法和《基本法》对香港实行全面管治权的制度,完善香港融入国家发展大局、同内地优势互补、协同发展机制,着力解决影响社会稳定和长远发展的深层次矛盾和问题。

第四,习主席讲话显示了中国政府反对任何外部势力干涉香港事务的坚定决心。近期香港事态不断升级,外部势力的姑息纵容和推波助澜难辞其咎。一些西方国家政客和西方媒体罔顾事实、颠倒黑白,把激进暴力犯罪分子称为所谓"和平示威者"和"民主抗议者",却对恪尽职守、维护香港法治、保护市民生命财产安全的香港警方百般指责。一些西方国家政客赤裸裸地为激进暴力违法分子撑腰打气。美国国会众议院通过所谓《香港人权和民主法案》,粗暴干涉香港事务和中国内政。英国政府和议会下院外委会出台涉华报告对香港问题说三道四。更有甚者,个别英国政客还要为鼓吹"港独"、鼓动极端暴力活动的"急先锋"授奖。如果有人还怀疑外部势力插手香港事务,这些事实难道还不够吗?!我们要正告那些外部势力,中国政府反对任何外部势力干涉香港事务的决心坚定不移!我们要奉劝那些外部势力,立即停止以任何方式干预香港事务和中国内政,立即停止纵容香港暴力犯罪，否则必将搬起石头砸自己的脚！

为了帮助各位更好地了解当前香港激进暴力犯罪事实，我们这次又制作了一个短片，让大家看一看那些被西方政客和媒体称为"和平示威者"和"民主抗议者"的真实面目，看一看今天的香港究竟面临什么样的危险局面。

（播放视频）

事实无法掩盖，真相击破谎言。这是我对这个短片的评价，希望大家看后也有同感。我曾多次向英国各界人士表示，香港保持繁荣稳定、维护"一国两制"，不仅符合中国的利益，也符合包括英国在内的各国共同利益。英国在香港有30多万公民、700多家企业。香港乱下去对英国有百害而无一利。我衷心希望，英国各界有识之士认清形势，看清大局，支持香港特区政府止暴制乱、恢复秩序、维护法治，抵制和反对任何干涉香港事务的言行，多做有利于香港繁荣稳定的事情，使香港乱局早日结束，使"东方之珠"重现光彩。

下面，我愿回答大家提问。

BBC： 此前我给贵使馆写过邮件，询问关于新疆"集中营"的情况，你能否告知真相？

刘晓明： 你的问题超出了今天记者会的主题，但我可以做出回答。首先我必须澄清，新疆没有你所说的"集中营"。新疆设立了职业技能教育培训中心，目的是预防恐怖主义。

BBC: 最近我看到一些中国政府发给"集中营"的命令，内容包括改变相关人员的行为，进行普通话培训，这是给他们洗脑。

刘晓明： 这完全是假消息。新疆是中国一个自治区，是一个风光美丽、和平繁荣的地方。但是从20世纪90年代到2016年不是这样的，新疆发生了几千起恐怖事件，数千名无辜群众遇害，当地民众强烈要求政府采取应对措施。设立教培中心后，新疆3年来没有发生一起恐怖事件，恢复了昔日的美丽、和平与繁荣。我倒是想问问，如果英国某个地方也集中发生恐怖事件、民众深受其害，英国政府会怎么做？

中方采取的预防性措施根本不是什么宗教清洗。新疆民众享有充分的宗教自由。希望你有机会去新疆走一走、看一看，体会一下当地民众享有的宗教自由和幸福生活。新疆有2.8万个宗教场所3万名宗教教职人员，平均每530个穆斯林就拥有1座清真寺，比例超过许多伊斯兰国家，也比英国基督教徒拥有教堂的比例高很多。所以说，新疆根本不存在所谓宗教清洗的问题，当地民众享有充分宗教自由。

设立教培中心是为了更好地帮助那些曾参与恐怖活动、极端主义活动但情节相对轻微的年轻人改邪归正，开展语言培训可帮助这些人成为合法公民和合格的劳动者。当地民众可以使用自己民族的语言，但为了改善生活水平、更好地与其他地区民众交流，需要掌握更多的语言技能和职业技能。缺乏法律知识也容易使他们成为恐怖主义的受害者。学习好语言有助于帮助他们更好地学习职业技能和法律知识，实现自食其力，这才是教培的目的。最重要的是，这一举措是成功的，新疆变得更加安全。去年，赴疆旅游人数增长40%，国内生产总值（GDP）增长超过6%。

BBC： 但据我掌握的文件，大量被关进"集中营"的人既没有接受审判，也没有被起诉，至少会在里面待一年。

刘晓明： 你所说的那些文件都是编造的虚假信息。中方已就新疆反恐去极端化斗争、职业技能教育培训工作等发布了7本白皮书，记者会后我们向你提供这些官方文件，希望你认真阅读，不要听信假消息。

英国电视四台： 我曾与一些"集中营"里的人交流过。如果主要是针对年轻人的话，为什么还有许多老年人和妇女被关进"集中营"？关于香港，中方要将香港"融入"内地，变成"一国一制"吗？

刘晓明： 教培中心的学员涉恐情节轻微，无须予以法律惩戒。政府希望给他们机会改正，离开教培中心后不会再发生犯罪行为。这才是设立教培中心的目的，事实证明这一举措十分成功。教培中心里大多数是年轻人，当然也有一些年龄较大的人，年龄不是问题，主要取决于他们的行为是否对社会构成威胁。

中国共产党十九届四中全会已再次重申将继续坚持"一国两制"，习近平主席在庆祝中华人民共和国成立70周年大会等多个场合予以重申。"融入"的意思是祖国要给香港提供更多发展机遇，如推进粤港澳大湾区建设。这些机遇可以帮助香港实现更好的发展，解决存在的一些深层次问题，如收入差距、年轻人就业等。我们会继续坚持"一国两制"的成功实践，但目前这一政策受到暴力极端分子的破坏。正如我刚才所说，"一国两制"是一个完整的概念，不能割裂。"一国"的含义是香港已经回归，是中国的一部分，我们不允许任何外部势力干涉香港事务。"一国"是"两制"的前提和基础，"一国"受到损害，"两制"也无从谈起。

《南华早报》：大使先生，刚才你在讲话中敦促国际社会支持香港特区政府止暴制乱。但实际情况是香港特区政府的举措效果有限，暴力活动还在升级。我想问的是，中国政府是否将考虑部署军队平息局势？

刘晓明：据我所知，包括特首在内，香港特区政府已采取多种措施与民众进行沟通，听取意见建议，举行各类活动逾百场。我们需要给他们机会和时间。开展对话需要和平的环境，但当前暴力活动猖獗，显然无助于特区政府与民众开展实质性、有成效的对话，我们需要创造有利的条件。驻港部队肩负着维护国家主权、安全、领土完整和香港安全的重任。此前记者会上我已多次说过，我们信任香港特区政府和林郑月娥特首。不久前，习主席会见林郑特首时高度肯定特首及特区政府管治团队的工作，表达了充分信任。特区政府正在努力控制局势，但如果事态失控，中央政府不会坐视不管，我们拥有足够多的办法和足够强大的力量平息动乱。

《南华早报》：第二个问题，香港立法会前主席、民建联前主席曾钰成是香港最亲内地的人士之一，几天前他在接受采访时表示，支持赦免轻微

有问必答
No Question Unanswered

犯罪的暴力分子并对警察开展独立调查。你对此有何评论？

刘晓明： 这个问题应该由香港特区政府回答，我不对具体的司法问题做出评论。

天空新闻台： 第一个问题，关于解放军是否会介入，你重复了上次记者会的表态，怎么理解"无法控制"？事态已经延续了5个月，仍未改善。放手香港特区政府处理事态的政策是否失败了？下一步是向抗议者做实质性的妥协还是中央政府会派军队干预？第二个问题是关于新疆。《纽约时报》周末公布了数百份文件并进行相关报道，你对此有何评论？

刘晓明： 关于第一个问题，我认为香港特区政府对当前事态仍在进行有效处理，在这种形势下，我要求外部势力停止干涉，停止煽动暴力，停止火上浇油，尊重特区政府，让特区政府依法施政。关于第二个问题，我的回答是，根本不存在这样的文件，有关报道纯属编造，一派胡言、用心险恶。这不是《纽约时报》第一次捏造假新闻了，不值一驳。

《每日电讯报》： 你提到外部势力煽风点火、"港独"等，你还提到英国政府，特别是英国议会下院外委会，你数次提到外部势力煽动暴力，你是否指责英国政府煽动暴力和支持"港独"？

刘晓明： 当英方发表不负责任的涉港言论时，我们向英方表明了立场。英国政府批评香港警察，批评香港特区政府处置事态，就是对中国内政的干涉。英方某些言论表面上看起来平衡，但实质是在偏袒暴徒。我们赞赏英方反对"港独"的立场。英国高级官员已数次表示，"港独"不是选项。我希望英方对"港独"进行更强烈的谴责，也希望英方遵守承诺，言行一致，采取实际行动反对"港独"。

独立电视台： 在过去24小时，我们看到香港形势急剧恶化，是否镇压已迫在眉睫？

刘晓明： 不存在所谓"镇压"。我认为香港警察在履行他们的职责。一些人指责香港警察，但在我看来，他们是最专业的警察，保持了极大的克制。比如说，如果在英国的校园里发生类似的事件，在英国议会及周边地区出现类似的事态，你可以想象一下英国警察会怎样应对。香港警察努力避免伤亡，他们不想伤害被极端分子洗脑的学生，如果不是这个原因，事情恐怕不会是现在的样子了。

《卫报》： 第一个问题关于香港局势，你认为下周的香港区议会选举会照常举行吗？第二个问题，为什么中国政府反对英国给予在香港的英国国民（海外）护照（BNO）持有者以英国公民身份、允许他们获得居英权并在英工作？

刘晓明： 根据中国国籍法，所有香港中国同胞，不论是否持有"英国属土公民护照"或"英国国民（海外）护照"（BNO），都是中国公民，中国不承认双重国籍。关于2019年香港特别行政区区议会选举，我们当然希望选举正常进行，但这将由香港特区政府来决定。我们希望香港局势能迅速稳定，港人能不受滋扰地去投票点投票，选举地方议员。这是我们的期望。

BBC： 你播放的短片让我们看到一个令人震惊、充斥暴力行为的香港，我们在英国电视以及社交媒体上也看到过类似的画面，但你的视频里没有香港警方针对这些暴行使用武力执法的画面。

刘晓明： 你是指警方应对暴力而采取的执法措施吗？

BBC： 我说的不仅是警方，也包括一些不明身份的人员，比如"白衣人"，他们今年夏天袭击地铁站的行人。换句话说，双方都有暴力行为。我只是想知道，你是否承认双方都实施了暴力？在某种意义上说，示威者的暴力是"以暴力还击暴力"。我的第二个问题是，2008年，北京举办奥运会时，多数香港人认为自己是中国人，他们表现出了很高的自豪感，后来比例大幅下降，现在很少人承认自己是中国人，越来越多的人认为自己是香港人。你是否担心中国会失去700万港人的信任？

刘晓明： 首先，我们反对任何形式的暴力。其次，你应该弄清这些暴力背后的原因，如果不知道暴力的起因，就无法应对。香港的暴力起源于极端分子的行径，他们应该受到法律的严惩。毫无疑问，其他违法犯罪者也应被绳之以法。法治是一个城市的基础。关于香港居民身份认同，我不认为失去了一代人，这些暴力分子并不能代表香港年青一代。一些青年学生不明真相，我们有责任与他们

香港问题 / Hong Kong

交流，帮助他们了解祖国，了解香港回归后的发展进步。我们应该帮助他们把今天的香港和22年前的香港做比较。回归前的香港没有自由、没有民主、没有权利，港督都是英国政府任命的。但现在香港能够定期选举特首。我们的制度并不完美，就像我说过的，世界上最大的空间就是不断改进的空间。但我们是开放的，我们坚定不移地努力工作，为的就是使香港更美丽、更安全、更民主。如果没有新的提问，今天的记者会到此结束，感谢大家出席。

What Would Be the Way out for Hong Kong?
——The Third Press Conference on the Situation in Hong Kong

On 18th November 2019, I held a press conference at the Chinese Embassy expounding China's principles and position on the escalating violence in Hong Kong. About 50 journalists from 22 media agencies attended the press conference, including BBC, ITV, Sky News, Channel 4, *Financial Times*, *The Daily Telegraph*, *The Guardian*, Reuters, Xinhua News Agency, CCTV, China News Service, CGTN, *China Daily*, *Science and Technology Daily*, *Global Times*, AFP, RT, Phoenix Infonews, the *South China Morning Post*, *European Times*, *UK Chinese Times*, and the *UK Chinese Journal*. The following is the transcript of the press conference.

Liu Xiaoming: Good morning! Welcome to the Chinese Embassy.
This is the third press conference that I have held on the Hong Kong question. In the past five months, the incident arising from the relevant amendments has evolved into incessant violence. The recent escalation of illegal, violent activities has pushed Hong Kong into an extremely dangerous situation.
Those who truly care about Hong Kong would ask these questions:
• What is happening in Hong Kong?
• How shall we see the current chaos?
• What would be the way out?
Four days ago, during the 11th BRICS Summit in Brazil, President Xi Jinping made clear the solemn position of the Chinese Government on the situation in Hong Kong. He said,
"The incessant extreme violent offences in Hong Kong trampled on the rule of law, disrupted public order, severely undermined the prosperity and stability in Hong Kong, and gravely challenged the bottom line of 'One Country, Two Systems'."
He pointed out: "The top priority for Hong Kong is to end violence and restore order. We will continue to firmly support the SAR Government under the leadership of the Chief Executive in governing Hong Kong in accordance with the law. We firmly support the Hong Kong police in their strict and rigorous enforcement of the law. We

firmly support the judicial institutions of Hong Kong in bringing violent offenders to justice in accordance with the law."

He further emphasized: "The Chinese Government remains unwavering in its determination to safeguard China's national sovereignty, security and development interests, implement 'One Country, Two Systems', and oppose any interference from external forces in Hong Kong affairs."

This important statement represents the most authoritative voice from the Central Government of China on the current situation and future of Hong Kong. Every word carries weight.

First, President Xi Jinping's speech reveals the nature and severe consequences of the extreme violent offences.

The current situation in Hong Kong has nothing to do with the so-called "democracy" or "freedom". The nature of the issue is that extreme violent offenders have disrupted law and order in Hong Kong, have attempted to destabilize Hong Kong and undermine "One Country, Two Systems". Their activities are extreme, violent and illegal.

These extreme violent offences have trampled on the rule of law and disrupted public order in Hong Kong.

For the past five months, the self-labeled "peaceful protesters" have resorted to senseless beating, smashing and arson; they have carried out premeditated attacks against police officers and made a failed assassination attempt on a member of the Legislative Council; and they have turned many universities into their strongholds and besieged and attacked students from the Chinese Mainland.

While claiming they stand with the weak, the rioters have indiscriminately hurt ordinary citizens and even doused a citizen who opposed their vandalism with flammable liquid and set fire to him.

While claiming they safeguard democracy and freedom, the rioters have restricted or even deprived others of personal freedom and freedom of speech.

Such inhuman, murderous violence in broad daylight tramples on the bottom lines of law, morality and civilization and must not be tolerated!

The anti-China extremists have also taken such violence abroad and into the UK. Some of them, wearing black masks, created trouble in front of the Chinese Embassy in the UK. They defaced the Embassy gate and painted "Hong Kong independence" slogans on both sides of the gate. Some besieged the Secretary for Justice of the Hong Kong SAR, who was invited to an event in London. She was pushed to the ground and sustained arm injury.

We express the strongest indignation and condemnation over these violent acts!

The extreme violent offences have severely undermined prosperity and stability in Hong Kong.

Hong Kong is known for its free and open economy, inclusive and diverse culture, professional and efficient management, and law-abiding and safe society.

But today,

- Hong Kong citizens live under the "black terror" created by violent extremists, with their life and property being under severe threat.
- Hong Kong's GDP, after contracting for two quarters in a row, shrank by 2.9% year-on-year in the third quarter. It is now in a technical recession. The Office of the Government Economist of the Hong Kong SAR revised down its growth forecast for the full-year to minus 1.3%.
- Hong Kong's international rating has been downgraded. Its international image and business environment are being severely impacted.

In media reports, Hong Kong is now associated with incessant violence and disorder. The success and achievements of the past 22 years since the handover are being eroded. The one time "oriental pearl" is turning into an "oriental scar". Hong Kong the "fragrant harbour" is sliding into "an abyss of chaos". The future of Hong Kong, if such a situation continues, will be unimaginably dreadful.

The extreme violent offences have challenged the principled bottom line of "One Country, Two Systems".

The opposition and the violent extremists in Hong Kong have advocated "Hong Kong independence" and publicly clamoured for the "liberation of Hong Kong".

This reveals their true, sinister political agenda behind the so-called public petition. They are actually aiming to undermine "One Country", which is the basis of "One Country, Two Systems". They attempt to destabilize Hong Kong and paralyze the SAR Government, so that they could seize administrative power and separate Hong Kong from the motherland.

"One Country, Two Systems" is one complete concept. "One Country" is the precondition and basis of "Two Systems". Without "One Country", "Two Systems" will no longer exist. Violent offences that undermine "One Country, Two Systems" will never be tolerated.

Second, President Xi Jinping's speech points to a way out for ending the chaos in

Hong Kong, namely, the top priority for Hong Kong is to end the violence and restore order.

The basic requirement of the rule of law is that laws must be observed and offenders must be brought to justice. No society would in any way tolerate or indulge extreme violence.

To restore law and order, violence must end and violent perpetrators must be brought to justice. This is the only way to safeguard the interests of the public, ensure a better future for Hong Kong, and cement the foundation of "One Country, Two Systems".

The SAR Government, the police and the judicial institutions of Hong Kong should be given strong support in upholding the rule of law, and in taking forceful measures to curb and combat all types of violent offences and terrorist activities. We firmly support them in bringing the offenders to justice as soon as possible, and in safeguarding the rule of law and public order, so as to bring stability to Hong Kong and tranquillity to the people.

Third, President Xi Jinping's speech demonstrates the strong determination of the Chinese Government to safeguard national sovereignty, security and development interests and implement "One Country, Two Systems".

At the fourth plenary session of the 19th Central Committee of the Communist Party of China concluded last month, it was reiterated that "One Country, Two Systems" is an important policy of the Communist Party of China in leading the Chinese people to realise the peaceful reunification of the motherland.

The Chinese Government will continue to implement fully and faithfully "One Country, Two Systems", "the Hong Kong people administering Hong Kong", and a high degree of autonomy. For this formula to work in Hong Kong, there are three bottom lines, namely, no tolerance for any activity that,

One, undermines national sovereignty and security;

Two, challenges the authority of the Central Government or the Basic Law;

and, three, uses Hong Kong for infiltration or sabotage against the Chinese Mainland.

At the same time,

• The Chinese Government will improve the system of overall jurisdiction over Hong Kong in accordance with the Constitution and the Basic Law.

• We will also improve the arrangements for Hong Kong to integrate into the overall development of the country, match complementary strengths with the Mainland and achieve coordinated development.

有问必答
No Question Unanswered

•And we will work to address deep-seated problems hampering social stability and long-term development.

Fourth, President Xi Jinping's speech shows the firm resolve of the Chinese government to oppose external interference in Hong Kong affairs.

External forces that have indulged and fanned violence in Hong Kong cannot absolve themselves of the responsibility for the recent escalation of violence in Hong Kong. They confuse right and wrong, and refer to the extreme violent offenders as "peaceful demonstrators" and "pro-democracy protesters". At the same time, they are piling blame on the Hong Kong police who are performing their duty, safeguarding the rule of law and protecting the safety of life and property of Hong Kong citizens.

Some Western countries have publicly supported the extreme violent offenders.

•The US House of Representatives adopted the so-called "Hong Kong Human Rights and Democracy Act" to blatantly interfere in Hong Kong affairs, which are China's internal affairs.

•The British Government and the Foreign Affairs Committee of the House of Commons published China-related reports, making irresponsible remarks on Hong Kong.

•What is worse, certain British politicians even planned to present an award to a chief propagandist for "Hong Kong independence" who has instigated extreme violence.

•To those who question external interference in Hong Kong affairs, aren't these facts enough to address their doubt?

We would like to tell these external forces solemnly that the Chinese Government remains unwavering in its resolve to oppose any external interference in Hong Kong affairs! We urge these forces to immediately stop any form of interference in Hong Kong affairs and in China's internal affairs, and immediately stop condoning violent offences. Otherwise, they will lift the stone only to drop it on their own feet!

Just as we did at my last press conference, we have made a short video clip to help you see the extreme violent offences in Hong Kong. This will show you the true face of the so-called "peaceful demonstrators" and "pro-democracy protesters", and how dangerous the situation in Hong Kong has become.

[Play video clip]

After watching this clip, I hope you will agree with me that the facts and truth will prevail.

I have said to the British people from all walks of life on many occasions that a prosperous and stable Hong Kong under "One Country, Two Systems" is in the interests of both China and the world including the UK. There are 300, 000 British citizens and more than 700 British companies in Hong Kong. Continued chaos in Hong Kong will bring nothing but harm to the UK.

I sincerely hope that the British people will keep the larger picture in mind and have a clear understanding of the current situation. I hope they will support the SAR Government in ending violence, restoring order and upholding the rule of law, resist and oppose any words or deeds that interfere in Hong Kong affairs, and do more things that are conducive to the prosperity and stability in Hong Kong, so that chaos will end as soon as possible and the "oriental pearl" will shine brightly once again.

Now I would like to take your questions.

BBC: I wrote an email to you this week, actually, about the labour camps in Xinjiang. Why won't you tell me the truth about those camps?

Liu Xiaoming: You jump to Xinjiang. Please sit down. I'll answer your question. First of all, I would say there are no so-called labour camps, as you described. There are what we call the vocational education and training centres. They are there for the prevention of terrorism.

BBC: I have seen the orders sent to camps. They changed the way people behave, and the language they speak. So they are brainwashing camps.

Liu Xiaoming: That's disinformation. Xinjiang is a very beautiful, very peaceful and prosperous region in China. But it had become a battleground. You know, thousands of terrorist incidents happened in Xinjiang between 1990s and 2016. Thousands of innocent people were killed. So there's been an enormous uproar among the people of Xinjiang for the government to take resolute measures to tackle this issue. So since the measures have been taken, there's not been a single terrorist incident in the past three years. Xinjiang has again turned back into a prosperous, beautiful and peaceful region. If the same thing happened in the United Kingdom, would you - let me ask you this: if a certain region had rampant terrorist extremist activities, and people suffered severely and called for actions from the UK government, what would you do?

And remember what we're doing, what we here called "preventative measures", have nothing to do with the eradication of religious groups. You know, religious freedom is fully respected. I hope that in the future you'll have an opportunity to visit Xinjiang. You will see with your own eyes what is happening in Xinjiang, and see that the people enjoy freedom, enjoy a prosperous life. You know, in Xinjiang there are about 28, 000 religious sites and 30, 000 clergymen. There is one mosque for every 530 Muslims in Xinjiang, many more than a lot of Muslim countries in terms of ratio, many more than here in Britain. So there's no such thing as the repression of freedom of religion. People enjoy full religious freedom. The purpose of setting up these training centres is because some young people have committed minor crimes that are not serious enough to be tried or for them to be sent to prison. The government gave them the opportunity to learn Mandarin. Uygur people have their own language, but if they want development, if they want to prosper, if they want to communicate with the other parts of the country, they need to have Mandarin language skills and also they need to learn some professional skills. Because you know, the lack of basic legal knowledge makes them vulnerable to extremist forces.

Mandarin is widely used. Language is just one of the courses. They also learn professional skills; they also learn legal knowledge, so that they can live off their own profession. That's the purpose. This measure has been successful. First, Xinjiang as I said is much safer. Last year, the number of tourists increased by 40%, and GDP increased more than 6%.

BBC: The documents that I've seen make it quite clear that people are held there without sentence, without even charge, and they will be there for at least a year before they are released.

Liu Xiaoming: I'm telling you the documents, the so-called documents you are talking about, are pure fabrication. If you want to see documents about this vocational education and training centre, we have many. We have her seven white papers published. So before you leave the Embassy, I hope you will take some documents, the official documents. Don't listen to fake news. Don't listen to fabrications.

Channel 4: Thank you Sir. If it's for young people, why are there so many elderly women and elderly men in the camps in Xinjiang that has been documented? I have talked to people who were in the camps. And, on Hong Kong, you talked about integration into the Mainland's development. With all that's happening in Hong Kong, is it your aim to integrate Hong Kong more into Mainland China to make it more "One Country, One System"?

Liu Xiaoming: I already said those students who are taking courses in the centre are those who have committed some minor crimes, not serious ones, not to be tried. So that's what I'm saying. So we want to give them better opportunities. We hope that they will not commit a serious crime that will put them in prison. That's the purpose. And it turned out this has been very successful. I think most of them are young people, and also some elderly people. Age is not a big issue. The issue is about their behaviour. Do they constitute a potential threat and risk to the society?

On Hong Kong, I think I said earlier in very clear-cut terms that the Chinese government is committed to "One Country, Two Systems". This policy has been reaffirmed by the Party during the Fourth Plenary Session of the 19th Central Committee and reiterated by the President on so many occasions including when we celebrated the 70th anniversary of the founding of the People's Republic of China. When we say "integration", we mean that the Mainland will provide more opportunities to Hong Kong. You know, especially in terms of economic development. You know this Greater Bay Area project that includes Guangdong, Hong Kong and Macau. It offers enormous opportunities. The opportunities will bring more development in Hong Kong that will address some deep-seated problems. You know, we all heard voices in the recent incidents in Hong Kong to address this disparity of the income, to address the problem of opportunities for young people, to make Hong Kong more prosperous. That's the basic idea. We will certainly continue with "One Country, Two Systems", which has been very successful. But what is happening now is "One Country, Two Systems" is being eroded by these violent extremist offenders. As I said in my opening statement, "One Country, Two Systems" is a complete concept. You can't separate the two. And "One Country" means Hong Kong is now part of China. Hong Kong has returned to China, it is part of China. Period. So we can't agree to external interference in Hong Kong affairs. So "One Country" is the precondition. It is the basis for "Two Systems". If "One Country" is undermined, there will be no "Two Systems".

South China Morning Post: Mr. Ambassador, just now you mentioned you urge the international community to support the SAR government in ending violence. What we've seen so far is the SAR government has not been successful in ending violence, and to the contrary, violence is escalating. May I ask if the deployment of PLA troops would be part of the Chinese government's consideration?

Liu Xiaoming: I would say the SAR government including Chief Executive herself has tried very hard to communicate with the local community and reached out to other citizens in Hong Kong. I think according to my count, they have held more than 100 events, engaging, communicating with local people, and I think they have tried very hard. You need to give them an opportunity. You need to give them time. But in order to have a civilized dialogue, you need to have a conducive environment. The current violent situation in Hong Kong is not conducive, is not favourable for the SAR government to have a serious, productive communication with local people. You can't put the cart before the horse.

With regard to the deployment of PLA, they are there, in the Hong Kong Garrison. They are there to safeguard China's sovereignty, security and territorial integrity and they are responsible for the security of Hong Kong. As I said in my previous press conference, we have full trust in the Hong Kong SAR government and the Chief Executive. When President Xi met the Chief Executive two weeks ago, he spoke highly of the performance of the SAR government, the Chief Executive and her team. We make full acknowledgement of their performance and express a high degree of trust in her and her team. So I think now the Hong Kong government is trying very hard to bring the situation under control. But if the situation becomes uncontrollable, the Central Government certainly will not sit on its hands and watch. We have enough solutions and enough power to end the violence.

South China Morning Post: And I have a second question if I may. Just a few days ago, Mr. Jasper Tsang, who used to be the Chairman of the Legislative Council of Hong Kong and a former Chairman of the DAB, the biggest pro-China party in Hong Kong, gave an interview and he supported the idea of pardoning those who committed a minor crime and launching an independent inquiry into the police. He is one of the most respected pro-China figures in Hong Kong. What do you think of his opinion?

Liu Xiaoming: I will leave this to the Hong Kong SAR government to handle and respect the independence of the judicial institutions in Hong Kong. I will not comment on the judicial procedures in Hong Kong. Thank you!

Sky News: You have kind of repeated what you said in your previous press conference in terms of that question about whether there will be PLA involvement, But what does "uncontrollable" chaos look like? It seems that we've had five months now, and it's not getting any better. Isn't the policy of allowing the Hong Kong authorities to deal with this actually failing and either there's going to have to be some serious compromises made and demands met of the protesters, or the Chinese government's going to have to actually get involved and send troops on the ground? And a second question. About Xinjiang, do you have a comment on *The New York Times*' reports over the weekend? It's released hundreds of documents. Thank you.

Liu Xiaoming: First question first. I think the Hong Kong government is still effective in dealing with the situation. But the important thing is, while the Hong Kong government is handling the situation, I would call on external forces to stop interfering in Hong Kong affairs. Stop inciting further violence. Stop adding fuel to the violence. We should respect the Hong Kong SAR government in governing Hong Kong in accordance with the law. Your second question is about *The New York Times*' so-called "report". I can categorically deny that there are such documents. Such a story is sheer, pure fabrication. And this is not the first time *The New York Times* has made up stories. I think the story was made up with ulterior motives, and it's not worth making any substantial comment on it. Thank you.

The Daily Telegraph: You've spoken about external forces fueling violence. You spoke about the true agenda being independence for Hong Kong among the protesters and then you talked about the British government, specifically the Foreign Affairs Select Committee. You keep talking about external forces inciting violence. Are you accusing the British government of inciting violence and promoting Hong Kong independence?

Liu Xiaoming: I will say that we have made our position known to the British side when they made irresponsible remarks on Hong Kong. I think that when the British government criticizes the Hong Kong police and criticizes the Hong Kong SAR government over their handling of the situation, they are interfering In China's internal affairs. And it looks like they are balanced, but as a matter of fact, they are taking sides. With regard to "independence", we appreciate the British government's position that they oppose Hong Kong independence. I think the senior officials said on several occasions that independence is not an option. Of course, I would like to see more strong condemnation of this so-called independence. That's number one. Number two, I hope the British side will live up to their words. So I said we do not want to see them merely pay lip service. I want to see them take actions against so-called Hong Kong "independence".

ITV News: We've just seen a sharp deterioration in the last 24 hours regarding the situation in Hong Kong. Are your words now some kind of warning that a crackdown may be imminent?

Liu Xiaoming: I'm not talking about crackdown. I think the Hong Kong police is carrying out their duties. Many people have complained about the Hong Kong police. But in my view, they are the most professional police force in the world. And they exercised great restraint. If similar things happened on a British campus, if similar things happened in the Palace of Westminster or its surrounding areas, what would you expect the British police to do? I'll leave you to answer that. But it is exactly because the Hong Kong police tried very hard to avoid casualties of the students who have been, I would say, "brainwashed" by some extremists that they have tried very hard. If it were not for this, we would probably have a different picture, a different situation.

The Guardian: Could I just ask you, given what's going on in Hong Kong at present, do you think it's feasible that the local elections can go ahead next week? And secondly, can you tell me why the Chinese government opposes the idea of British National Overseas passport holders being given a right of abode and a right to work permanently in the UK?

Liu Xiaoming: I will start with the last question. According to China's nationality law, all Hong Kong compatriots, born in Hong Kong, are regarded as Chinese nationals. And also in China, we do not recognize dual citizenship. So I think that's my answer to your last question. What is your first one? The election. We certainly would like to see the election go ahead. I think it's up to the Hong Kong SAR government. I do hope that the situation will improve and people will be able to go to the polls, without fear. I do hope that the order will be restored and people can have the freedom to select their council members. So that is certainly our hope.

BBC: Two questions, Mr. Ambassador. First of all, you showed us a very emotive edit of violence on the streets of Hong Kong, violent scenes that we've all seen on our TVs, on social media for months. What you didn't show us was any violence being committed against the protesters, violence which has been going on for months and started a long time before.

Liu Xiaoming: You are talking about the police?

BBC: I'm not actually just talking about the police. I'm talking about police, but I'm also talking about unknown groups of people, the famous "white shirts" who attacked people on the Hong Kong Metro back in the summer. In other words, the violence is occurring on both sides. And I just wondered whether you would acknowledge that there has been violence used on both sides, and that what we're seeing in some ways is a response to that process. And my second question is, back in 2008, slightly more people in Hong Kong saw themselves as "Chinese" than "Hongkonger". It was at the time of the Beijing Olympics. People expressed enormous pride. That number has gone down ever since to the point now where very, very few people describe themselves as "Chinese" and more and more people describe themselves as "Hongkonger". Are you worried that you are losing the faith, the trust, the citizenship if you like, of 7 million Hongkongers?

Liu Xiaoming: First, I would say we are opposed to violence of all kinds. That's number one. Number two, you have to understand the cause of this violence. So if you do not understand the cause, you do not know how to handle it, so you do not know how to address this problem. I think these extreme forces, they are the starters of all violence. They should be brought to justice. And all the law breakers should be brought to justice. There can be no doubt that if you want to have rule of law in a city, in a society. With regard to the Hongkongers versus Mainlanders, I think people would reflect. I can't say we are going to lose a generation. You know these rioters do not represent the young generation, even the students. As I said, some of them do not understand the full picture. I think we have a responsibility to communicate with them to tell them about their motherland and what has changed since the handover. We should compare Hong Kong today with Hong Kong 22 years ago. When Hong Kong was under British colonial rule, it had no liberty, no freedom, and no rights. The governor of Hong Kong was appointed by the British government. But now Hong Kong has their fifth Chief Executive elected by the Hong Kong people. Even though the system is not perfect, as I said on many occasions, the largest room in the world is the room for improvement. We are open. We are committed to doing a better job to make Hong Kong a more beautiful, safe, and democratic place. Thank you.

It seems to me that time's up, and I have taken all the questions. Thank you for your attention.

"法者，治之端也"
—— 关于香港维护国家安全法中外记者会

（2020年7月6日，中国驻英国大使馆）

刘晓明： 大家上午好！欢迎大家出席今天的中外记者会。

6月30日，在香港回归23周年之际，中国全国人大常委会通过《中华人民共和国香港特别行政区维护国家安全法》，并将该法列入香港基本法附件三，由香港特别行政区在当地公布实施。香港国安法的实施，为"一国两制"行稳致远提供了强大支撑，为香港居民的权利和自由提供了坚实保障，堪称"一国两制"实践进程中的重要里程碑，具有重大现实意义和深远历史意义。

香港国安法通过后，英国媒体做了大量报道和评论。但坦率地讲，其中充斥着误读、误解甚至歪曲。

今天，我举行中外记者会，就是希望帮助英国各界全面、客观、准确地认识和理解香港国安法。针对英国媒体的报道和评论，我想着重回答5个问题：

第一，为什么要出台香港国安法？维护国家安全是香港繁荣稳定的基础和前提。基本法第23条，授权香港特区就维护国家安全自行立法。但23年来，由于反中乱港势力勾连阻挠，相关立法迟迟未能完成，导致香港在维护国家安全方面法律制度空白，执行机制缺失，长期处于"不设防"状态。去年6月香港"修例风波"发生以来，反中乱港势力公然鼓吹"港独""自决"，打砸抢烧，暴力袭警，冲击香港立法会，叫嚣"武装建国"，严重践踏香港法治，严重破坏社会稳定，重创香港经济，严重危害国家安全。香港民众痛心疾首，迫切希望香港转危为安、变乱为治、绝境重生。在此形势下，国安法从国家层面立法建立健全香港维护国家安全的法律制度和执行机制，得人心、顺民意，势在必行、刻不容缓。

第二，香港国安法是否违反"一国两制"？该法不仅完全符合"一国两制"方针，并将保障"一国两制"行稳致远。香港国安法开宗明义指出，坚定不移并全面准确贯彻"一国两制"、"港人治港"、高度自治方针。"一国两制"是一个完整概念，"一国"是"两制"的前提，"两制"从属和派生于"一国"。只有"一国"安全，"两制"才有保障。何为"一国"，它既体现在中国对香港恢复行使主权，也体现在中央政府对香港拥有全面管治权。维护国家安全历来是各国中央事权。中国中央政府通过《基本法》第23条授权香港特区维护国家安全的部分立法权，并不改变国家安全立法是中央事权的属性，也不影响中央政府继续建构维护国家安全的法律制度和执行机制。香港出现了挑战和破坏"一国两制"的活动，香港国安法正是为了捍卫"一国"权威，最终是为了坚持和完善"一国两制"，而不是要改变"一国两制"。

第三，香港国安法是否破坏香港高度自治和香港居民权利自由？该法充分体现了中央全面管治权和香港特区高度自治权的统一，不改变香港实行的资本主义制度，不改变香港高度自治和特区法律制度，不影响特区行政管理权、立法权、独立的司法权和终审权。该法明确规定，香港特区维护国家安全应当尊重和保障人权,依法保护香港特区居民根据《基本法》和《公民权利和政治权利国际公约》《经济、社会及文化权利国际公约》适用于香港的有关规定享有的言论、新闻、出版、结社、集会、游行、示威等权利和自由。该法规管的是分裂国家、颠覆国家政权、组织实施恐怖活动、勾结外国或者境外势力危害国家安全四类罪行,惩治的是极少数犯罪分子,保护的是绝大多数民众。正因为如此,短短8天,近300万香港民众签名支持国安法,充分体现出求稳定、保安全的主流民意。

第四,香港国安法是否违反中方国际义务?今年是联合国成立75周年,中国是第一个签署《联合国宪章》的国家,参加了100多个政府间国际组织,签署了500多个多边条约。中国始终致力于维护国际法和国际关系基本准则,认真履行自身承担的国际责任和义务。中国从未"退群""毁约",从不谋求本国利益优先。"不履行国际义务"的帽子扣不到中国头上。英方将《中英联合声明》与"一国两制"混为一谈,指责中方未履行国际义务,这完全是错误的。"一国两制"的版权属于邓小平先生,中国政府治理香港的法律依据是中国宪法和香港《基本法》,绝非《中英联合声明》。中国政府关于"一国两制"的方针政策,已充分体现在《基本法》中,并得到全面贯彻。因此,根本不存在所谓香港国安法违反中方国际义务问题。

第五,究竟谁在违反国际义务、践踏国际关系准则?主权平等、不干涉内政是国际法和国际关系的基本准则。中国从不干涉别国内政,包括英国内政,也希望英方不要干涉中国内政。英方应当十分清楚,香港已经不是英国殖民统治下的香港,香港早已回归中国，是中国的一部分。英国对回归后的香港无主权、无治权、无监督权。然而，英国政府仍不停地发表所谓《香港问题半年报告》，对香港事务说三道四，现在又对香港国安法指手画脚，甚至声称将改变对香港"英国国民（海外）护照"（BNO）持有者的安排。这是对中国内政的粗暴干涉，是对国际关系基本准则的公然践踏，中方对此表示强烈不满和坚决反对，并已就此向英方提出严正交涉。我想强调指出的是，香港是中国的香港，香港事务是中国内政，任何外国无权干涉。香港国安法的一项重要任务就是防范、制止和惩治勾结外国或境外势力危害香港国家安全的行为。任何人都不要低估中国捍卫国家主权、安全发展利益的坚定决心，任何干扰和阻挠香港国安法实施的企图都必将遭到14亿中国人民的坚决反对，都注定失败！

"法者，治之端也。"香港国安法是香港恢复秩序、由乱到治的治本之策。我们坚信，在中国中央政府的坚强领导下，在包括广大香港同胞在内的全体中国人民的共同努力下，在香港国安法的有力保障下，香港一定会更加安全、更加美好、更加繁荣！

谢谢！下面，我愿回答各位的提问。

中国国际电视台： 英方称，将为持有英国国民（海外）护照（BNO）的香港居民提供更多居留权限，中方表示将保留采取相应措施的权利。你能否谈一谈中国是否将就此采取具体措施以及何时宣布？英国首相约翰逊表示，自己是喜爱中国的，但香港国安法明显严重违反《中英联合声明》。你认为如何避免英中关系进一步恶化？

刘晓明： 我在开场白里已经回答了你的问题。关于BNO以及中方要采取的具体举措，你应该先问英国政府下一步要干什么。我刚才讲过，中英之间以及任何国家之间的关系必须建立在国际法和国际关系基本准则之上。国际法的基本原则是主权平等，互不干涉内政。这一原则已被写入《联合国宪章》，并在40多年前被纳入中英建立大使级外交关系的联合公报，是中英关系的基本准则。

70年前，英国政府宣布承认中华人民共和国。70年来，中英关系虽有起伏，但总体保持发展。实践证明，只要上述基本准则得到遵守，中英关系就向前发展，甚至是跨越式发展；反之，两国关系就遭遇挫折，甚至出现倒退。

BBC： 香港国安法第38条规定，该法还适用于非香港居民和身处香港以外的人。根据国际法的通行做法，域外法权一般只适用于最严重的犯罪，国安法该条规定将如何与国际法保持一致？在香港的记者、活动分子以及其他相关人士将如何在继续坚持言论和新闻自由的同时，确保自己免于被起诉？

刘晓明： 你提到的第38条是国际通行做法。即便根据英国法律，犯了罪和侵犯了英国国家利益的人都应被追究责任。如果他们的行为威胁英国国家安全，无论行为是发生在英国国内，还是国外，都应被追责。香港国家安全法在香港维护国家安全，没有超出国际通行做法。

你提到记者的工作。香港国安法规定得很明确，列出了危害国家安全的四种犯罪行为。记者们只要遵守法律，就没什么可担心的，就可以正常开展工作。国安法还规定，香港居民和在香港生活工作的所有人的人权都将得到充分尊重和保障，这些权利包括新闻自由和言论自由。因此，只要你守法，就无须担心。

天空新闻台： 英国政府正在研究是否在5G网络系统中使用华为，有传言称他们会推翻此前的决定，禁止在英国的5G网络中使用华为。这将对英中关系产生怎样的影响？你提到中国不干涉英国的内政，但有人不这么认为，他们认为中国正采取颠覆性措施，试图影响英国政商学界，以扩大中国的影响、推进中国的利益。对此你如何回应？

刘晓明： 我反对任何关于中国干涉英国内政的说法。我出使英国已超过10年，从未遇到过英国政府或机构指责中国政府干涉英国内政的情况。如果你有证据，请拿出来。但请不要制造有关中国的假消息并进行无端指责。

正如我在开场白中所说，中国一贯、全面遵守国际法和国际关系基本准则。我已就华为问题多次表态、撰文和发表演讲。一言以蔽之，华为是中英合作双赢的范例。我认为，英国使用华为，不是为了中国，而是基于英国自身的利益。英国政府已经制订雄心勃勃的计划，要在2025年实现5G全覆盖。华为可以为此做出贡献。但如果英国愿意高价购买质量不如华为的产品，这是英国自己的决定。我们要争取最好的结果，同时也要做最坏的准备。

华为在170个国家开展业务，没有一个国家能证明华为安装了后门。华为很透明，他们建立了完全由外国人、而非华为人员运营的安全评估中心，这证明他们很有信心。除了华为，世界上还有哪家公司建立了由东道国运营、专门检测公司自己产品的中心？没有。华为没什么好怕的，用不用华为是你们自己的决定。英语有句成语："当一扇门关上时，另一扇门会打开。"我们中国也有一句俗语："西方不亮东方亮。"近来，我听到不少有关华为的噪声，但我们不怕。我对在英中资企业说，你们应该保持信心。一旦你有拳头产品，你就不应该担心没有市场。世界足够大，足以让华为发展。我相信，华为能带来双赢，不仅有利于华为，也有利于英国。我们已尽己所能讲述华为的故事，但最终决定要由英国政府来做。我们不能替英国政府做决定。确实有很多猜测，我们已为可能的结果做好准备。我相信，华为不仅能生存下来，而且会日益发展壮大。越是面临来自所谓超级大国及其盟友的压力，华为就越变得强大。我对此坚信不疑。

彭博社： 还是关于华为的问题，英国政府即将做出的决定，很明显出于安全关切，而非你所说的商业考虑。众所周知，美国对华为也存在严重安全关切，而你说中方不认为存在安全问题，也不担心英方会在政治层面做出相关决定。

刘晓明： 最终决定要由英方来做。关于安全问题，我认为华为已经尽其所能，回应各方关切。谈到安全问题，要看是出于政治角度还是技术角度。安全有很多种，例如在通信方面，我们的技术是否足够安全可靠，能够保护我们免受来自某些国家或黑客或公司的攻击。不要片面谈安全问题。华为为解决安全问题和关切采取了所有必要措施，不断改进他们的技术。英国情报机构的分析报告也显示，华为的安全风险是可控的，华为的技术总体上是安全的，这也是为什么英国政府虽然设定了35%的市场份额上限，仍然决定允许华为参与5G。现在是否要决定放弃华为，这取决于英方自己。正如我所说，世界很大，足够让华为发展。目前华为已在170个国家运营，一个国家放弃华为，还有169个国家。我一直鼓励华为人，要向前看。首先你要努力向英国政府、商界和人民证明，你拥有最先进的技术和最具竞争力的价格，坚持不断改进，解决大家的关切，做行业的领军者。但如果他们不选择你，那是他们的决定，你们还要继续发展。华为历经种种阻碍仍不断进步，我对他们充满信心。

你提到安全问题，我也正想谈谈这一点。一些英国政客一提到华为，就炒作中英关系。他们中的一些人将中国视为威胁，甚至是敌对国家，这是完全错误的，这与两国领导人达成的共识不符。很多人谈及中英关系"黄金时代"，但他们对到底什么是"黄金时代"毫无概念。事实上，"黄金时代"是英国领导人首先提出的，我们认为这符合两国的共同利益，就同意将其作为中英关系的定位。如果英方放弃"黄金时代"、将中国视为敌人，这就大错特错了，也不符合英方自身利益。美国战略家布热津斯基曾说，如果你把中国当作敌人，那么中国就可能真的成为敌人。中国希望成为英国的朋友、伙伴，但如果你们把中国当作敌人，就要承担由此产生的后果。

《泰晤士报》： 中方会采取措施阻止拥有英国国民（海外）护照（BNO）的香

港人接受英方的安排来英居留吗？

刘晓明： 最近我们听到很多关于英方改变BNO立场的说法。1984年，中英双方通过交换备忘录达成一致，英方明确承诺不会给予持有BNO护照的香港中国公民在英居留权。但英方执意单方面改变这一立场，中方视之为违反国际法和国际关系准则，将保留做出进一步反应的权利。首先，中方坚决谴责英方此举，因为它违背了英方自身承诺；其次，中方认为这是对中国内政的干涉，是针对香港维护国家安全法的政治操弄；最后，中方将视英方具体实际行动，决定将采取何种反制措施。

《经济学家》： 能否请你介绍一下英方在香港问题上的相关立场将带来什么样的后果？例如，在华经营的英国企业和英中贸易是否会面临这些后果？将涉及哪些行业？英国银行和服务消费行业的英国公司在华经营是否会面临风险？

刘晓明： 正如我在开场白中所说，国家间的关系应建立在一些基本原则之上，包括相互尊重主权和领土完整、互不干涉内政、尊重彼此核心利益和重大关切等。上述原则也得到中英两国领导人的认可。疫情期间，习近平主席和约翰逊首相两次通电话，重申了有关基本原则。但是，一旦这些原则被违背，必将带来相应后果，双方的互信将受损，信心将遭到削弱。至于具体在哪些领域带来哪些后果，我们还要看。中方切实希望英方从维护中英双方根本利益出发，停止错误做法。我们要好好把握中英关系根本利益的大局。

有问必答
No Question Unanswered

新华社： 最近一项调查发现，英国超越美国，成为中国学生"首选留学目的地"。若中英关系因政治分歧而进一步恶化，中国对学生来英留学的态度和政策会改变吗？

刘晓明： 包括留学生交流合作在内的中英正常关系将会继续发展。我看到了有关报道，由于美国的一些原因，转到英国学习的中国学生正在增多。我们欢迎并鼓励更多中国学生到英国留学。驻英国使馆教育处一直非常忙碌，向中国学生提供信息，回答他们的各类咨询，帮助他们与英国的大学建立联系。目前，我还未看到对中英教育合作的负面影响。目前，中国有20多万留学生在英学习。疫情期间，我给英国154所有中国留学生的大学校长写信，除了要求他们照顾好中国留学生，我也重申中方致力于发展同英国各大学的合作关系。

路透社： 当前，英国一些人正重新审视对华为政策。英国政府表示将提出关于外国收购和兼并法案，外界认为这是针对中国公司的。你之前提到英中关系"黄金时代"。在中方看来，英中关系"黄金时代"是否已经终结？如果没有终结，英方怎么做才能推动"黄金时代"向前发展？

刘晓明： 中英关系"黄金时代"最早是由英方提出，随后中英双方均予以认可。我希望"黄金时代"没有终结。但是，是否终结并非取决于中方。在中英合作抗击新冠肺炎疫情期间，英国领导人表示致力于推动两国关系"黄金时代"。我常说，"一个巴掌拍不响"，国家间的关系需要双方去呵护。因此，我衷心希望中英关系能够健康稳定发展，造福两国人民。这需要中英双方共同努力。中方视英国为伙伴，我们希望与英国发展良好关系。我们从来不会用"潜在的敌对国家"这样的说法来形容英国，不论是中国领导人，还是政府官员从来未用过这种说法。因此，我真诚提醒英国领导人和政府官员，希望他们谈到中英关系的性质时，务必谨言慎行。

《卫报》： 大使先生，你说香港国安法得到香港社会广泛欢迎，近300万香港民众签名支持国安法。但在去年的香港区议会选举中，我们看到"泛民"成绩不俗。你能否保证，今年秋天香港立法会选举也能如往年一样保护参选和竞选的自由？

刘晓明： 对于去年以来香港发生的事情，我们有不同解读。你们认为那是支持民主。我们认为那是暴乱、违法行为，甚至是恐怖主义行径。如果有人冲击英国议会，相信你不会称之为支持民主。过去几周，英国街头举行了大量游行示威活动，但我没见哪家英国媒体说这是支持民主，你们把一些游行示威人员称作违法分子和暴乱分子。那么，为什么提到香港时，你们的评判标准就变了呢？这是赤裸裸的双重标准！今年9月香港立法会选举将依法举行。关于香港国安法，我想强调，该法会依法实施。香港国安法充分体现了中央全面管治权和香港特区高度自治权的统一，不改变香港实行的资本主义制度，不改变香港高度自治和特区司法制度，不影响特区行政管理权、立法权、独立的司法权和终审权。香港居民的权利自由将得到良好保障。只要不触犯香港国安法，一切都不会改变。你应该对香港抱有信心。

《每日电讯报》：刘大使早上好！如果英国继续推行其给予香港英国国民（海外）护照（BNO）持有者来英计划，中方将采取哪些报复举措？你能告知英方具体安排吗？另一个问题，英国通信管理局（OFCOM）今天或将严厉批评中国国际电视台此前播放英国人韩飞龙（Peter Humphrey）被迫认罪的有关视频，你对此有何评论？

刘晓明：我已回答过关于英国国民（海外）护照（BNO）的问题。我的回答还是一样，中方已向英方表明立场，我们希望英方重新考虑其立场。至于中方将如何应对，我们将视英方采取的措施而定。

关于中国国际电视台的问题，中国国际电视台已批驳了韩飞龙的指控，韩的指控毫无事实根据。我认为中国国际电视台已经非常清楚地表明了立场。

美国全国广播公司：非常感谢大使先生。你刚才讲，新的香港国安法与已执行几十年的"一国两制"政策不冲突。但"一国两制"在很大程度上保障了香港的政治和言论自由。今天早上有报道称，香港公共图书馆下架了部分香港活动人士撰写的书籍，一些活动人士被拘留，你们称其为暴徒和恐怖分子。我的问题是，香港国安法的颁布是否意味着香港几十年来享有的言论自由的终结？

刘晓明：完全不是。香港民众的言论和新闻自由将得到充分保障。你提到一些书在香港公共图书馆下架，这完全取决于书的内容。如果一本书的目的是煽动分裂和颠覆，按照香港国安法就可能被视为犯罪，建议你仔细阅读香港国安法。英国有很多涉及国家安全的法律，如果有人发表支持恐怖主义和仇恨的言论，将被视为犯罪行为。为什么英国可以有这样的法律，而中国却不能有自己的国家安全法来惩罚煽动分裂国家、颠覆国家政权、危害国家安全的人？为保护国家安全而制定法律是各国的普遍做法。至于香港言论自由和新闻自由，我认为，香港国安法将保障绝大多数香港人的新闻、游行、示威等权利和自由。但任何人都不能做破坏国家安全的事情，不能从事香港国安法规管的四类犯罪行为。权利和自由都是有边界的。尽管《公民权利和政治权利国际公约》保护言论自由等权利，但这些权利也是受限制的。公约明确规定，行使这些权利不能破坏国家安全和公共秩序。我建议你仔细阅读有关公民权利的国际公约。因此，只要香港民众遵守国安法、不触碰国安法底线，他们将享受充分的自由，完全不用担心权利和自由问题。英美部分媒体危言耸听，妖魔化香港国安法的行径是完全错误的。他们并未仔细阅读香港国安法。该法详细规定了四种犯罪行为，只要不触碰法律底线，在宪法、基本法和有关国际公约所规定的范围内行使权利，就不会有任何问题。

《金融时报》：很多在中国内地和香港经营的英国企业对香港国安法表示担心，如果企业拒绝香港警察查看或使用其数据和系统将会有什么后果？

刘晓明： 香港警方将依法执行香港国安法。香港国安法写得很明确，包括香港警察、国安相关工作人员在内的执法人员，都要遵守香港法律，执法部门将依法行事。

今日俄罗斯电视台： 约翰逊政府正打算给几百万香港人居英权，帮助他们逃离中国法律管辖。为什么英国认为香港是前殖民地，可以给予居英权，却不肯给其他前殖民地人民同样的权利呢？例如伊拉克遭受了非法战争，成千上万人逃离了伊拉克。

刘晓明： 首先，一些英国政客抱守很强的殖民心态。他们不愿意相信香港已经不是英国殖民统治下的香港，无视香港已经在23年前就回归中国的事实。正因为如此，他们总是"好事"，仍把香港看成是英国的一部分，对香港事务指手画脚、大肆干涉。但他们彻底错了，香港早已是中国的一部分。其次，他们没有意识到香港的稳定和繁荣不仅符合中国的利益，也符合英国的利益。英国有30多万公民在港生活，有700多家企业在港经营。香港有近300万人署名支持香港国安法，其中就包括汇丰、太古、怡和、渣打等英国企业。但他们却遭到了一些英国政客的批评。这些政客又错了，因为没有和平的环境，英国公民和企业根本无法正常生活和经营。去年的"修例风波"已经说明了这一点，在"黑色恐怖"笼罩下，人们甚至都不敢上街，因此民众呼吁尽快止暴制乱。在这一背景下，香港国安法的诞生将帮助香港恢复稳定和繁荣。

英国电视四台： 谢谢刘大使。我能否回到关于华为的问题？如果英国把华为排除在其5G建设之外，会面临什么样的后果？你认为这是敌对行为吗？

刘晓明：可能面临多种后果。第一，这会损害英国标榜的开放、宜商、自由、透明的形象。中国的工商界人士认为，英国的营商环境良好，适合在这里做生意。这也是为什么过去5年中国对英投资超过此前30年投资总和的原因。但是一旦英国将华为剔除，就会发出非常错误的信号。这会损害英国坚持自由贸易的形象。第二，这会损害英国独立自主的国家形象。这意味着英国屈从外国压力，不能坚持独立自主的外交政策。我经常说，只有拥有独立自主的外交政策，"不列颠"才能成为"大不列颠"。如果没有独立自主的外交政策，随他国起舞，大不列颠之"大"又该如何体现呢？第三，我认为这也会向在英中国企业发出非常负面的信号。他们都在看英国如何对待华为。禁止华为将不仅向其他中国企业，也将向其他外国企业释放负面信号。第四，这关系到基本的信任问题。国与国关系必须建立在相互尊重、相互信任的基础上。中国有句俗话叫"朝令夕改"。如果你变来变去，别人怎么信任你？因此，这关系到信任问题。我希望英国政府做出不仅有利于中英合作，而且符合其自身利益的决定。

《中国日报》：谢谢大使。有人认为，香港国安法也将有助于保护英国投资及其在香港的合法权益。大使先生，你对此有何看法？

刘晓明：确实是这样。我想我在此前的讲话和问答中已经回答了你的问题。做生意需要稳定与和平的环境。这就是为什么香港国安法会受到欢迎，它不仅受到非常关注自身安全的普通民众的欢迎，也受到包括英国企业和许多其他国家企业在内的工商界的欢迎。近期美国商会有一份报告称，美国商会对香港有信心。这是因为香港国安法可以为各国工商界保障良好的营商环境。因此，我希望包括英国媒体在内的英国公众能够客观、正确和准确地看待香港国安法，不要试图妖魔化这部法律。国安法将为香港的安全与繁荣提供保障和保护。正如我在开场白中所说，在香港国安法的有力保障下，香港将成为一个更加安全、更加美好、更加繁荣的地方。谢谢大家出席今天的中外记者会。

Law is Beginning of Order
—— An On-line Press Conference on the Law on Safeguarding National Security in the HKSAR

On 6th July 2020, I held an on-line press conference at the Chinese Embassy on the Law on Safeguarding National Security in the HKSAR.
Some 50 journalists from 33 media agencies attended, including BBC, BBC Radio 4, Sky News, Channel 4, ITV, *Financial Times*, *The Daily Telegraph*, *The Times*, *The Guardian*, *The Economist*, Reuters, Xinhua News Agency, *People's Daily*, CCTV, CGTN, CRI, China News Service, *China Daily*, AP, Bloomberg, NBC, CBS, AFP, RT, CBC, Phoenix Infonews, the *South China Morning Post*, *European Times*, *UK Chinese Times* and *UK Chinese Journal*. BBC, Sky News, and CGTN broadcast the press conference live.
The following is the transcript of the press conference.

Liu Xiaoming: Good morning! Welcome to today's press conference.
On June 30th, one day before the 23rd anniversary of Hong Kong's return to China, the Standing Committee of the National People's Congress adopted the Law of the People's Republic of China on Safeguarding National Security in the Hong Kong SAR. This law is now added to the list of laws in Annex III of the Basic Law. It will be applied by promulgation in Hong Kong SAR.
This law is an important milestone in the implementation of "One Country, Two Systems", because it provides powerful support for the steady and sustained implementation of "One Country, Two Systems" and it is a strong safeguard for the rights and freedoms of Hong Kong residents. It is of both practical and historic significance.
After the law was adopted, the British media carried massive reports and comments, which, to be frank, were full of misinterpretation, misunderstanding and even distortion.
Today, I want to use this press conference to help the British public understand this law comprehensively, objectively and accurately. I would like to begin by answering the five questions frequently asked by the British media.

Question one: Why is the National Security Law for the Hong Kong SAR necessary?
National security is the basis and precondition for prosperity and stability in Hong Kong. Article 23 of the Basic Law authorizes the Hong Kong SAR to enact laws on safeguarding national security. However, 23 years after Hong Kong's return, nothing has been done and there is no legal framework or enforcement mechanism in terms of national security in the Hong Kong SAR. As a result, the city is left "defenceless" against the anti-China forces seeking chaos and disruption.

Since the turbulence over the proposed amendment bill in June last year, these forces have openly clamoured for "Hong Kong independence" and "self-determination". They have taken actions such as beating, smashing, looting, arson, confronting police enforcement with violence, and storming the Legislative Council of the Hong Kong SAR. They have even called for "waging armed revolution to gain independence". Such activities trampled on rule of law, undermined social stability, hit the economy hard and put national security at serious risk.

The situation has been distressing for the people of Hong Kong. They cried out for the chaos to end quickly, for order to be restored and for Hong Kong to walk out of this desperation. In light of such a situation, establishing at the national level a sound legal framework and enforcement mechanism for safeguarding national security in the Hong Kong SAR meets people's aspiration. The National Security Law must be enforced without delay.

Question two: Does the National Security Law for Hong Kong SAR contravene "One Country, Two Systems"?
The answer is a definite "No". This law is not only in line with "One Country, Two Systems". It also ensures the sustained implementation of this policy.

The National Security Law for the Hong Kong SAR declares at the outset that:
It is enacted for the purpose of "ensuring the resolute, full and faithful implementation of the policy of "One Country, Two Systems" under which the people of Hong Kong administer Hong Kong with a high degree of autonomy".

"One Country, Two Systems" is a complete concept. "One Country" is the precondition for "Two Systems". "Two Systems" is subordinate to and derived from "One Country". Only when "One Country" is safe and secure can "Two Systems" be safeguarded. What is the meaning of "One Country"? "One Country" not only embodies China's resumption of the exercise of sovereignty over Hong Kong. It also means that the Central Government has comprehensive jurisdiction over Hong Kong. As is true in all countries, the Central Government is responsible for upholding national security. Through Article 23 of the Basic Law, the Central Government of China authorizes the Hong Kong SAR to enact laws on safeguarding national security. This authorization, however, does not change the fact that by it nature legislative power belongs ultimately to the Central Government. Nor does it prevent the Central Government from establishing a legal framework and enforcement mechanism for safeguarding national security in Hong Kong SAR.

In response to the activities that challenge and harm "One Country, Two Systems", the National Security Law for the Hong Kong SAR was enacted to safeguard the authority of "One Country" for the purpose of upholding and improving, rather than changing, "One Country, Two Systems".

Question three: Will the National Security Law for the Hong Kong SAR impair the high degree of autonomy in the SAR or the rights and freedom of the Hong Kong people? The answer is again a definite "No".

The National Security Law fully integrates the comprehensive jurisdiction of the Central Government and the high degree of autonomy enjoyed by Hong Kong SAR:

- It does not alter the current capitalist system in Hong Kong.
- It does not change the high degree of autonomy or the legal system in the SAR.
- And it does not affect Hong Kong's administrative, legislative or independent judicial power, including that of final adjudication.

This Law clearly stipulates:

"Human rights shall be respected and protected in safeguarding national security in the Hong Kong Special Administrative Region. The rights and freedoms, including the freedoms of speech, of the press, of publication, of association, of assembly, of procession and of demonstration, which the residents of the Region enjoy under the Basic Law of the Hong Kong Special Administrative Region and the provisions of the International Covenant on Civil and Political Rights and the International Covenant on Economic, Social and Cultural Rights as applied to Hong Kong, shall be protected in accordance with the law."

This Law outlined four types of criminal activities that jeopardize national security. They are: secession, subversion, terrorist activities and collusion with a foreign country or with external elements to endanger national security. The Law targets a very few criminals but protects the great majority of the Hong Kong people.

That is why, in only eight days, nearly three million Hong Kong people signed the petition in support of the Law. This bears full witness to the overwhelming aspiration of the Hong Kong people for stability and security.

Question four: Has China failed to fulfill its international obligations by enacting the National Security Law for the Hong Kong SAR?

My answer again is a definite "No".

This year marks the 75th anniversary of the founding of the United Nations. China was the first country to put its signature on the UN Charter. China is now a member of more than 100 inter-governmental international organisations and signed over 500 multilateral treaties.

- China has been committed to upholding international law and the basic norms governing international relations.
- It has faithfully fulfilled its international responsibilities and obligations.
- It has never withdrawn from international organisations or treaties. Nor does it believe in "us first" at the expense of others. This label is more suited to some other countries.

It is completely wrong to confuse the Sino-British Joint Declaration with "One Country, Two Systems" and accuse China of failing to honour its international obligations.

The "copyright" for "One Country, Two Systems" belongs to Deng Xiaoping. The Chinese Government governs the Hong Kong SAR in accordance with the Constitution of China and the Basic Law, not the Joint Declaration.

The policies for "One Country, Two Systems" of the Chinese Government are fully embodied in the Basic law and faithfully implemented. There is no question of China having failed to fulfill its international obligation!

Now let me turn to the fifth question: Who has failed to fulfill their international obligations and who has trampled on the norms governing international relations?

Sovereign equality and non-interference in other countries internal affairs are fundamental principles of international law and basic norms governing international relations. China has never interfered in the internal affairs of other countries, including the UK, and we hope the UK will also abide by this principle.

The UK side well knows that Hong Kong is no longer under its colonial rule, and that Hong Kong has returned to China and is now part of China. The UK has no sovereignty, jurisdiction or right of "supervision" over Hong Kong after the handover.

However, the UK Government keeps making irresponsible remarks on Hong Kong affairs through its so-called "six-monthly report on Hong Kong". It makes unwarranted accusations against the National Security Law for the Hong Kong SAR, and even talks about changing the arrangements for "British National (Overseas) " (BNO) passport holders in Hong Kong.

These moves constitute a gross interference in China's internal affairs and openly trample on the basic norms governing international relations. The Chinese side has lodged solemn representation to the UK side to express its grave concern and strong opposition.

I want to emphasize that Hong Kong is part of China. Hong Kong affairs are China's internal affairs and brook no external interference. One important task of the National Security Law for the Hong Kong SAR is to prevent, suppress and punish collusion with a foreign country or with external elements which endanger national security.

No one should underestimate the firm determination of China to safeguard its sovereignty, security and development interests. Attempts to disrupt or obstruct the implementation of the National Security Law for the Hong Kong SAR will be met with the strong opposition of 1. 4 billion Chinese people. All these attempts are doomed to failure!

Law is the beginning of order. The National Security Law for the Hong Kong SAR is the fundamental solution that will end the chaos and restore order in Hong Kong.

I am confident that, under the strong leadership of the Central Government of China, with the concerted efforts of all the Chinese people, including Hong Kong compatriots, and with the strong safeguards of the National Security Law for the Hong Kong SAR, Hong Kong will become a safer, better and more prosperous place.

Thank you!

Now I would like to take your questions.

CGTN: China has said it reserves the right to take corresponding measures to the UK's decision to offer citizenship to 3 million Hong Kong residents. Can you give us more details about what those measures would be and when they will be announced? Secondly, if I may, Boris Johnson says that he is still a sinophile but the National Security Law for HK is a clear and serious breach of the Sino-British Joint Declaration. How do you think the relations between China and the UK could be saved from deteriorating any further?

Liu Xiaoming: I think I already answered your question in my opening remarks. With regard to BNO, with regard to specific moves, you have to ask the British government what they are going to do next. I also said that the relationship between China and the UK, or between any countries, has to be based on international law and the norms governing international relations. The fundamental principles of international law are sovereign equality and non interference in each other's internal affairs. This was incorporated into the UN charter. It was also included in the Joint Communiqué on the Agreement on an Exchange of Ambassadors between the UK and China about 40 years ago. These are the basic norms of the relationship.

This year is the 70th year since UK recognized the New China. In the past 70 years, we've seen ups and downs in the relationship, but on the whole, the relationship has moved forward. The reason why we have seen downs is because these principles were violated. When we have had ups in the relationship, it means these principles were abided by. So when the principles are abided by, we will witness the leaps and bounds in the relationship. But when these principles are violated, the relationship will suffer setbacks and even backslide. Thank you.

BBC: Article 38 in this new law says that it applies even where the individual is neither a Hong Kong resident nor physically in the territory. How does this use of universal jurisdiction fit alongside international law where it's kept normally for the most serious crimes? And how can journalists, activists, and others be sure that they're able to continue exercising their freedom of speech without being prosecuted if they set foot in Hong Kong?

Liu Xiaoming: You mentioned Article 38. That is a common practice. Even by British law, those who commit a crime, who work against the interest of the UK, should be accountable no matter where they are. If they conduct activities that endanger national security either inside the UK or outside the UK, they will be held responsible. I don't think there's anything new to the National Security Law when it comes to safeguarding Hong Kong security.

With regard to journalists, I think the law is very clear. It outlines the four categories of crime against the national security of China. As long as a journalist abides by the law, you should have nothing to worry about. You can conduct your work. Also, as mentioned, human rights are fully respected. That applies not only to Hong Kong residents but also to every resident and every person working and living in Hong Kong. And those human rights include freedom of the press and freedom of speech. So there's nothing to be worried about as long as you abide by the law.

Sky News: The UK government is looking again at the decision of allowing Huawei into the UK network. They are actually going to make a U-turn on the decision on Huawei and not allow Huawei anymore into the 5G network. What impact would that have on UK-China relations? If I may, you said that China does not interfere with UK affairs, and yet some people would disagree with that and say that China is actually conducting subversive activity, trying to influence elements of UK politicians, academia and even business to further its influence and interests. How do you respond to that?

Liu Xiaoming: I would totally reject any accusation of China interfering in the UK's internal affairs. I've been ambassador here for more than 10 years, and I never came across any incident in which we've been accused by the UK government or any institutions with hard evidence of China's interference in the UK's internal affairs. If you have evidence, please show me. But do not spread disinformation and make false accusation against China. As I said in my opening remarks, China is fully committed to the basic norms governing international relations and that has been our consistent policy.

With regard to Huawei, I have written many articles and made many speeches on Huawei. I don't think we have enough time to talk about that. So I want to be brief on Huawei. Huawei is a win-win example of China-UK collaboration. We believe that to embrace Huawei, to include Huawei, is not only in the interest of China. I think it's also in the fundamental interests of the UK. The British government has its ambitious plan for full 5G coverage for the UK by 2025. I think Huawei can do the job. But if the UK chooses to pay a higher price for less advanced products, it's up to you. I always say that we have to work for the best and prepare for the worst. Huawei has operations in 170 countries and no country has found evidence that they are operating by the back door. They have been very transparent. They set up the center for analyzing their products that is completely managed by British people, not people from Huawei. They have built confidence. Throughout the world, can you give me the name of another company that sets up a center for itself to be examined by the host country? No. So they have nothing to fear. If you do not want Huawei, it's up to you. I always say when one door shuts, another door opens. In China, we have a saying when the West turns dark, the East will be brighter. I heard a lot of fuss and noises about Huawei, but we have nothing to fear. I told our business community here, you have to be more confident; once you have good products, you should not worry that they don't have the market. I think the world is big enough to accommodate Huawei. I really believe that having Huawei is a real win-win situation, not only for Huawei but also for the UK. But of course, at the end of the day, it's up to the British government. We have tried our best to tell the story of Huawei, but we cannot control the British government's decision. I heard there is a lot of speculation. We are ready for any scenario and consequences. I think Huawei will survive and prosper. The more pressure from the so-called "superpower" and its allies, the stronger Huawei will grow. That is my belief.

Bloomberg: Thank you, Ambassador. Just a very brief follow-up on the Huawei question. The decision taken by the UK government is quite clear that it will be based on security concerns, rather than on the commercial relations you bear in mind. And it is also quite clear that the United States is concerned about Huawei's security. What you are saying is that China doesn't see it as a security issue at all, and that it wouldn't be concerned at the political level that the UK will make such a decision.

Liu Xiaoming: I think it's up to the UK to make the final decision. In terms of security, I think Huawei has done their best to address the concerns about security. When you talk about security, are you talking about security from the political perspective? There are many kinds of security. One is about telecommunications, whether the technology is safe enough and resilient enough to protect you, not only from the so-called states, but also from some individual hackers or other companies. So you cannot generalize security. But Huawei has made every effort to address security concerns and tried to improve their technology. Analysis of intelligence agencies said the risks are manageable and the technology in general is safe. That's why the UK government made the decision to include Huawei, even though they have imposed a 35% cap. If it is decided that Huawei will be rejected, it's up to them. As I said, the world is big enough to accommodate Huawei. They have operations in 170 countries. If the UK gives up, they still have 169 countries. I tried to encourage people from Huawei to look forward. First, you have to work and convince the UK partners and UK people, government and business that you have the best technologies and your price is the most competitive, and you are addressing their concern by keeping improving your technologies. You are the leader. But if they decide not to choose you, it's up to them. You still have to develop. Huawei has been developing despite so many measures. I have full confidence in them.

So you mentioned security, this is also the point I want to make. When some British politicians talk about Huawei, they link Huawei to UK's relations with China. Some of them regard China as a threat, even as a hostile country. I think that is totally wrong. That is inconsistent with the consensus reached by the two leaders of our countries. When President Xi was here, many people talked about the "Golden Era", but they have no idea what the "Golden Era" is about. Actually the "Golden Era" was proposed by the British side, it was proposed by the British leader. We think that it is in the interests of the two countries, then we agreed with terming our relationship a "Golden Era". But if you do not want the "Golden Era", if you treat China as an enemy, that is completely wrong and not in your interest. That reminds me of Brzezinski, the American strategist who helped to normalize the relationship between China and the US. Dr. Brzezinski had a very fine line: If we make China an enemy, China will become an enemy. So we want to be your friend and partner. But if you want to make China a hostile country, you have to bear the consequences. Thank you.

The Times: I want to know whether there will be any attempts to prevent Hong Kong holders of British National (Overseas) status from taking up Britain's offer to come to UK.

Liu Xiaoming: We have heard quite a lot of talk about revoking British position on BNO. When we reached the agreement in 1984, the British government promised, in the exchange of MOU, that they would not give citizenship to BNO holders in Hong Kong. But now they have decided to revoke their position, which we regard as walking away from their international obligations. People talk about China's response. Our first response is that we criticize the British move. We don't think they have honoured their commitment. Secondly, we think it is an interference in China's internal affairs and a political manipulation against the National Security Law. Thirdly, we will have to wait and see, and have to decide our counter measures in accordance with the actual actions to be taken by the British side.

The Economist: Ambassador, can I ask you please to elaborate on the consequences for the UK in response to its position on Hong Kong? For example, do you foresee consequences for British companies operating in the Chinese market, for bilateral trade and in what sectors in particular? Do you see risks for British banks or for companies serving consumer industries to operate in China? Thank you.

Liu Xiaoming: As I said in my opening remarks, the relationship between states has to be based on basic principles, including respect for each other, respect for sovereignty and territorial integrity, non-interference in each other's internal affairs and respect for the core interests and major concerns of each other. That has been reaffirmed by our top leaders. During the pandemic, President Xi and Prime Minister Johnson had two telephone conversations. They both reaffirmed their commitment to these basic principles. But once these principles are violated, there will certainly be consequences for the relationship. Mutual trust will be weakened. Confidence will be weakened. But with regard to specific consequences in specific areas, we have to wait and see. We do hope that the UK side will stand by the fundamental interests between China and the UK. We should bear in mind the big picture of the fundamental interests of the relationship. Thank you.

Xinhua News Agency: A recent survey found that the number of the Chinese students who would choose the UK as the first country to study abroad has for the first time overtaken that of the US. Will China's attitude and policy regarding Chinese students studying in the UK change if the Sino-UK relations are further dented by political differences?

Liu Xiaoming: We would certainly like to say that normal relations between China and the UK will move forward, including the exchanges of the students. I have also read some reports. Because of what is going on in the US, there is more demand from Chinese students to study in the UK. We welcome this and encourage more students to come here. The education section of the Embassy has been very busy, providing information and answering questions and enquiries from Chinese students. We are helping them to get in touch with various universities. Right now, I have not seen any negative consequences from educational cooperation. We have 200, 000 Chinese students studying in the UK. During the pandemic, I wrote letters to the presidents or vice chancellors of 154 universities which host Chinese students. In addition to asking them to take good care of Chinese students, I also expressed my commitment to a stronger relationship between China and their respective universities.

Reuters: We've got some Brits looking again into Huawei. The British government is talking about introducing new laws about foreign takeover and acquisition, which is believed to be specifically aimed at Chinese firms. You spoke earlier about the "Golden Era". From China's point of view, is the "Golden Era" over between the two countries? If it isn't, what does Britain need to do to keep it going?

Liu Xiaoming: The "Golden Era" was an idea proposed by the UK side and endorsed by both sides. Whether it's over or not -- I certainly hope not -- but whether it's over or not is not up to Chinese side. I think, during the pandemic, we still heard the British leaders express their commitment to the "Golden Era". You know, I always say, for any kind of relationship, you need two to tango, you need two hands to clap. So I do hope that our relationship will develop further and will enjoy steady growth in the best interests of the two countries. But, as I said, it's up to both sides. We have every reason to share a good relationship with the UK, and we regard the UK as a partner. We never use the words that "the UK is potentially a hostile country". You've never heard this word from any Chinese leader nor any Chinese official. So I really want to remind the British leaders, the British officials, they have to be careful with regard to how to characterize the nature of the relationship.

The Guardian: Ambassador, you mentioned that the Security Law is very popular in Hong Kong. You said that three million people have signed the petition. But you know, in the district elections last year, we've seen pro-democracy movements doing very well. Can you guarantee the election this autumn will be held on the same basis as the ones that were held, and will increase the freedom to stand and freedom to campaign?

Liu Xiaoming: We have a different interpretation of what was going on in Hong Kong. You regard it as a pro-democracy movement. But we think they are violent, rioting and law-breaking activities, even terrorism. If people were to storm the UK parliament, I don't think you would regard them as a "pro-democracy movement". We've seen so many things happening on the streets of London in the past few weeks. I never read the British media describe them as a "pro-democracy movement". You regard them as law-breakers and rioters. But why, when it comes to Hong Kong, do you have a different standard? So I think this approach absolutely exposes a double standard. And with regard to the election in September, I think the election will be conducted in accordance with the law in Hong Kong. And, you know, when we talk about the National Security Law, it will be implemented according to the law. As I said, this Law has incorporated fully both the comprehensive jurisdiction of the Central Government and the high degree of autonomy of Hong Kong. So Hong Kong people will administer their affairs. Nothing has changed as long as you do not violate the National Security Law. Hong Kong's social system, legislative system and legal system will all remain unchanged. Nothing has been altered. You should have confidence in Hong Kong.

The Daily Telegraph: Morning, Mr. Ambassador. I am reporting on retaliatory measures if the UK pressed ahead with a plan on passports and residents back to the UK, but we are short of detail. Can you offer any detail on what measures might be taken? Can I also ask you another issue? Ofcom today will severely criticize CGTN over its broadcast involving a Briton, Peter Humphrey, saying he was forced to confess on air while under duress, can you offer a comment on that please?

Liu Xiaoming: On the BNO, I think I answered previous questions. My answer will be the same. We have made our position clear to the British side. We hope that they will reconsider their position. With regard to what the response China is going to make, we have to wait and see what will be the specific actions from the British side.
With regard to CGTN, I think they already made a rebuttal to the accusation of Mr Humphrey. The accusation is totally not based on fact. And I think they have made their position very clear. Thank you.

NBC: Thank you very much, Mr. Ambassador. You talked about how this new National Security Law doesn't violate the decades-old policy of "One Country, Two Systems" but the spirit of that agreement on "One Country, Two Systems" allows a great deal of political freedom and freedom of expression in Hong Kong. There are reports this morning that books are being removed from public libraries written by activists. There have been activists — you've described them as "rioters" and "terrorists" — who have been detained. So my question is, is this the end of freedom of expression as people have known it in Hong Kong for the last several decades?

Liu Xiaoming: Not at all. Hong Kong people will be protected in their freedom of speech and freedom of press. You mentioned some of the books. It really depends on what the book is about. If a book is aimed at inciting secession and subversion, that will be tantamount to a kind of crime. You'll have to read the National Security Law carefully. In the UK, there are many laws governing national security. If you voice opinion in support of terrorism and hatred, that can be regarded as a criminal act. Why can the UK have this law but China cannot have a National Security Law to punish those who incite secession and subversion, who incite actions that endanger the national security? I think this is a common practice. When you talk about freedom of speech and freedom of the press, I think, as I said, this law will protect the majority, the great majority, of Hong Kong people in exercising their rights of freedom of the press, freedom to march, freedom of demonstration. But you can't do things to endanger national security, i.e. only four categories of crime. There is a boundary. Even with regard to the freedom of expression, freedom of speech, protected by the International Covenant, there is also limit. You can't do this at the expense of national security and public order. It's clearly stipulated. I do recommend you to go back to read this Covenant on Civil and Political Rights, an international document. So people have nothing to worry about. As long as they abide by the National Security Law, as long as they do not cross the line prohibited by the National Security Law, they should be one hundred percent free. They should have nothing to fear.

So that's the problem. The British media, and the American media too, exercise what I would call a scaremongering practice. They demonise this law. That's totally wrong. They don't read the law carefully. There are four categories of crime. They have been very carefully stipulated in a very detailed way. As long as you do not cross the boundary, as long as you exercise your rights within the limits protected by the Constitution, by the Basic Law, by the International Covenant, you should have no problem at all. Thank you.

Financial Times: Thanks very much Ambassador. A lot of British businesses in Mainland China and Hong Kong are worried about the law. What will happen if the Hong Kong police request to use their data or system and they refuse?

Liu Xiaoming: The Hong Kong Police will carry out the National Security Law in accordance with the law. The National Security Law has made it very clear that the law enforcement people, including the police, including the people working in the national security office based in Hong Kong, have to abide by the law in China and also the law in Hong Kong. The police enforcement people will carry out the National Security Law in accordance with all laws on the ground. Thank you.

RT: Thank you, Mr. Ambassador. The Boris Johnson government is looking to give millions of Hongkongers citizenship to escape Chinese laws. Why is the UK so ready to give citizenship to Hong Kong as a former British colony but not to other former British colonies, such as Iraq which suffered an illegal war that thousands fled.

Liu Xiaoming: Firstly, some of the politicians in UK still have a very strong colonial mindset. They fail to recognise that Hong Kong is no longer under British colonial rule. Hong Kong was returned to China 23 years ago. That's their problem. That's why they have this passion. They still regard Hong Kong as being under British colonial rule, they try to make irresponsible remarks, and they try to interfere in Hong Kong affairs. But that's totally wrong. They fail to realise that Hong Kong is now part of China.
Secondly, they fail to realise that the stability and prosperity of Hong Kong is not only in the interest of China. It's also in the interest of the UK. The UK has 300, 000 citizens living in Hong Kong and more than 700 businesses there. So the prosperity and stability of Hong Kong is in their best interest. That's why, I am talking about how 3 million people in Hong Kong signed a petition to support the National Security Law, including major British business people from HSBC, Swire, Jardine and Standard Chartered. But those politicians try to criticise them. That's wrong because that stability and prosperity in Hong Kong is in their interest. You can't do business or live a normal life without a peaceful environment. Look at what happened last year. People did not even dare to walk in the streets under this so called "black terror". People cried for chaos to end as quickly as possible. That was what gave birth to the National Security Law.

Channel 4: Thank you, Ambassador. Can I just get back to the issue of Huawei? What are the consequences for Britain if Huawei is removed from 5G (development in the UK)? And would you consider that a hostile act?

Liu Xiaoming: The consequences, there might be many. First, it damages Britain's image as an open, business-friendly, free and transparent environment as it claims to be. So that's why in the past 5 years, the Chinese investment in the UK has been bigger than the Chinese investment in the previous 30 years. Because Chinese business people believe the UK is business-friendly, and they can do business here. But if you get rid of Huawei, it will send out a very wrong message. It will tarnish Britain's image as a free trade country. That's number one.

Number two, it will tarnish your image as a country which follows independent policies. It means you have succumbed to foreign pressure. You can't make your own independent foreign policy. I always say, Britain can only be Great when you have your independent foreign policy. If you do not have an independent foreign policy and you have to dance to the tune of another country, how can you claim to be Great Britain?

Thirdly, I think it will also send out a very bad message to the Chinese business community here. They are all watching how you handle Huawei. If you get rid of Huawei, it will send out a very bad message for other Chinese businesses. It will also send out a very bad message for other foreign businesses.

Fourthly, there is also an element of trust. When you have a sound relationship, it has to be built on mutual respect and mutual trust. In China, we have a saying: You can't make your policy in the morning and then change it in the evening. How would people be able to trust you? So I think it's a matter of trust here. I do hope that the British government will make decisions in the best interest -- not only in the interest of China-UK cooperation -- but also in the interest of itself. Thank you.

China Daily: Thank you, Ambassador. Some people think the National Security Law in Hong Kong will also help protect British investments and their legal rights in Hong Kong. Mr. Ambassador, what is your opinion?

Liu Xiaoming: Absolutely. I think I have answered your question in my previous remarks. You can only do business in a stable and peaceful environment. So that's why the National Security Law is welcomed, not only by the ordinary people who are very concerned about their security, but also by the business communities; not only British businesses but also many other businesses. There is a report that the American Chamber of Commerce expressed their confidence in Hong Kong. That is because

有问必答
No Question Unanswered

the National Security Law can guarantee a business environment for people including the British. So I do hope the British public, including the British media, approach the National Security Law from an objective, correct and accurate perspective. Do not try to demonize this law. This law will provide a guarantee and protection for safety and prosperity of Hong Kong. As I said in my opening remarks, with the safeguard of the National Security Law, Hong Kong will become a safer, better and more prosperous place. Thank you.

Thank you for your attention and thank you for attending today's press conference.

▲ 2015年1月12日，看望中国海军第十八批护航编队

▼ 2015年1月12日，在"长白山舰"甲板上就中国海军第十八批护航编队访问英国举行中外记者会

▲ 2015年11月13日，在英国剑桥大学发表演讲：《为中英关系"黄金时代"增光添彩》

▼ 2015年11月13日，在英国剑桥大学发表演讲后回答师生提问

▲ 2016年5月20日，在伦敦国际战略研究所发表演讲：《中国是维护南海和平稳定的中坚力量》

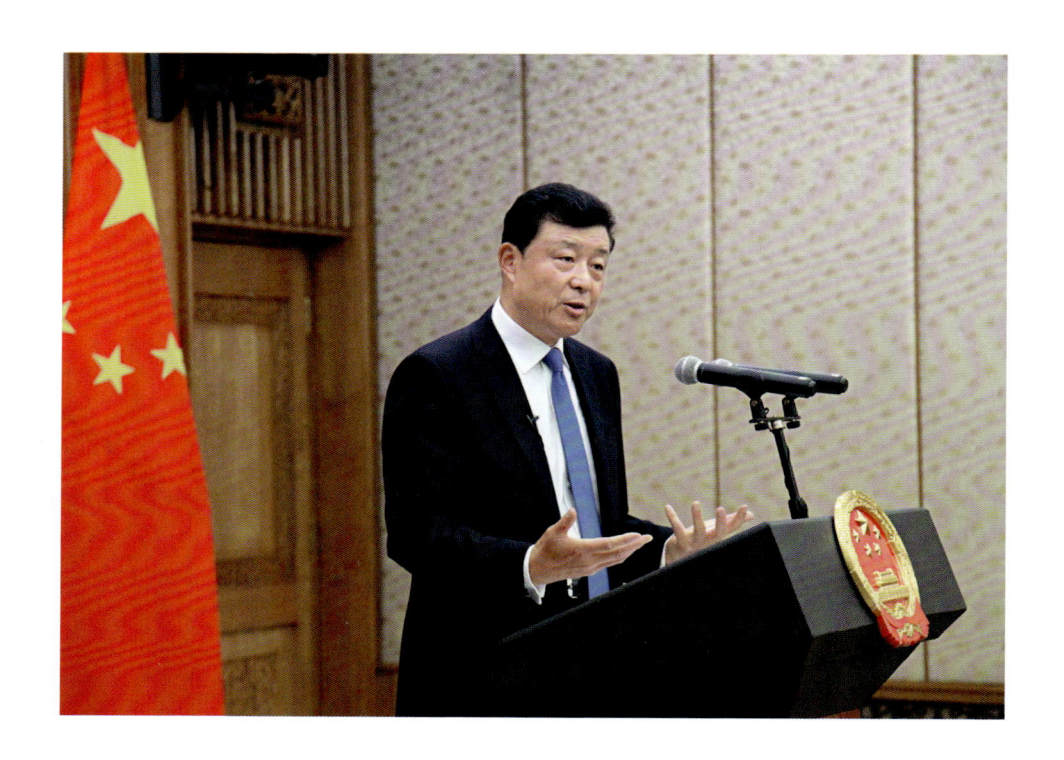

▲ 2016年7月19日，在中国驻英国大使馆就南海仲裁庭裁决结果举行中外记者会

▲ 2016年7月25日,在英国皇家国际问题研究所发表主旨演讲:《浮云难遮望眼,正道总是沧桑》

▲ 2017年11月7日，对英国工商界宣介中共十九大精神并回答提问

▲ 2017年11月21日，在英国议会发表主旨演讲，宣介中共十九大精神并回答议员提问

▲ 2018年9月10日，在英国议会就"一带一路"发表主旨演讲并回答议员提问

南海问题

South China Sea

2016年5月20日，我在伦敦国际战略研究所就南海问题发表题为"中国是维护南海和平稳定的中坚力量"的主旨演讲，并就如何看待美军机对中国抵近侦察活动、美亚太再平衡战略对地区局势影响、中美在亚太地区如何管控分歧、中国对南海仲裁案裁决结果的立场等回答了现场听众提问。英国政界、工商界，英美学术界以及俄罗斯、美国、法国、巴西、澳大利亚、印尼、新加坡、文莱、日本、加拿大、波兰、以色列、土耳其、塞浦路斯等国驻英使节和外交官100多人出席。路透社、BBC、《泰晤士报》《每日电讯报》《经济学家》、天空新闻台、独立电视台等英国主流媒体，中国中央电视台、《人民日报》、新华社等驻英央媒及主要华文媒体对演讲进行报道。

伦敦国际战略研究所是国际著名智库，成立于1958年11月，主要从事国际战略、国防安全和防务政策研究，每年出版《全球军力平衡报告》《战略研究》等重要刊物。许多国家的政要及战略界知名人士曾在该所发表演讲。该所每年与新加坡、巴林政府分别合作举办"香格里拉对话会"和"麦纳麦对话会"，在国际问题研究领域具有重要影响。

7月19日，我在驻英使馆就南海仲裁庭裁决结果举行中外记者会，阐述中国政府对南海仲裁庭裁决结果的严正立场。指出裁决结果是无效的，没有拘束力，中国不接受、不承认任何基于该仲裁裁决的主张和行动。中国坚定致力于维护南海和平稳定，致力于同直接有关的当事国在尊重历史事实的基础上，根据国际法，通过谈判协商和平解决有关争议。23家中外媒体近40名记者出席。

7月25日，我在英国皇家国际问题研究所（简称"皇研所"）就南海问题发表题为"浮云难遮望眼，正道总是沧桑"的主旨演讲，阐述中方对南海仲裁案的立场和中国在南海问题上的政策主张。英国政界、工商界、学术界、外交界及中外主流媒体300多人出席。演讲后，我回答了听众关于美国大选对中美关系的影响、南海仲裁案的性质、南海断续线的法律地位、"南海各方行为准则"谈判、中国岛礁建设、南海资源开发、仲裁案对中国与邻国关系的影响、中日钓鱼岛争端、中国外交走向等提问。

皇研所成立于1920年，是英国规模最大、历史最悠久的国际问题研究机构之一，拥有高水平的研究队伍，主要从事国际战略、国际关系和外交政策研究，在英国和世界国际关系学界享有较高声誉，会员超过3000人。皇研所与英国政府、企业、媒体和学术界联系密切，对英国外交政策具有一定影响。该所主要刊物有《国际事务》《今日世界》等。

中国是维护南海和平稳定的中坚力量
——在伦敦国际战略研究所发表演讲并回答提问

（2016年5月20日，伦敦国际战略研究所）

2016年5月20日，我在伦敦国际战略研究所发表题为《中国是维护南海和平稳定的中坚力量》的主旨演讲并回答听众的提问。演讲和答问实录如下：

刘晓明： 很高兴时隔三年之后再次应邀来到伦敦国际战略研究所。三年前，我应齐普曼所长的邀请在这里就"新时期的中国外交"发表过一次演讲。今天，我要讲的主题还是中国外交，不过这次集中谈一个问题，这就是南海问题。

南海问题的热度最近几个月来不断升温，很多人在关注南海问题，很多媒体也在炒作南海问题，但对于南海问题的真实情况人们却往往不甚清楚，有时甚至存在误解。因此我特意选伦敦国际战略研究所这样一个研究国际政治和安全问题的知名智库，来阐述中国对南海问题的立场和政策，并回答大家的提问。希望通过今天的交流，让各位对南海问题能有一个比较全面和准确的了解。首先我还是要从中国与南海的历史渊源说起。

我们要想客观、公正、理性地看待南海问题，就要追本溯源，从源头上弄清事情的本来面貌。

南海诸岛自古以来就是中国领土，之所以强调"自古以来"，是因为南海诸岛属于中国这一历史事实源远流长，可以用四个"最早"来概括：

一是最早发现：一些国家宣称南海岛礁是"无主地"，企图以所谓"先占原则"据为己有。事实上，早在公元前2世纪的汉代，中国就已经有了大规模、频繁的远洋航海及渔业捕捞活动，南海自古就是中国重要的海上航路，当时的中国人频繁航行于南海地区，最早发现了南海诸岛。著名南海问题学者马文·塞缪尔斯在20世纪80年代的著作《南海争端》中明确提出："是南海和南海上的岛礁帮助中国人在地理上形成了对世界秩序的认识。"

二是最早命名：现在西方人多用SPRATLY群岛称呼中国的南沙群岛，这缘于1843年英国船长Richard Spratly所谓"发现"并"命名"了南沙群岛。而事实是，2000多年前，中国人就已经开始认识南海，并在各种历史文献中将这片海域称为"涨海"，把海中的岛、礁、滩、沙称为"崎头"。后来历朝历代均出现了专指西沙、南沙群岛及其具体岛屿的古地名。明清时期形成的航海指南《更路簿》，更是详细记载了包括南沙群岛在内的南海诸岛数十处地名，不少沿用至今并被各国航海家广泛承认和采用。

三是最早实施行政管辖：自1200多年前的唐代开始，中国历代政府就不断通过行政设治、水师巡视、资源开发管理等方式对南海诸岛进行有效管辖。到公元10世纪的宋代，地方志明确记载南海诸岛属琼州也就是现在的中国海南省管辖。公元1279年，元代著名天文学家郭守敬曾到南海开展测量活动并建立天文观测据点。明清两代也均将南海纳入水师巡防范围。

四是最早开发利用：中国人民长期以来一直在南海诸岛及海域从

事捕捞、种植和其他生产活动，许多岛礁上都曾留下中国渔民生产生活的遗迹。英国海军部测绘局1868年编制的《中国海指南》一书中就明确记录了南沙群岛仅有中国人生产、生活的事实。

以上四个"最早"均有充分史实作为支撑，这说明中国在历史上早已将南海诸岛并入中国版图并持续和平有效行使管辖。事实上，直到20世纪70年代之前，南海诸岛属于中国是国际社会普遍认知。举两个典型的例子：1883年，德国曾派军舰到西沙、南沙群岛附近进行测量，清朝广东地方政府以主权为依据提出抗议，德国被迫停止测量活动并撤走；1958年，中国政府发表关于领海的声明，并宣布声明中的规定适用于包括西沙、南沙等南海诸岛在内的所有中国领土，时任越南政府总理范文同就此专门照会时任中国国务院总理周恩来，明确承认西沙和南沙群岛属于中国。类似这样的例子还有很多。

既然南海诸岛属于中国是无可争辩的历史事实，那么南海争端又是怎样产生的？

从20世纪70年代开始，一些南海周边国家由于觊觎南海的丰富自然资源，开始对中国南沙岛礁提出领土要求。越南、菲律宾等国先后派兵非法侵占了南沙部分岛礁，南海问题就此产生。迄今为止，越南共侵占29个岛礁，菲律宾共侵占8个岛礁，马来西亚共侵占5个岛礁。

进入80年代以来，《联合国海洋法公约》经过9年的谈判于1982年签署。随着现代海洋法制度的发展，各国又逐步提出了专属经济区和大陆架等海洋权益主张，这些主张覆盖的范围有部分重叠，从而又产生了海域划界的问题，这就使得问题进一步复杂化。

由此可见，南海争端的根源：一是一些国家非法侵占中国南沙群岛部分岛礁而产生的领土争议；二是一些国家提出的海洋管辖权主张重叠而产生的海域划界争议。这两方面原因相互交织，使南海问题异常复杂。但无论从哪方面原因看，中国都不是挑起事端的一方，恰恰相反，中国是南海争端的受害方。

那么，中国对南海问题的立场和政策是什么？

面对一些国家的侵权挑衅行为，中国始终保持克制和忍让，以建设性态度负责任地处理南海争端。事实上，如果不是中方长期保持克制态度，南海地区的局势早已不是今天的样子。中方在南海问题上的态度和立场，主要体现在五个"坚持"上：

一是坚持维护南海的和平稳定。中国是地区和平稳定的坚定捍卫者和维护者，始终奉行"与邻为善、以邻为伴"的周边外交政策。这既是因为中国人民血液中流淌着的爱好和平的基因，也是中国自身利益和发展的现实需要。30年来，中国在和平稳定的环境中实现了人类历史上从未有过的高速度、大规模工业化。中国的发展得益于和平稳定的国际和周边环境，中国当然不希望南海生乱，也决不允许南海生乱。

二是坚持当事国通过友好谈判协商和平解决争议。世界上领土问题的最终解决，无论经过哪些机制和过程，最后都要由当事方通过平等谈判达成协议，才能获得根本、长久的解决。谈判协商最能体现国家主权平等原则，最能体现当事方的意愿，是最行之有效的解决争端方式。新中国成立以来，中国与14个陆地邻国中的12个签订了边界条约，划定和勘定的边界长度达2万余公里。这些邻国中绝大多数都是中小国家，从来没有哪一国说过中国在谈判中以大欺小，以强凌弱。这些都是中国与当事国通过直接谈判协商解决问题的范例，解决南海问题同样也不例外。实践证明，有关各方只有通过谈判协商，才能不断增进互信、管控危机、缩小分歧、促进合作。处理南海问题，必须坚持谈判协商这一现实有效途径。

三是坚持通过规则机制管控分歧。中国和东盟国家2002年签署《南海各方行为宣言》，2013年启动"南海行为准则"磋商。"准则"磋商启动以来，已经取得了积极进展。中国与东盟国家还积极推动建立"海上紧急事态外交热线"和"海上联合搜救热线"。各方同意积极探讨制定"海上风险管控预防性措施"，从而在"准则"最终达成前有效管控海上局势，防止不测事件发生。事实证明，地区国家间通过规则机制管控分歧的努力是有效的。

四是坚持维护南海航行和飞越自由。中国作为南海最大的沿岸国，每年有大量的能源和海上货物贸易运输经过南海，没有哪个国家比中国更关心南海地区的航行和飞越自由。近一段时间，航行自由成了热门话题，一些人大谈所谓保护航行自由，仿佛在该地区的航行安全遇到什么问题。但事实是，每年有十万多艘船只经过南海地区，从未听说有哪艘船只抱怨过航行自由受到过任何影响。如果南海存在威胁海上航行的风险，通常会导致航运保费瞬间上涨。但是这样的情况并没有发生。据今年初英国路透社报道，没有迹象显示南海地区商业航运受到了任何影响。报道还称，英国知名保险机构"劳合社联合战争险委员会"（Lloyd's Joint War Committee）并未将南海列入高风险地区，保险公司也不会向通过该地区的船只多收保费。常识告诉我们，商人特别是保险商们对风险的嗅觉是最灵敏的，连他们都没有察觉出南海航行自由受到了威胁，我不知道一些人所声称要"保护"的是什么样的航行自由？

近来，个别国家打着"行使航行和飞越自由"的旗号，不断在南海炫耀武力，派遣军用舰机抵近中国南沙群岛有关岛礁邻近海空域进行挑衅，制造紧张局势，威胁中国主权和安全。就在10天前，美国"劳伦斯号"驱逐舰未经中国政府许可，非法进入中国南沙群岛有关岛礁邻近海域。这些行为所要维护的恐怕不是航行自由，而是凭借力量优势行使海上霸权的"横行自由"，这才是南海地区和平稳定以及真正航行自由的最大威胁。我要奉劝这些国家，如果它们真的关心航行和飞越自由，就应遵守国际法，尊重沿岸国主权、安全和相关权益。

看美国的行为，要看其对待国际法的态度。如果美国认真致力于国际海洋法，那么早就应该签署包括中国在内的广大国际社会均已签署的《联合国海洋法公约》。尊重国际法，和平谈判解决争端，对于维护南海和平稳定至关重要。借航行自由之名，行军事挑衅和威胁之实，是极其危险的行为，它直接扰乱地区的和平稳定。

五是坚持通过合作实现互利共赢。中国一贯致力于发展与周边各国的友好合作关系，主动提出了"搁置争议，共同开发"，这为解决南海争议提供了有益思路，也充分考虑到各方的实际利益。根据这一思路，中国与有关各方相继开展了一系列合作。例如：中、菲、越三国石油公司于2005年签署《在南海协议区三方联合海洋地震工作协议》，推动共同开发南海地区的油气资源；2011年，中国宣布设立总额30亿元人民币的中国—东盟海上合作基金，支持海上务实合作项目；近两年，中国又提出以东盟国家为枢纽建设"21世纪海上丝绸之路"战略构想，进一步深化海上务实合作。这些倡议和措施充分展示了中方开展合作的努力和诚意，受到周边国家的普遍欢迎。

从上述五个"坚持"可以看出，中国是在真心实意地寻找南海问题的解决办法，从而促进南海地区的和平稳定和周边国家的共同发展。

刚才我向大家介绍了中国与南海的渊源以及中国对南海问题的基本政策，现在我想就当前几个南海热点问题谈一些看法。

第一个问题是菲律宾仲裁案。菲律宾单方面提起南海仲裁一事最近闹得沸沸扬扬。我想首先说一说接受菲律宾仲裁请求的仲裁庭。一些媒体报道对该仲裁庭的性质缺乏清晰的认识。其中最关键的一点在于，该仲裁庭只是一个非常设的仲裁机构，与真正意义上的"法庭"有着本质区别。此外，就仲裁机制而言，只有当争议双方自愿达成一致，仲裁程序才能启动。但中国自始至终都已明确表达了不参与、不接受的立场。

一些媒体和政客伺机炒作，称中国必须接受仲裁，否则就是"不遵守国际法"，就是"破坏基于规则的国际体系"，这种说法是完全错误的。中国拒绝接受和参与仲裁，是在行使国际法赋予的合法权利。与此相反，菲律宾方面的做法则是在挑战国际社会的法律和道德底线，既不合情，也不合理，更不合法。

说它不合情，是因为菲律宾破坏了它对中国和其他东盟国家做出的庄严承诺。中菲两国早在一系列双边文件中就通过双边谈判解决争端达成协议。包括菲律宾在内的东盟各国和中国所共同签订的《南海各方行为宣言》中也明确规定，要通过当事国和平谈判解决争议。菲律宾在2011年还与中国发表共同声明，承诺坚持通过谈判协商解决问题，一年后就突然变卦，在事先未告知中方，更未征得中方同意的情况下单方面提起仲裁。国际关系中有一条成文的规则："约定必须遵守"，这是每个国家自立于国际社会所必须严守的道德底线。中国有一个成语："出尔反尔"，用来形容菲律宾的所作所为再合适不过。

说它不合理，是因为菲律宾拿到仲裁庭上要求裁决的岛礁都是我前面所说中国自古以来的固有领土。这就好比邻居抢走了你家的东西，然后就堂而皇之地要求法院把东西判给他。敢问世间哪有这样的道理？英国个别政客总是在强调"基于规则的国际秩序"，请问如果每个国家都如此行事，何谈规则？何谈国际秩序？

说它不合法，原因更明显。一则,《联合国海洋法公约》明文规定：缔约国享有自主选择争端解决方式的权利。菲律宾未经中国同意单方面强行仲裁，侵犯了中国的这一合法权利。二则,《公约》规定：缔约国如果已协议自行选择和平方法解决争端，则只有在这种方法未得到解决以及争端各方之间的协议并不排除其他程序的情况下，才适用第三方争端解决程序。而中方对双边谈判的态度在任何时候都是开放的，中菲之间还远未穷尽双边手段。三则,《公约》还规定，如果缔约国之间对本公约的解释或适用发生争端，应迅速就以谈判或其他和平方法解决争端一事交换意见。而菲律宾从未就此与中国进行过任何协商。中菲两国同为《公约》缔约国，但菲律宾单方面提起仲裁的做法明显违背了上述《公约》规定，是明目张胆的违法行为。

与菲律宾的所作所为相比，中国才是在真正践行和维护国际法。菲方所提15项仲裁诉求涉及领土主权和海洋划界，主权问题不属于《公约》的调整范围；至于海洋划界问题，中国早在2006年就依据《公约》第298条有关规定做出排除性声明，将有关海洋划界等争端排除在《公约》强制争端解决机制之外。中方的行为是在行使《公约》赋予的合法权利，完全符合国际法规定。

我还要指出的是，做出了类似排除性声明的除了中国之外还有30多个国家，其中也包括英国。这些声明构成了《公约》不可分割的组成部分，这些国家合理合法的关切和诉求也应该得到重视。如果南海仲裁案形成了惯例，那就意味着只要有人愿意，上述任何一个国家都可能在毫不知情的情况下被拉入仲裁。这将对各国主权、国际秩序和国际法的尊严和权威造成严重打击。媒体称仲裁案的结果即将公布，但中方对仲裁坚持不参与、不接受、不承认、不执行，并不是因为担心所谓不利结果，而是为了坚守国际法治的底线。

让我们担忧的是，对上面所列举的有关仲裁案的种种不合情、不合理、不合法之处，仲裁庭心知肚明，却仍然坚持按照菲律宾的要求强推仲裁程序，这不能不让人质疑其公正性、合法性，对其背后的政治目的提高警惕。仲裁案实质上是一起披着法律外衣的政治闹剧，无论其结果如何，中方都不会接受。

尽管不接受仲裁，但中国与菲律宾之间直接谈判解决问题的大门依然是敞开的。两国毕竟是近邻，两国人民之间也有传统友谊。我们注意到菲律宾近期举行了大选，希望新一届菲政府能与中方共同努力，妥善处理分歧，使南海局势重回以《公约》和国际法为主导的正常轨道。

第二个问题是中国的岛礁建设。近年来，中国在南沙群岛几个岛礁上开展了建设活动。中方的建设除了为改善驻岛人员的生产生活条件之外，主要目的是为各类民事需求服务，以便向本国、本地区乃至国际社会提供必要和急需的公共产品。中方在岛礁建设中安排了很多公益设施，包括大型综合灯塔、海上安全通信设施、海上应急救捞设施、综合性医疗设施等，从而更好地履行中国在海上搜救、防灾减灾、海洋科研、气象观察、生态环境保护、航行安全、渔业生产服务等方面承担的国际责任和义务。同时，中国也根据所处的安全环境，在自己的岛礁上部署了必要的防御设施，这是在行使国际法赋予主权国家的自保权。据英国路透社报道，一些东南亚船东认为，中国在南海的活动有利于海域的安全，中国在南海岛屿部署援救力量，会缩短营救时间，增加营救机会。刚才我提到，南海地区的航行安全与自由对国际贸易意义重大，我想任何秉持公正立场的人都能看到，中国在南海的岛礁建设，将使这条国际经济大动脉更加安全。

有人说，中国的岛礁建设太大，规模太快。我想说，规模和速度从来不是评判对错的标准。中方建设活动的规模、速度与其在南海承担的国际责任和义务相匹配。中国不能因为自己块头大，就自缚手脚，不做正确的事。

也有人说，中国的岛礁建设是改变现状。我想问，所谓"现状"是什么？中国的岛礁建设完全是在自己领土上进行的，根本不存在所谓"改变现状"的问题。我还想问，当一些国家非法侵占中国岛礁，并在这些非法侵占的岛礁上大兴土木的时候，那些大喊不要改变现状的人跑到哪里去了？

第三个问题是所谓南海"军事化"。近来，外界关于南海"军事化"问题的炒作不绝于耳，其中美国的声音叫得最凶。事实上，只要认真观察一下事实，就能看出到底是谁在南海搞"军事化"。美国将一半以上的军力部署在本来和平稳定的亚太地区，拉帮结派，不断开展针对性极强的军事演习，频繁派遣军用舰机到中国岛礁邻近海空域炫耀武力。正是美国的这些挑衅和敌对行动，加剧了南海紧张局势，同时也助长了菲律宾等国家在非法侵占的岛礁上大肆部署军事设施。由此可见，美国才是南海"军事化"的最大推手。我们希望美方作为负责任的大国，在南海这一复杂敏感问题上谨言慎行，与中方相向而行。因此，要解决南海"军事化"问题，美国首先要停止损害中国主权和安全的危险挑衅行动，其次要停止恶意炒作和渲染南海"军事化"问题，再次要严格遵守国际法，最后要以实际行动做一些有利于南海地区和平稳定的事。

女士们、先生们，南海问题尽管复杂敏感，但在中国和周边国家的共同努力下，南海地区局势一直保持稳定。随着中国国力的增强，我们将会为维护南海地区的安定与繁荣做出更大贡献。正如习近平主席所说，中国将通过和平、发展、合作、共赢的方式推进海洋强国建设。中国的成就得益于和平发展道路，我们绝不会舍弃这一宝贵财富。展望未来，我们有信心也有能力通过友好谈判协商解决争议，通过合作共同维护好南海的和平稳定，我们愿与各国共同携手，把南海真正建设成"和平之海、友谊之海、合作之海"。

谢谢！下面我愿回答大家的提问。

毕马威会计师事务所： 我想请你再澄清一点，你刚才提到美国军舰经过中国岛礁临近区域是非法的。但根据《联合国海洋法公约》规定的"无害通过权"条款，外国船舶享有无害通过他国领海的权利。

刘晓明： 我认为美国军舰抵近中国有关岛礁临近海域的做法是在滥用"无害通过权"。美方没有尊重中国的主权，没有事先通知中方，也未寻求获得中方的许可。因此美方的做法是违反国际法和国际惯例的。

伦敦政治经济学院： 非常感谢你的演讲。你刚才在演讲中提到中美之间存在一定的紧张关系。在我看来，中国与菲律宾、中国与越南之间的紧张关系都是可控的，但中美关系并非如此。从国际体系演变角度看，美国作为现行国际体系的守成力量一直试图维持现状，不少美国官员和研究报告则认为中国将取代美国。你如何看中美管理这种"权力转移"过程？双方能否确保这一转移过程是和平与稳定的？

刘晓明： 正如我在演讲开始时所说，在南海问题上，中国并不是麻烦制造者，而是受害者。相信我已对此进行了清楚解释。在美国实施所谓亚太再平衡战略之前，整个南海地区局势是稳定的。中国与包括菲律宾、越南在内的周边邻国进行双边谈判，我们与东盟国家也在稳步落实《南海各方行为宣言》，有效管控分歧。南海争议已经存在30多年，但整个地区保持了稳定局面。然而，自从美国在2009年实施亚太再平衡战略以来，南海形势出现变化。一些地区国家受到了怂恿，认为有美国为其撑腰打气。例如，菲律宾改变了对南海问题的立场,颁布了所谓"领海基线法案",越南也改变立场。菲方甚至拒绝与中方谈判,并单方面提出涉南海仲裁案。解决主权争议的方法有很多,根据《联合国海洋法公约》,国际仲裁只是辅助途径。解决主权争议问题的最主要途径是当事国进行和平协商谈判。菲方舍本逐末,拒绝与中国和平协商谈判,单方面挑起所谓国际仲裁,就是因为有美国为其撑腰。

关于中美关系,中方历来致力于建设良好的中美关系。这是毋庸置疑的。我的外交生涯中有一半多的时间参与对美关系,两次在中国驻美使馆工作,深知中美关系的重要性。中方认为,如果中美关系出现问题,亚太地区将难以实现稳定与繁荣。我们一贯主张积极发展中美关系,推动双方密切合作。目前中美副外长级安全对话正在华盛顿举行。中美之间有很多对话与沟通渠道,但重要的是,美方应从根本上改变那种认为中国有朝一日要取代美国成为全球领导者的思维定式。这并不是中国追求的目标。我们追求的是实现中华民族伟大复兴的中国梦。作为一个拥有13亿多人口的大国,我们对前进道路上的挑战有清醒认识。我出使埃及之后,曾在中国西部的省份之一甘肃省担任省长助理,我知道中国的一些贫穷地区有多穷,我也深刻体会到中国发展任务之艰巨、挑战之巨大。中国不愿意看到中美交恶,对当超级大国不感兴趣。英国曾当过超级大国,当超级大国是有代价的。而我们中国现在的首要任务是实现自身的发展、提高本国人民的生活水平。

伦敦国际战略研究所: 昨天美国五角大楼对外表示,中国派遣两架战机对美EP-3侦察机进行了"不安全"拦截。我想请问你,这也属于美方的敌对行为吗?

刘晓明: 我认为,美方行为十分危险。美国打着"航行自由"的旗号,挑战中国对南海诸岛的主权,这种做法十分危险。我们都知道,海洋那么宽阔,足够军用舰机自由通行,但美方却偏偏选择对中国抵近侦察,企图挑战中国的国防能力,这种行为十分危险。至于你提到的具体事件,中国外交部发言人已对此阐明了立场。中国有充足的理由维护国家主权,中国军机有权查明美国军机想干什么,但我们始终保持安全距离,有关操作符合专业和安全标准。中方努力避免发生意外,特别是避免发生冲突。但如果美方一意孤行,将会陷入危险境地。

BBC: 两个问题。刘大使,你在演讲中批评仲裁庭,我也曾听到中方官员表示中方不会接受仲裁结果。你刚才的意思是不是也是这样,即不管结果如何,中方都不会接受仲裁判决?

另外一个相关的问题是,你好像将仲裁庭判决和主权问题联系到了一起。据我所知,仲裁内容是南沙海域部分岛礁的地位问题,和主权并无关系。你一直说,中国数百年来在南海海域开发利用,那么仲裁庭的判决一定会对中方有利,为什么中方仍拒绝接受仲裁案和仲裁庭判决?

刘晓明: 让我来告诉你为什么。仲裁庭从一开始就是非法的,一个非法的仲裁庭怎么能判出好的结果?!中方对仲裁庭不承担任何义务。我们始终认为,仲裁案本身即违反了《联合国海洋法公约》和国际法。

BBC： 中方不承担哪些义务？

刘晓明： 中方对仲裁案不承担任何义务。我可以明确地告诉你，不论仲裁结果如何，都不会影响中方对南海岛礁的主权，仲裁案判决结果对中方不具任何约束力。关于仲裁内容，我说过，这就好比邻居抢走了你家的东西，然后堂而皇之地拿到法官面前，要求法官进行判决。不管判决对象是物品所有权，还是物品性质，只要法官受理，都与所有权密不可分。菲律宾曾向仲裁庭提出了15项仲裁申请，其中8项遭到了拒绝，原因就是这些仲裁申请明显违背了《公约》，仲裁庭不希望卷入其中。虽然菲律宾变换手法，对仲裁案进行包装，给它披上合法的外衣，但这不能改变问题的实质。仲裁案始终与主权问题和海洋划界问题密切相关，超出了仲裁庭的管辖范围，违反了《公约》的规定。仲裁庭的设立本身即违反了《公约》规定，是不合法、不合理的。中国坚持不接受仲裁的立场恰恰是为了遵守国际法，恰恰是为了维护国际法的权威。

伦敦政治经济学院： 你如何看待美国对南海地区经济影响。安全方面，美国国防部部长卡特等人在南海问题上不断提高调门，步步紧逼。但在经济方面，美国虽达成了跨太平洋伙伴关系协定，但美国能否在大选前后签署该协定还是个未知数。中国同东南亚开展了卓有成效的合作，经济领域尤其如此，你认为美国总统大选结果是否会影响中国同东南亚的经济合作态势？

刘晓明： 我们一直密切关注美国总统大选情况。当然，没有人能够预测大选结果。不论美国人民选择了谁，不论白宫椭圆形办公室的新主人是谁，我们都愿意并准备与之打交道。与竞选期间的言论相比，我们更注重其上台后的所作所为。我希望，美国新一届政府能以中美关系大局为重。中方愿与美方新领导人一道，共同推动中美关系发展。

因克斯特主任（主持人）： 刘大使，非常感谢。我们已经超时了，今天的活动只能到此为止。请允许我分享一点体会。近来，伦敦国际战略研究所的人普遍有一种感受，就是中国的国际战略影响越来越大，研究所很大一部分精力放在研究中国上。我们还发现，研究所的系列研究报告1/3以中国为题。所有这些都十分说明问题。最后，让我们再一次以热烈的掌声感谢刘大使内容详细、全面的演讲。

China is a Staunch Force for Peace and Stability in the South China Sea
—— A Keynote Speech and Q&A at the International Institute for Strategic Studies

(International Institute for Strategic Studies, 20th May 2016)

On 20th May 2016, I delivered a keynote speech entitled "China is a Staunch Force for Peace and Stability in the South China Sea" at the International Institute for Strategic Studies (IISS), after which I took questions from the audience. The transcript of the keynote speech and Q&A is as follows:

Liu Xiaoming: It is truly a delight to be back again at the International Institute for Strategic Studies (IISS) after three years. Back then, I was invited by Dr. John Chipman to deliver a speech about China's Diplomacy in the New Era. Today my speech is also about China's diplomacy, but I shall focus on one issue - the South China Sea.

Recently the South China Sea issue has attracted much attention and media coverage. However, the articles and reports show that the truth and the facts behind the issue remain unclear to most people. Misunderstandings still exist.

So I have chosen to speak about this issue at the IISS, a prestigious institution that focuses on international security. I shall expound on China's position and policy, and then take questions from you. In this way, I hope our interaction today will help you to gain a more comprehensive and accurate understanding of the issue.

In order to be objective, impartial and rational on the issue of the South China Sea, one must get to the root of the issue and put it in perspective. So I would like to begin with the history of China and the South China Sea.

The islands and reefs in the South China Sea have been Chinese territory since ancient times. I emphasize 'ancient times' to highlight the historical facts that put the South China Sea firmly on the map of China. To elaborate on this, let me share with you four "Firsts".

China was the first to discover the islands in the South China Sea.

Some countries attempt to claim some of the islands on grounds of "prior possession". They try to get away with their illegal occupation by referring to the Nansha Islands as *Terra Nullius*. In fact, as early as 200 BC, during China's Han Dynasty, the Chinese undertook large-scale and frequent sea-faring and fishing activities in the South China Sea. There is clear evidence that the South China Sea was already used by China as an important shipping route since ancient times. It follows that, because of frequent shipping, the Chinese became the first to discover the islands in the South China Sea.

Marwyn Samuels is known for his studies on the South China Sea. He wrote a book in the 1980s called *Contest for the South China Sea*. In this he wrote:

"Along the way, both literarily and figuratively, the South China Sea and its islands helped shape the geographical cognita of the Chinese world order."

Second, China was the first to name the islands in the South China Sea.

Today, the Nansha of the South China Sea are called the Spratly Islands in the West. This name comes from a British sea captain called Richard Spratly who thought it was he who had "discovered" and "named" the islands in 1843. But actually the Chinese had named the Nansha Islands about 2,000 years before he did.

In various Chinese historical records dating back to over 2000 years, the South China Sea is known as *Zhang Hai*, or "rising sea", and the islands, reefs, shoals and sands as *Qi Tou*, or "rugged peaks". In historical documents of later dynasties after the Han Dynasty, ancient names referring to today's Xisha Islands, the Nansha Islands and individual islands in the archipelagoes are clearly recorded.

A popular sailing guide called *Geng Lu Bu* was compiled by Chinese fishermen. This was during the Ming and Qing Dynasties between the 14th and 20th century. In this book, the names of dozens of islands of the South China Sea, including those in Nansha, are recorded. Many of these names have been widely adopted and used by international sailors until this day.

Third, China was the first to exercise administrative jurisdiction in the South China Sea.

Ever since China's Tang Dynasty, about 1,200 years ago, successive Chinese governments have exercised jurisdiction over the South China Sea. This included islands and the waters around them. China's sovereignty was established through administrative establishment, naval patrol, resource development and management.

In the 10th century, during China's Song Dynasty, local chronicles explicitly recorded that the islands in the South China Sea were under the administrative jurisdiction of Qiongzhou, which is present-day Hainan province.

In 1279, China's famous astronomer Guo Shoujing was recorded traveling to the South China Sea and building observatorial facilities. The Governments of the Ming and Qing dynasties both placed the South China Sea under the supervision of naval patrols.

Fourth, China was also the first country to develop the islands in the South China Sea. For centuries, the Chinese have been engaged in fishing, planting and other activities on the islands and in the nearby waters. The traces of this continuous habitation can be seen through archaeological evidence found on many islands. The fact that only Chinese people lived on the Nansha islands is recorded clearly in the book called *The China Sea Pilot* published by the British Navy in 1868.

The aforementioned four "Firsts" are based on substantial and concrete historical evidence. They testify to the fact that the islands of the South China Sea have long been Chinese territory under successive, peaceful and effective administration.

Until the 1970s, it was widely recognised by the international community that islands in the South China Sea belonged to China. Let me give you two examples:

• In 1883, Germany sent military vessels to Xisha and Nansha for surveys. The Government of Guangdong Province protested to the Germans, citing Chinese sovereignty. Germany had to stop the survey and withdrew their team.

• In 1958, the Chinese government issued a declaration on territorial waters applicable to all Chinese territory including the Xisha, the Nansha and other islands in the South China Sea. Vietnam's then prime minister, Phạm Văn Đồng, sent the Chinese Premier Zhou Enlai a diplomatic note which explicitly recognizes that the Xisha and the Nansha belonged to China.

I could give you more examples like these if we had more time.

History speaks for itself as to who owns those islands in the South China Sea. Then how did the disputes arise?

Since the 1970s, some countries have tried to lay claim on the natural resources in the South China Sea. It was then that some nations began to make territorial claims. Vietnam and the Philippines sent troops and illegally occupied some of the islands. That is how the disputes started. Up till today, Vietnam has occupied 29 islands, the Philippines eight and Malaysia five.

In 1982, the United Nations Convention on the Law of the Sea (UNCLOS) was concluded after 9 years of negotiations. With the development of the maritime legal system in the 1980s, countries around the South China Sea gradually made further claims. These include the Exclusive Economic Zone (EEZ), the continental shelf and other maritime rights and interests. The overlapping claims in some cases gave rise to disputes over maritime delimitation. This has caused further complications to the issue of the South China Sea.

It is clear that there are two disputes at the centre of the South China Sea issue:
- One is the territorial dispute caused by illegal occupation of Chinese territory.
- The other is the dispute over maritime delimitation caused by overlapping claims of maritime jurisdiction.

These two disputes are intertwined and have made the issue highly complex. However, one thing is clear: from whichever angle one chooses to look at the issue, China has never been the troublemaker. Quite the opposite, China has been a victim.

Then what is China's position and policy?

For a long time China has exercised a high-level of self-restraint and forbearance when it comes to this issue. We have always approached the disputes in a constructive and responsible manner. If China had not maintained self-restraint, the South China Sea would not have been what it is today.

I would like to summarize China's position through five "commitments":

First, China maintains a strong commitment to peace and stability in the South China Sea.

For years, China has been a staunch force safeguarding and maintaining regional peace and stability. Building friendship and partnership with neighbours has always been a top priority in China's policy towards neighbouring countries.

The Chinese people are a peace-loving nation. Moreover, China's development requires a peaceful environment. In the past three decades it has been peace and stability that have enabled China to industrialise at a speed and scale unprecedented in human history. This advance by China can be largely attributed to the peaceful and stable environment in its neighborhood and beyond. So, China would be the last to wish to see instability in the South China Sea. It means that China would be the first to oppose conflicts in the South China Sea.

Second, China maintains a strong commitment to solving disputes peacefully through friendly consultations and negotiations.

The ultimate resolution of territorial disputes, regardless of their mechanisms or processes, has to be agreed between parties directly involved. The dialogue must be based on negotiations on an equal footing if such a resolution is to be fundamental and lasting. Negotiations and consultations are the most effective way of resolving disputes. This is because they can, to the greatest extent, reflect the principle of sovereign equality and the will and wishes of the parties involved.

Since the People's Republic of China was founded in 1949, we have signed boundary treaties with 12 of our 14 neighbors with land borders. These treaties involved over 20,000 kilometers of boundary. Most of the neighbors are medium-sized or small nations, but none of them has ever complained about the approach of China in the negotiations. These are examples of how China has resolved disputes through face-to-face negotiations with other countries directly involved in the disputes.

The South China Sea disputes do not need to be an exception. Experience shows that only negotiation and consultation could help the parties concerned to constantly build mutual trust, manage problems, narrow differences and advance cooperation. Negotiation and consultation are the most realistic and effective approach to the South China Sea issue.

Third, China maintains a strong commitment to rule-based dispute management.

China and the ASEAN countries signed the "Declaration on the Conduct of Parties in the South China Sea" in 2002 and are now working closely on the drafting of the "Code of Conduct in the South China Sea", or COC for short. Since the start of the COC consultation, there has already been much progress.

China and the ASEAN countries have worked actively to set up the "Senior Officials' Hotline" in response to maritime emergencies, and the "Point-to-Point Hotline Communication" on search-and-rescue. All sides have also agreed to establish "Preventive Measures to Manage Risks at Sea", which will serve as the interim measure prior to the final conclusion of the COC. What has happened over the years testifies to the efficiency of rule-based dispute management.

Fourth, China maintains a strong commitment to the freedom of navigation and over-flight.

China is the biggest littoral state in the South China Sea. The vast majority of China's energy supply and trade pass through the South China Sea. This means China cares more than any other nation about freedom of navigation and over-flight in the South China Sea.

Recently "freedom of navigation" has become a hot subject. Some people talk about "protecting the freedom of navigation".

This creates a dangerous misunderstanding as it implies that the safety and security of ships passing through the region are under immediate threat. The reality is that more than 100,000 vessels pass through the South China Sea every year. None of them has ever run into any problem with freedom of navigation.

If there were a real threat to maritime traffic in the South China Sea then this would immediately result in a leap in shipping insurance rates. This has not happened. The Reuters news agency reported in January that there are no signs of commercial shipping being affected in the South China Sea. The report went on to say that the South China Sea area was not listed as a high risk area by the industry's influential Lloyd's Joint War Committee. This means insurers do not charge additional premiums for vessels operating in the region.

Business people, particularly insurers, are the most responsive to risks. Yet they haven't sensed any threat to freedom of navigation in the South China Sea. This makes me wonder what kind of "freedom of navigation" some people are feeling so eager to protect.

The fact is, "freedom of navigation" has recently been used as an excuse by the United States to flex its military muscles in the South China Sea. The United States sends military jets and warships on close-in reconnaissance missions in the waters and air space adjacent to China's islands and reefs. Such dangerous actions have increased tension and posed a threat to China's sovereignty and security.

For example, just ten days ago, the USS William P. Lawrence, a guided missile destroyer, illegally sailed into the waters near China's Nansha islands. The ship manoeuvered in the sovereign waters of China without the permission of the Chinese government.

Actions such as this, I am afraid, cannot be regarded as protection of "freedom of navigation". They are a manifestation of superior military power and the assertion of maritime dominance. These actions have posed the biggest threat to the real freedom of navigation and the peace and stability in the South China Sea.

To those who claim that they care about freedom of navigation and over-flight, I hope they will act in strict accordance with the international law and respect the sovereignty and security of coastal state.

The actions of the United States should be judged at all times by its approach to international law. If the United States had a serious commitment to maritime law then it would have signed the UNCLOS. China has signed UNCLOS along with most other member nations.

Respect for international law and peaceful dialogue on disputes is crucial to the stability and peace in the South China Sea.

Military provocation and intimidation in the name of "freedom of navigation" is highly dangerous. Such actions directly undermine regional peace and stability.

Turning to my next point, about China's commitment.

Fifth, China maintains strong commitment to win-win cooperation.

China values friendly and cooperative relationships with its neighbours. We have taken the initiative to call on all parties involved to "shelf differences and engage in joint development" in the South China Sea. This provides a useful approach to the resolution of the issue. And it is an approach that takes into consideration the interests of all parties concerned. To put this into practice, China has engaged in a series of cooperative initiatives with relevant countries.

In 2005, oil companies from China, Vietnam and the Philippines signed the "Agreement for Joint Marine Seismic Undertaking in Certain Areas in the South China Sea". This was an effort for the joint development of oil and gas resources in the South China Sea.

In 2011, China announced the establishment of China-ASEAN Maritime Cooperation Fund with a total of 3 billion RMB yuan, or more than £300 million. This was set up to fund maritime cooperation projects.

Two years ago, China put forward the initiative of the 21st century Maritime Silk Road. This demonstrated the mutual benefits which the ASEAN countries can enjoy by becoming regional hubs of development. These measures and initiatives are evidence of China's efforts and good faith in seeking further and deeper maritime cooperation with its neighbours.

The aforesaid five "Commitments" constitute China's position on the South China Sea. They demonstrate China's sincerity:

- Resolving the issues.
- Securing the regional peace and stability.
- And promoting the common development in neighboring areas.

Recently a number of hot issues have cropped up with regard to the South China Sea. In turn I will share with you my views.

The first one is about the "arbitration"

The reference to the Arbitral Tribunal was unilaterally initiated by the Philippines.

Many media reports are creating misunderstanding by not explaining clearly the circumstances of the "arbitration".

A crucial point is that the Tribunal was not a permanent arbitration body nor was it a court of law.

For any arbitration to work it requires the proactive participation and agreement of both sides. Another critical point is that China refused to participate in the arbitration. From the very start of the reference from the Philippines for the arbitration China made it clear this was not an acceptable way to resolve the dispute.

Some media and politicians are now ramping up this topic of arbitration. They are erroneously making the following claims:

• If China does not accept the ruling of the arbitration panel it will be breaking international law.

• It would be seen as "violating the international law" and "undermining the rule-based international system".

These claims are completely wrong.

China's rejection of the arbitration and its non-participation in the arbitral process is an act of exercising its legitimate rights empowered by the international law.

By contrast, it is the Philippines who is challenging the legal and moral bottom line of the international community because the arbitration is totally unreasonable, unfair and illegal.

My second point about the arbitration is that it was unreasonable.

It was not reasonable because the Philippines went against its commitment to China and other ASEAN countries. Let me briefly summarise the logic of this point. China and the Philippines reached a number of bilateral agreements long ago on resolving disputes through bilateral negotiations. In the Declaration of Conduct reached between China and Philippines and other ASEAN countries, it is clearly stipulated that "the parties concerned undertake to resolve their territorial and jurisdictional disputes by peaceful means."

In 2011, the Philippines issued a joint statement with China to reaffirm its commitment to negotiations and consultations. However, a year later, it suddenly went back on its clearly written commitment. Without notifying China, or even asking for consent from China, the Philippines unilaterally initiated the arbitration against China. *Pacta sunt servanda* is a basic rule in international relations. This is the bottom line of morality that every country must strictly observe. To put it simply, the Philippines has reneged on its words and deeds.

Another point is that the arbitration was unfair.

It was unfair because the islands in the arbitration case have been the sovereign property of China since ancient times. What the Philippines is doing is robbing its neighbour and asking the court to rule in its favour over the ownership of the booty. No one in the world should find this reasonable.

Here in Britain, there is always an emphasis on a "rule-based international system". But if rules can be abused, as they are in the Philippine arbitration, what should we expect from such rules and order?

The arbitration is illegal for three apparent reasons:

First, the UNCLOS stipulates that State Parties have the right to settle a dispute by any peaceful means of their own choice. The aforementioned arbitration was unilaterally forced ahead by the Philippines, who did not seek consent from China. This violates China's legitimate right under the international law.

Second the UNCLOS also states:

"If the States Parties have agreed to seek settlement of the dispute by a peaceful means of their own choice, the (arbitration) procedures apply only where no settlement has been reached by recourse to such means and the agreement between the parties does not exclude any further procedure."

China has always been open to bilateral means and clearly bilateral means between China and the Philippines has not been exhausted.

Third, the UNCLOS states:

"When a dispute arises between State Parties concerning the interpretation or application of this Convention, the parties to the dispute shall proceed expeditiously to an exchange of views regarding its settlement by negotiation or other peaceful means."

However, the Philippines has never had any consultations with China. Its unilateral initiation of the arbitration is an overt violation of law.

It should also be noted, for the record, that both China and the Philippines signed and ratified the UNCLOS. Compared with what the Philippines did, China has truly implemented and championed the international law.

The 15 submissions made by the Philippines concern territorial sovereignty and maritime delimitation. The UNCLOS has no jurisdiction over issues related to sovereignty.

As for maritime delimitation, China made a declaration in 2006 in accordance with Article 298 of the UNCLOS. This made it very clear China would exclude disputes on maritime delimitation from compulsory arbitration. So China has exercised its legitimate rights conferred by the UNCLOS. China's action complies with the international law.

It should be noted that over 30 other countries, including the UK, have made similar declarations on the same principle of exclusion. These declarations have constituted an inseparable part of the UNCLOS. The reasonable and legitimate appeals and concerns of these countries should be considered. If the Philippines' arbitration case became a convention to be followed, then any of these 30 countries could be dragged into arbitration without prior notice. This would be a serious damage to state sovereignty, international order and the dignity and authority of international law.

There has been speculation in the media that the Tribunal may soon make public its report on the so-called "arbitration" triggered by the Philippines.

China is not hiding from any outcome. China has been totally consistent in its respect for international law. What China refuses to do is participate, accept, recognize or implement any arbitration that has no legitimacy in upholding international law.

The Tribunal is running a risk of undermining its authority and legitimacy. The Tribunal has created a situation where the arbitration is clearly unreasonable, unfair and illegal. Despite this the Tribunal has still chosen to proceed with the arbitration with only the Philippines participating. This raises grave concern about the Tribunal's impartiality and legitimacy. It also calls into question the political intention behind the arbitration. The arbitration in essence is a political initiative under the cloak of law. China will never accept the result whatever comes from the Tribunal.

Although China rejects the arbitration, the door to bilateral negotiation remains open. China and the Philippines are close neighbors. The Chinese and the Philippine peoples have had a long tradition of friendly ties. The Philippines has just elected a new President. We hope that the new Philippine government will work with China on a proper settlement of differences and bring the situation in the South China Sea back on track following the principles established by the UNCLOS and international law.

Another issue I want to talk about is the developments on China's islands in the South China Sea.

Development on some of the Nansha islands began a few years ago. The building efforts will improve the living conditions on the islands and will serve mainly civilian purposes. This includes providing necessary and emergency public services to China and to other countries in and from outside the region. The facilities built include lighthouses, maritime communication facilities, search-and-rescue facilities and medical centers. They will enable China to better fulfill its international responsibility and obligations, such as maritime search-and-rescue, disaster prevention and relief, scientific maritime research, meteorological observation, eco-environmental protection, navigation safety and fishing services.

There are necessary defence facilities deployed according to Chinese security assessments. Such deployment on China's own islands falls within the right of self-protection that every sovereign state is entitled to under international law.

In January 2016, according to Reuters news agency, "some shipowners believe a greater Chinese presence could actually improve safety."

The Reuters report quoted ship owners saying: "If China is to base search-and-rescue assets on the (disputed) islands then there would potentially be faster response times, improving the chances of rescue and survival."

Earlier I described the crucial importance to international trade of the safe and free of navigation for ships through the South China Sea. Reasonable observers would then applaud China's investment and actions to make this critical international artery safer.

However, some people complain about the scale and speed of the building efforts. I want to remind these people that scale and speed are not the benchmark for right and wrong. The scale and speed of China's building efforts match China's international responsibility in the South China Sea. Why would China sit on its hands and refrain from doing the right things simply because of its size?

Some others accuse China of "changing the status quo". I would like to ask this question: What is the "status quo"?

China is undertaking construction work on its own islands. China is not changing any "status quo".

And I also like to ask those who are so keen on not "changing the status quo": Why are they silent when some countries illegally occupy China's islands and go in for large-scale construction activities there?

The third issue is the so called "militarisation" of the South China Sea.

Recently the "militarisation" has been hyped up and the United States shouts the loudest. However, it is not difficult to see who is "militarising" the South China Sea.

More than half of the US military force is deployed in Asia-Pacific. Yet, this is a region that has been largely peaceful and stable for many years.

In addition to this huge military force, the USA, together with its allies in the region, frequently flexes its military muscles. This is shown with the conduct of highly-targeted military drills. Then there are the military jets and warships on in-close reconnaissance missions in the waters and air space adjacent to China's islands and reefs. It is these provocative and hostile actions that have raised the tensions in the South China Sea. These acts have sent wrong signals to the Philippines and others who have recklessly deployed military facilities on their illegally occupied islands.

The answer to the question of who is "militarising" the South China Sea is nothing but self-evident. Going forward it is the hope of China that the United States:

- Will act as a big country with responsibility.
- Be prudent in what it says or does on this complicated issue.
- Commit to and respect widely agreed international law, such as the UNCLOS.
- And work with China to safeguard stability and peace.

Therefore, to solve the "militarisation" issue, the United States needs to:

- First of all, stop its dangerous provocations that challenge China's sovereignty and security.
- Secondly, stop being provocative with its "militarisation".
- And thirdly, take concrete steps to facilitate peace and stability in the region.

Ladies and Gentlemen,

Complicated and sensitive as the South China Sea issue is, the region has maintained overall stability thanks to the joint efforts of China and its neighbours. China will, as it grows in strength, make greater contribution to the stability and prosperity of the South China Sea region. As President Xi Jinping once said, China pursues maritime capability through peace, development and win-win cooperation.

What China has achieved today can be largely attributed to its path of peaceful development. And China will keep to this path.

Looking into the future:

- China is confident and capable of resolving disputes through negotiations and consultations.
- China has shown a steadfast commitment to upholding international law.
- China has been steadfast in safeguarding peace and stability of the South China Sea through cooperation.

- China is ready to join hands with other countries to create a peaceful resolution.
- And China can always be counted on to build the South China Sea into a sea of peace, a sea of friendship and a sea of cooperation.

Thank you.

Now I am pleased to take your questions.

KPMG: Sir, I just want you to clarify one point. You said that the US warships' transiting near the islands was illegal and is not covered by the right of innocent passage set out in the UNCLOS, which does say warships can go through other people's territorial waters provided certain conditions are maintained.

Liu Xiaoming: I think the US abused the so-called right of "innocent passage." They didn't show respect for China's sovereignty. They did not notify China first of all. And they didn't seek to get permission from China. So that is totally against international law and international practices.

LSE: Thank you for sharing your insights. Towards the end of your presentation, you hinted at the tension between the US and China. It seems to me that the tensions between the Philippines and China, between the Vietnamese and China could be managed. At the systematic level, as you can see, the US is seen as the system manager, which is to maintain the status quo, and China has been described for over a decade in analysis by semi-official documentations as the "near peer rival". It seems that the fundamental thing is managing the tensions between the US and China. What is China doing to make the transition of the relations between China and US peaceful, calm and stable?

Liu Xiaoming: As I said in my presentation, from the very beginning, China has not been a trouble-maker. Instead, China is a victim in all this. I hope I made myself clear. Before the so-called "rebalancing strategy" of the US, the South China Sea and the region had been peaceful. China and the neighboring countries including the Philippines and Vietnam have been talking to each other. We have the "Declaration of Conduct" and we have managed our differences effectively. This dispute has been there for 30 years. The area has been quiet and stable. But when it comes to the so-called US "rebalancing" strategy in 2009, I think some countries became emboldened and they thought they had the US behind them. The Philippines changed their approach and submitted the so-called "baseline". The Vietnamese also changed their approach. The Philippines refused to talk to us and then they unilaterally went in for the so-called "arbitration". There are many ways to resolve disputes. According to the UNCLOS, arbitration is only supplementary, while the main method for resolving disputes is peaceful negotiations and consultations between member states. Yet the Philippines resorted to the so-called supplementary measures which are not the main course. I think they thought they had the support of the US.

China wants to have good relations with the US. There is no doubt about it. Over half of my diplomatic career has been devoted to working for a better relationship between China and the US. I was posted twice in Washington DC. We want to have good relations. We also know that without a good relationship between China and the US, there will be no peace or prosperity in the Asia-Pacific region. So we tried very hard and we tried to engage them in consultations. I'm very pleased to see that currently the Security Consultation is right now taking place in Washington DC. The Deputy Minister of Foreign Affairs of China is talking to US Deputy Secretary of State. We do have these channels. But the important thing is that the Americans should change the stereotypical mindset of regarding China as a threat. I think that is the problem, that they have been haunted by the fear that China would someday take their place as the leader of the world. That is not China's dream. China's dream is to revitalize the Chinese nation. We know what we are doing and we know the tremendous challenges ahead of us. We have 1.3 billion people to take care of. After my tour in Egypt, I was seconded to Gansu, one of the western provinces in China, as an assistant governor. I know how poor that area is. I know there are challenges and tremendous tasks for China to achieve its modernization. China is the last country who wants to have bad relations with the US. We are not interested in becoming a superpower. The UK used to be a superpower. A superpower should take on a lot of responsibilities. Our primary task is to achieve development and to take good care of our people.

IISS: I just want your thoughts on the recent incident that the Pentagon went on record to say yesterday that China made an "unsafe" intercept by sending two aircrafts to make unsafe intercept, to US EP-3 reconnaissance aircraft. In your opinion, is this US antagonism?

Liu Xiaoming: I think it is a dangerous move on the US part. The Americans are trying to challenge China's sovereignty over these reefs. That is a very dangerous move. They do it under the cloak of the so-called "freedom of navigation". We know the ocean is wide enough for the military aircraft and vessels to have freedom of passage. But they made a close reconnaissance. They want to challenge China's defence capabilities. So this is a very dangerous move. The case you mentioned in fact has been refuted by the spokesman of the Chinese Foreign Ministry. China has every reason to defend its sovereignty. Chinese aircraft wanted to find out what the American aircraft wanted to do. But they did it in a very professional way. They moved within safe boundaries. We've tried to avoid anything unexpected happening, especially conflict. But if the Americans keep on doing this, I think they will be walking into very dangerous waters.

BBC: I have two questions. Ambassador, you criticized the Court of Arbitration. I have heard Chinese officials do that before, but I can't remember when, saying that it wouldn't accept the result. Can you confirm that that is what you are saying: you are not going to accept the results of the rulings of this court regardless of what they are? Another related question, you seem to be linking the tribunal's rulings with sovereignty. It's my understanding that it's got nothing to do with sovereignty. They are merely going to rule on the status of reefs, islands, rocks, islets in the South China Sea. You've already said that China has been planting and fishing on these islands for many centuries. Why do you then reject that narrow definition they are looking at? Because that for sure will help your case. If you are certain and you see to it that your claims are right, why don't you accept their results?

Liu Xiaoming: Let me tell you why. As for your first question, the arbitration tribunal you refer to from the very start is illegal. How could you expect an illegal tribunal to result in a good case? We have had no obligation at all, from the very beginning. We think the tribunal itself is a violation of the UNCLOS and international law.

BBC: What are the obligations that you are not going to accept?

Liu Xiaoming: We are not obligated at all by this arbitration. I can say in very clear-cut terms: no matter what decision the arbitration is going to make, it makes no difference to China's sovereignty over these islands, and is not binding at all as it is illegal and unfair as I said clearly in my presentation. With regard to what decision will the arbitration make, I already gave the example. When some people rob you and put their booty from the robbery before a court, asking the judge to make a decision, whether on ownership or status of this booty, as long as the judge handles this case, it has an impact on the ownership and on the sovereignty. The Philippines tried to divert the attention on this case. They tried to wrap up the case under the cloak of law. Of the first 15 submissions, 8 have been rejected because the tribunal is concerned about getting involved in the dispute. That is too obvious for them to be seen to violate the UNCLOS. Despite the change in tactics, it doesn't change the essence of this case. So from the very beginning, this case has been about sovereignty and delimitation. It is beyond the authority and jurisdiction of arbitration, even by the UNCLOS. The establishment of the arbitration tribunal itself is a violation of the UNCLOS. China is fighting this case according to international law. It is fighting this case in order to protect the international law.

LSE: I'd like to ask your view on US economic narrative in the South China Sea. Where do you think it stands now? On the security side, Ashton Carter and others are quite proactive in escalating their rhetoric. But on the economic side, the American narrative, the TPP, now stands in jeopardy. Whether or not it will be ratified either before or after the change in presidency is very much up in the air. China's successful narrative in Southeast Asia has been primarily economic. Do you see the change in the presidency as working toward China's continuing successful conversation with Southeast Asia?

Liu Xiaoming: Of course we will watch US presidential election very closely and with great interest. No one can predict the outcome of the election. But I would say, we are ready to deal with whoever is elected by the American people, and whoever is the new occupant of the Oval Office. We put more emphasis on what they will do after the election. I hope the new administration will set store by and bear in mind the interest of China-US relations. China stands ready to work with the US to move China-US relations forward.

Director Inkster (Moderator): Thank you very much. I'm afraid we have run out

有问必答
No Question Unanswered

of time so I have to draw a halt to the proceedings here. Let me make one brief observation, which is, we found in the IISS now that the strategic salience of China is such that it is taking an increasing amount of our time. I think we concluded recently that one in every three of our books has China as a topic, which I think tells you something. I'd like to invite all of you to join me again in thanking Ambassador Liu for the very detailed and comprehensive speech.

中国不接受、不承认南海仲裁庭裁决结果
—— 关于南海仲裁庭裁决结果的中外记者会

（2016年7月19日，中国驻英国大使馆）

刘晓明： 各位记者，大家上午好。

欢迎出席中国驻英国大使馆举办的中外记者会。今天的记者会只有一个主题，就是解读中国对所谓南海仲裁庭裁决结果的政策立场。7月12日，菲律宾南海仲裁庭公布了所谓裁决结果，中国政府第一时间重申了不接受、不承认的严正立场。中国国家主席习近平强调，南海诸岛自古以来就是中国领土。中国在南海的领土主权和海洋权益在任何情况下不受所谓菲律宾南海仲裁案裁决的影响。中国不接受任何基于该仲裁裁决的主张和行动。中国坚定致力于维护南海和平稳定，致力于同直接有关的当事国在尊重历史事实的基础上，根据国际法，通过谈判协商和平解决有关争议。为进一步宣示中国的政策主张，中国政府发表了《中华人民共和国政府关于在南海的领土主权和海洋权益的声明》，中国外交部发表了《中华人民共和国外交部关于应菲律宾共和国请求建立的南海仲裁案仲裁庭所作裁决的声明》，中国国务院新闻办发表了《中国坚持通过谈判解决中国与菲律宾在南海的有关争议》的白皮书。国务委员杨洁篪接受专访，外交部部长王毅发表谈话，外交部副部长刘振民介绍情况，对声明和白皮书进行深入解读。上述声明和白皮书全面、清晰、权威地阐述了中国的政策主张。在此，

我愿向各位做简要介绍。

《中华人民共和国政府关于在南海的领土主权和海洋权益的声明》重点是重申中国在南海的领土主权和海洋权益，强调中国最早发现、命名和开发利用南海诸岛及相关海域，最早并持续、和平、有效地对南海诸岛及相关海域行使主权和管辖，明确指出中国在南海的领土主权和海洋权益包括中国对南海诸岛拥有主权；中国南海诸岛拥有内水、领海、毗连区、专属经济区和大陆架；中国在南海拥有历史性权利。强调中国一向坚决反对一些国家对中国南沙群岛部分岛礁的非法侵占及在中国相关管辖海域的侵权行为。同时指出中国愿继续与直接有关当事国通过谈判协商和平解决争议，共同维护南海和平稳定，维护南海国际航运通道的安全和畅通。

《中华人民共和国外交部关于应菲律宾共和国请求建立的南海仲裁案仲裁庭所作裁决的声明》重点指出菲律宾提起仲裁事项超出《联合国海洋法公约》管辖范围，侵犯中国作为《公约》缔约国享有的自主选择争端解决程序和方式的权利，违反中菲两国以及中国与东盟国家通过谈判解决南海有关争议的协议与承诺，揭露仲裁庭扩权、越权、滥用仲裁程序的本质，强调该裁决是无效的，没有拘束力，中国不接受、不承认。

《中国坚持通过谈判解决中国与菲律宾在南海的有关争议》的白皮书，全面阐述中国对南海诸岛主权的历史形成过程以及中国维护在南海的领土主权和海洋权益的努力，展现中菲南海争议来龙去脉，溯本清源，以正视听。同时重申中方坚持通过谈判协商解决争议，强调只有谈判取得的成果才更容易获得当事国人民的理解和支持，才能够得到有效实施，才具有持久生命力。正如杨洁篪国务委员在接受媒体专访时指出的，只要中菲都坚持《南海各方行为宣言》的原则和精神，通过对话协商妥善处理分歧，坚持互利友好合作，就一定能为两国关系开辟美好未来。

为了便于各位记者全面深入了解中方主张，我们准备了中方声明、白皮书、专访和谈话的中英文版本，欢迎大家会后领取。

下面我愿意回答各位的提问。

《中国日报》：我们注意到，习近平主席表示中国致力于通过直接谈判解决有关争议，但他同时表示，中国在南海的领土主权和海洋权益在任何情况下不受所谓菲律宾南海仲裁案裁决的影响。请问，中国愿在哪些领域开展谈判？

刘晓明：习主席阐述的是中国一贯的政策立场。在南海问题上，中方的立场是明确的、一贯的。我们对包括南沙群岛在内的南海诸岛拥有主权，同时我们也注意到存在争议，因此我们主张将争议搁置起来，着手共同开发。中方有12个字："主权在我，搁置争议，共同开发。"中国不会就主权问题进行谈判，但我们意识到争议的存在，始终坚持通过谈判协商和平解决争议。

新华社：我的问题是关于英国外交部前副法律顾问霍默斯雷发表的一份法律研究报告。他在报告中指出，仲裁庭的观点"不能令人信服"，仲裁庭的裁决"将撼动国际关系的整体稳定"，因为该裁决允许菲律宾放弃其在正式法律文件，如《南海各方行为宣言》中的立场。你能谈谈对霍默斯雷观点的看法吗？你认为他的观点正确吗？

刘晓明： 我同意这个观点。中方坚决反对仲裁庭的裁决，该裁决开了一个"恶例"。有人认为裁决书是废纸一张，也有人认为应当束之高阁。我是学国际法的，我看这份判决只能作为国际法教学的反面教材，作为"恶例"收录到历史书里。这份裁决在多个方面违反了国际法。首先，它违反了《公约》的宗旨。《公约》旨在维护国际海洋和国家间关系的和平与稳定。但仲裁庭不但背离《公约》的宗旨，还加剧了国家间的紧张关系。仲裁庭不仅否定了谈判解决的外交渠道，而且否定了《南海各方行为宣言》的法律地位，而《南海各方行为宣言》是中国和东盟十国达成的一份庄严的官方文件。因此这份裁决根本不能达到和平解决争议的目的。相反，它给相关国家间的紧张关系火上浇油，给地区形势火上浇油。正如我在开场白中所说，中方不承认、不接受裁决，裁决没有拘束力。没有一个国家会把这份裁决当真，任何国家都不应在所谓裁决的基础上提出新的主张。裁决是非法的，没有任何法律地位。如果有人在裁决基础上提出新的主张，这将导致新的违法行为，将进一步损害地区和平与稳定。

普罗派乐卫视： 我来自普罗派乐卫视。你认为，菲律宾新一届政府是否暗示中菲关系将转圜？

刘晓明： 我们当然期望如此。杜特尔特总统就职后，我们听到了一些积极的表态，比如他希望中菲双边关系保持友好，希望中菲能通过双边谈判解决有关争议等。事实上，这也是我们多年来一直努力的方向。因此中方从一开始就强烈反对这个强加的仲裁。我们认为仲裁无助于问题的解决，只有谈判才是解决问题的唯一出路。我们愿意同菲律宾新一届政府开展合作，也期待菲律宾新政府能够采取进一步的行动。中国有句老话叫作"听其言，观其行"。我们希望通过对话协商妥善处理分歧，使两国关系回到正确的轨道上。中菲两国作为隔海相望的近邻，有着上千年友好交往历史，我们深信这些争议不应影响两国保持友好关系，也希望杜特尔特总统领导的新一届政府为中菲关系带来新的气象。

《金融时报》：我希望能请你解释一个关于仲裁庭的问题。据我所知，中方反对该仲裁庭主要有两项理由：第一，仲裁应由当事国双方同意后才能提出；第二，仲裁庭对菲律宾提出的仲裁事项没有管辖权。但是《公约》有两项条款似乎与中方上述立场相悖。一是《公约》第286条指出，事关《公约》的解释或适用问题可由任意争端一方提出仲裁，无须双方共同提出。二是《公约》第288条指出，仲裁庭自己有权决定是否有管辖权。请问中方对此有何看法？

刘晓明：关于《联合国海洋法公约》第288条和286条，中方有不同解读。中方反对仲裁庭的理由不仅限于你提到的两项。我希望你能认真研读《中华人民共和国政府关于在南海的领土主权和海洋权益的声明》《中华人民共和国外交部关于应菲律宾共和国请求建立的南海仲裁案仲裁庭所作裁决的声明》《中国坚持通过谈判解决中国与菲律宾在南海的有关争议》白皮书。我认为菲律宾南海仲裁案至少从八个方面违反了国际法。

第一，它违反了《联合国海洋法公约》对领土主权争端没有管辖权的规定。尽管南海仲裁案被菲律宾精心包装成一个关于解释公约的技术性案件，但其实质是关于领土主权争端。从仲裁庭的裁决过程和结果看，任何人都能得出结论，此案事关中国在南海领土主权。

第二，它违反了中国做出的排除性声明。中国早已声明将有关海洋划界、历史性海湾和历史性权利、军事和执法等活动排除出《公约》强制争端解决程序，其他30多个国家也做出了类似声明。这些排除性声明被视为是《公约》不可分割的一部分，而仲裁庭裁决显然与海洋划界有关。这一裁决证明仲裁庭肆意扩权，侵犯了中国根据排除性声明所享有的合法权益。《公约》缔约国之所以做出排除性声明，是因为预见到各国有可能就海洋划界问题产生争端。如果此类声明被拒绝，将会构成不良先例，造成严重后果。今天是中国，试问明天会是哪个国家？

第三，它违背了中国与菲律宾达成的双边协议。菲律宾已与中国就如何通过外交谈判解决争端达成了一系列协议，包括双边签署的文件、宣言和协议。

第四，它违背了中国与东盟国家签署的《南海各方行为宣言》。该宣言是国际法的一部分，各方承诺通过友好磋商和谈判，维护南海地区和平稳定。宣言的作用十分重要，一直为中国和东盟国家所尊重并遵守。

第五，仲裁旨在否定中国对南海有关岛礁的主权，否定中国包括断续线在内的历史性权利，挑战了《联合国宪章》关于维护国家主权、独立和领土完整的基本准则，因此严重违反了国际法。

第六，仲裁庭曲解《公约》第286条，非法受理菲律宾单方提出的仲裁案，却否定了中国作为《公约》缔约国自主选择争端解决方式的权利。

第七，仲裁庭对《公约》断章取义，破坏了《公约》的完整性和严肃性，树立了"坏典型"。

第八，仲裁背离了《公约》促进争端和平解决的初衷。相反，它加剧了地区局势紧张。

回到你刚才所提的两个条款。仲裁庭虽然可以自行对管辖权做出解释，但并不意味着它可以不顾事实乱做解释。南海仲裁案仲裁庭只看到《公约》赋予的权利，却看不到应当履行的义务，包括对《公约》管辖权的尊重，对中国就海洋划界所做排除性声明的尊重，对中国主张通过双边外交谈判解决争议的立场及为之做出努力的尊重，对中国与东盟十国达成的《南海各方行为宣言》的尊重，等等。所以，在管辖权问题上，仲裁庭没有绝对权力，更没有不履行《公约》规定义务的权力。

《人民日报》： 我有两个问题。第一个问题是，仲裁案对中菲关系有何影响？今后中菲关系将如何发展？第二个问题是，就我们所知，过去许多个世纪，甚至在过去数十年，南海是非常和平、安宁的海域。但如今南海局势越来越复杂，成为越来越受关注的热点。你认为其原因是什么？

刘晓明： 首先，仲裁结果不会对中国在南海的领土主权和海洋权益产生任何影响，也没有任何拘束力，它是非法的，不能作为未来谈判的基础。如果菲律宾同意我们的意见，我想我们可以很快恢复双边谈判。如果菲律宾将裁决作为谈判的基础，那是行不通的。

我希望地区国家站在中国的一边。已经有一些国家表示支持中国的立场，一些国家对裁决所产生的后果表示担忧。怎样做最符合中国和东盟国家的利益？怎样做最有利于该地区的和平与稳定？我希望中国和东盟国家能够达成共识。我们注意到菲律宾新政府的一些积极表态，但还不清楚他们就裁决结果持什么立场。可以明确的是，我们不会执行这个裁决。希望有关方面不要借所谓仲裁结果采取进一步的非法行动，使本已紧张的局势进一步升级。那是我们所不想看到的。

关于第二个问题，在20世纪70年代前，没有人对中国南海主权提出挑战。断续线受到普遍承认，美国、英国、法国、苏联和许多其他国家印制的官方地图都标明了断续线。随着70年代南海发现了石油和天然气，一些地区国家趁机非法侵占南海岛礁。我们就这些非法侵占问题向有关国家提出了强烈抗议。但不幸的是，当时中国正在进行"文化大革命"，因为内乱，中国无暇顾及维护对这些岛屿的主权。

最近几年南海发生的事和美国所谓的亚太再平衡战略有关。尽管我们和菲律宾、越南、马来西亚等一些邻国之间存在一些问题，但我们之间仍然保持着双边沟通的渠道。中国和越南完成了北部湾海上划界。我们与包括菲律宾在内的地区国家签署三方联合海洋地震工作协议。但美国所谓的亚太再平衡战略提出后，这些项目中断了。有美国撑腰，这些国家更大胆地向中国提出挑战。现在美国不再满足于幕后操纵，而是跳到台前，派出战舰和飞机到中国南沙群岛有关岛礁邻近海、空域抵近侦察，挑战中国的主权。这些行为造成了局势紧张。我们希望南海消除紧张局势，希望和美国在内的有关国家一道努力，使南海成为和平之海、合作之海、友谊之海。这是中国国家领导人一再强调和重申的，是中国对该地区和平与稳定的承诺。

中国国际广播电台： 海牙仲裁庭是《公约》框架下设的法律机构。中国宣称"不接受""不承认"该仲裁庭裁决，你做何解释？中国"不接受""不承认"仲裁庭裁决，究竟意味着什么？是否意味着中国将不会就此做出任何反应？

刘晓明： 首先，我要纠正一下这个仲裁庭的性质。该仲裁庭不是国际法院的一部分，与联合国没有关系，甚至也与常设仲裁法院（PCA）关系不大。该仲裁庭是应菲律宾政府请求为本次仲裁案临时组建的，据我所知，它与常设仲裁法院唯一的关系，就是使用了后者的场地，并且借用了其秘书处的一些人员，仅此而已。它的法律基础十分薄弱。

我愿进一步介绍一下这个仲裁庭的组成。这个仲裁庭由5名仲裁员组成，除了菲律宾自己指定的仲裁员外，其他4名仲裁员都是由国际海洋法法庭时任庭长、日本籍法官柳井俊二指定的，此人曾任日本驻美国大使。我对其政治动机非常怀疑。他是日本首相安倍晋三的政策顾问，在协助安倍修改和平宪法、解禁集体自卫权、挑战"二战"后国际秩序等方面起了很大作用。我认为本次仲裁案为他再次挑战战后国际秩序提供了新的机会。

中国拥有南海诸岛主权的历史可追溯至2000多年前。日本在"二战"期间曾非法侵占中国南海诸岛。"二战"结束后，日本根据《开罗宣言》和《波茨坦公告》的规定，将其归还中国。如果任由该仲裁庭否定《南海各方行为宣言》，这将鼓励其他南海国家争相效仿，并引发一系列类似事件。或许终有一天，他们会宣布《开罗宣言》和《波茨坦公告》也没有法律依据。我不知道届时事态将如何演变。

根据《开罗宣言》，日本必须归还所窃取的所有中国领土和岛屿，其中包括南海诸岛。事实上，当年中国政府的军队正是乘坐美国军舰收复了南海诸岛。仲裁庭此次试图将中国南沙群岛太平岛定性为"岩礁"而不是"岛"，暴露出其提起仲裁的目的是企图否定中国对南沙群岛的主权及相关海洋权益，这是违反国际法的，完全不能接受的，受到了台湾海峡两岸中国同胞的一致强烈谴责。

中国不参与南海仲裁，是因为从第一天起，我们就坚信这是一场政治闹剧。只要你对仲裁庭的组成及其仲裁背后的政治动机有所了解，就会立即判断出其结果会是什么。我们清楚这场闹剧不会有任何结果，自然也没有兴趣参与其中。仲裁庭的裁决没有法律拘束力，中国决不会接受该仲裁裁决，并且希望其他国家不会执行所谓的裁决。你怎么能指望如此毫无公信力、不具合法性的仲裁庭，能做出有公信力的裁决？如果该裁决得到执行，势将对地区形势造成进一步破坏。

《每日电讯报》：许多不是南海争端当事方的人士指出，中国是在有选择性地遵守国际法。中国声称将和平崛起，中国既然能遵守其他领域的国际法，是否在南海问题上也应遵守国际法？有观点认为是美国鼓励菲律宾提出南海仲裁案，你如何看待美国在南海争端中扮演的角色？

刘晓明： 我不同意你关于中国有选择性地遵守国际法的看法。中方立场有坚实的法律基础。正如我刚才谈到，南海仲裁庭在八个方面违反了国际法。而中国完全遵守《公约》规定。中国坚定遵守双边达成的协议，包括中菲之间曾达成的协议。中国同样致力于遵守与东盟国家达成的《南海各方行为宣言》。中国严格遵守国际法，依照国际法行事。国际法的基础之一是《联合国宪章》，中国作为联合国安理会常任理事国，肩负维护宪章的重要责任。这是毫无疑问的。

关于美国，我认为应给美国在南海问题上的所作所为画上一个"大问号"。首先，美国迄未批准《公约》，不断违反《公约》的条款，但却自诩为所谓的《公约》"守护者"。如果美国真的如此热爱《公约》，为什么不立即批准《公约》？这是因为美国担心《公约》可能会妨碍他们所谓"航行和飞越自由"。美国要的是完全不受国际法限制为所欲为的权利。其次，南海仲裁案完全是政治操纵的产物。这是美国战略的一部分。一方面，美国不断派军舰和军机抵近中国领土。另一方面，美国希望利用针对中国的南海仲裁案，借此在外交上侮辱中国，损害中国的国际形象，并为挑战中国主权寻找法律基础。但美国的上述图谋是注定会失败的，因为其所作所为从一开始就没有法律基础，而南海仲裁案已完全演变成为一场政治闹剧。迄今为止，我们没有听到多少国家支持仲裁庭的裁决，与此相反，已有70多个国家、290个政党和组织表达了支持中国通过外交谈判解决争端的立场。我们希望仲裁案结束后，常识和理性终将占据上风，相关沿岸国能够重返谈判桌，接受中国提出的"搁置争议，共同开发"倡议，进行认真严肃的外交谈判。这样做符合有关各方的共同利益。中国希望美方能切实尊重中方的关切和权利。美国在亚太地区有利益，但是不能为维护自身利益而损害他国的正当合法权益。中国和邻国在南海地区是命运共同体。中国最不希望看到南海地区动荡。南海是重要的国际航运通道，中国将继续确保该地区的和平稳定，并维护航行及飞越自由。

《欧洲时报》：有人认为南海争端是中国历史性权利与美国基于规则的国际秩序观之间的冲突。你如何看待这个问题？你认为争端是否将长期化？你提到谈判是解决争端的唯一途径。中方是否已经开始这方面的准备？

刘晓明：首先回答你的第一个问题，我们谈历史性权利，这是中方在长期历史过程中形成的。有人称，中方已经抛弃了"韬光养晦"的战略，不再单纯关注经济发展，正在谋求更多权利。这种看法是不正确的。我们捍卫的是中方自古以来拥有的领土主权。断续线是1948年中国政府正式公布的，并且得到国际社会的承认，不是创设新的权利。直到南海地区发现了资源才引发一些国家竞相侵占中国的岛礁。中国过去没有，现在和将来也不会寻求属于自己的领土主权以外的东西。正如我在接受路透社采访中指出的，别人的领土，我们一寸都不要。我们对别人的领土不感兴趣，也不羡慕，但我们珍视、捍卫自己的领土。中国曾经失去太多领土，当时中国积贫积弱，遭受外强入侵，被迫接受割地赔款等不平等条约。所以，捍卫国家主权权益是中国与生俱来的基因决定的。我们希望国际社会能尊重中国拥有的历史性权利。

20世纪70年代以前，美国是承认中方历史性权利的，许多历史、法律和国际法文件均对此予以确认。但是，现在情况变了。他们有新的盟友，新的利益。我曾在《世界邮报》撰文谈到，"超级大国历来是来了又走，走了又来"。应当知道，邻国比超级大国更重要。邻国无法选择，必须相处。

中国无意挑战美国的地位，但也不能接受不平等的国际秩序。中国尊重现有国际秩序，中国也是这一秩序的受益者。中国多次重申愿与国际社会合作，共同维护战后国际秩序。我们无意改变现有秩序，无意"重起炉灶"。但今天世界发生了很大变化，需要与时俱进，需要改革过时的国际秩序，特别是要适应发展中国家的需求。中国也是发展中国家的一员。

习近平主席指出，宽广的太平洋有足够空间容纳中美两个大国。我们希望中美携手合作，而不是走向对抗。我们希望美国认识到中国无意挑战其地位。我们承认，美国虽然不是域内国家，但在地区拥有经济和安全利益。我们尊重美国的利益，也希望美国尊重中国的利益。中美两个太平洋大国可以携手合作，共同维护地区和平与稳定。

谢谢各位出席今天的记者会。我们下次再见。

China Does Not Accept or Recognize the Award
—— A Press Conference on the Award of the South China Sea Arbitration

(19th July 2016, Chinese Embassy in the UK)

Liu Xiaoming: Ladies and Gentlemen:

Good morning. Welcome to the Chinese Embassy. Today's press conference will focus on one subject. That is China's position on the South China Sea arbitration ruling.

On 12th July, the so-called tribunal for the South China Sea arbitration unilaterally initiated by the Philippines announced its award. The Chinese government immediately reaffirmed its solemn position that China does not accept or recognize the award.

Chinese President Xi Jinping stressed the following points:

The relevant islands and reefs in the South China Sea have been the territory of China since ancient times.

China's territorial sovereignty and maritime rights and interests will in no circumstances be affected by the ruling of the Philippines'-initiated arbitration.

China will not accept any proposition or action based on the ruling.

China remains firmly committed to safeguarding the peace and stability of the South China Sea.

China remains committed to settling disputes with the countries directly involved through peaceful negotiations based on the recognition of historical facts and in accordance with international law.

To further elaborate on China's position, the Chinese government issued two statements and a white paper and interpretations of these documents by senior officials have also been released.

The Chinese Government issued the "Statement on China's Territorial Sovereignty and Maritime Rights and Interests in the South China Sea".

The Chinese Foreign Ministry issued the "Statement on the Award of 12th July 2016 of the Arbitral Tribunal in the South China Sea Arbitration Established at the Request of the Republic of the Philippines".

China's State Council Information Office published a white paper entitled "China Adheres to the Position of Settling Through Negotiation the Relevant Disputes Between China and the Philippines in the South China Sea".

The Statements and White Paper provide authoritative, comprehensive and clear-cut elaborations on China's position.

In-depth readings of these documents have been provided by State Councillor Yang Jiechi in an interview, by Foreign Minister Wang Yi in his remarks, and by Vice Foreign Minister Liu Zhengmin in a press briefing on the White Paper.

Here, I would like to talk very briefly about these documents.

The Statement by the Chinese Government reaffirms China's territorial sovereignty and maritime rights and interests in the South China Sea.

The Statement underscores the facts that China is the first to have discovered, named, and explored and exploited the Nanhai Zhudao, or the South China Sea islands, and relevant waters. China is the first to have exercised sovereignty and jurisdiction over them continuously, peacefully and effectively.

The Statement explicitly points out that China's territorial sovereignty and maritime rights and interests in the South China Sea include its sovereignty over the Nanhai Zhudao.

China has internal waters, territorial sea, a contiguous zone, an exclusive economic zone and a continental shelf, based on the Nanhai Zhudao.

China has historic rights in the South China Sea.

The statement also emphasizes that China is always firmly opposed to the invasion and illegal occupation by certain states of some islands and reefs of China's Nansha Qundao, or the Nansha Islands, and firmly opposed to activities infringing upon China's rights and interests in relevant maritime areas under China's jurisdiction.

At the same time, China stands ready to continue to resolve the relevant disputes peacefully through negotiation and consultation with the states directly concerned. China is ready to work with them to jointly maintain peace and stability in the South China Sea and to ensure the safety of and unimpeded access to the international shipping lanes in the South China Sea.

The Statement by the Chinese Foreign Ministry focuses on the arbitration.

It points out that the subject-matter raised by the Philippines for arbitration are beyond the jurisdiction of the UNCLOS.

The arbitration infringes on China's right as an UNCLOS state party, namely the right to choose the procedures and means for dispute settlement by its own will.

The arbitration also violates a series of bilateral agreements between China and the Philippines and the commitment made by China and ASEAN member countries to resolve relevant disputes through negotiation.

The tribunal has in essence expanded its power, exceeded its authority and abused arbitration proceedings. Its ruling is therefore null and void and has no binding force.

China will neither accept nor recognize it.

The White Paper offers an overall elaboration of how China's sovereignty over the Nanhai Zhudao was established in the course of history, and what China has been doing to uphold its territorial sovereignty and maritime rights and interests.

The White Paper sheds light on the origin and development of the disputes between China and the Philippines.

It aims to get to the root of the issue and set the record straight.

At the same time, the White Paper reiterates China's unchanging commitment to negotiation and consultation as the right way to settle disputes.

China believes only a negotiated result can gain understanding and support from the people of the countries concerned.

Only a negotiated result can be effectively implemented.

And only a negotiated result can be enduring.

As State Councilor Yang Jiechi said in his interview, as long as China and the Philippines stay committed to the principles and spirit of the DOC, stay committed to dialogue and consultation to manage differences properly, and stay committed to friendly and win-win cooperation, Sino-Philippine relations will have a bright future.

I have copies of these documents and transcripts of the interview and remarks prepared for your reference, in both Chinese and English. These should help you to gain an indepth and comprehensive understanding of China's position. Please feel free to take the copies with you after the conference.

Now I would like to take your questions.

China Daily: The Chinese President Xi Jinping said that China is committed to peacefully resolving relevant disputes through direct negotiations. But he also said that national sovereignty and maritime interests will not be influenced under any circumstances by the ruling. So my question is, outside these two areas he mentioned, what are the areas that China is willing to negotiate? Thank you.

Liu Xiaoming: The position that President Xi elaborates is the consistent policy of China. When it comes to the issue of The South China Sea, our position is clear and consistent. We have sovereignty over the islands in the South China Sea. And we also realize there are disputes over some of the islands. So we propose to "shelf the differences and seek joint development. " This principle consists of twelve words: "Sovereignty belongs to China, differences can be shelved, parties seek joint development." So, China will not negotiate its sovereignty on the islands of the South China Sea, but we realize that there are disputes over some of the islands and we are ready to have negotiations and consultations to ensure that disputes will be resolved by peaceful means and through diplomatic negotiations.

Xinhua: My question is about a law research paper by former deputy legal advisor to the Foreign and Commonwealth Office, Chris Whomersley. Chris Whomersley argued in a recent research paper that the tribunal's argument is "not convincing" and the way the tribunal handles the arbitration case is "potentially destabilizing" to international relations because it actually allowed the Philippines to resile, abandon its undertakings in a formal document like the DECLARATION ON THE CONDUCT OF PARTIES IN THE SOUTH CHINA SEA (DOC) . Could you briefly comment on this argument of Chris Whomersley, and to what extent do you think it is true?

Liu Xiaoming: I agree with him. I always oppose arbitration. I would say, it sets a very bad example. Some people believe it belongs to the dustbin. Some people believe it is useless. I was a student of international law. I believe it should be regarded as a negative example for teaching because it will be remembered in the history books as a failed case. It has violated international law in many aspects. To begin with, I would say it violates the basic purpose of the UN Convention on the Law of the Sea (UNCLOS). The purpose of UNCLOS is to ensure a stable and peaceful environment in the oceans and also stable and peaceful relations between states. Yet this tribunal, instead of serving the purpose of the UNCLOS, caused further tension between countries. It denied the diplomatic channel of negotiations for solution. It even denied the legal status of the DOC which is a very solemn official document reached by China and 10 ASEAN countries. So it did not fulfill the purpose of finding a peaceful solution. Rather it added fuel to the fire in the tension between the countries concerned. Also it added fuel to the fire in the tense situation within the region. So it is a very bad practice. As I said in my opening remarks, China will not recognize it, or accept it. It has no binding force. And we also hope that no country will take the ruling seriously. No country will make further claims based on the so-called ruling. The ruling is illegal. It has no legal status. If new claims were to be made based on the ruling, it would lead to new illegal actions that will further endanger regional peace and stability.

Propeller TV: I am from Propeller TV. Do you think there have been any implications from the Philippine government about a turnaround in China-Philippines relations? Thank you.

Liu Xiaoming: We certainly hope so. Since President Duterte took office, we have heard some encouraging words, positive comments, that he'd like to see China and the Philippines maintain good relations, that he'd like to see China and the Philippines resolve these disputes through bilateral negotiations. In fact, that is what we have been working for over many years. That is why we have strongly opposed this imposed arbitration from the very start. We believe this arbitration will lead nowhere. So we still believe, as I said, that negotiation is the only path that can lead to a solution. So we are open to cooperation with the new government of the Philippines, and we certainly expect further actions from the new Philippine government. As you know, there is a saying in Chinese, "listen to what you say, but watch out for what you are going to do. " I do hope that their actions will match their words, and we can start bilateral negotiations and set relations back to its normal track. China and the Philippines are neighbouring countries across the sea. And China and the Philippines have enjoyed very good relations for thousands of years. We always believe that disputes will not prevent the two countries from having good relations. And, we do hope that President Duterte and his government contribute to new prospects in China-Philippine relations.

Financial Times: I would like to just ask you for a bit more explanation on the question of the tribunal itself. From what I've read, China's main objection to the tribunal is, first of all, that an arbitration should be agreed to by both parties, and secondly, that the tribunal has no jurisdiction over the ruling that it had. But I've looked at the UNCLOS and there are two articles which appear to run counter to China's position. The first article is Article 286, and it says that the interpretation of the UNCLOS can be brought by any party to the tribunal. So it doesn't say 'both parties' but 'any party'. The second is 288, which says the question of jurisdiction should be settled by the tribunal itself. So could you explain China's position on that please?

Liu Xiaoming: We have different views with regard to how Articles 288 and 286 should be interpreted. Let me first say that our opposition to this tribunal is not only confined to the points you've made. I advise you to read carefully the Chinese Government statement, the Foreign Ministry statement and the white paper. I have summarized after reading these documents that this tribunal at least violated international law in eight aspects.

Firstly, it violated the UNCLOS. The UNCLOS has no jurisdiction over the matter of territorial sovereignty. This arbitration is about territorial sovereignty, although it has been meticulously packaged by the Philippines as being a technical case. From the way it ruled, everybody must come to the conclusion that it is about China's sovereignty over the islands and the adjacent waters.

Secondly, it violated the UNCLOS in terms of maritime delimitation. China and over 30 countries have already made optional exception statement to exclude from arbitration matters concerning maritime delimitation, historic bays or titles, military nature and law enforcement activities and so on. This declaration of optional exception is regarded as part of the UNCLOS. Everybody, I believe, agrees that this ruling is pertinent to maritime delimitation. So that is why we are saying the result shows that the tribunal has wilfully exceeded its power and violated China's right under this declaration. The reason why the parties belonging to the UNCLOS made such declaration is they realized that disputes might arise from the differences in maritime delimitation. If this declaration is denied, it will set a bad example. Today it's China, but who will be the next one tomorrow?

Thirdly, it denied the bilateral agreements that we have already signed. The Philippines has a series of bilateral agreements with China with regard to how to resolve the disputes through diplomatic negotiation. There are a series of bilateral documents, declarations, agreements signed between our two countries.

Fourthly, it violated the DOC signed by China and ASEAN countries. The DOC is part of international law and this declaration ensures that the parties are committed to maintaining peace and stability in the region through peaceful consultation and negotiation. It plays a very important role and has been respected and adhered to by China and ASEAN countries.

Fifthly, The arbitration denied China's sovereignty over the islands, denied China's historical rights, including the "dotted line", and challenged the basic norms enshrined in the UN Charter, namely safeguarding state sovereignty, independence and territorial integrity. So the arbitration is a serious violation of international law.

Sixthly, the arbitration, based on a distortion of Article 286, accepted the case and denied China's right to choose its own means of settling the dispute.

Seventhly, it set a bad example by misinterpreting the Convention and undermining the integrity and seriousness of the UNCLOS.

Eighthly, this arbitration deviated from the purpose of the UNCLOS to promote peaceful settlement of disputes. Rather, it intensified tensions in the region.

To come back to the articles you mentioned, the arbitration has its own right to interpret whether it has jurisdiction or not, but it should reach its judgments based on the facts. When it comes to the interpretation of an article, in addition to what rights you have, you also have to realize the obligations you have to live up to. So the arbitration only capitalized on the rights but failed to recognize the obligations. The obligation is to respect the UNCLOS provisions on jurisdiction and respect the declaration that China has made to exclude maritime delimitation. So the tribunal itself is not given the absolute right to determine whether it has the jurisdiction or not. Nor is it exempt from its obligations under the UNCLOS.

People's Daily: I have two questions. Firstly, what do you think is the impact of the so-called "arbitration" on Sino-Philippine relations? In your opinion, how will Sino-Philippine relations develop in the future? The second question is, as we all know, over the centuries, even over the recent decades, the South China Sea has been a very peaceful, and very quiet sea. But now it becomes hotter and hotter, and more complicated. What do you think is the reason for that?

Liu Xiaoming: First of all, the ruling of arbitration certainly has no impact, with no binding force, because we regard it as illegal, and not to be taken as the basis for future negotiations. If the Philippines agrees with us, I think we can resume our bilateral negotiations very soon. If the Philippines takes the ruling as the basis for negotiations, I don't think that will lead us anywhere.

I do hope countries in the region will share China's position. We already have some countries which share and support China's position, and some countries have expressed concerns over the consequences of the ruling. I do hope that China and ASEAN countries will reach consensus with regard to what serves the best interests of China and ASEAN, and what serves the best interests of maintaining peace and stability in the region. We've heard positive comments from the new Philippine government, but we do not know yet what their position is regarding the ruling. There is no way that we will implement the ruling. I hope the parties concerned will not take further illegal action, which will further escalate the already tense situation. That's something we do not want to see.

With regards to the second question, before 1970s nobody had challenged China's sovereignty over the South China Sea. The dotted-line was widely respected. It had been printed in many official maps published in the U.S., Britain, France, the former Soviet Union and many other countries. After oil and gas were found in 1970s, some regional countries rushed to invade and illegally seize the islands. We mounted strong opposition to this kind of illegal occupation by the countries concerned. As you know, during that time China was going through the Cultural Revolution, and the internal disruption prevented China from reaffirming and safeguarding its sovereignty over these islands. That was very unfortunate.

What happened in recent years, I think, had something to do with the so-called "rebalancing strategy" of the United States. Even though we had some problems in these years with neighbouring countries, the Philippines, Vietnam, Malaysia, to name a few, we did have bilateral discussions. China and Vietnam had reached agreement on maritime delimitation of the Beibu Bay. We even had a joint development project which includes the Philippines. This was a tripartite agreement on seismic survey and joint exploitation. But the projects failed to be implemented when the so-called U. S. "rebalancing strategy" came into being. Those countries were emboldened to challenge China's sovereignty. Now, instead of working behind the scene, the U. S. jumps to the front to challenge China's sovereignty by sending their warships and airplanes to have those close-in reconnaissance on China's air space, territorial sea and waters. These moves are causing tensions. We do hope these tensions will be reduced. We hope to work together with countries concerned, including the United States, so that we can make the South China Sea a sea of peace, a sea of cooperation and a sea of friendship. That is what has been reiterated by the Chinese leaders when they reaffirmed China's commitment to peace and stability of the region.

China Radio International: The Hague Tribunal is a legal institution set up under the framework of a UN convention. What is China's justification for "not accepting" and "not recognizing" its ruling? And what does it really mean to "not accept" or "not recognize" the arbitration ruling? Does it imply that China will do nothing whatsoever about it?

Liu Xiaoming: First of all, I like to correct this argument by pointing out that this tribunal has no relationship with the United Nations. It's not part of the International Court of Justice. It even does not have much to do with the Permanent Court of Arbitration (PCA) . This tribunal was set up on a temporary basis at the request of the Philippine government for this arbitration case. Its only relation to the PCA, to my knowledge, is that they use the PCA's office building, and they borrowed some staff from the PCA secretariat. That's all. Its legal basis was very weak.
What I should further mention is the composition of the tribunal, namely the five arbitrators. Apart from one arbitrator designated by the Philippines, all the other four arbitrators were appointed by the Japanese judge Shunji Yanai, who was the then ITLOS President. He used to be the Japanese ambassador to Washington. I am very suspicious of his political motives. He is a policy advisor to the current Japanese Prime Minister Shinzo Abe, and he has helped Abe to change Japan's peaceful constitution and the status of the Japanese armed forces and assisted in lifting the ban on the collective self-defence strategy. This is a person who wanted to challenge the post World War II order, and I think this case gave him another reason to do so again.
China's sovereignty over the islands of the South China Sea dates back 2,000 years. In recent times, these islands were illegally seized by Japan during the Second World War. Later, after the Second World War, they were returned to China under the authority and articles of the Cairo Declaration and this was reaffirmed by the Potsdam Proclamation. If this tribunal were allowed to deny the DOC, and if this case were

established, this would embolden other coastal countries to follow suit and incur a string of similar tribunal cases. In the next ruling, maybe they would say that the Cairo Declaration and the Potsdam Proclamation had no legal status. I do not know where it would lead.

According to the Cairo Declaration, all the territories and islands occupied by Japan must be returned to China, including the South China Sea islands. In fact, the military officers of China used the American ships to recover the islands. That the arbitral tribunal characterized the Taiping Dao of the Nansha Islands as a "rock", not an island, exposed that the purpose of arbitration is to deny China's sovereignty over the Nansha Islands and relevant maritime rights and interests. This violates international law, and is totally unacceptable. It has been strongly condemned by the Chinese people from both sides of the Taiwan Strait.

China did not participate in the arbitration because from day one, we believed this was a political farce. When you look at the composition of the tribunal and the political motives behind the ruling, you will know what the outcome will look like from the very beginning. We know it will lead to nowhere. We naturally showed no interest in it. When China says the ruling has no binding force, it means China will certainly not be bound by this ruling and we also hope that no other country would implement the so-called "ruling". As I said, how do you expect this discredited, illegitimate tribunal to make credible rulings? If the rulings were implemented, it would cause further damage to the situation.

The Daily Telegraph: What would you say when people who are not part of the disputes are saying that China is cherry-picking international law, and yet China is talking about its peaceful rise, it has to follow international law, as China is following in other areas? Secondly, can you give your thoughts on the way you perceive America's role in these disputes, in the sense that America encourages the Philippines to make this claim?

Liu Xiaoming: I can't agree with you when you say China is "cherry-picking". I think we have a legal basis to argue. Like I have said, there are eight areas in which this tribunal violates international laws. China abided by all the regulations of UNCLOS. China stood behind bilateral agreements, including those signed with the Philippines. And China is committed to the DOC with the ASEAN countries. So I would say, China is a country which abides by international law, plays by the rules. A basis of international law is the UN Charter, and China, being a Permanent Member of Security Council, bears the responsibility of safeguarding the UN Charter. There should be no doubt about it.

With regard to the United States, I think there should be a big question mark over US behaviour with regard to the South China Sea. They have not ratified the UNCLOS, and they have kept on breaching the UNCLOS, yet they acted as if they were the guardian of the UNCLOS. If they love the UNCLOS so much, why couldn't they ratify the UNCLOS? I think they are concerned that the UNCLOS might prevent their so-called "freedom of navigation and overflight". They want to go anywhere they want, and they do not want to see any restrictions on them. That's number one.

Number two, I think this arbitration case is politically motived. It is part of their strategy. On the one hand, they sent their warships and airplanes to areas close to China. On the other hand, they seized this legal case launched against China, so as to humiliate China diplomatically, damage China's image, and also give them a legal base to challenge. But I think this intention is doomed to failure, because they do not have a good legal base from the beginning. This has already turned out to be a political farce. So far, we have not heard many countries voice their support for this ruling. By comparison, we have over 70 countries supporting China's approach. We have about 290 political parties and organizations from over 70 countries expressing their support for China's position, the position that we believe the diplomatic negotiation between sovereign states is the only solution, rather than forced arbitration. We do hope that after this ruling, common sense will prevail. All the coastal countries will come to the negotiation table and accept China's proposal to shelve disputes, and to have serious diplomatic discussions and work for the joint development. That serves the interests of the countries concerned. We also hope the United States will respect the concerns and rights of China. We believe the U.S. has its interests in the region. But they cannot protect their interests at the expense of other countries' interests. China and our neighboring countries share a common destiny and common interests. China is the last country that is willing to see instability in this region. A lot of trade and commercial commodities pass through these channels and shipping lanes. China will continue to safeguard peace, stability, and freedom of navigation and overflight in this region.

European Times: Some people say the South China Sea dispute is a case of China's view of historical sovereign rights versus America's idea of rule-based international order. How do you view this? Do you think it will be a protracted dispute? My second question is that you mentioned negotiation is the only solution to the dispute. Are you already in preparation for it?

Liu Xiaoming: First on your first question about the historical rights that we must safeguard. "Historical" means the rights and interests of China have been formed through the course of history. Some people say China discarded its strategy of "keeping a low profile" and China no longer focuses on its economic development. China is seeking more power. I think that is incorrect. In fact, what we are defending is basically what has been ours since ancient times. The dotted line is not a creation of new rights. It was there since 1948 and has been recognized by the international community. It was not until something precious was found under the sea that countries began to seize and invade China's islands. China does not ask, has not asked and will not ask for anything more than what belongs to us. As I said in an interview with the Reuters, we are not interested in an inch of land that belongs to others. We are not jealous of others. But we treasure what we have. China lost so many territories when the country was very poor and when it was invaded by foreign powers and was subjected to foreign occupation as a result of unequal treaties. So it really is in China's DNA. We will defend China's sovereignty, rights and interests. So I would say we hope that the historical rights will be reaffirmed by the international community.

China's historical rights had been respected before the 1970s by the United States in many historical documents, legal documents, and international law. But things have changed. They have new allies and new interests. In an article I contributed to the *World Post*, I said "Superpowers are used to coming and going. " Countries should know that your neighbours are more important than superpowers. You cannot choose your neighbours. You have to live with your neighbours.

China does not want to challenge America's position in the world. But we cannot accept an unequal international order. China respects the current international order and China is a beneficiary of this international order. So that is why we have said time and again that China would like to work with the international community to safeguard the post-war order. We have no interest in disrupting this order or in starting a new order. But the world has changed. You need to keep up with the times. You need to make adjustment in order to meet demands, especially from the developing countries.

有问必答
No Question Unanswered

China regards itself as one of the members of the developing countries.

As President Xi said, the Pacific Ocean is big enough to allow China and the United States to work together, rather than have conflicts with each other. We do hope that the United States will realize that China has no interest in challenging U.S. dominance. We acknowledge that although the U.S. is not a regional country, it has economic and security interests in the region. We respect that. We hope the United States will also respect the interests of China, so that the two largest Pacific countries can work together to maintain peace and stability in the region.

Thank you for your presence. I look forward to seeing you again.

浮云难遮望眼，正道总是沧桑
—— 在英国皇家国际问题研究所发表主旨演讲并回答提问
（2016年7月25日，英国皇家国际问题研究所）

刘晓明： 很高兴再次来到皇家国际问题研究所。这是我担任中国驻英国大使以来第五次到访皇研所。

听说近来皇研所最热的议题是"英国脱欧"，我没想到今天会有这么多人来听我的演讲，这说明南海问题确实很重要，我通过皇研所这个讲坛介绍中国对南海问题的政策主张也确实很必要。

关于南海问题，最近最突出的事件就是菲律宾南海仲裁案。所谓仲裁庭裁决结果一出台，中方在第一时间发布了《中华人民共和国政府关于在南海的领土主权和海洋权益的声明》、《中华人民共和国外交部关于应菲律宾共和国请求建立的南海仲裁案仲裁庭所作裁决的声明》以及《中国坚持通过谈判解决中国与菲律宾在南海的有关争议》的白皮书，中国领导人和多位政府高官也分别发表谈话、接受采访，重申中国在南海的领土主权和海洋权益，揭露仲裁庭扩权、越权、滥用仲裁程序的本质，阐明中方对非法裁决结果不接受、不承认的严正立场。

今天，我愿向大家面对面地进一步阐述为什么中方坚持认为仲裁庭的裁决结果是非法的、无效的。我们认为：

第一，仲裁庭对有关事项没有管辖权。菲律宾前政府单方面提起仲裁的有关事项，其背后的本质和真正目的都指向领土主权和海洋划界问题，领土主权问题不在《联合国海洋法公约》的调整范围内，海洋划界问题也早已被中国根据《公约》第298条规定而作的排除性声明所排除。因此仲裁庭首先是在自身无权管辖的领域随意扩权、滥权，又何谈此后会程序公正和实体公正？

第二，仲裁程序与《公约》规定相违背。在《公约》设计的争端解决机制中，缔约国通过双边渠道解决争议应予以优先适用，只有穷尽双边渠道仍未得到解决时才适用第三方解决机制。中菲之间早已选择通过谈判协商解决争端，两国也根本没有就菲律宾所提的仲裁事项进行过双边沟通，仲裁庭何以认定双边渠道已经用尽？在诉诸仲裁所需的所有条件都不成熟的情况下，仲裁庭却强行推进审理。这种做法不合常理，很不正常，违反《公约》的一般实践，在程序上本身就是违法。大家知道，程序正义是实体正义的前提和基础。

第三，仲裁结果背离了《公约》合理解决争端的基本宗旨。《公约》诞生的初衷是公正地解决问题、化解矛盾，仲裁庭的做法却与此背道而驰，带有明显倾向性和政治目的：对菲律宾的非法主张照单全收，对中国的合理关切则一概拒绝。为了给菲律宾违反双边谈判解决争议的承诺开脱，仲裁庭不惜贬低《南海各方行为宣言》和中菲之间的一系列双边文件。为了最大程度否定中国的合法权利，仲裁庭竟把太平岛硬称为"礁"。

这让我想起一个中国成语："指鹿为马。"这个成语讲的是2000多年前中国秦朝一位丞相专横跋扈、越权滥权的故事，没想到在21世纪的今天，这一幕又在菲律宾仲裁案仲裁庭上演。明明是鹿，为什么硬要说是马呢？明明是岛，为什么硬要说是礁呢？时代不同，但手法如出一辙，动机都是不可告人。仲裁庭这种毫无顾忌的偏袒不是在解决问题，而是在制造问题；不是在化解矛盾，而是在挑起矛盾。因此本案不具实体正义。

基于以上管辖权、程序和实体三大违法事实，所谓仲裁案自始至终就是一场非法的政治闹剧。难怪一些知名法学家认为这一仲裁"必将会被视为毒树之果，无法得到认可和支持"。如果有些人非要拿仲裁结果当作什么"宝贝"，我奉劝他们，这就是一剂花高价买来的"精神幻药"，开始会让他们亢奋一阵，后面会让他们饱受折磨。

中方坚决反对仲裁案及其结果，同时将坚定既定政策，不会让仲裁案成为南海局势走向的所谓"分水岭"，更不会让仲裁案来干扰当前南海地区总体和平稳定的局面。

第一，仲裁结果对中国在南海的领土主权和海洋权益没有任何影响。国际法的基本规则是"非法行为不产生合法效力"，因此非法的裁决结果对包括中国在内的南海问题各当事方而言只是一纸空文。中国不会接受任何未经中方同意的第三方解决方式，也不会接受任何强加于中国的解决方案。

第二，仲裁结果对中国以谈判协商和平解决南海问题的既定方针没有任何影响。正如我不久前在一篇文章中的标题："中国无意统治南海。"中国一贯致力于与直接当事国在尊重历史事实的基础上，依据国际法通过谈判协商和平解决有关南海争议，主张有关各方在解决争议的过程中均应保持克制，不采取使争议扩大化、复杂化的行动，倡导有关各方在争议最终解决前基于谅解和合作精神做出临时性、过渡性的安排。中国也一直主张"搁置争议，共同开发",这一点没有改变,以后也不会变。

仲裁案没有改变中国与菲律宾谈判解决争议、改善双边关系的愿望。虽然菲律宾前政府执意单方面提起仲裁,给中菲关系造成损害,但中菲毕竟是隔海相望的近邻,我们仍希望菲新政府从中菲共同利益和两国关系大局出发,回到对话协商解决问题的轨道。

仲裁结果也没有改变中国和东盟之间的合作势头。今年是中国与东盟建立对话关系25周年。双方将于9月举行纪念峰会,并以此为契机全面规划未来合作战略,更加紧密地团结在一起,造福双方人民。在南海问题上,中国愿与东盟国家保持坦诚友好的沟通,按照"双轨思路",全面、有效落实《南海各方行为宣言》,稳妥推进"南海行为准则"磋商进程,共同维护南海的和平稳定。就在今天,中国和东盟外长发表联合声明,重申《南海各方行为宣言》是具有里程碑意义的文件,各方再次承诺由直接有关主权国家通过友好磋商和谈判,以和平方式解决领土和管辖权争议,同时鼓励其他国家尊重《南海各方行为宣言》所包含的原则。

第三,仲裁结果对中国走和平发展道路的方针没有任何影响。中国始终是国际法和国际秩序的维护者、建设者、贡献者。中国在南海的主权和权益本身就是"二战"后确定的国际秩序的一部分,中国的有关主张也从未超出该秩序所涵盖的范围。中国坚持对仲裁说"不",就是为了捍卫战后国际秩序,就是为了防止《联合国海洋法公约》被政治绑架,就是为了维护包括《公约》在内的国际法的权威性和完整性。自新中国成立以来我们已通过协商谈判与14个陆地邻国中的12个签订了边界条约,并与越南完成了北部湾海上划界。这些都是中国遵守国际法,捍卫国际秩序,维护地区和平安宁的生动体现。

南海是世界重要航道，是包括中国在内众多国家利益聚焦的地方。中国理解国际社会对南海问题的关注，也从来不排斥域外国家在南海地区的合法权益，一直致力于维护该地区的航行自由。但我们反对个别国家以"航行和飞越自由""维护地区和平"之名，行"炮舰政策"之实，借仲裁案渲染甚至制造南海紧张局势。南海不应成为域外大国"秀肌肉"的竞技场。威胁、恐吓动摇不了中国人民维护国家领土主权和海洋权益的决心。

浮云难遮望眼，正道总是沧桑。

南海问题既是历史遗留问题，也是现实利益问题，同时被一些国家掺杂了地缘政治因素，解决这个问题需要时间、耐心和当事方之间的相互谅解与尊重。只有当事国在尊重历史事实的基础上，根据国际法通过平等谈判协商和平解决有关争议，才能根本、长久地解决问题。南海应成为"和平之海、友谊之海、合作之海"，这是中国致力于实现的目标，也需要周边各国与中国一道做出努力！

谢谢。下面我愿回答大家的提问。

听众： 美国未批准《联合国海洋法公约》，但在南海问题上有重要影响。美国将举行总统选举，克林顿或特朗普当选总统将对中美关系和南海问题带来什么样的机遇或挑战？

刘晓明： 现在做预测还为时尚早，但我们需要做好与他们两人之一打交道的准备。希拉里·克林顿曾担任美国国务卿，多次访华。我们对特朗普了解不多，一些西方媒体报道称中国可能对特朗普担任总统感到担忧，但我并没有那种担心。我曾从事对美工作，经历过多次总统选举，对美国选举政治有一定了解。我们要听其言，更要观其行，关注他们当选后会做什么。我认为，不管谁担任美国总统，都要从美国的国家利益出发，重视中美关系，对这一点我是有信心的。中美关系涉及方方面面，双方可能有一些分歧，关系可能有一些起伏，但我相信中美之间的共同利益远远大于分歧。

听众： 大使阁下，感谢你的演讲。你提到中国愿意就南海争议进行谈判，我想问中国是否能够澄清断续线的含义是什么？比如，中国是否对断续线内的一切拥有权利？中国在南海国际水域拥有的海洋权益是否源于断续线？这将有助于谈判进程。我还想问另外一个问题。仲裁庭裁决书提到了中国渔民在南海这个世界上渔业资源最丰富的渔场使用炸药捕鱼。中国将采取什么措施阻止类似情况发生？

刘晓明： 首先，我想指出的是，中国一直主张在尊重历史事实的基础上，根据国际法，通过双边谈判解决与周边邻国的争议，这是中国的一贯政策，现在仍然如此。我们希望周边邻国与中国通过外交谈判找到双方都能满意的解决方案。

关于断续线，我想说明的是，中国的领土主权、海洋权益、历史性权利是在长期的历史过程中形成的，是基于中国对南海诸岛最早发现、命名、开发及有效管辖的历史事实，其中当然也包括中国渔民的捕鱼活动。因此，1948年中国政府公布断续线后，国际社会普遍予以承认，没有国家提出挑战。20世纪70年代，南海发现了丰富的油气资源，一些国家争先恐后地非法侵占南海中国岛礁，共侵占中国南沙群岛的42个岛礁。其中，越南侵占了29个，菲律宾侵占了8个，马来西亚侵占了5个。中国对这些岛礁拥有主权，它们是南沙群岛的一部分。如果你查阅一下历史记录，就会发现美国、法国、英国等国官方公开发行的地图上标注了断续线，表明它们对中国在这一区域主权的尊重。

关于渔业问题，我们当然要有序地管理南海渔业活动。中国政府反对任何对渔业资源造成破坏的渔业活动，这也是中国与周边国家讨论如何共同维持良好渔业秩序的原因。当我们讨论这一问题时，我也想提醒你注意，一些周边国家的渔民在进行大量非法、破坏性的捕捞活动，因此这需要中国与周边国家共同努力，寻找解决问题的方法。

听众： 大使阁下在刚才演讲中指出，由于主权问题不属于《联合国海洋法公约》调整范围，仲裁庭裁决结果没有任何效力。在南海当前的紧张局势下，需要以国际法和平解决有关争议。中方将仲裁这一和平解决的方式排除在外。当你谈到大国与小国之间的双边谈判时，这某种程度上是否将重演19世纪"强权即真理"的逻辑？

刘晓明： 所谓没有任何效力，是指仲裁庭所谓裁决结果对中国的领土主权和海洋权益没有任何影响。我已清楚表明这一点。如果你认为仲裁会对中国上述权益产生影响，那将是一种误判。这种事情永远不会发生。仲裁只是解决争端的辅助手段。《公约》规定，缔约国通过双边渠道解决争议应予以优先适用，只有穷尽双边渠道时才适用仲裁机制。仲裁庭的做法违反了这一规定，因此是非法的，中方不会接受。所以，我不能同意所谓仲裁庭是以国际法和平解决争议的说法。

中菲之间早已达成通过谈判协商解决争端的协议，但双方从未举行此类谈判，因为菲方认为自己得到了美国支持，能够通过仲裁得到利益，对与中方谈判不感兴趣。仲裁庭违反了《公约》基本程序，尽管如此中方仍坚持通过双边谈判解决争议。今天（7月25日），中国与包括菲律宾在内的东盟十国外长共同发表了联合声明，承诺全面有效完整落实《南海各方行为宣言》，重申由直接当事方通过对话协商和平解决争议的立场。但另一方面，菲律宾一些人仍对仲裁抱有幻想，相信所谓裁决会产生效力。我希望菲方尽早从这样的矛盾心态中走出来，越早越好。仲裁结果对中国在南海的领土主权和海洋权益没有任何影响，对中国以谈判协商和平解决南海问题的既定方针没有任何影响。我相信，唯一、长久的解决方式是由直接当事国进行面对面的谈判，而不是将所谓裁决结果强加给一个主权国家。我相信，英国也希望与其他国家通过谈判和平解决争议，不会在谈判开始之前接受一个强制仲裁结果。主权国家有通过谈判寻找解决方式的权利，这就是我想表达的意思。

关于你所说的大国小国关系问题，中国体量大一些，但中国始终主张大国小国一律平等。中国与14个邻国中的12个划定了边界，其中很多是小国，如尼泊尔、缅甸等。但我们通过和平、友好、平等的方式解决了困难的划界问题。中国是国际秩序和国际法的维护者，中方仍然希望与菲律宾、越南、马来西亚等国找到解决争议的方式，共同维护地区和平稳定。

听众： 我对中国向南海岛礁派驻部队的做法持不同看法，但对中国应对南海问题的总体方式持积极态度。大使先生，你认为在无人生活的岛礁上修建飞机跑道，并安排成批的游客去参观，是否比单边仲裁结果更为加剧地区紧张局势？

刘晓明： 中国对南海有关争议一直呼吁各方保持克制，但有关国家却变本加厉，在非法侵占的中国岛礁上修建军事设施。菲律宾和越南在非法占据的岛礁上修建跑道，西方媒体却刻意保持沉默，一些西方政客更是视而不见。中国对这些挑衅行径忍无可忍，不得不采取措施应对。中国的岛礁建设是在自己的土地上进行的，这一点我希望你注意。而有关国家背弃了与中国达成的共识，在非法侵占的岛礁上修建军事设施，并部署导弹、坦克、大炮，中国不得不加以应对。

中国岛礁建设并未给地区带来损害。相反，中国修建的设施将在气象、海洋研究、环境保护等领域提供更好的服务。修建的灯塔也有助于南海的航运安全。每年大量船舶经过南海，当地的船东都十分赞同修建灯塔。今年初路透社做了一个调查，结果显示很多船东都十分感激中国提供的海上公共服务，认为修建灯塔及其他救援设施大大缩短了海上救援时间，并极大改善了海上运输环境。这都是中国正在努力做的事情。

说到这，我建议你读一读今天刚刚发布的中国与东盟国家外交部部长关于全面有效落实《南海各方行为宣言》的联合声明。中国与东盟国家外长一致同意，有关各方保持克制，这体现了中国致力于地区和平与稳定的承诺。我手边就有这份声明，我现在就读其中一段，帮助你增进对地区局势的理解：

"各方承诺保持自我克制，不采取使争议复杂化、扩大化和影响和平与稳定的行动，包括不在现无人居住的岛、礁、滩、沙或其他自然构造上采取居住的行动，并以建设性的方式处理它们的分歧。"

听众： 大使先生，你刚才谈到了中国利用南海海底资源的有关计划。外界认为中国有意开发这些资源。你能进一步解释有关开发计划并提供一些数据吗？

刘晓明： 正如我提到的，中国在本地区享有合法的海洋权益。目前确有一些中国石油公司在南海进行海上勘探开发。当然，你会看到这些开发活动都在中方主权范围内。同时，中国也认识到在有些区域存在争议，愿意与有关国家搁置争议，开展对话并进行共同开发。

事实上，中国与越南已经就海上共同开发达成协议。中国、越南、菲律宾也曾确立三方合作项目。在争议地区开发自然资源问题上，中国愿与有关国家进行讨论。

听众： 我研究中国有很多年了，现在正在研究法律政策问题。我认为大使先生的演讲十分精彩。我的问题是，你认为某个未加入《联合国海洋法公约》的国家，可以通过代理人，以十分隐秘的方式滥用国际法吗？

刘晓明：　这当然不可以。

听　众：　非常感谢大使先生的演讲。我认为你已将中国政府的立场阐释得极其清楚，我们也对仲裁结果毫无法律效力这一事实有了进一步的认识。你已经解释了中国不接受仲裁结果的原因，阐述了中国在南海的历史性权利，介绍了中国提供的修建灯塔等公共服务。但为什么很多中国邻国，如菲律宾、越南、日本等，均不认可中国上述政策？

刘晓明：　当你提到不认可中国政策的邻国时，你用了"很多"这个词。我必须纠正你，因为这样的邻国并不多。

事实上，中国与周边国家关系很好。俄罗斯作为最大的邻国，与中国关系十分友好。我曾常驻过的朝鲜，以及韩国、蒙古、巴基斯坦、印度、哈萨克斯坦、尼泊尔、孟加拉国、越南等也都与中国有非常好的关系。当然，国家间关系有起有伏很正常，共同利益将双方紧密地联系在一起。

的确，有少数邻国不认可中国的政策，那是因为它们与中国存在海上争议。譬如日本，两国在钓鱼岛问题上存有明显分歧。根据《开罗宣言》，钓鱼岛应归还中国。当年中日关系实现正常化的时候，中方不希望钓鱼岛问题影响两国关系正常发展，邓小平先生提出了搁置争议，他指出下一代比我们更聪明，一定会找到彼此都能接受的方法。中日建交40多年来，钓鱼岛问题没有大的起伏。但近年来，日本政府对钓鱼岛实施所谓"国有化"，一些右翼势力甚至提出通过"购岛"进行非法占领，正是由于日方动摇了中日两国在钓鱼岛问题上达成的共识，中方才不得不对日方挑衅行为做出回应。

在南海问题上，中国一直是受害者，但中国始终认为国家不论大小，都应在平等基础上通过谈判寻求解决方案。中越之间已成功解决了部分领土争议，双方就北部湾划界问题达成了协议。中国与其他国家不一定照搬中越解决争议的模式，但只要有信心和耐心，就一定能够找到解决方法。

现在南海还面临地缘政治问题。某个域外大国，一个比中国强大得多的国家，想利用南海问题为其所谓"再平衡"战略服务。它展示"肌肉"，显示存在，反而使问题更加复杂，这是我们不愿看到的。

听众： 大使阁下，没有国家比中国更强大。你的演讲很有说服力，可以说是我听过的最有说服力的演讲。中方对仲裁案很愤怒，我认为中方有理由感到愤怒。但中方应该保持耐心，尽量避免发怒。

我想了解中方在"势力范围"问题上的长期政策立场。未来20至30年，中国的政策立场会不会因南海仲裁案而改变？你谈到战后国际秩序，你认为太平洋哪些部分属于这一秩序？哪些部分属于中国的"势力范围"？中、美、俄三方有许多问题需要共同应对，应该加强合作，而不是就南海岛礁争吵。你如何展望中国"势力范围"的未来？

刘晓明： 恕我直言，我认为你仍在用冷战思维评判形势。我在演讲中提及的战后国际秩序，指的是第二次世界大战后，而不是冷战期间的秩序，战后国际秩序的基本原则是由《联合国宪章》等所确定的。

我不同意你关于"势力范围"的看法，中国对建立"势力范围"没有兴趣。你认为没有国家比中国更强大，这明显不符合事实。尽管中国已成为世界第二大经济体，中国仍是一个发展中国家，人均GDP仅排在全球80多位，比英国落后，与美国差距更大。人均GDP直接关系到人民的生活水平，比经济总量更重要。

我担任中国驻埃及大使之后，曾在甘肃省担任省长助理。你可能连甘肃省的名字都没听说过，那是中国最贫困的省份之一。当地生活条件十分艰苦，最基本的饮用水都非常匮乏，许多人依靠水窖蓄存雨水来满足基本生活需要。我去过甘肃许多这样的地方，这使我更好地了解国家贫困地区的情况，对我做好外交工作很有帮助。上海、天津、广州等大城市并非中国的全部，就如同伦敦不能代表英国一样。如果你访问英格兰北部地区或苏格兰地区，就会发现它们与伦敦存在不小差距。在发展经济和改善民生方面，中国仍面临巨大挑战。

中国对挑战美国"领导地位"没有兴趣，也无意构筑所谓"势力范围"。我们的目标是实现中国现代化，提高人民生活水平，使13多亿中国人生活得更好，生活得更幸福。为什么我们如此看重南海这些岛礁？新中国成立前100多年，中国屡遭列强欺凌，被迫签订了不少不平等条约，大片土地被割让侵占。如今中国实现了国家独立，民族解放，中国人民看重自己的领土主权，别国的土地中国一寸不要，但中国的领土我们寸土不让。中国人常讲，寸土寸金。维护中国的主权和领土完整，已经成为中国人民的基因，中国将采取一切必要措施,捍卫领土主权和海洋权益。

听众： 我来自日本驻英使馆。因为你谈及了日本和"尖阁列岛"，[1]所以我必须有所回应。首先，你提到了受害者问题。中国成为受害者的经历是七八十年前的事，现在我们不是在讨论受害者，而是在讨论法治问题。中国是《联合国海洋法公约》缔约国，《公约》对通过仲裁解决争端有明确规定，中方理应接受。对于"尖阁列岛"问题，中国虽不接受1951年签署的《旧金山对日和约》，但直到1971年之前，中方都未对"尖阁列岛"归属日本提出异议。中国似乎在操纵历史议题，而且有些过分。

布朗院长（主持人）： 你是在演讲，还是在提问？

刘晓明： 你应该向皇研所申请演讲。今天是中国大使在发表演讲，你的问题是什么？

听众： 我想问中方为什么不设定完成"南海行为准则（COC）"谈判的具体日期？请你明确说明这一日期是什么时候。

刘晓明： 我认为你没有资格提这个要求，因为日本并非COC谈判当事国。你要求中方设定结束谈判的日期，这很过分，而且充满了傲慢。COC谈判是中国与东盟国家之间的谈判，日本却急着要定谈判结束日期，岂有此理？COC谈判非常复杂，涉及中国与东盟十国的共同关切。中方已就积极推进谈判做出庄重承诺，也希望尽早达成协

---

[1] "尖阁列岛"是日本对中国钓鱼岛的称呼，中国不予承认。

议。但中国要与东盟国家平等相待、相互尊重。

关于钓鱼岛问题，我们可以花一整天时间讨论。简言之，中日两国政府高层和工作层已经多次讨论钓鱼岛问题。中方从未承认和接受《旧金山对日和约》。钓鱼岛是中国的一部分，是日本用战争手段从中国窃取的。"窃取"这个词不是我首创的，而是在中、美、英三国领导人共同签署的《开罗宣言》中明确阐明的，即日本所窃取于中国之领土，全部归还中国。随着战后国际形势发生变化，特别是冷战开始后，日本成为美国盟友，美国因此改变了立场，不愿将钓鱼岛归还中国，事实就是这样。

听众： 感谢大使就南海问题所做的强有力的阐述。你认为仲裁庭对领土主权和海洋划界问题没有仲裁权，这没有错。但仲裁庭反复重申其裁决不涉及领土主权和海洋划界问题，为什么中方反复指责仲裁庭所作裁决实质是主权问题？

刘晓明： 首先，仲裁庭的裁决关系到主权问题，事实非常清楚。这也恰恰是菲律宾前政府提出仲裁的目的所在，其想通过仲裁否定中国对南海诸岛的主权。有人说，菲方为此次仲裁花销高达3000万美元。有谁会相信花这一大笔钱仅仅是为了裁决一些无人居住岛礁的地位问题。我想，菲方还不至于愚蠢和疯狂到这个地步。事实上，菲律宾想通过仲裁否定中国对有关岛礁的主权，这一目的非常明确。任何没有偏见的人，即便不是专家学者，也能从常识角度认清其真实目的。

其次，你怎么能将有关岛礁的地位属性与国家主权割裂开呢？仲裁庭表面上未直接就主权问题进行裁决，但实质上其否定中国维护主权和海洋权益的权利。中国将南海诸岛视为一个整体，中国拥有无可争辩的主权。仲裁庭却要把中国的主权与岛礁分割开来，以便否定中国的领土主权和海洋权益。对这一险恶用心，我们看得非常清楚。

仲裁庭还完全否定中国包括断续线在内的历史性权利，这违背了《联合国海洋法公约》的精神。中方已声明将涉及海洋划界、历史性海湾或所有权等方面的争端排除出《公约》强制争端解决程序，包括英国在内的30多个国家也做出了类似声明。为什么《公约》认可排除性声明？因为《公约》的出发点，是为主权国家处理海洋划界等方面的争端创造和平环境，并不是想给主权国家制造麻烦。

布朗院长（主持人）：非常感谢刘大使就中国在南海问题上的政策立场所做的全面详细的介绍。我们期待今后有机会第六次或第七次邀请你来皇研所发表演讲。再次非常感谢！

刘晓明：不客气。

Let No Fleeting Clouds Block Our Vision
—— A Keynote Speech and Q&A at Chatham House

On 25th July 2016, I delivered a keynote speech entitled "Let No Fleeting Clouds Block Our Vision" at Chatham House. expounded China's position on the award of the South China Sea arbitration and China's policy initiatives on the South China Sea issue. Present at the event were over 300 people from the political, business, academic and diplomatic circles of the UK as well as major media organizations. Following the speech, I answered questions from the audience on issues including the impact of the US presidential election on China-US relations, the nature of the South China Sea arbitration, the legal status of the dotted line in the South China Sea, the negotiations on the Code of Conduct in the South China Sea, China's construction on its islands and reefs, resource development in the South China Sea, the impact of the arbitration on China's relationship with neighboring countries, disputes between China and Japan over the Diaoyu Islands, trends in China's diplomacy, etc.

Founded in 1920, Chatham House, the Royal Institute of International Affairs, is one of the largest research institutes on international affairs in the UK, boasting of a high-level research team and enjoying prestigious reputation in international studies both in the UK and worldwide. With more than 3,000 members and close connections with the British government, business, media and academia, it has considerable influence on UK foreign policy. Its research mainly focuses on international strategies, international relations and foreign policies. The full text of the speech and Q&A are as follows:

Liu Xiaoming: It is a great pleasure to be back. This is my fifth visit to Chatham House since I began my term as Chinese Ambassador to the UK.

Recently Brexit has been the hottest topic at the Chatham House. I did not expect such a big turnout for my speech. This shows the importance of the issue of the South China Sea and the necessity for me to share with you where China stands on this issue.

With regard to the South China Sea, one issue has been a headline maker recently. That is the arbitration unilaterally initiated by the Philippines. Right after the arbitral tribunal announced its ruling, China made a series of responses.

The Chinese Government issued the "Statement on China's Territorial Sovereignty and Maritime Rights and Interests in the South China Sea".

The Chinese Foreign Ministry issued the "Statement on the Award of 12th July 2016 of the Arbitral Tribunal in the South China Sea Arbitration Established at the Request of the Republic of the Philippines".

China's State Council Information Office published a white paper entitled "China Adheres to the Position of Settling Through Negotiation the Relevant Disputes Between China and the Philippines in the South China Sea".

Chinese leaders and senior officials also made remarks or gave interviews to highlight and interpret the above two statements and the white paper.

They reaffirmed China's territorial sovereignty and maritime rights and interests in the South China Sea. They disclosed the nature of the arbitral tribunal which expanded and exceeded its power and abused the arbitration proceedings. They expounded on China's solemn position of not accepting or recognizing the illegal ruling.

Today, I want to discuss with you face-to-face about why China believes the ruling is illegal, and why it is null and void.

First, the tribunal has no right of jurisdiction. The subject on which the Philippines unilaterally initiated this arbitration, and the real intention behind it, are in essence related to territorial sovereignty and maritime delimitation. Issues of territorial sovereignty are clearly beyond the scope of the UN Convention on the Law of the Sea (UNCLOS). And issues of maritime delimitation have been excluded by the declaration that China made years ago in accordance with the UNCLOS. From the very beginning, the tribunal enlarged and abused its power recklessly to areas outside of its jurisdiction. How could a tribunal thus established go ahead to ensure procedural and substantive justice?

Second, the arbitral proceedings are against the rules of the UNCLOS. According to the dispute settlement mechanism of the Convention, bilateral channel between state parties comes before arbitration. The third party settlement will be applied only when bilateral means have been exhausted. China and the Philippines have long agreed to resolve relevant disputes through bilateral consultations and negotiations. The two countries have never shared any bilateral communication over the filing of the arbitration. On what basis did the tribunal conclude that bilateral means have been exhausted? However, the tribunal disregarded the fact that none of the pre-conditions for initiating the arbitration had been met and forced ahead with the case. Such a procedure is utterly unreasonable and unusual. It contravenes the general practice of international arbitration under the Convention. Hence, the proceedings of the arbitration were illegal. And as everyone knows, procedural justice is the pre-condition and foundation for substantive justice.

Third, the arbitration ruling is an aberration from the fundamental purposes of the Convention. The Convention is aimed at settling disputes and differences in a reasonable and equitable way. But the tribunal's practice, overtly biased and politically motivated as it was, went the opposite way. The tribunal accepted every illegal claim made by the Philippines while all of China's reasonable concerns were rejected. To save the Philippines from breaching of its own commitment to bilateral negotiations, the tribunal belittled and nullified the Declaration on the Conduct of Parties in the South China Sea (DOC) as well as a series of bilateral agreements reached between China and the Philippines. To maximize its denial of China's legitimate rights, the tribunal even shrank the Taiping Island into a rock.

This indeed reminds me of a Chinese idiom: Calling a stag a horse. This idiom comes from the story of a high-handed prime minister during the Qin Dynasty who exceeded and abused his power. But that was a story from over 2,000 years ago. Today, in the 21st century, it is inconceivable that the arbitral tribunal could relive the same story. Two thousand years ago, by the order of a prime minister, a stag could be deliberately called a "horse". Today, at the hands of the tribunal, an island suddenly becomes a "rock". Time has changed. But the tribunal is playing exactly the same trick and its motive is just as hidden from the broad daylight. The obvious bias of the tribunal has solved no problem or dispute. Rather, it has created problems and intensified disputes. The arbitration thus has no substantive justice.

The arbitration is therefore illegal in jurisdictional, procedural or substantive terms. So, from the very beginning, it has been nothing but an illegal political farce.

It was not surprising when some prestigious jurists concluded that the ruling "will be widely regarded as the fruit of a poisonous tree, and it will fail, therefore, to garner the necessary support."

To those who insist on regarding the ruling as a "treasure", I would say that this ruling created nothing but a costly "hallucination": the excitement may last a while but what follows would be endless suffering.

China is firmly opposed to the arbitration and its ruling, and will stick to its consistent policy. The arbitration has zero possibility of becoming a "watershed" in developments in the South China Sea. Nor will it be allowed to disturb the overall peace and stability the region now enjoys.

First, the arbitration ruling will by no means affect China's territorial sovereignty and maritime rights and interests in the South China Sea. In international law, the principle *ex injuria jus non oritur*, says that illegal acts cannot create legal effect. The illegal ruling is nothing but waste paper, not only to China, but to any party concerned. China will not accept any third-party dispute settlement that does not have China's prior consent. Nor will we let others impose solutions on us.

Second, the arbitration ruling will by no means affect China's commitment to finding a peaceful solution through bilateral negotiations and consultations. I wrote an article on this subject. As its title says, China is not motivated by a desire to rule the South China Sea. China has always been committed to settling disputes through peaceful consultation and negotiation with countries directly concerned based on respecting historical facts and international law. China calls on all parties to exercise self-restraint in the process of resolving disputes, and to refrain from taking actions that will intensify or complicate the disputes. Pending an ultimate settlement of the disputes, China supports the creation of a temporary and transitional arrangement, agreed by all relevant parties based on mutual understanding and the spirit of cooperation. China has all along called for "shelving differences and engaging in joint development". This commitment has not changed and will not change.

China remains committed to negotiation with the Philippines for the sake of dispute resolution and the improvement of bilateral relations. This hasn't been changed by the arbitration. The arbitration unilaterally initiated by the former Philippine government has caused damage to China-Philippines relations. But the Philippines is one of China's close neighbours. We therefore hope the new Philippine government will consider the overall interests of China-Philippine relations and the common interests of both countries. We hope it will come back to the track of dialogue and consultations.

The momentum of cooperation between China and the ASEAN has not been changed by the arbitration, either. This year marks the 25th anniversary of the dialogue partnership between China and the ASEAN countries. The two sides will co-host a special commemorative summit in September. This will be an opportunity to outline the future cooperation strategy for closer unity and greater benefit for the people of both sides. With regard to the South China Sea issue, China is always ready to engage in friendly and candid communications with the ASEAN countries. China will comprehensively and effectively implement the DOC and steadily advance the consultation of the Code of Conduct in the South China Sea. China will follow the "dual track approach". This means the relevant disputes will be settled properly by the countries directly concerned through friendly consultations and negotiations, while peace and stability of the South China Sea shall be jointly maintained by China and the ASEAN countries.

Today, the foreign ministers of the ASEAN member states and China issued a Joint Statement. In the Joint Statement,

The parties reaffirmed that the "Declaration on the Conduct of Parties in the South China Sea" (DOC) is a milestone document;

The parties concerned undertake to resolve their territorial and jurisdictional disputes by peaceful means, through friendly consultations and negotiations by sovereign states directly concerned;

At the same time, the parties encourage other countries to respect the principles contained in the DOC.

Third, the arbitration ruling will by no means affect China's commitment to peaceful development. China has long been working to build, uphold and contribute to international law and the international order. China's sovereignty and maritime rights and interests in the South China Sea are in fact part of the international order established after the Second World War. China's relevant claims have never exceeded the scope of the current international order. In this sense, China's rejection of the arbitration is to uphold the post-war international order. It is to prevent the Convention from being politically hijacked. It is to protect the authoritativeness and the integrity of international law, including the Convention. Since the founding of the People's Republic of China in 1949, we have signed boundary treaties with 12 of our 14 neighbours with land borders through consultation and negotiation. We have completed maritime delimitation with Vietnam, also through consultation and negotiation. These powerful examples demonstrate that China abides by international law, upholds international order and works for regional peace and stability.

The South China Sea is an important shipping lane. It has a bearing on the interests of many countries, including that of China. Therefore we understand the international concerns over the South China Sea issue. We have never rejected the legitimate rights and interests of non-regional countries. We have always been committed to safeguarding the freedom of navigation in the South China Sea. However, we are opposed to the "gunboat diplomacy" of certain countries operated under the pretext of "protecting the freedom of navigation and overflight" and "maintaining regional peace". We are opposed to them taking advantage of the arbitration to hype up or create tensions in the South China Sea. The South China Sea must not become an arena for some big powers from outside the region to flex their muscles. The Chinese people are firmly determined to protect our national sovereignty and maritime rights and interests. Our determination will not be swayed by threats or intimidation.

Let no fleeting clouds block our vision. Let the right way lead us on.

The South China Sea issue is a legacy from history. At the same time it concerns the real interests of today. Geopolitics is also involved. Resolving this issue will take time, patience and mutual understanding and respect between countries concerned.

For a solution to be fundamental and enduring, it has to be peaceful, it has to have gone through an equal-footed consultation and negotiation between the countries directly concerned, and it has to be based on respecting historical facts and international law.

The South China Sea should be a sea of peace, a sea of friendship and a sea of cooperation. This is China's commitment. And it takes the joint efforts of China and its neighbours to turn this into reality.

Thank you. Now, I would like to take your questions.

Question: We know that there is an important election in America. America's role on the South China Sea issue is very significant, even though it has not ratified the UNCLOS. So what kind of opportunity or challenge do you see from a Clinton presidency or a Trump presidency for China-US relations and the issue of the South China Sea?

Liu Xiaoming: I think it's still too early for me to make predictions, but we have to be ready to deal with either of the two. Hillary Clinton was the Secretary of State, and she has visited China many times. We don't know Donald Trump that well. I have read some Western media reports saying that China might be concerned about a Trump administration. I'm not that worried. I had been working on China-US relations for years and had followed many presidential elections. I think I understand American electoral politics. We listen to what they are saying today, but we must pay more attention to what they are going to do after the election. I'm confident that whoever becomes US president will set store by the national interests of the United States, and will attach importance to the relationship with China. I am confident about that. I believe that China and the US have a broad relationship. We may have some differences, there may be up and downs in the relationship, but I believe what unites China and the United States is more important than what divides us.

Question: Ambassador, thank you very much for your statement. You say that China is happy to negotiate on the South China Sea, and I think it will assist the negotiation if China could clarify the meaning of the "dotted line," what is intended by the line? Whether it is a claim for the rights of everything within the line, or it is the basis for China to generate for themselves maritime rights? It will be great for China to clarify it. And if I may ask another thing that the arbitration tribunal report also reviewed several fishing practice by Chinese fishermen, including the use of explosives in the South China Sea, one of the world's richest fishing grounds. So would you tell us what kind of steps China will take to put an end to these actions?

Liu Xiaoming: First I will say that China has long stood on the side of resolving disputes through bilateral negotiations with our neighbouring countries on the basis of respect for historical facts and in accordance with international law. It is not something that we have only put forward recently, and we are still behind the commitment. We do hope that the neighbouring countries and China will engage in diplomatic negotiations to find solutions with which both sides can be content.

Regarding the "dotted line", this is something inherited from history, as are our territorial sovereignty and maritime interests as well as historical rights. It is based on many facts that China was the first to discover, to name, to explore these islands and areas, including development and jurisdiction on these islands, and also including the fishing activities by Chinese fishermen. So the dotted line has been recognized by the international community since it was announced in 1948. No country, I know you are shaking your head, but no country challenged the dotted line until the 1970s, when natural gas was found. Then some countries rushed into this area and illegally seized, invaded, and occupied 42 islands or reefs, 29 by the Vietnamese, 8 by the Philippines, 5 by the Malaysians. China has sovereign rights over all these islands. They are part of the Nansha Islands. So I think the dotted line has been on the map, if you check your record, the maps published officially by a variety of authorities by the US, France and even Britain. They all show the dotted line, which is regarded as showing respect for the Chinese sovereignty over this area.

With regard to the fishing activities, we are of course regulating the fishermen's activities. The government does not support any fishing activities that damage fishing resources. That's one reason why we are also in discussions with neighbouring countries in order to find solutions on how together we can bring good order to fishing activities. With regard to the fishing activities, I want to remind you that fishermen of some neighbouring countries indulge in a lot of illegal damaging activities. So efforts are called for from China and its neighbouring countries to find a solution to this problem together.

Question: Some people might have actually seen you saying there's zero possibility of the ruling of the international law being enforced, given that sovereignty has been ruled out of the UNCLOS. I was very concerned. You know a peaceful resolution of this very tense dangerous situation requires international law to be respected by all. But your side ruled out the possibilities for the peaceful solutions for all the parties. And when you talk about the bilateral negotiation between a big power and a small power, does it mean some kind of might is right in the 19th-century-style? Thank you!

Liu Xiaoming: When I say there is zero effect, I'm talking about the effect they have on China's territorial sovereignty, maritime rights and interests. You would not expect that China's territorial sovereignty and maritime rights would be affected at all by this arbitration. I think I made this point very clear, you could not expect there would be change because of the arbitration. If you expect there to be an impact on China's territorial sovereignty and maritime rights and interests, I think you will be proved wrong. You should never expect anything to happen in this respect.

Arbitration is a very unsatisfactory way to resolve this issue. China will not accept it. It violates the UNCLOS, and it is illegal. The UNCLOS places the bilateral agreements, bilateral discussions ahead of arbitration. Arbitration will only apply when the state parties of the UNCLOS cannot resolve their problems by bilateral negotiations. So, I cannot agree with the argument that the tribunal is resolving disputes in accordance with international law.

南海问题 / South China Sea

China and the Philippines agreed that we were going to have bilateral negotiations. These negotiations never took place because the Philippines thought they received support from the United States. They believe they can get something from the arbitration case and are no longer interested in talking with China. The tribunal violated the basic proceedings of the UNCLOS, but we remain committed to bilateral negotiations. It is endorsed again today by Foreign Ministers from China and the ten ASEAN countries, including the Philippines, in a joint statement pledging to implement the DOC in full. It's very interesting that the Philippines is one party that has agreed to the new joint statement, which is also supportive of the bilateral negotiations between directly concerned parties as a means to solve disputes peacefully through dialogue and consultation. But on the other hand, they (the Philippines) still have illusions about these rulings. I do hope that they can get out of this dilemma, the sooner the better. So that's why I'm saying that these things have no effect on China's rights and China's sovereignty over the South China Sea, and will not have impact on China's commitment to bilateral negotiations with neighbouring countries. We believe the only solution that can be lasting and enduring is that the related countries meet face to face rather than to hold a tribunal arbitration that is imposed on a sovereign state. Just like here in this country, I do not foresee that if Britain wanted to negotiate with the other countries through peaceful means to find solutions to their disputes, you would accept an arbitration imposed on yourselves before these negotiations had even started. I don't think you would accept that. You would believe that a sovereign country has the right to find a solution rather than to be faced with having a tribunal case imposed on it. So that's what I'm saying.

You talked about big country and small country. Although China is big in size, we always stand for the position that countries big or small should be equal. Out of the 14 countries which neighbour China, we have reached boundary agreements with 12. Some of them are small countries, such as Nepal and Myanmar, but we have resolved the difficult border issues through peaceful and friendly methods on an equal footing. I think China is a guardian of international order and international law. We are still hoping that we can find a solution to the disputes with the Philippines, Vietnamese, Malaysians and other countries. We can work together to ensure peace and stability in this region.

Question: I have some strong words about the utility of the troops, and nice words about China's approach. But Mr. Ambassador, don't you think that building air strips on unoccupied reefs and sending ships full of tourists create more tension than unilateral arbitration in the region?

Liu Xiaoming: China has always called for restraint. But some countries even started building military facilities on their illegally-occupied islands. When the Philippines or Vietnam built air strips on the illegally-occupied islands, the Western media kept silent. Some Western politicians turned a blind eye to this. In face of the provocations, China could not help but to build facilities to counter their measures. We are doing this on our own land. I hope you understand my point. Those countries went back on their word, built military facilities and deployed missiles, tanks and artillery on the territory they illegally seized and occupied. And China is forced to make a response to this.

So I don't think China's actions have caused any damage to the region. On the contrary, China is building facilities that will provide public services in terms of meteorological research, oceanic research, and environmental protection. Building lighthouses is very beneficial for the safety of shipping in the South China Sea. Hundreds of thousands of vessels pass through the South China Sea. This has been appreciated by local business people. I read earlier this year that the Reuters conducted a poll. Many ship owners appreciate China's efforts and they believe the public services and public goods provided by China in building these services, like lighthouse and other rescue facilities, really shorten the time of rescue, and have done a great deal to improve the environment for shipping in the area. And I think China is really committed to this.

Having said this, I would encourage you to read the statement published today. Both China and the ASEAN countries agreed that the parties concerned will exercise self-restraint. That shows the commitment China has made to maintain peace and stability in the area. Let me read this line, and I hope this helps you to understand the situation.

"The Parties undertake to exercise self-restraint in the conduct of activities that would complicate or escalate disputes and affect peace and stability including, among others, refraining from action of inhabiting on the presently uninhabited islands, reefs, shoals, cays, and other features and to handle their differences in a constructive manner."

Question: Mr. Ambassador, would you just explain a little bit more about how China plans to use the resources in the South China Sea, those resources under the sea bed, because presumably you do have ambitions for those resources? Could you explain a bit more about your plans?

Liu Xiaoming: As I said, China has legal maritime rights and interests in this area. And of course, there are some Chinese oil companies doing the drilling. You know that all these activities are within the scope of China's sovereignty. We realize the disputes in some areas and we are ready to talk to relevant countries about joint exploration and joint development.
In fact, China and Vietnam reached agreement on some joint development programmes. In fact there is a project between China, Vietnam and the Philippines. When it comes to the natural resource exploration in disputed areas, we are open to discussions with neighbouring countries.

Question: I have been studying China for a number of years, I found, your Excellency, that your speech was an excellent presentation. Now to the question, do you think it is right for countries that do not sign the UNCLOS, or shall we say by proxy, make utilization of international law in a very disguised way. Is that indeed correct?

Liu Xiaoming: Absolutely incorrect.

Question: Thank you very much. Ambassador, I think you have explained China's position extremely well, and I think all of us have got a much better understanding on the arbitration decision that has zero legal effect. You don't accept it for the reasons you explained. On the territorial claims, you explained China's historical territory rights and you also explained China is developing public services in the South China Sea, building lighthouses and other beneficial things. So why are your neighbours Vietnam, the Philippines, not to mention Japan not accepting these issues?

Liu Xiaoming: I noticed when you say China's neighbours are not accepting China's policy, you used plural forms. I would say they are not in the majority.
The truth is, we have a very good neighbourhood. Our largest neighbour, Russia, has good relations with China. The DPRK where I had worked, South Korea, Pakistan,

India, Kazakhstan, Nepal, Bangladesh, Vietnam, they all have very good relations with China. Relations between countries sometimes have ups and downs. What binds us together is interest.

Indeed, some countries do not accept China's policy because they have maritime disputes with us. Take Japan for example. We have problem with Japan over the Diaoyu Islands. The islands should be returned to China, according to the Cairo Declaration. We believe the Diaoyu Islands are ours, but when we normalized relations with Japan, we did not want the issue standing in the way. Deng Xiaoping proposed shelving the disputes. He believed future generations would be wiser and would find a solution finally. So the status quo has been there for over 40 years. It was not until recently that the Japanese government wanted to, in their words, "nationalize" the island, and the right wing segment wanted to buy this island to achieve illegal occupation. They rocked the boat, and they forced us to respond to their provocative actions.

The South China Sea is the same thing. China has been the victim, but we still believe countries, big or small, should be placed on an equal footing in bilateral negotiation to find solutions. We have been successful with Vietnam in settling some territorial disputes. We reached agreement on the maritime delimitation of the Beibu Bay. I am not saying we are trying to copy what we have achieved between China and the Vietnam, but we are confident that we can find solutions. But we should be given time on these very complicated issues. Confidence and patience are required.

Now we have the geopolitical factor. Some big countries, much bigger than China, want to use the issue of the South China Sea as an excuse for so-called "rebalancing strategy", to flex their muscles and to show their presence. That makes things more complicated. That is something that we would not like to see.

Question: Ambassador, nobody is bigger than China. You made very strong statement there. It's one of the strongest I've ever heard and China is very angry.

To some extent, I think the Chinese are very right to be angry. You're going to have to be very patient, and try not be angry. Let's talk about the sphere of influence. How does your long-term policy look in the sphere of influence? Where China will be 20 to 30 years from now? Which parts of the Pacific do you feel you will consider as part of the post-war world order and as your sphere of influence because you have concerns about that? China, the US and Russia have huge problems in common and we should be working with one another, not arguing about these islands of South China Sea. Could you talk a little bit on how you foresee China's sphere of influence evolving?

Liu Xiaoming: Sorry for saying this. I think you are still using a Cold War mentality to judge things. I am talking about the post-war order after the Second World War, not the Cold War order. This basic order is part of the international order that is guaranteed by the UN Charter.

And I can't agree with you when you say China's "sphere of influence". China has no interest in having a "sphere of influence". The number one reason is that, you said no country is bigger than China, and you are wrong from the very beginning. China is still a developing country. China is the second largest economy, that's for sure, but in per capita income, China ranks lower than 80th in the world, much poorer than the UK, to say nothing about the U.S. per capita GDP is more important than total GDP, because that concerns the livelihood of the people.

After my tour in Egypt, I was seconded to Gansu, one of the poorest provinces in China, as an assistant governor. You probably have never heard the name of that province. It is so poor that people even have problem getting drinking water. Many local people have to depend on purified rain water collected in a cell. There are still hundreds of thousands of people living under such conditions. I traveled a great deal in that province. One of the purposes is to get to know the reality of the country that I represent. Shanghai, Tianjin, Guangzhou do not represent all of China, just like London is not all of the UK. If you go to the north of England or Scotland, you will find a different country. That's the same with China. So China must face enormous challenges in developing its economy and allowing 1.3 billion people to have a better and happier life.

We are not interested in challenging the so-called American "leadership". We are not interested in building the so-called "sphere of influence". We are only interested in building our country to make China a more advanced and modernized country. Why do we care about these islands? China had been the victim of foreign aggression for over 100 years before the founding of the PRC. A lot of unequal treaties were imposed on China. China lost a large portion of its land. Now China is an independent country standing on its own feet. People care about their territory. As I said, we are not interested in a single inch of foreign land that does not belong to us. We are not jealous of it. But we will defend every inch of the land that belongs to us by every means available to us. So if you have been to China, you will understand a saying in China, that is, "an inch of land is more precious than an ounce of gold". So it is in the DNA of the Chinese people to defend our sovereignty, territorial integrity, and maritime rights and interests.

Question: I am from the Japanese Embassy. Since you talked about Japan and the Senkaku Islands (the Diaoyu Islands of China), so I have to respond. First of all, on the matter of victimhood, we are not talking about history from 70-80 years ago. So I do suggest we do not talk about victimhood but talk about the rule of law. China is a big country within the UNCLOS. By becoming a party of the UNCLOS, China has to accept articles on dispute settlement and it must comply with them. The UNCLOS has stated that the matter should be decided by the tribunal. So it is very clear that China is bound by the treaty and by acceding to the UNCLOS. You cannot make both deals at the same time. In terms of the Senkaku Islands, in 1951 when the San Francisco Treaty was concluded, China objected, but from 1952 to 1971 China never claimed the Senkaku Islands. So we can sense a kind of manipulating use of history. It's a bit too much.

Kerry Brown (Host): Do you have any questions?

Liu Xiaoming: You could apply for another opportunity to make a speech. I think this time the floor is given to me. What is your question?

Question: I want to ask why don't you declare by which date that COC can be concluded? Please if you can specify the date of COC conclusion?

Liu Xiaoming: I think you have no right to ask me this question, because as I said, Japan is not a party to the negotiations of the COC. So when you ask China to set a deadline, I think that's too much. It's too arrogant, because this matter is up to China and the ASEAN countries to negotiate. China already made a commitment to working actively with the ASEAN countries to reach the COC as soon as possible. Because this matter is very complicated -- it not only concerns China but also concerns the ten ASEAN countries -- and since China always treats others as equals and always respects others' views, China cannot set a date.

As far as the Diaoyu islands are concerned, we could spend a whole day on this. This topic has been debated many times at the very top level and working level between China and Japan. One thing is certain, that is, you mentioned, the San Francisco Treaty has never been accepted or recognized by China from day one. The Diaoyu Islands is part of China and was illegally stolen by Japan by means of war. This is the term used by the Cairo Declaration signed by the leaders of China, UK and US. Namely, that these islands, i.e., all islands in the Pacific Ocean stolen by Japan should be confiscated and returned to China. After the Second World War, the Cold War followed. Japan became America's ally. So they changed their mind and thought, why should they return the islands to China? I don't need to refer back to history on that.

Question: Thank you very much Ambassador. You made a very strong argument on the issue of the South China Sea. You began by saying that the Tribunal does not have jurisdiction over territorial sovereignty and maritime demarcation and you are right. The tribunal says repeatedly that it does not have. My question is that why do Chinese government representatives keep on talking about how the tribunal has violated the territorial sovereignty and maritime delimitation? Actually it has not.

Liu Xiaoming: Talking about sovereignty, I think it's very clear that this is the whole purpose of the Philippines' arbitration case. They want to use the arbitration to deny China's sovereignty over the islands. That's the basic logic. I don't know how much they have spent. Some say they spent 30 million U.S. dollars on lawyers' fees. They spent that large sum of money just for a ruling on the status of uninhabited islands? I think they are not that stupid and mad. I think the purpose is to use this tribunal's ruling to deny China's sovereignty and maritime rights. That's very clear. Anyone who has no bias, to say nothing about the experts, should realize their real intention behind this.

Secondly, how can you separate the land features from the country who owns it? In appearance, the ruling was not on China's sovereignty, but in the essence, it says you can't claim sovereignty and maritime rights. We regard the South China Sea islands as a whole, but they single out each feature. They want to dismantle China's sovereignty bit by bit. The ruling actually deprives China of our sovereignty over the islands. I think their aim is obvious.

They also deny China's historical rights. The dotted line is one of them. Such denial goes against the basic principles of the UNCLOS. The UNCLOS respects the historical entitlements. China made exceptional declarations to exclude any compulsory arbitration on matters concerning maritime delimitation and historical rights. The exceptional declaration has been made not only by China but by more than 30 countries including the UK. Why does the UNCLOS accept the exceptional declaration? This is because they do not want to create a problem for a sovereign state. The whole purpose of the UNCLOS is for sovereign countries to live in a peaceful environment with regard to maritime delimitation.

Kerry Brown (Host): We are extremely grateful to you for bringing China's perspective on the South China Sea. We hope you will have the sixth and seventh time to speak at Chatham House in the future. Thank you very much.

Liu Xiaoming: My pleasure.

新冠肺炎疫情
COVID-19

2020年新冠肺炎疫情发生不久，以美国为首的西方势力编造各种谎言和谣言，对中国进行污名化、妖魔化，企图把病毒源头的帽子扣在中国头上。2月6日，我在驻英使馆举行中外记者会，介绍中国防控疫情工作成效，阐明中方政策立场，揭穿谎言，说明真相，激浊扬清。27家中外媒体50余名记者出席。菲律宾、柬埔寨、加拿大、芬兰、西班牙、韩国等国驻英使节及外交官也出席了记者会。BBC、天空新闻台、中国国际电视台和今日俄罗斯电视台对记者会进行了现场直播。

4月23日，我出席"亚洲之家"网上座谈会，发表题为《坚定信心，加强团结，携手战胜疫情》的主旨演讲，并与"亚洲之家"主席格林勋爵进行对话交流，回答听众提问。英国政府"一带一路"特使范智廉爵士，议会上院议员鲍威尔勋爵，英中贸协名誉主席沙逊勋爵，英国候任驻华大使吴若兰及英内阁办、外交部、财政部、国际贸易部、国际发展部、商业能源与产业战略部等部门官员，20多个国家驻英使节或外交官，以及英国、美国、欧洲、亚洲等工商、媒体、学术等各界人士近250人出席。BBC和天空新闻台进行了现场直播和转播。

"亚洲之家"是英国非营利、非政治性机构，旨在增进英各界对亚洲的认识理解，深化与亚洲各国政治、文化、商业、教育等各领域交往联系，定期举办演讲、座谈、展览等活动，其会员多为英知名机构、大型企业及各界精英人士。

说明真相，激浊扬清
——关于抗击新冠肺炎疫情中外记者会
（2020年2月6日，中国驻英大使馆）

刘晓明： 大家上午好！今天，我们举办中外记者会，通报中国防控新型冠状病毒肺炎疫情的最新情况。

疫情发生以来，中国政府果断采取一系列有力防控举措，行动之快、力度之大、范围之广，举世罕见。我认为，可以从"三个高度"看中国政府采取的有力措施：

一是高度重视。习近平主席多次做出重要指示，始终把人民群众生命安全和身体健康放在第一位；两次召开中共中央政治局常务委员会会议，成立应对疫情工作领导小组，全面部署防疫工作。李克强总理受习主席委托，亲赴武汉指导疫情防控工作。中国举国上下，已形成全面动员、全面部署、全面加强的防控工作局面，全力打赢疫情防控阻击战。

在国家层面，政府有关部门各司其职，军队积极支援地方，各地区成立党政主要官员挂帅的领导机制；在诊疗一线，广大医务人员无私奉献、英勇奋战，涌现出不胜枚举的感人故事；在社会基层，广大民众众志成城、团结奋战，打响了疫情防控的人民战争。疫情防控工作有力开展，逐步取得成效。总地看，疫情是可防、可控、可治的。

二是高度负责。疫情发生之后，中国政府采取了最全面、最严格的防控举措，很多举措远远超出《国际卫生条例》要求，这不仅是对中国人民的生命安全和身体健康高度负责，更是对维护世界人民的健康和全球公共卫生安全做出的最大努力。例如，中国在武汉等地暂时采取集中隔离举措，全力遏制病毒扩散；来自全国各地超过6000名专业医务人员驰援武汉和湖北其他地区，口罩、防护服、药品等医疗用品及肉类、蔬菜、日用品等生活必需品及时陆续运抵；武汉火神山、雷神山两家专门医院在短短10天内建成并投入使用，集中收治、救治重症病人。需要指出的是，此次疫情虽然感染人数较多，但中国境内病死率非常低，仅为2.1%，远低于埃博拉（40.4%）、非典（SARS，10%）、中东呼吸综合征（MERS，34.4%）。美国本流感季已有1900万人感染，至少1万人死亡，从死亡人数看比新型冠状病毒感染肺炎疫情更加严重。目前中国治愈人数在增加，我们对打赢疫情阻击战充满信心。

与此同时，中国也努力承担应对疫情的国际责任和义务。世界卫生组织总干事谭德塞充分肯定中方防控工作，高度赞赏中国抗击疫情为世界做出的巨大贡献，认为中国举措"设立了应对疫情的新标杆"。中方高度重视疫情对其他国家和地区的影响，加强了中国公民海外旅行的管控，呼吁公众在防止疫情传播方面积极承担社会责任，努力减少疫情对其他国家的影响。截至2月3日，中国境外确诊病例153例，占所有病例不到1%，这表明中方为控制疫情传播、保护中国人民和全世界人民的健康和卫生安全，采取了最有力的举措，做出了重要贡献。

三是高度合作。中方始终本着公开、透明、负责任的态度开展疫情防控国际合作。第一，我们第一时间向世卫组织、有关国家及中国港澳台地区通报疫情，分享病毒基因序列，以利于各方及时、有效应对疫情，世卫组织及许多国家对此予以高度评价。我们还在双边层面与多国就疫情防控等问题保持密切沟通。第二，我们高度重视在华外国人安全，通过各种渠道向各国驻华机构通报疫情，解决好他们面临的困难。截至2月6日中午，19名在华外国公民确诊感染新型冠状病毒肺炎，2人已治愈出院，17人正接受隔离治疗，病情平稳。近期，包括英国在内的一些国家决定从武汉撤侨，中方给予协助。第三，我们正同国际社会一道，加强科学研究、疫苗研发等合作，共同维护全球和地区公共卫生安全。疫情无情人有情。面对突如其来的疫情，很多国家政府官员和各界人士都对中国抗击疫情表达了同情、信任和支持，多国政府及国际组织向中方捐助疫情防控物资。除了英国政府援助外，英国工商界、华人社团、留学生纷纷通过各种渠道捐资捐物。就在几天前，中国驻英国使馆举行仪式，接受全英20多个侨学界社团捐款、捐物，这些帮助让我们深受感动。我们对这些来自英国各界的爱心和善举表示衷心感谢！

女士们、先生们，中国政府遏制疫情扩散的决心是坚定的，措施是有力的，我们将继续把疫情防控作为当前最重要的任务。

一是全力以赴救治患者。生命重于泰山。生命权、健康权是最基本，也是最大人权。中国各地医疗机构正努力提高收治率和治愈率，降低感染率和病死率。

二是着力做好重点地区疫情防控工作。湖北省特别是武汉市仍是疫情防控的重中之重，当地正进一步完善和加强防控，严格落实早发现、早报告、早隔离、早治疗措施，加强疫情监测，集中救治患者，加大对密切接触人员医学观察力度，全力防止疫情向外扩散。

三是加大疫情国际防控合作和科研攻关力度。中方将继续同世卫组织、相关国家和地区保持密切合作，共同做好疫情防控工作。近日，中国将《新型冠状病毒肺炎公众防护指南》翻译成多语种，通过社交媒体等多种形式快速传递给世界各国，这体现了中国与国际社会合作应对疫情的诚意和负责任大国的担当。据我所知，中国、英国等国科研人员正加紧论证病毒来源和传播途径，密切跟踪病毒变异情况，实施相关数据和病例资料的开放共享，共同研究防控策略和措施，医药和疫苗研发也在有条不紊推进中。

女士们、先生们，目前，英国和国际社会对疫情还存在一些担忧，一些人担心疫情对中国经济乃至世界经济产生不利影响。我们也注意到，个别国家最近对疫情做出过度反应，一些国家还出现针对中国公民的恐慌甚至侮辱性、歧视性的言行。对此，我想强调四点：

一是各方应全面看待对中国经济的影响。从目前情况看，疫情对交通运输、文化旅游、酒店餐饮和影视娱乐等服务消费方面的影响较大。我想指出，这种影响在短期内的确存在，但是阶段性的、暂时性的，不会改变中国经济长期向好的基本面。中国经济极具韧性，中长期看仍具有巨大的发展潜力。我们完全有能力、有信心把疫情对经济的影响降到最低。世界银行、国际货币基金组织及国际知名经济学家普遍认为，疫情对中国经济的冲击是暂时的，对中国经济的未来充满信心。

二是各国政府应客观理性地评估疫情。世界卫生组织反复强调，不赞成甚至反对采取旅行和贸易限制措施。近日，英方在双边层面亦表示充分肯定中方为抗击疫情付出的巨大努力和采取的有力措施，并愿同中方加强合作，尽可能向中方提供协助。希望包括英国在内的各国政府，理解支持中方努力，尊重世卫组织专业建议，不要过度反应，不要人为制造恐慌，确保国家之间正常合作和往来不受影响。

三是各国媒体应客观公正报道疫情。我们注意到，近期包括英媒在内的多国媒体对疫情做了大量报道，不少报道积极评价中国抗击疫情的努力，一些建议客观中肯，我们对此表示赞赏。但也有一些报道存在偏见，有些甚至恶意中伤、蓄意造谣。谣言和恐慌比病毒更可怕，信心和决心对战胜疫情至关重要。公共卫生安全问题超越国界，需要各方携手应对，媒体也应为此肩负起应有的社会责任。

四是各方应共同反对任何侮辱性、歧视性言行。我十分赞同世卫组织总干事谭德塞所说，"这是一个需要事实而不是恐惧的时刻，是需要科学而不是谣言的时刻，是需要团结而不是羞辱的时刻"。希望各界能够理性、冷静地认识这场疫情，并做出科学、恰当的应对，同舟共济、共迎挑战。

女士们、先生们，中国人常说"人心齐，泰山移"。我坚信，有中国共产党的坚强领导，有中国特色社会主义制度的巨大优势，有中国人民团结一心、众志成城，有国际社会的大力支持，我们一定能战胜疫情！

每次记者会，我都会播放一段视频。今天我也想和大家分享一段暖心的视频，它讲述了中英两国人民共克时艰、共迎挑战的感人故事。

（播放视频）

现在，我愿回答各位记者提问。

中国国际电视台： 能否请你详细介绍一下中英在研制疫苗方面开展合作的情况？约翰逊首相个人尚未表达对中方抗击疫情的支持，你对此是否感到不满？

刘晓明： 中英科学家确实正在积极推进相关合作。疫情发生前，中国的研究机构与包括牛津大学、帝国理工学院在内的英国大学建成联合研究中心等合作平台。目前他们正在争分夺秒地加紧工作，着手开展药物研发和疫苗开发，希望在不久的将来能取得实质性成果。中国政府十分支持这项工作，中国驻英国使馆正在尽我们所能促进两国科学家的沟通交流。

中方对英国政府的支持表示感谢。疫情发生以来，两国政府保持了密切联系。英国内阁秘书兼首相国家安全事务顾问塞德维尔和外交大臣拉布分别与中央外事工作委员会办公室主任杨洁篪、国务委员兼外长王毅通电话。英方高度赞扬中方防控疫情的举措，并表示愿意提供帮助，我们对此表示感谢。因此，并不存在中方对英国政府感到失望和不满的问题。

BBC： 你刚才提到中方对包括英国在内的一些外国政府的过度反应和恐慌感到失望，你能具体谈一下是哪些过度反应吗？你指的是不是英国政府警告在华英国公民尽快离开中国？

刘晓明： 中英两国政府间的沟通渠道是开放的，包括最高层和工作层。我与英国外交部官员保持良好沟通，包括代理常务次官和总司长。我的副手及使馆主管官员与英国外交部几乎每天保持联系。中方已明确表达相关立场，中国采取的防控措施是有效的，各方不应恐慌或过度反应，建议英方遵循世界卫生组织的专业意见。英方对此表示赞同，高度肯定中方举措取得的实效，并表示将采纳世卫组织意见。

然而，我也看到，英方并未完全做到言行一致。相信你们也注意到，世卫组织总干事已经公开批评英国政府通告提醒英国公民全部离开中国的行为，认为这种"一刀切"的做法无助于解决问题。我们只对疫情集中发生地区实施了隔离，并不是整个中国都是疫区，中国的大部分地区生活正常进行。我多次在公开和私下场合讲，中方希望英国政府和公众客观冷静看待中国国内形势。疫情是全世界面临的共同威胁，需要国际社会合作应对。我们应该相互支持，而不是削弱他国的努力，这就是我的建议。

英国电视五台： 大使先生，你表示你对中国与英国政府的合作和密切联系感到满意，但指责英方过度反应。

刘晓明： 我并不是指责，而是希望英方能够言行一致。

英国电视五台： 既然英中双方保持密切联系，那么当你听到英国政府向在华英国公民发布警告时，你是否感到十分惊讶？

刘晓明： 我们认为不应有如此的恐慌情绪。英方正式发布警告前向我们做了通报，中方明确表示，这样做是不妥的，我们认为疫情是可防、可控、可治的，要求英方客观、冷静反应，保障双方正常往来与合作不受影响。

独立电视台： 你是否担心英国出现第三例确诊病例？如果出现这种情况，是否表明中国并不是像你刚才说的那样有能力控制疫情？

刘晓明： 不能排除英国出现新的病例，因为我们对这个新型病毒并不十分了解，这也是为什么包括中英在内各国科学家正在密切合作，努力研发治疗药物和疫苗。中方认为疫情可治可防，因为到目前为止，治愈病例是死亡病例的两倍，中国全国的治愈病例仍在稳定增加。正如习近平主席所说，我们在同时间赛跑，与病魔较量，我们有信心！目前累计已有1150多例治愈出院，死亡病例563例，治愈病例数远高于死亡病例数。

天空新闻台： 有报道称，疫情发生以后，针对在英中国公民和中国留学生的歧视和仇恨在增加，你怎么看？

刘晓明： 总地看，英国民众对中国是同情和支持的，比如刚才播放的视频，来自北爱尔兰一所小学，师生们表达了他们对中国的支持。我们赞赏英国民众对中国的支持。的确，有针对中国人歧视和仇恨的个案发生。我们向英国政府和警方表达了关切。我们也向中国公民发布旅行建议，提醒他们注意此类事件，做好自我保护。

我们发布了英国警方和中国使领馆的联系方式，出现此类情况，他们要先报警，同时向中国使领馆寻求领事保护。我们收到一些有关大学存在校园歧视的报告，中小学也有。

引发歧视现象的原因是多方面的，有的是由于对疫情缺乏了解，有的是媒体不实报道误导造成的。媒体应该以负责、科学的态度报道疫情，不能加剧公众的恐慌。当然，根深蒂固的种族歧视也是存在的，在英国和其他国家都有。我们面对的是人类共同的敌人，在疫情面前，所有国家的人们应该团结起来，共同反对歧视和仇恨。我呼吁包括媒体在内的各行各业的人们共同应对挑战。

彭博社： 你刚才提到，与非典、中东呼吸综合征、美国流感疫情相比，新型冠状病毒引发的肺炎并不严重。

刘晓明： 我比较的是死亡病例的数字。

彭博社： 现在疫情还处于初期阶段，你想向中国和中国以外的人传递什么信息？是否与其他流行病相比，当前形势并不严重？

刘晓明： 我想传递的信息是，我们不应该恐慌。对传染病应该高度重视，但我们有信心、有资源、有能力战胜疫情。现在，中国举国上下都已经动员起来应对疫情，治愈病例在增加。昨天，习近平主席又一次主持召开会议，他要求医务人员全力以赴提高收治率、治愈率，降低死亡率，民众信心倍增。

我们有中国共产党的坚强领导，有中国特色社会主义的制度优势，有全国人民的众志成城，有国际社会的大力支持，我们一定能够战胜疫情。我无法预测拐点，但希望尽快到来。一方面，我们必须依靠自己的力量，中国科学家和研究人员正在努力工作；另一方面，我们也与其他国家，包括英国的科学家开展合作。英国在防治传染病方面处于领先地位。在疫情发生前，中英两国科学家就已经开展长期合作，我们有合作基础。这次英国已经提供了支持。我希望公众不要恐慌。

英国电视四台：你是否已要求英国外交部重新考虑要求英国公民离开中国的建议？

刘晓明：我们已向英国外交部表示，过度反应无助于应对当前疫情。我们希望英国外交部听从世界卫生组织的建议，理性应对，不要过度反应。

《卫报》：武汉"封城"已经两周，一些人可能钱物都将用尽，中国政府会提供援助吗？"封城"会一直持续下去吗？有报道说，武汉的医疗系统压力很大，很多人得不到及时的诊断，你们如何保证所有的病例，至少大部分病例得到收治？

刘晓明：隔离措施不是永久的，但目前看仍是必需的。各级政府正全力以赴采取行动。面对疫情，我们采取的是综合解决办法。全国上下已经动员起来，为患者提供治疗的一线医务人员正在紧张工作，物流运输部门也在日夜奋战。我想问一问，《卫报》在北京有常驻记者吗？看来他的工作还不够努力，没有抓住报道的关键。中国国家卫生健康委员会每天召开新闻发布会对外公布疫情最新情况并回答人民群众关心的问题。我每天都在跟踪进展，尤其关注在哪些方面能与英方开展合作以共同抗击疫情。中国交通部、海关总署、工业和信息化部等部门每天都在公布物资供应信息。尽管民众正常的生产生活会受到一定影响，但基本物资供应还是有保障的。

习近平主席和李克强总理指示各级政府要把人民群众的生命安全和身体健康放在第一位，关心包括受感染者在内的全体民众，竭尽全力保障生活必需品供应。中方所做努力均需要一定时间，但当前举措在遏制病毒传播方面已凸显成效，得到世界卫生组织的高度评价。

你提到一些人有抱怨，我认为这是可以理解的。疫情发生得十分突然，令人措手不及，但从中央到地方各级政府都充分动员，采取了切实有效的应对策略。假以时日，人们会了解疫情的本质，理解形势的急迫性，最终得出正确结论。

疫情刚刚发生时，我们的应对资源确实有些捉襟见肘，没有足够的医院和床位。正因如此，我们在10天之内建成两家医院，全力收治更多病患。世界上没有其他任何国家能做到这一点。在基层，广大民众都在努力防控疫情，医务工作者都在尽力救治病患，全国上下都在全力以赴防控疫情。

今日俄罗斯电视台：大使曾经提到病毒对中国经济发展有影响。这是否由于一些媒体的不公正报道造成的？你所说的这些媒体，包括在座记者，其中是否有人在蓄意诋毁、破坏中国经济？

刘晓明： 我注意到了英国媒体的相关报道，总的来说他们对中国经济仍保有信心。我举几个例子，《每日电讯报》的一篇报道认为中国经济仍充满弹性和活力。《金融时报》也做了一些积极报道。我并没有说英国媒体唱衰中国经济，我只是用事实说明中国经济仍具活力。我希望你在报道中国的时候也能采取客观理性的态度。

《金融时报》： 目前有多少被困英国的中国公民向使馆方面报告？这些人可能是来旅游、出差、过农历新年，或因交通困难无法回家。如果此类人员数量很多，中国政府如何向他们提供有效帮助？是否为他们提供经济和住宿等支持？

刘晓明： 我们正尽最大努力去帮助他们。一些来自湖北特别是武汉的民众被困国外，中国政府尝试用包机接他们回家。驻英国使馆也在努力与来自湖北特别是武汉的同胞取得联系，询问他们是否需要帮助，是否有意愿尽快回家，但遇到实际困难。他们当中许多人或有自己的生意，或有未竟的工作，表示仍需留在国外。使馆尊重他们的意见并尽力予以协助。

《泰晤士报》： 世界卫生组织发出警告，要求对疫情的反应不应过度，不以政治为目的。在当前中美存在贸易争端背景下，英国政府紧随美方公布旅行限制。你认为是否有一些国家采取了政治手段？你对此有何评论？

刘晓明： 我赞同你的观点。一些别有用心的政客利用当前形势以达到其政治目的。中方对这些不负责任的言行及时表达了不满和反对。这种行径不符合美国利益，更不用说破坏中美合作了。我相信中美双方会共同致力于落实第一阶段经贸协议。正如我在不同场合反复强调的，协议对中美双方有利，对世界有利。但是"一个巴掌拍不响"，我们会继续落实协议，希望美方与中方相向而行。

伦敦广播电台： 据报道，你对约翰逊首相未能就疫情与中国政府直接沟通表示关切，能否谈一谈看法？第二个问题，你对英国政府建议在华英国人尽量离开中国有何看法？这与世界卫生组织的建议背道而驰，你认为英国政府为何会提出这样的建议？

刘晓明： 我认为，中方与英国首相的沟通渠道是畅通的。约翰逊首相在唐宁街10号举办了中国春节招待会，我和夫人受邀参加。我们谈得很愉快。我转达了习近平主席和李克强总理对约翰逊首相的问候，首相请我转达对中国领导人的问候。约翰逊当选首相后，李克强总理向他发了贺信。约翰逊首相向我表示，他致力于中英关系"黄金时代"，这是一个坚定的承诺。我认为，中英两国政府的沟通渠道是畅通的。关于第二个问题，你应该向英国外交部或外交大臣本人求证，他们为什么会提出这样的建议？我的回答是，不要做出过度反应。

《每日电讯报》： 我最近刚从北京回来，此前也曾去过武汉，当地处于"封城"状态。今天你讲了当地民众的总体情况是正常的，但实际上除了正式宣布隔离的地区外，其他很多城市也封锁了交通，民众不能随意离开，这跟你刚才介绍的情况并不一样。

刘晓明： 全国各地的疫情和湖北及武汉的疫情有区别。中国和其他国家也不一样。其他国家可能不需要举国动员。我并不是说中国国内一切如常，但不应将中国所有地方都看作疫区。所以不要做出过度反应，这就是我的建议。

《每日电讯报》： 事实是，中国国内民众反应过度了，他们对正在发生的疫情感到担心。我曾经在中国采访过一些人，他们的家人在感染了病毒后短短几天就去世了，甚至来不及检测是否感染了新型冠状病毒，也没有被纳入官方统计数字。中国国家卫健委的统计数字是否可信？

刘晓明： 我对你的建议是，要相信中国官方发布的数字。不信谣，不传谣，不要制造恐慌。正如我刚才所讲，现在需要保持冷静，不要恐慌。我对《每日电讯报》的建议是，可以关注个案，但更要看大局，否则就看不清中国目前的总体情况。这就是我给你的建议。

《每日电讯报》： 我想问中央政府给地方的指示是什么？因为很多地方并没有感染病例，也采取了封闭交通、设立体温检测点等措施。这些做法是地方政府决定的还是由中央决定的？

刘晓明： 总体上，各级政府应承担起应有责任。各地都已成立了主要党政领导人挂帅的疫情应对工作机制。中央的指示很明确，习近平主席两次主持召开中央政治局常委会会议，这是很少见的。昨天，习主席还召开另一个会议，对疫情防控做出重要指示。建议你们仔细阅读。地方政府必须听从中央的指示，地方政府及官员如不能有效履职，将为失职承担责任。

BBC： 有人说此次疫情凸显了中国"一党专政"国家的优势和弱点。一方面，中国在极短时间建起两所医院，展示了强大的资源动员能力。但另一方面，中共中央政治局常委会会议也提到疫情暴发之初的一些短板和不足，换句话说，就是缺乏透明、推卸责任、试图掩盖事实而不是迅速应对疫情等。你如何看待这种挑战？上述挑战对中国政治体制有多大影响？

刘晓明： 首先，我要纠正你的说法，中国不是"一党专政"国家。中国是由中国共产党领导的国家，我们还有8个民主党派参政议政。所以建议你了解一下中国政治制度的基本知识。民主党派积极参政，有不少民主党派成员是著名科学家，为政府应对疫情出谋划策。当然，没有任何一种制度是完美的。你也不能说英国的制度就是完美无缺的，否则你们怎么花了3年时间才搞定"脱欧"，当然我没有批评你的意思。任何制度都有不断改进的空间，所以我常说，世界上最大的空间就是不断改进的空间。

我高兴地看到，你仔细阅读了中共中央政治局常委会会议的新闻稿。正是认识到了短板和不足，我们才可以在未来做得更好。我们的确面临挑战，但我们对挑战的看法不同，我们认为挑战能够敦促我们改进工作、完善制度。我们对自己的制度充满信心，如果没有我们今天这样的制度，难以想象疫情会发展到什么程度。设想一下，如果类似的事情发生在英国，会是怎么样一种境况？

如果没有其他问题，今天记者会到此结束。谢谢大家出席，我们下次再见。

Facts Speak Louder than Words
—— A Press Conference on China's Fight against Novel Coronavirus Epidemic

On 6th February 2020, I held a press conference at the Chinese Embassy on China's fight against the Novel Coronavirus. More than 50 journalists from 27 media agencies attended the press conference, including BBC, ITV, Sky News, Channel 4, 5 News from Channel 5, Reuters, *Financial Times*, *The Daily Telegraph*, *The Times*, *The Guardian*, *The Evening Standard*, *The Daily Mail*, Leading Britain's Conversation of the UK, Xinhua News Agency, CCTV, China News Service, CGTN, *China Daily*, and Bloomberg, AFP, RT, the National of United Arab Emirates, *South China Morning Post*, Phoenix Infonews, *European Times*, *UK Chinese Times* and *UK Chinese Journal*. Also present at the press conference were envoys and diplomats from the diplomatic missions of the Philippines, Cambodia, Canada, Finland, Spain and the ROK to the UK. BBC, Sky News, CGTN and RT broadcast the press conference live.

The following is the transcript of the press conference.

Liu Xiaoming: Good morning! Thank you for joining us at the Chinese Embassy for today's press conference on updates about the novel coronavirus situation and the prevention and control measures in China.

Since the outbreak of the disease, the Chinese Government has taken a series of decisive and rigorous prevention and control measures. The speed, intensity and coverage of China's response have been unprecedented in the world. Let me use three "greats" to expound China's actions.

First, the Chinese Government has attached great importance to epidemic prevention and control.

President Xi Jinping has made important instructions on many occasions, emphasising that the safety of life and the health of the people are the top priority. He also twice called the meetings of the top leadership and set up a taskforce to map out plans for epidemic prevention.

Premier Li Keqiang, entrusted by President Xi, went to Wuhan to lead the counter-

virus efforts. The whole nation has been mobilized; prevention and control efforts have been deployed and strengthened across the country. China has gone all out to fight the disease.
- At the national level, the relevant government departments are shouldering their responsibility; the military has been mobilised to help;
- In all the places, the counter-virus taskforces are led by key Party and government officials.
- At the very frontline of treatment and care, medical workers are making selfless sacrifices and showing tremendous courage.
- In communities, the people stand united to wage a "people's war" against an invisible enemy.

The vigorous measures are taking effect gradually. On the whole, the epidemic is preventable, controllable and curable.

Second, the Chinese Government has demonstrated a great sense of responsibility.

Since the outbreak, the Chinese Government has taken the most comprehensive and strict prevention and control measures, many of which go far beyond the requirements of the International Health Regulations. By taking these measures, China is safeguarding the lives and health of not only the Chinese people, but also the people of the whole world. China is doing its best to safeguard global public health.

- Temporary measures for collective quarantine have been implemented in Wuhan and other places to prevent the further spread of the disease.
- More than 6, 000 medical professionals from all over the country have arrived in Hubei Province, including Wuhan.
- Medical supplies such as masks, hazmat suits and medicines, and daily necessities such as meat and vegetable have been transported to the affected areas without delay.
- Two specialised hospitals, the Huoshenshan Hospital and the Leishenshan Hospital, were built in ten days and have started to receive and treat the critically ill.

I want to emphasize that, although a large number of people have been infected with this virus, the mortality rate in China, which stands at 2. 1%, is very low. This is much lower than Ebola (40. 4%), SARS (10%) and MERS (34. 4%). In the United States, more than 19 million people have fallen ill with the flu so far this season, with the death toll being ten thousand. This is more serious than the coronavirus infection. Currently in China, the number of cured patients is rising. We are fully confident about beating the virus.

China is also honouring its obligation. Dr. Tedros, the Director General of the World Health Organisation, has expressed full recognition for China's prevention and control efforts, and spoken highly of the tremendous contribution that China has made to the world in fighting the disease. He said that China "is setting a new standard for outbreak response."

China attaches great importance to containing the potential spread of the virus to other countries and regions. It has strengthened management and control on the overseas travel of Chinese citizens, and called on the Chinese people to take up their social responsibilities to help prevent the further spread of the disease.

As of 3rd February, there were 153 confirmed cases outside China, which accounted for less than 1% of all cases. This is a testament to the efficiency of the measures that China has taken its important contribution to preventing the spread of the disease and protecting the health and safety of the people of China and the whole world.

Third, the Chinese Government has attached great importance to enhancing international cooperation.

China is open, transparent and responsible in its cooperation with the world.

First, China has shared with the WHO, the relevant countries, and the regions of Hong Kong, Macao and Taiwan the information about the epidemic, including the genetic sequence of the virus. This has been highly appreciated by the WHO and many countries. China has also kept in close touch with many countries at the bilateral level on the prevention and control of the disease.

Second, China has attached great importance to the safety of foreign nationals in China and tried its best to address the difficulties they face by keeping them informed about the epidemic through various channels, including through foreign representative institutions. As of midday on 6th February, 19 foreign nationals in China have been tested positive for the disease, of which, two have been cured, and 17 are under quarantine and treatment. All are in a stable condition. China has also offered assistance to other countries, including the UK, that decided to evacuate their nationals from Wuhan.

Third, China is enhancing its cooperation with the international community on the research and development of the vaccine. We are working together to safeguard the safety of public health around the world.

In face of the epidemic, people have shown great care towards each other.

Government officials and people from all walks of life in many countries have expressed their sympathy, trust and support for China. Many governments and international organisations have donated supplies for epidemic prevention and control. Here in the UK, in addition to government aid, the business community, the Chinese associations and Chinese students have donated money and supplies through various channels. A few days ago, a ceremony was held here at the Chinese Embassy, where more than 20 Chinese community and student associations in the UK made donations in funds and kind. We have been deeply touched and greatly encouraged. We would like to express our heartfelt thanks to all those in the UK who have shown their care and kindness!

Ladies and Gentlemen:

The Chinese Government has the firm resolve and has taken vigorous measures to prevent the spread of the disease. This will continue to be its most important work.

First, we will try our best to treat the infected.

Every life counts. The right to survival and health is the most basic and important human right. Medical institutions all over China are doing their very best to increase the hospitalization rate and cure rate, and reduce the infection rate and mortality rate.

Second, we will strengthen epidemic prevention and control efforts in key areas.

By key areas, we mean Hubei Province, especially Wuhan City. Prevention and control measures are being improved and strengthened in this Province.

- Patients are being diagnosed, reported, isolated and treated in a most timely manner.
- Monitoring of the epidemic development is strengthened.
- The infected are treated in specialised hospitals.
- People who have had close contact with patients are under close medical observation.

All these are aimed at preventing the further spread of the disease.

Third, we are enhancing international cooperation on epidemic prevention and control, and on scientific research.

China will continue working closely with the WHO and the relevant countries and regions.

A few days ago, China published multi-language versions of the *Guide for General Public to Prevent Pneumonia Caused by the Novel Coronavirus*, which has been shared with all countries in the world through social media and other channels at top speed. This demonstrates China's sincerity in working with the international community to fight the disease. This also shows China's determination to take up its responsibilities as a reliable global player.

As I understand, researchers from China, the UK and other countries are working round the clock to trace the transmission route of the virus, to follow closely its evolution, share the relevant data and case information, to design prevention and control strategies and measures, and develop new drugs and vaccines.

Ladies and Gentlemen:

It is understandable that there are concerns in the UK and the rest of the world about the epidemic. Some people are worried that it might have a negative effect on China's economy or even the world economy. Overreactions have been seen from individual countries. There has been panic among the public, and even insulting and discriminatory remarks and behaviors targeting the overseas Chinese community. With regard to these issues, I want to stress the following four points:

First, the impact on China's economy should be seen against a larger picture.

At the moment, the epidemic is exerting a relatively severe impact on the service sector, including transport, tourism, hospitality, catering, films and entertainment.

But the impact will be short-term and temporary. It will not change the fundamentals of China's economy, which will maintain sound growth in the long run.

China's economy is highly resilient and has enormous potential for growth in the mid-to-long term. China has the capability and confidence to minimise the economic impact of the epidemic.

The World Bank, the IMF and well-respected economists across the world have all agreed that the impact of the epidemic on China's economy is temporary, and they have full confidence in the future of China's economy.

Second, understanding of the epidemic should be objective and reasonable.

The WHO has reiterated that it disapproves of and is even opposed to travel and trade restrictions on China. In recent days, the UK, at the bilateral level, has fully recognised China's tremendous efforts and effective measures in fighting the virus. It also expressed the willingness to enhance cooperation with China and do its best to assist China in these efforts.

It is our hope that governments of all countries, including the UK, will understand and support China's efforts, respect the professional advice of the WHO, avoid overreaction, avoid creating panic, and ensure normal cooperation and exchanges between countries.

有问必答
No Question Unanswered

Third, media reports of the epidemic should be objective and fair.

The Coronavirus has been hitting the headlines in many countries, including the UK. Many of the reports speak highly of China's counter-virus efforts or offer objective and reasonable advice. We appreciate that. However, some reports are biased, or even contain malicious slander and disinformation.

Rumours and panic are worse than the virus itself. Confidence and determination are of vital importance in overcoming the epidemic. The issue of public health suppresses national borders and requires the joint efforts of all sides, including the media, who should shoulder their due social responsibility in this battle against a common enemy of all mankind.

Fourth, we should join hands to oppose any insulting or discriminatory words and behavior.

I fully agree with Dr. Tedros, the Director General of WHO, who said, "This is the time for facts, not fear. This is the time for science, not rumours. This is the time for solidarity, not stigma."

I believe this is a time for reason and cool-headedness. This is the time for a scientific approach and a rational response. It is my hope that people from all quarters of society will stand up against this challenge and pull together.

Ladies and Gentlemen:

A Chinese saying goes, "When people are of one mind, they can move Mount Tai."

I am confident that under the strong leadership of the Communist Party of China, and given the strengths of socialism with Chinese characteristics, the solidarity and perseverance of the Chinese people, and the broad support from the international community, we will beat the virus!

Every time I hosted a press conference, I played a video clip. Today, I want to share a heartwarming clip showing how our British friends are standing with us to meet the challenges.

(Video is played.)

Now I would like to take your questions.

CGTN: First of all, Ambassador, You mentioned cooperation with the British (on vaccine). Can you just elaborate on that?

Secondly, is it true that you are unhappy that Prime Minister Boris Johnson hasn't sent a personal message showing support for China?

Liu Xiaoming: Yes, we have been collaborating with British scientists. There were already some joint labs between China and the UK, before the outbreak of the disease, on prevention of the epidemics, between Chinese institutions and universities here, such as Oxford University and Imperial College. And now they have begun to work around the clock. Now they have a target to work towards a vaccine and medicines to fight this coronavirus. So we hope that it won't be long before they will have made substantial success in their joint efforts. The governments are very supportive of their efforts, and my Embassy tried our very best to facilitate the communication and the exchanges between the scientists of our two countries.

We are thankful to the British government for their support. Since the outbreak, our two governments have maintained very close contact. Cabinet Secretary Sedwill and Foreign Secretary Raab had telephone conversations with their counterparts, Director Yang Jiechi, and State councilor and Foreign Minister Wang Yi. The British side spoke highly of the prevention and control measures taken by China, and also offered to help, and we appreciate that. There's no such issue with regard to disappointment or discontent about the British government's response.

BBC: You spoke just now about your frustration at what you call the "overreaction" and "panic" that has been generated by some foreign governments including the UK. Can you be more specific? What was it that you felt was an overreaction? Are you referring to the British government's warning to British nationals in China, saying "if you can, leave".

Liu Xiaoming: As I said, the channel of communication between China and the UK at the government level is very open, not only at the top level, but also at the working level. I have had very good communication with my counterparts in the Foreign Office, including the Acting Permanent Under-Secretary and the Director-General. And my deputy and counselors also maintained almost daily contact with their counterparts. In our conversations, we express our position that the measures taken by China are effective. There should be no panic, and there should be no overreaction. We advise the British side to follow the professional advice of the WHO. And the British side agreed with us. Of course they spoke highly of our efforts, and recognized the effectiveness of the measures taken by China. They also told us they would follow the WHO advice.

It seemed to me that the words do not match with the deeds. I noticed, probably you also notice, that the WHO Director-General has spoken publicly about his reservation, or maybe his criticism, of the British government's latest advice to ask all British nationals to leave China. He does not think this is helpful. He does not think this, what he described as, "blanket approach" towards the epidemic in China, is helpful. Because there's quarantine in one city, but not the whole of China. Life is still normal in most parts of China. And so I do say again, in private and in public, that I hope the British government and the British public should take an objective, cool-headed view of what is going on in China. And I do hope that they should regard it first as a threat to the whole world that calls for international effort. We should support each other, rather than weaken the others' efforts. So that is my advice.

5 News: Mr. Ambassador, you say you're very pleased with the British cooperation and there is close contact, and yet you accused overreacting.

Liu Xiaoming: I'm not accusing. I like to see their words meet their actions.

5 News: Given that close contact you spoke about, how surprised were you when that advice was given to British nationals in China?

Liu Xiaoming: We don't think there should be such a panic. We were given notice before they made a formal announcement. So that's why we keep close contact. And we advise them. We don't think it is a good idea. We believe that the epidemic is controllable, preventable and curable. And so we asked the British side to take an objective, cool-headed approach, and also to ensure the normal exchanges and cooperation between the two sides. That should not be interrupted.

ITV News: Are you concerned that, if there are further cases confirmed in the UK, it will discredit everything you just said about China's ability to contain this virus?

Liu Xiaoming: I cannot rule out new cases, because this is really something we do not know well. That's why there are intensive efforts by scientists from all countries, especially in China and the UK, to work together and try to find a cure, medicines and vaccines. I give one example why we said it's curable and controllable. So far twice as many cases have resulted in cure rather than death,and the number of the cure is still increasing. The whole country is mobilised. Just as President Xi said we are racing against time, and we will try our best to keep ahead of the further spread of the disease. So, I think we are confident. Since there are about 1, 150, or something like that, cured cases. Of course I know the death toll now is 563. But if you compare the two, we have had more cured cases than cases of death.

Sky News: There has been reports of an increase in hate crimes against Chinese students, Chinese citizens in the UK, including the universities, ever since the outbreak of this virus. What's your reaction to that? What do you think of that?

Liu Xiaoming: I would say, in general, the public is very supportive of and sympathetic towards China. As we see in the video clip, the pupils and teachers in this primary school show their solidarity with China. So I think the general public here is very supportive. We appreciate that. There are some cases of hatred and discrimination against Chinese nationals. We have raised this issue with the British government and the police. We have also issued advice and warning to Chinese citizens, either living here or traveling to this country, about these incidents, so that they will stay alert and keep safe. And also we give contact information. If such cases occur, they should first report to the police and get in contact with the Embassy. We will provide consular protection.

We did receive some reports from universities and even some middle schools and primary schools. I think there are many reasons for it, such as a lack of understanding of the epidemic and also misinformation by some of the media. I think you should take up your responsibility to report the epidemic in a responsible and scientific way, so people will know there is nothing to worry about. Of course, there is also some deep-seated racism, not only in this country, but elsewhere too. I think at the time of crisis like this, countries should stand together. People should realise that we as mankind have a common enemy. We should say no to discriminatory words and behaviour. That's why I am calling for the public, the media and people from all walks of life to stand together, to pull together, in face of the same challenges.

Bloomberg: Several minutes ago, you made a comparison between this Coronavirus and MERS, SARS and the US seasonal flu. And really what you said is that this is not as serious.

Liu Xiaoming: I am talking about the death tolls.

Bloomberg: Are you trying to get across the message that this is not significant? This outbreak is still at a very early stage. Is this not a message to people in China and to people wherever that this is not as serious as these other outbreaks?

Liu Xiaoming: The message I am trying to get across is that there should not be a panic. It's a disease. It's an epidemic. We attach great importance to the seriousness of this epidemic. But we believe that we have the confidence, resources and capability to overcome this virus. Now the whole nation has been mobilized from the top to the very grassroots level. I have shown you there has been an increase in the number of cured cases. That gave us the reason. Just yesterday, President Xi convened another meeting, in which he called the medical personnel to work around the clock, to make sure the death toll is reduced, and the cure rate increased. That will give people more confidence that we can win this battle. I definitely think that we have a strong leadership, we have the strength in our system to mobilise the whole country, our people are united, and also, we have the support of the international community. Of course I can't predict when the inflection point will come. We do hope it will come sooner. But I can't say when we will get there. On the one hand, we have to depend on ourselves. The scientists and researchers are working very hard. And also we are engaging with scientists and researchers from other countries including the UK, who have offered generous support. The UK is a leader in epidemic prevention. I'm pleased that we have this foundation of cooperation. The scientists started to work together long before the outbreak of the disease. I do hope that people would not panic about it.

Channel 4 News: Have you formally or informally approached the Foreign Office at any point over the past few days to ask them to review their request for British nationals to get out of China as soon as they can?

Liu Xiaoming: Yes. We did tell them overreaction is not helpful. We asked them to take the advice of the WHO to make a reasonable response. Do not overreact.

The Guardian: It has been two weeks now of quarantine of Wuhan. Is this quarantine indefinite? Is the Chinese government planning measures to support people who are actually going to run out of money? And the other report we hear from Wuhan is that there are a lot of people who are saying that the hospitals are so overwhelmed that they are just not able to get tested. How are you confident that you are picking up all of the cases or even the majority of the cases?

Liu Xiaoming: Definitely, the quarantine cannot be permanent, but it is currently still necessary. As I said the government has gone all out to take actions. And also, you know, it's a comprehensive approach. So that's why I'm saying that the whole nation has been mobilised, not only the medical staff -- the medical staff are on the very frontline, giving treatment to the critically ill and the people who need medical care -- but also the logistics and transportation. Do you have a correspondent based in Beijing? It seems to me that he's not doing a very good job. I am not critical of your reporting. You know, the departments concerned give daily briefing these days. I follow what is going on, closely. Of course my focus is to engage with the British government in order to coordinate other efforts.

The Minister of Transportation, the Customs Inspector General and the Minister of Industry gave all the briefings about the supply, as I said, the supply of basic needs, food and vegetables. And I think there shouldn't be a panic. With regard to this, I can't say people enjoy a normal life, but daily necessities are guaranteed. And the President and Premier both emphasised that, as I said, the safety of life and health are top priorities of the government. So this is not only referring to the people who are ill, but also to the people who are not infected, so we have to make sure that they have the daily necessities. Of course, it will take some time. The quarantine efforts really have been effective in preventing the further spread of this disease. It's necessary and these measures have been spoken highly of by the WHO.

You talk about some complaints. And I think it's understandable. You know this outbreak of disease comes so unexpectedly. It's a crisis, I would say. I think the central government has made a very effective response. At the grassroots, at the local level, I would say people have also been mobilised, but it will take time for people to understand the nature and the urgency of this outbreak. I think, they have all come to know now. I can't say that China is prepared for this outbreak. We don't have enough beds, hospitals, that's for sure. So that's why we have built two emergency hospitals within just 10 days. I don't think any other country can do this, but we tried. We tried our best to treat as many patients as possible. And there have also been some efforts at the grassroots level. In communities, clinics have made every effort to take care of the patients as well. We will do our best.

Russia Today: Ambassador, you did say there was economic damage caused by coronavirus. Is it the case that the bias in misinformation, as you alleged, on the part of media, maybe some of the journalists here, is designed to damage China economically?

Liu Xiaoming: I've read some reports in the local media. They, on the whole, still have confidence in China's economy.I just gave you an example. I think *The Daily Telegraph* carried one piece; they believe Chinese economy is still resilient. And I think The *FT* also carried similar reports. So, I'm not saying the media in the UK are talking down China's economy. I'm just stating the fact that China's economy is resilient. I hope you will also adopt an objective, reasonable approach when reporting on China.

Financial Times: Ambassador, how many reports you've had of Chinese citizens in this country being stuck here -- people who may have come as tourists, may have come for the Lunar Festival, not able to get home because of transport difficulties, may have come for business trips -- is that a significant number? How are you helping them if it is a significant number? Are you looking after them to make sure that they have money and accommodation, etc.

Liu Xiaoming: We are trying our best to help them. Some people from Wuhan and Hubei got stranded. The government tried to get chartered flights to take them home. And here we are also trying to get in touch with the people from Wuhan and Hubei to see if they encounter difficulties and if they have a request to get home, but faced with the difficulties. But many of them told us they would like to stay. They still have business. They haven't finished their work here. So we are very open. We try our best to help them.

The Times: There have been some warnings from the WHO about ensuring that the global reaction to the crisis are driven by medical need and not political need, and I wonder if you had any sense of any countries taking more political approach? I'm thinking in particular of the context of the trade dispute with the US, and the fact that the travel advice issued by the British government came on the heels of similar advice from the US?

Liu Xiaoming: You are absolutely right. There are some people who tried to take advantage of this for political gains. We have expressed our resentment and opposition to some American politicians. We think it's harmful to the interest of the United States, not to say damaging to the collaboration between the two countries. I am confident that the two sides will continue to work together to implement the Phase One economic and trade agreement because, as I have said on several occasions, this is a good agreement. It's beneficial not only to China and the US, but also to the world. Of course, you need two to tango. So, we are committed to implementing this agreement. And I hope the other side will do the same.

LBC: It's been reported that you have some concerns about Boris Johnson's failure to engage with the Chinese government directly on this issue, so I wonder if you could say a little bit more about that. And secondly, what is your take on the advice that was given to British citizens living in China? As you said, that's against the WHO's advice. What's your sense of why that advice was given by the UK government?
I think the channel of communication is good. The Prime Minister held a Chinese New Year Reception at Number 10. Both my wife and I were invited. We had a good conversation. I conveyed greetings from the Chinese President and Premier. As a matter of fact, when he was elected, Premier Li sent him a message of congratulations. And I took this occasion to convey greetings from the top leaders from China face to face, and he also reciprocated his greetings to Chinese leaders. And he told me he was still committed to the "Golden Era" of China-UK relations. So it's a very affirmative commitment. I think the channel of communications between our two governments is very good.
As for your second question, the second question is not that difficult to answer, I think. You'll have to ask the Foreign Office, or maybe the Foreign Secretary himself, what is the reason for him to give this advice? I can't read their minds. I can only say my advice is: do not overreact.

The Daily Telegraph: I just want to clarify something. I was in Beijing for two days. You said that life in China is very much normal, but that was not the case. I have traveled in your cities in the last few weeks since the outbreak occurred. The cities are shut down, the ones outside of the official quarantine zone. All the transport has been closed. People are afraid to go outside. So what you said before isn't really true? And I just want to make that clear.

Liu Xiaoming: What I'm saying that you can't regard the whole country as being in the same situation as Hubei and Wuhan. The whole country is different. In other countries you do not need the whole nation to be mobilised. I'm not saying everything is normal in China. I'm just saying you shouldn't overreact to what is going on in Hubei and Wuhan, as if the whole of China were an epidemic zone. So do not overreact. That is what I'm saying.

The Daily Telegraph: Your people at home are overreacting. They are very worried about what's going on. I've interviewed people whose family members have died within days of the onset of symptoms, who were never tested for the coronavirus and thus are not included in the official count. So how confident are you that these numbers that are coming out from the National Health Commission are indeed capturing all the cases that could be out there?

Liu Xiaoming: My advice to you is to stay with official figures. Do not believe in rumors. Do not spread rumors. Do not spread panic. I think this is the time, as I said in my presentation, the time for cool headedness. Do not panic. And also my advice to you -- you are from *The Daily Telegraph*, right? -- It's okay that you focus on individual cases, but do not miss the big picture. When you miss the big picture, you will not know what the real situation is in China. That is my piece of advice to you. Thank you.

The Daily Telegraph: I wanted to know what kind of directives the central government is giving to local governments, because a lot of provinces and cities are also implementing basically quarantine situations. Even if the city itself has not announced as such, they're shutting down the transport including roads, there are temperature checkpoints, you know, there are compounds where people cannot get back in if they had traveled anywhere in the country for the last 14 days. So where are these actions coming from, are they coming from the local governments, or is the central government asking the local officials to do this?

Liu Xiaoming: Generally speaking, the government should shoulder their responsibility. As I said, in all places, the key Party and government officials are now leading taskforces to address this crisis. That is their responsibility.

And the instruction from the central government is very clear. I think the President twice called the top leadership meeting, that is the Standing Committee of the Political Bureau. It's very rare in Chinese history to have two top leadership meetings in such a short period of time. And he called another meeting yesterday to issue important directives. I hope you will read them, word for word, sentence by sentence. These are the instructions from the central government. We asked local government to follow the central government instructions. And, of course, if the local government, including officials, failed to do their duties, they will be accountable for their misconduct.

BBC: Somebody said that this crisis has shown both the strength and weakness of the Chinese one-party state. On the one hand, the astonishing mobilisation of resources in a very short space of time -- the two emergency hospitals you referred to.

But equally, the Chinese Politburo Standing Committee has referred explicitly to the shortcomings and deficiencies of the initial response -- in other words, the lack of transparency, the blame culture, the desire to close it down rather than actually get to grips with this virus -- very, very quickly. So how do you respond to that challenge? How much does this crisis challenge the political model of the Chinese state?

Liu Xiaoming: First, I should correct you: China is not a one-party state. China is a country led by the Communist Party, but we have eight democratic parties working together with the Communist Party. So I recommend that you should read about some of the basics of China's political system. And they are also very active. Many of the members of the democratic parties are top scientists and they offer their opinions. They advise the government on what to do in fighting this virus.

No system is perfect. I don't think you can say, in the very affirmative way, that the British system is perfect. It has taken three years to figure out Brexit. I don't want to be critical. But I think every system has room to improve. So, that's why I always say the largest room on earth is the room for improvement.

And I'm pleased that you read very carefully the press release of the top leadership meeting that we recognize there are shortcomings. There is room for improvement so that we can do a better job in the future. And you're right. This is a challenge.

Maybe we have a different understanding of the challenges. My understanding of the challenges is that they challenge us to improve our work and our system. But we are very confident in our system. As I said in my opening remarks, if it were not for this system, I do not know what kind of situation we will be facing. If you imagine a similar situation happening in the UK, I would not try to second guess what you are going to do with regard to this situation.

If there is no more question, that's the end of the press conference. Thank you very much for coming to the Embassy. I look forward to seeing you in the future.

坚定信心，加强团结，携手战胜疫情
——与英国智库谈新冠肺炎疫情
（2020年4月23日，中国驻英国使馆/英国"亚洲之家"）

2020年4月23日，我出席"亚洲之家"网上座谈会，发表题为《坚定信心，加强团结，携手战胜疫情》的主旨演讲，并与"亚洲之家"主席格林勋爵进行对话交流，回答听众提问。演讲和答问实录如下：

刘晓明： 感谢格林勋爵的盛情邀请和刚才的热情介绍。正如格林勋爵所说，我担任中国驻英大使10年，曾多次做客"亚洲之家"，但通过连线这种特殊方式与大家交流还是第一次。

当世界迈入21世纪第3个十年，新冠肺炎疫情大暴发，给人类带来前所未有的挑战，给世界经济带来前所未有的冲击，给国际格局带来前所未有的影响。这是一场没有硝烟的战争，对每个国家都是一场大考。

今天，我想从三个方面谈一谈，中国是如何应对这场大考的：一是中国的抗疫斗争对全球抗疫意味着什么；二是疫情背景下的中国经济将如何为世界经济注入更大动力；三是为什么中国认为，"团结合作是国际社会战胜疫情最有力武器"。

当前，疫情仍在全球扩散蔓延，全球抗疫斗争进入关键阶段。中国是最早向国际社会报告疫情、最早取得疫情防控重要阶段性成效的国家，我认为中国抗疫斗争对全球抗疫具有三大重要意义。

一是中国抗疫为全球健康安全构筑了坚固的"中国防线"。中国本着对人民负责、为世界担当的精神，迅速采取最全面、最严格、最彻底的防控举措。全国14亿人民团结一心，众志成城，打响一场抗击疫情的人民战争。经过艰苦奋战，承受巨大牺牲，中国成为世界上率先控制住国内疫情的国家之一，境内已连续1个月仅呈现零星散发态势，本土疫情传播基本被阻断。中国用力量、智慧与牺牲为世界筑牢了捍卫生命和健康的第一道防线。

二是中国抗疫为全球防疫斗争积累了宝贵经验。坚持以人民为中心，一切为了人民，一切依靠人民，始终是抗疫斗争中最鲜明的中国特色；中国迅速构建起从中央到地方、全方位、多层次网格状的防控体系，发挥"一方有难，八方支援"的精神，共同打赢武汉保卫战；中国始终坚持向科学要答案、要方案，坚持早发现、早报告、早隔离、早治疗的防控要求和集中患者、集中专家、集中资源、集中救治的原则，坚持中西医结合、中西药并用；中国高度重视统筹疫情防控和经济社会发展，统筹国内效应和全球影响，精准有序推进复工复产。不少国家领导人称赞，中国抗疫经验值得世界借鉴。

三是中国为全球抗疫提供了巨大支援。中国始终秉持公开、透明、负责任的态度，积极开展抗疫国际合作。中国第一时间通报疫情信息，迅速测出并分享病毒基因序列。中国毫无保留地与各国分享防控诊疗经验，开设了向所有国家开放的新冠肺炎疫情防控网上知识中心。中国向世卫组织提供2000万美元捐款。今天，中国又宣布增加3000万美元捐款，用于新冠肺炎疫情防控，支持发展中国家卫生体系建设等工作。中国向15个国家派遣17支医疗专家组，已经或正在向包括英国在内的150多个国家和国际组织提供了口罩、防护服、检测试剂、呼吸机等急需的医疗物资援助。中国克服自身困难，加大力度向国际市场供应原料药、防疫物资等产品，从3月1日到4月10日，中国共出口口罩约72亿只，防护服5557万件，红外测温仪359万件，呼吸机2万台，护目镜1300万副。"中国支援"为国际社会战胜疫情提振了信心，为全球抗疫斗争注入源源不断的正能量。

现在，我想谈谈各位关心的疫情背景下的中国经济。近来国际货币基金组织大幅下调今年世界经济增长预期，警告此次疫情对世界经济的冲击可能超过20世纪大萧条。疫情对中国经济社会发展带来严峻的冲击，第一季度经济同比下降6.8%。面对前所未有的风险、挑战和不确定性，我们更要坚定信心和勇气，努力化危为机，推动经济社会不断发展。

一是中国经济长期向好的态势没有改变也不会改变。中国经济基础雄厚，中国是世界第二大经济体，2019年国内生产总值达到14.4万亿美元，是2008年国际金融危机时4.6万亿美元的3.1倍和2003年非典时1.67万亿美元的8.6倍。中国是全世界唯一拥有联合国产业分类当中全部工业门类的国家。中国经济发展空间广阔，有14亿人口、9亿劳动力、4亿多中等收入群体。中国人均国内生产总值刚超过1万美元，仅为英国的1/4、美国的1/6，中国城市化率仅有60%，未来增长潜力巨大。中国高度重视统筹疫情防控和经济社会发展，生产生活秩序加快恢复，复工达产正在逐步接近或达到正常水平。目前，全国规模以上工业企业平均开工率达到99%，3月制造业采购经理人指数（PMI）比上月回升16.3

个百分点。根据IMF最新的《世界经济展望》报告，2021年中国经济增速将强劲回升至9.2%。

二是中国经济更高质量发展的方向没有改变也不会改变。中国在疫情防控常态化前提下，坚持新发展理念，坚持以供给侧结构性改革为主线，完善要素市场化配置体制机制，坚持以改革开放为动力推动高质量发展。我们以更大的宏观政策力度对冲疫情影响，加大"六稳"工作力度，保居民就业、保基本民生、保市场主体、保粮食能源安全、保产业链供应链稳定、保基层运转，维护经济发展和社会稳定大局。我们坚定实施扩大内需战略，积极扩大有效投资，敏锐抓住"宅经济""云办公"等发展机遇，借助互联网、大数据、人工智能等新兴技术，推动数字经济、智能制造、医疗健康等新兴产业快速成长，促进传统产业改造升级，扩大战略性新兴产业投资，积极促进绿色经济发展，加快经济高质量发展步伐。

三是中国作为世界经济"动力源"和"稳定器"的担当没有改变，也不会改变。中国坚定不移扩大对外开放，放宽市场准入，优化营商环境，积极扩大进口，扩大对外投资，保障国际物流畅通，推进共建"一带一路"高质量发展。中国历史最悠久的广交会将于6月中下旬首次在网上举办，中国还将于11月举办第三届中国国际进口博览会，为各国互利合作提供更大机遇。中国推动加强宏观经济政策协调，稳市场、保增长、保民生，确保全球供应链开放、稳定、安全。作为"世界工厂"的中国经济率先重回正轨，将为世界经济复苏注入强大动力。

最后，我想谈谈国际社会应如何携手应对疫情。当下，人们都在争论，疫情使世界变得更团结了，还是更分裂了？我的回答是：疫情使我们再次深刻感受到，人类是一个休戚与共、命运相连的命运共同体。团结合作是最有力武器，国际社会只有团结合作、共克时艰，才能最终战胜疫情。

一是加强全球行动，打好全球疫情防控阻击战。在不久前举行的二十国集团领导人特别峰会上，习近平主席提出坚决打好疫情防控全球阻击战、有效开展国际联防联控、积极支持国际组织发挥作用、加强国际宏观经济政策协调四点重要倡议，推动开展药物和疫苗联合研发、发起二十国集团抗疫援助倡议、共同维护全球产业链供应链稳定等一系列务实合作，为各国合作应对疫情指明方向。中国将继续与各国加强抗疫合作，展现大国胸怀与担当，为全球抗疫做出应有贡献。

二是凝聚团结共识，坚定战胜疫情的信心。病毒没有国界，疫情不分种族。危机面前，指责与推诿无济于事，傲慢与狂妄害人害己。刻意将病毒标签化、抗疫政治化以及对特定国家污名化，更是违背人类道德良知，加剧国际社会分裂，侵蚀国际抗疫合作成果，损害全人类的利益。各国应该坚决摒弃意识形态偏见，把保护和拯救生命放在第一位，切实形成抗击疫情的最大合力。

三是坚持多边主义，支持国际组织发挥积极作用。中国坚持多边主义原则，加强和完善以联合国为核心的全球治理体系。疫情发生以来，世卫组织秉持客观科学公正立场，为协调推动国际抗疫合作发挥了重要作用，得到国际社会普遍赞誉。中国将一如既往支持世卫组织工作，支持世卫组织在全球抗疫合作中发挥领导作用。中国将积极加强与各国"一带一路"卫生合作，共建"健康丝绸之路"。

四是促进开放合作，维护开放型世界经济。越是面对困难和挑战，我们越要坚持以开放促合作、以合作促发展。有人鼓噪搞"人为脱钩"和"科技封锁"，这是自我封闭、自我设限、自我倒退。中国将坚定不移扩大改革开放，积极推动各方加强宏观经济政策协调，着眼"后疫情时代"，采取一切必要举措，维护全球产业链供应链稳定，促进贸易投资自由化便利化，共同建设开放型世界经济。

女士们、先生们，中英是国际抗疫合作的重要伙伴。习近平主席与约翰逊首相一个多月来两次通电话，共同传递了携手战胜疫情的坚定决心。中英正加强防疫信息分享和经验交流，加强科研攻关合作。中英两国都坚定支持多边主义，支持世卫组织在全球抗疫中发挥重要作用，支持加强在二十国集团框架内的抗疫合作，推动完善全球卫生治理。在这个抗击疫情的重要时刻，中英要展现担当，守望相助，排除杂音和干扰，为双方合作增加正能量，为全球公共卫生安全做出新贡献。我相信，疫情过后，中英关系将更加成熟、强劲，双方合作将更加广泛、深入，两国人民友谊将更加牢固、持久！

中国有一句古语，"积力之所举则无不胜，众智之所为则无不成"。中国愿与包括英国在内的国际社会一道，坚定必胜信念，加强团结合作，携手共克时艰，共同战胜疫情，共创世界美好未来！

下面我愿回答各位的提问。

"亚洲之家"主席格林勋爵： 欢迎刘大使！非常感谢各位与会者！随着新冠肺

炎疫情在全球蔓延，我们正面临非同寻常的形势，更多人呼吁开展建设性的国际合作。我认为，现在的形势至少是第二次世界大战以来"前所未有"的，给每一个国家都带来了各种挑战。中国第一个受到疫情冲击，看来也将是第一个摆脱疫情影响的国家。我认为，保持谨慎仍是非常必要的。现在英国仍在与疫情做斗争，欧洲也在与疫情做斗争。

当前，我们面临短期、中期和长期的挑战，其中一些挑战源于新冠疫情的深刻影响，另一些则不是。在我看来，短期内，我们面临如何退出封锁隔离措施的问题。这一问题在英国乃至整个欧洲引起了广泛讨论，并在美国和东亚一些地区引发诸多焦虑。日本采取了特殊的防疫路径，但极有可能引发病毒"二次冲击"。在研制出有效疫苗仍需时日的情况下，不同的抗疫策略会带来不同的挑战。疫情对经济也产生短期挑战。例如，旅游业如何能重新成为重要的经济力量？小型零售企业在多大程度上会因疫情影响而倒闭？

从整个宏观经济看，各国纷纷推出庞大的财政和货币刺激政策，这些措施会产生什么样的中期后果？随着各国试图修复财政状况，这是否意味着新一轮财政紧缩？是否意味着将推高税收或通胀？无论是经济正在复苏的中国，还是英国、欧洲国家或者美国，都面临这样的问题。当然，由于美元的特殊性，美国的情况可能会有所不同。这些都是疫情带来的中期挑战。

同时，在疫情影响之外还存在一些中长期挑战，国际贸易秩序就是其中之一。在疫情发生前，由于缺乏足够的上诉法官，世界贸易组织正在丧失有效解决争端的能力。我注意到，今年3月30日，欧盟和中国以及其他一些国家达成了"多方临时上诉仲裁安排"（MPIA）。这是支持世贸组织工作的重要一步。我很关注英国将如何参与这一安排。

刘大使刚才在演讲中谈到为什么要支持世卫组织。世卫组织是一个重要的国际组织，而世贸组织同样是一个重要的国际机构，是当前国际多边秩序的一部分，我们都应予以关注。对于这两个国际组织，美国目前采取了"非建设性态度"。我认为，重建对国际多边秩序的信心，符合各方共同利益。

最后，还有一个绕不开的长期性问题，就是生物多样性、环境退化、气候变化。疫情导致经济活动下降，世界各地城市的污染状况暂时得到改善，二氧化碳排放减少。但由于持续的人口、城市化和经济发展等压力，人类将不得不继续面对环境、气候等长期挑战。短期内，疫情可能增加应对气候变化的困难，比如英中双方均不得不推迟举办《联合国气候变化框架公约》第26次缔约方会议（COP26）和《生物多样性公约》第15次缔约方会议（COP15）。刘大使提到这两次会议是中英共同的重要议程，我也希望会议只是暂时推迟，我们不能因疫情和眼前的困难而忽视长期挑战。

我们生活的时代非同寻常。疫情带来的挑战是多方面的，国际关系也不可避免地受到影响。对于中美关系这一重大问题，我们欧洲人以期待和祈愿的心态关注其发展，认为中美关系只有在建设性基础上才能向前发展。因此，我们今天的对话可谓恰逢其时。"亚洲之家"一直积极为开展各类对话发挥重要的平台作用，这些对话既包括从微观经济到宏观经济，也包括贸易秩序等中期问题，以及气候变化及其对经济发展影响等长期问题。我就讲到这里。刘大使，不知你是否与我"君子所见略同"？

刘晓明： 感谢格林勋爵！对于你谈到的很多问题，有不少方面的观点我都赞同。你谈到了疫情对各个国家的挑战。我认为每个国家的情况各不相同，英国不同于德国、意大利或法国。我们正在密切关注疫情情况。尽管存在差异，但我认为各国在抗击疫情方面仍存在共同之处。我在演讲中谈到中英合作，这同样适用于中国与其他国家的合作。当我们面对这些共同威胁时，各国应该共同合作应对。

第一，我们应该加强互相支持。在医疗物资领域，当中国处于抗疫关键阶段时，英国政府向中国提供了两批急需的医疗物资。现在英国正与疫情做斗争，我们同样向英方提供了大力支持。正如英国内阁办大臣戈夫所说，英方收到中方的防疫医疗物资远远超过英方给中方的防疫捐赠。目前，英国急需呼吸机，中国已经将750台呼吸机运到英国，未来还会更多。我们还准备向英国及世界其他国家提供更多其他医疗物资和设备。

第二，我们要开展抗疫经验分享。中国是最早取得疫情防控重要阶段性成效的国家之一。我们愿与其他国家分享在疫情防控和诊疗方面的经验。我很高兴地看到，中英双方就此保持密切沟通。英国卫生大臣汉考克昨天与中国卫生健康委主任马晓伟通了电话，双方就中英抗疫合作进行了非常富有成果和深入的讨论。

第三，我们要加强抗疫国际合作。在演讲中，我已经谈到这方面内容。刚才，格林勋爵以"英国绅士式"的措辞——"非建设性态度"来形容美国的立场和做法。我们对美国宣布暂停资助世卫组织的决定深感失望。在当前抗疫关键时刻,世卫组织扮演着重要角色,我们需要支持世卫组织在全球抗疫合作中发挥领导作用。我很高兴地看到,英国政府决定继续支持世卫组织,中英双方在这方面持相同立场。中国已向世卫组织提供2000万美元捐款。就在我们今天活动开始前数个小时,中国又宣布向世卫组织增加3000万美元现金捐款,用于支持非洲和发展中国家卫生体系建设等工作。中国政府有关部门好像知道今天"亚洲之家"要举办这一活动,使我能够第一时间跟各位分享这个信息。(众人笑)

第四,我们要加强宏观经济政策协调。包括中英在内的国际社会可加强宏观经济政策协调,促进世界经济恢复增长。目前,中国全国规模以上工业企业平均开工率已达到99%,中国政府还采取了更多支持中小企业的政策。同时,中国致力于支持世界贸易组织,推进贸易自由化和便利化。我们愿就此与英方加强合作。

中方同样高度重视气候变化问题。令人遗憾的是,中英双方均不得不推迟COP15与COP26。今年初,我曾讲,今年是中英气候变化合作之年。尽管面临疫情挑战,中英两国仍就此保持密切沟通。会议虽然推迟,但工作仍在推进。我同英国商业、能源与产业战略部大臣兼COP26主席夏尔马保持密切沟通,积极推动他与新上任的中国生态环境部部长黄润秋建立工作联系,两国工作组也通过网上保持沟通。

另一个重要问题是,当我们加强抗疫国际合作时,也应共同反对"政治病毒"。正如我在演讲中所说,一些政客和一些势力试图寻找"替罪羊",企图对外"甩锅"、转嫁责任。各国政府应集中精力应对疫情，保护本国人民生命安全，而不是相互攻击和破坏国际合作。对一些美国政客对中国的指责，我们坚决反对。这种针对中国的抹黑无助于国际社会合作抗疫。

关于中美关系，我们完全有理由建立稳定和良好的关系。近一个时期，习近平主席与特朗普总统多次通话。我们始终认为中美合则两利、斗则俱伤。一个稳定和良好的中美关系不仅符合中美两国利益，也符合世界各国的利益。我们希望在不冲突不对抗、相互尊重、合作共赢的基础上与美国保持良好关系，但是这需要中美双方相向而行。当中国领导人和中国的驻外使节、外交官们在全世界大力倡导构建人类命运共同体，支持国际社会增强抗疫必胜信心的时候，一些国家的政客和官员在干什么？他们到处散布假消息和谣言——这毫无助益！我们真诚希望中美加强合作，也希望国际社会加强合作，以实现符合全人类利益的共同目标。

怡和集团董事亚当·凯瑟克： 刘大使，你好！感谢刘大使和格林勋爵，你们刚才的发言令人鼓舞。我相信，我们为抗疫而建立的沟通网络，在战胜疫情后同样能促进世界经济发展。刘大使在演讲中对中国所做努力做了全面介绍，令人欣慰。现在，国际社会都很关注中国全国人民代表大会何时召开。有消息称，这次大会可能会在今年5月晚些时候召开。你认为这次大会将对外传递什么具体信息？这些信息将如何增强国际社会抗疫信心、推动世界经济恢复到正常状态？希望听听你的看法。

刘晓明： 你提到的会议很重要。每年的"两会"是中国政治生活中的一件

有问必答

大事。今年的"两会"受疫情影响推迟了。今年的"两会"将不只为今年中国发展制订规划，还将制订未来五年的"十四五"规划，意义更加深远。当然，抗击新冠肺炎疫情将是"两会"的重要议程。正如我在演讲中所说，疫情既带来挑战，也为中国进一步发展提供机遇。我认为，"两会"的代表们将会聚焦中国未来发展的新领域和新增长点。我建议你密切关注今年中国"两会"。

必和必拓公司国际关系和公共事务副总裁埃罗伯茨：很高兴听到刘大使全面介绍中国经济正走出危机。必和必拓与中国客户保持着非常密切的联系。截至目前，我们感到即使在中国疫情高峰期，中国客户对我们公司产品的需求仍保持稳定，这让我们能够继续向中国提供产品。当然，我认为难免还会有一些关切。例如，近期部分媒体关注中国对外需求在今年下半年会否放缓。同时，西方国家正尝试退出封锁隔离措施，实现经济恢复运转仍很艰难，中国从西方国家的进口可能下滑。你对中国经济走出危机和保持快速发展势头有何看法？受西方经济复苏乏力影响，中国经济面临的风险会增加，是否还会保持稳定和强劲呢？

刘晓明：我认为，随着逐步复工达产，中国仍将是世界经济发展的动力源。目前全国规模以上工业企业平均开工率已达到99%，中国将继续扮演"世界工厂"的角色。中国市场规模巨大，将为促进全球经济恢复增长做出贡献。此次疫情也为中国经济加快转型带来机会，包括"宅经济"、数字经济、人工智能及医疗卫生等领域都具有很大的发展潜力。例如，从3月1日到4月10日，中国出口了约71.2亿只口罩、5557万件防护服、2.01万台呼吸机和1369万副护目镜。中国已经成为全球医疗用品的主要供应地，这不仅是中国对全球抗疫的贡献，也有助于打造未来的产业链、供应链。

中国致力于构建开放型世界经济。中国过去40多年来取得巨大成功，得益于改革开放。我认为，中国未来继续成功，同样有赖于坚持改革开放。对中国而言，没有任何理由关上大门，也没有任何理由停止改革。因此，中国的改革将继续推进，对世界开放的大门只会越开越大。第127届广交会将于今年6月在网上举办，第三届中国国际进口博览会将于11月举办，这些为中国与世界加强互利合作提供了宝贵机会。我已与英国国际贸易部高级官员和商界领袖进行沟通，邀请他们出席这两场重要活动。这将为中英两国共同推动重振世界经济提供重要机遇。

阿斯利康公司英国政府与国际关系副总监曼： 感谢刘大使所做的精彩演讲。阿斯利康公司一直高度重视对华合作。疫情发生以来，我们与中国以及世界卫生组织、世界经济论坛合作，向全球有需要的国家捐赠了900万只口罩。你认为未来深化英中关系有哪些重要机遇？例如，在医疗卫生、生命科学等领域的合作。

刘晓明： 正如我刚才所讲，中英两国高层保持密切沟通。习近平主席与约翰逊首相一个多月内两次通电话，这非常罕见。我担任中国驻英国大使10年有余，从未见过两国领导人在这么短的时间内进行如此密集的沟通。中央外事工作委员会办公室主任杨洁篪与英国内阁秘书兼首相国家安全事务顾问塞德维尔、王毅国务委员兼外长与英国外交大臣拉布等两国高官也保持密切沟通。我在伦敦也与英国有关部门大臣、国务大臣等就中英合作交换意见和建议。未来中英很多领域的合作都充满机遇。

在疫苗研发和经验交流方面，目前中英两国科学家正紧密合作加快研发，帝国理工学院、牛津大学、剑桥大学与中国科研机构密切合作。不久前，中国山东联合工作组来英国期间，与英国医疗专家进行线上交流，开展密切合作。除医疗物资外，疫苗是我们打赢这场全球疫情防控战的最终解决方案。习近平主席和约翰逊首相都很支持两国科学家在这一重要领域开展合作。

在国际领域，中英两国合作密切。双方都支持多边主义，支持世卫组织和世贸组织，格林勋爵对此十分关注。我们把英国视作共建"一带一路"的"天然合作伙伴"。中英还可共同推动"一带一路"沿线国家加强卫生合作，共建"健康丝绸之路"。

在气候变化领域，中英也可加强合作。双方都是环境保护的全球领军者。中英今年原计划分别主办的COP15与COP26虽因疫情推迟，但双方准备工作并没有停止。疫情过后，两场会议将再次提上日程，为气候变化、环境保护领域国际合作设定议程和方向。两国在这些领域合作面临巨大机遇。

在贸易领域，中英合作前景广阔。去年，尽管全球贸易增长放缓，中英双边货物贸易额同比增长超过7%，创历史新高。目前，英国是中国在欧洲第三大贸易伙伴，中国是英国第三大货物出口市场。英国是中国在欧洲地区最大投资目的地国，过去5年中国对英投资超过了过去30年的总和，中资企业在英国非常活跃。前不久，我在线出席了英国中国商会首批援助英方医疗物资捐赠仪式，英国中国商会向英国国民医疗服务体系捐赠了呼吸机、防护服、口罩等医疗物资，这充分体现了在英中资企业的全球视野和社会责任。我们鼓励中英之间加强这样的交流互动。

毕马威会计师事务所金融服务副主席塞耶：我想谈谈现在了不起的技术。刘大使，你刚才说，每个挑战中也蕴含着机遇。现在通过技术，我们不仅与英国客户，也能与中国公司进行更快、更直接的对话。我们现在能更容易、更好地与中国伙伴进行视频会议。而以前，要与中国伙伴对话，我们必须经过近20个小时飞行，还得有其他安排。我认为此次疫情挑战所带来的一个机遇，就是英中各领域对话将加速。在这方面，我们应如何更好地利用新技术？中国驻英国使馆为此能发挥什么作用？

刘晓明：很高兴你成为新技术的获益者之一。华为公司参与英国5G网络发展后，在线会议速度一定会更快、质量会更高。约翰逊首相提出雄心勃勃的计划，要在2025年前在全英实现5G网络全覆盖，华为将为此发挥重要作用。我希望，不仅中英两国领导人保持沟通，两国工商界人士也要加强对话。除了与"亚洲之家"对话外，我最近还参加了其他在线会议。不久前，我与英国中国商会进行视频座谈，接下来我还将与英国工商业联合会、英中贸协进行视频座谈。我们能进行即时讨论，得益于新技术发展。同时，我们应致力于维护自由贸易，共同营造良好营商环境。英国素以自由和开放经济著称，这是英国能成为中国在欧洲最大投资目的地国的重要原因。我曾问中国企业家，你们为什么要到英国来投资，而不是去其他国家。我不久前参加中国河北敬业集团收购英国钢铁公司交割仪式时，问过敬业集团负责人同样的问题。他们表示，英国非常开放、透明，英国从中央政府及地方政府领导人，到工商界人士和地方社区，都张开双臂欢迎中国投资。这是英国成功的秘诀。因此，我希望这一势头能继续保持，这不仅有利于中英合作，也符合英国自身的利益。

BBC记者兰德尔： 刘大使，你非常重视国际合作。中国是否支持针对病毒源头的独立国际调查？是否会完全向调查者开放所有的相关数据、地点和证据？

刘晓明： 中国对疫情从一开始就采取公开、透明、负责任的态度。我们邀请世卫组织专家来华，他们不仅访问了武汉，还访问了其他城市。访问后他们发布了一份非常全面翔实的报告，不知道你是否读过。我听到关于所谓中国掩盖和隐藏疫情的猜测和虚假信息，这些都不是事实。一些人抱有先入为主的偏见，每当听到美国政客指责中国掩盖事实的时候，都会随波逐流。但是，当中国外交部发言人讲出事实真相的时候，西方媒体却很少报道，因为他们对中国抱有很深的偏见。这就是问题的症结。

我建议包括英国媒体在内的西方媒体要秉持平衡、客观立场。我并非要求你们对中国友好，只是要求你们保持平衡、公正的立场。你们报道美国国务卿对中国的所谓"批评"，实际上他是在对中国污名化。同时，你们更应该报道中国的反驳论点，更应该报道世卫组织对此的评论。那些固守偏见的媒体，只会报道他们想听的东西，而不会报道故事的另一面。这就是问题之所在。

中国政府对抗疫公开、透明、负责任并且反应迅速。美国抱怨中国在疫情发生后一个月没有分享信息，也没有向世卫组织和其他国际组织报告，这不是事实。新冠病毒最早由张继先医生于2019年12月27日首次报告，要早于李文亮医生。李文亮医生是个英雄，为抗击疫情而牺牲了。在张继先医生向当地卫生部门报告3天后，中国政府采取了非常严格和迅速的行动，4天后就通知了世卫组织，7天后与美国分享了疫情信息。所以美国才能采取撤侨等行动。如果你查阅中国抗疫的时间线，你会发现我们所有疫情信息都是公开、透明的。

你谈到独立调查，这应该取决于世卫组织。我们支持世卫组织在全球抗疫合作中发挥重要作用。我们应该遵循国际规则，而非某个国家的规则。个别国家甚至在地方法院"起诉"中国，这完全是荒唐至极。我曾两次在美国常驻。这已不是第一次某些政客想当"世界警察"了。当今时代已不是"炮舰外交"的时代，也不是中国处于半殖民地半封建社会的时代，而是21世纪的第3个十年。但这些政客还生活在过去，无法理解今天的世界，自认为能像过去一样欺负中国、欺负世界。如果世卫组织不能按其意志行事，他们就停止支持世卫组织，指责世卫组织"以中国为中心"，这完全是错误的。因此，我们呼吁加强国际合作，这是赢得抗疫斗争的唯一武器和唯一出路，而不应找"替罪羊"，不应玩政治游戏，不应把病毒政治化，不应传播"政治病毒"。我们在与病毒这个"无形的敌人"做斗争时，必须对"政治病毒"保持警惕。

我想强调的是，中国不是美国的敌人，而是美国的朋友，是美国

有问必答
No Question Unanswered

与病毒做斗争的伙伴。如果这些美国政客将中国视为敌人,就是选错了对象。尽管一些美国政客散布关于中国的虚假信息,我们仍在美国人民需要时伸出援手。中国已向美国提供超过18亿只口罩,意味着每个美国人可获得6只口罩。

中国国际电视台记者戴维德: 刘大使,你提到了中国在疫情之后的一些优先关注领域。具体看,你认为这些优先领域有哪些?

刘晓明: 首先,要全面实现复工达产。中国高度重视统筹推进疫情防控和经济社会发展工作。我们在常态化疫情防控中全面推进复工复产达产,恢复正常经济社会秩序。我们将以更大的宏观政策力度对冲疫情影响,加大"六稳"工作力度,保居民就业、保基本民生、保市场主体、保粮食能源安全、保产业链供应链稳定、保基层运转,坚定实施扩大内需战略,积极扶持中小企业,维护经济发展和社会稳定大局。

其次,要确保疫情不反弹。中国政府始终把人民群众生命安全和身体健康放在第一位。针对国外输入病例带来的风险上升,中国政府正完善各项措施并切实抓好落实,但还需要与其他国家加强合作来实现防疫目标。我们现在已经开放离开武汉的通道,但在其他领域仍存在一些限制。我们必须确保来之不易的抗疫成果不会发生逆转,不断巩固疫情防控持续向好态势。

再次,要坚持推动改革开放。我们坚持用改革的办法解决发展中的问题,完善要素市场配置体制机制,坚定不移扩大对外开放,保障国际物流畅通,继续为国际社会提供高质量的防疫物资,推动共建"一带一路"高质量发展。

最后,要进一步加强国际合作。正如我刚才谈到的,中国将继续就重要国际议程与各方保持沟通。例如,在气候变化领域我与英国商业、能源与产业战略部大臣夏尔马及其他高级官员进行交流,保持双方合作势头,共同推进相关工作。我们正与英国国际贸易部就英国"脱欧"后推进中英自贸协定保持密切沟通。因此我们的工作日程是很满的,许多工作都在网上进行。我们时刻做好准备,确保疫情一旦结束,相关工作就可以尽快重回正轨。

格林勋爵： 刘大使,这是一次非常精彩的讨论。我感到收获颇丰。你最后的发言是非常好的总结,充分展示了我们在广泛领域有机会开展有效合作,我们需要保持这一积极势头。在新冠肺炎疫情之后,我们将总结经验教训,短期内看,我们还有许多修补宏观经济等工作要开展;从长期看,我们在根本性问题上有很多共同点,也有很多合作的机会。因此,我代表"亚洲之家"衷心感谢你抽出宝贵时间与我们一起讨论,也期待着更多交流。你提到你出任中国驻英国大使已超过10年,这意味着你非常了解英国。我一直很赞赏你对英国的看法,因为你总是对英国和英中关系有深刻的见解。在这场疫情危机中,我们面临许多重大机遇。我们永远不要忽略这一点。

再次感谢刘大使,感谢所有嘉宾出席这场非常有意义的座谈会。

刘晓明： 不客气。

A Keynote Speech and Q&A with "Asia House": Confidence and Solidarity Will See Us through to Final Victory

(Chinese Embassy/Asia House, 23rd April 2020)

On 23rd April 2020, I attended an "Asia House" webinar and delivered a keynote speech entitled "Confidence and Solidarity Will See Us through to Final Victory". This was followed by a discussion with Lord Green, the Chairman of "Asia House" and Q&A with online participants. The event was chaired by Michael Lawrence, the Chief Executive of "Asia House", and attracted an audience of nearly 250, including Sir Douglas Flint, the UK's Special Envoy to the BRI, Lord Powell, Lord Sassoon, the Honorary Chairman of the China-Britain Business Council, Caroline Wilson, Ambassador-designate to China, officials from the UK's Cabinet Office, the Foreign and Commonwealth Office, HM Treasury, Department for International Development, and the Department for Business, Energy and Industrial Strategy, ambassadors and diplomats from more than 20 countries, and representatives of the business, media and academic communities from the UK, the US, Europe and Asia. The conference was broadcast live on my Twitter, and covered live and reported by the BBC and Sky News. The full text of the speech and Q&A are as follows:

Liu Xiaoming: Thank you, Lord Green, for your kind invitation and warm introduction. As Lord Green said, having been Chinese Ambassador to the UK for more than 10 years, I am no stranger to Asia House, but this is the first time I have joined you online.
As the world enters the third decade of the 21st century, the outbreak of COVID-19 is posing unparalleled challenges to mankind, striking an unprecedented blow to the world economy and having a profound impact on the international landscape. In this battle, every country in the world is facing a severe test.
How well is China performing in this test? Today I would like to share with you my views by answering the following three questions:
- First, what does China's experience mean to the global response to COVID-19?
- Second, will China continue to be an engine for world economic growth in the

context of the pandemic?

• Third, why does China believe international solidarity is the most effective weapon against the virus?

Currently COVID-19 continues to ravage the world, and the global response to this challenge is at a critical moment. China was the first country to report the virus, and also the first to have achieved preliminary but important success in containing the virus. I think, China's efforts bear three-fold significance to the global response to this public health crisis.

First, China has built a strong "line of defence" for global public health.

In the early days of the outbreak, China acted responsibly and quickly by adopting the most comprehensive, strict and thorough measures of prevention and control in the interests of the Chinese people and the rest of the world. Across the nation, 1.4 billion people have rallied behind the government and are waging a "people's war" against the virus.

After strenuous efforts and enormous sacrifices, China became one of the first countries in the world to have brought the epidemic under control. For one whole month, there have been only sporadic cases and the spread of the virus within China has been basically cut off.

Through persistent efforts, wisdom and sacrifice, China has built the first line of defence for the world, offering protection for life and health.

Second, China has accumulated valuable experience for the global response to the pandemic.

In fighting its battle against the virus, China has always focused its efforts on the welfare of the people and relied fully on the support of the people. This has become the most salient Chinese experience in this battle.

In record-short time, China established a multi-dimensional and multi-layered network of prevention and control involving everyone from the Central Government to the local communities. The whole nation was mobilized to support Wuhan, the epicenter of the outbreak.

The measures that China has taken are based on science. The principles of early diagnosis, early report, early quarantine and early treatment have been followed. COVID-19 patients were admitted into designated hospitals with the best experts and sufficient resources for timely and tailored treatment. And both traditional Chinese medicine and Western medicine have been used to treat patients.

China attaches great importance to balancing counter-epidemic measures and ensuring normal economic and social activities. We have kept in mind both domestic and global impacts when taking actions. And we have been working to gradually bring economic activities back to normal.

Leaders of many countries have spoken highly of China's efforts, and recognized that China's experience offers useful lessons to the world.

Third, China has provided assistance to other countries in the spirit of solidarity.

China has engaged actively in international cooperation in an open, transparent and responsible manner to deal with the crisis.

China notified the world about the outbreak without delay, and acted quickly to identify and share the genetic sequence of the virus. At the same time, China has been sharing its experience of prevention, control and treatment with other countries without reservation, and set up an on-line knowledge centre, which is open to all countries.

China has donated $20 million to the WHO. Today, China announced a further donation of $30 million, which will be used to contain COVID-19 and bolster the public health system in developing countries.

China has also sent 17 teams of medical experts to 15 countries. It has provided or is in the process of providing much-needed medical supplies, including masks, protective gowns, testing kits and ventilators, to more than 150 countries and international organizations, including the UK.

Despite the difficulties at home, China has been increasing supply of pharmaceutical ingredients and medical and protective equipment and materials to the international market. From 1st March to 10th April, China exported about 7.2 billion masks, 55.57 million protective gowns, 3.59 million infrared thermometers, 20,000 ventilators and 13 million pairs of goggles.

The assistance from China has injected positive energy into the global response to COVID-19 and shored up international confidence in winning this battle against the virus.

Now I would like to move on to the second part of my speech and talk about China's economy in the context of the outbreak, which I know you have all been following closely.

A few days ago, the IMF downgraded this year's growth expectations by a big margin, warning that the impact of COVID-19 on the world economy might surpass that of the Great Depression.

The outbreak has also taken its toll on China's economy and social conditions. In the first quarter, China's GDP contracted by 6.8% year-on-year.

In face of the unprecedented risks, challenges and uncertainties, it is all the more important that we shore up confidence, keep up our courage, and work hard to turn challenges into opportunities and ensure continued growth. I think we can draw confidence from the following three facts:

First, China's economy will maintain steady growth in the long run. This momentum has not changed and will not change.

China has a solid economic foundation:

- As the world's second largest economy, China's GDP reached $14.4 trillion in 2019, 3.1 times compared with that of 2008 during the international financial crisis, which was $4.6 trillion, and 8.6 times compared with that of 2003 amid the SARS outbreak, which was $1.67 trillion.
- China is the only country in the world that has all the industries under the United Nations classifications.
- With a population of 1.4 billion, including 900 million workforce and more than 400 million middle-income earners, China enjoys broad prospects for economic growth.
- China's economy has enormous potential for further growth. The per capita GDP has just crossed the $10,000 line, which is only one fourth that of the UK and one sixth that of the US. The urbanization rate stands at only 60%.

As I said earlier, China attaches great importance to balancing counter-epidemic measures and economic and social activities. Within the country, life is gradually returning to normal, and economic activities are approaching or have already returned to the normal track.

As of today, 99% of major industrial companies have resumed operation. March manufacturing PMI increased by 16.3 percentage points over February. According to the latest IMF World Economic Outlook, China's economy growth will rebound to 9.2% in 2021.

Second, China's economy will pursue high-quality development. This goal has not changed and will not change.

While COVID-19 will remain on the government agenda for some time to come, China has lost no time in turning our attention to the economy.

- We will continue to follow the new development concept.
- We will press ahead with supply-side structural reform.
- We will improve the market-based allocation of production factors.
- We will pursue high-quality growth through further reforms and by opening up further to the world.

We have stepped up macro-policy regulation to counter-act the impact of COVID-19. Measures have been taken to safeguard employment, the financial market, foreign trade, investment, FDI and expectations stable. On this basis, we have taken further steps to protect basic livelihood, market entities, food and energy security, stable industrial and supply chains, and the normal operation of the grassroots communities. All these efforts are aimed at ensuring overall economic growth and social stability.

We have also taken measures to expand domestic demand and increase effective investment. The battle against this pandemic has created new opportunities for development, such as the "stay-at-home economy" and the "cloud office". China is seizing these opportunities. We will leverage the internet, big data, artificial intelligence and other new technologies to accelerate the development of emerging industries, such as the digital economy, smart manufacturing, and medical and health care. Efforts are also being made to transform and upgrade traditional industries, a expand investment in strategic and emerging industries, and to develop the green economy.

These efforts will ensure that China's economy remains on the track of high-quality growth.

Third, China will continue to be the powerhouse and stabilizer for the world economy. Our commitment has not changed and will not change.

China has been committed to opening its market wider to the world. Measures have been taken to:
- increase market access,
- improve the business environment,
- expand import,
- increase outbound investment,
- facilitate the unimpeded flow of goods around the world,
- and promote high-quality cooperation on the Belt and Road Initiative.

The 127th China Import and Export Fair will take place online in mid-to-late June. This will be the first time that this longest-running trade event in China will be held online. In November, China will hold the third China International Import Expo. Both events will create huge opportunities for the mutually-beneficial trade and cooperation between countries of the world.

China is also calling on the international community to step up macro-policy coordination in order to stabilize the market, secure growth, protect wellbeing, and ensure that the global supply chain is open, stable and safe.

On top of that, China is the "factory of the world". Steady economic growth in China provides a strong support for global recovery.

Now I would like to move to the third part of my speech and talk about how the international community should work together to win the battle against COVID-19.

The question being asked or debated around the world today is this: Has the pandemic united or divided the world?

My answer to this question is this: The on-going battle is living proof that countries of the world belong to one and the same community with a shared future. In the battle against the pandemic, cooperation is the most effective weapon if the international community wants to claim final victory over the virus.

First, we need global, unified action to win the battle against COVID-19.

At the Extraordinary G20 Leaders' Summit last month, President Xi Jinping put forth four important proposals:

- First, we need to fight a global war.
- Second, we need to take international collective action.
- Third, we need to support international organisations in playing their active roles.
- Fourth, we need to enhance macro-economic policy coordination.

He also made a number of specific proposals regarding intergovernmental cooperation, including joint R&D into drugs and vaccines, a G20 COVID-19 assistance initiative and joint efforts to stabilize global industrial and supply chains. These could be the areas where the countries of the world could work together to meet the challenges of the global public health crisis.

China will continue to enhance its cooperation with other countries, shoulder its due responsibilities and contribute to the final victory of this battle.

Second, we should enhance solidarity and shore up confidence.

This virus does not respect borders or discriminate between races. In face of the crisis, playing the blame game is futile; arrogance and insolence will only poison the cooperation between countries.

It is against human conscience to deliberately affix the "virus" label to a specific region, to politicize public health issue and stigmatize a specific country. Such moves will only drive a wedge between countries, undermine international cooperation and harm the interests of all mankind.

It is important that countries of the world reject ideological bias, place human lives above everything else and form the maximum synergy to bring the pandemic under control.

Third, we should uphold multilateralism and support international organisations in playing an active role.

China is committed to multilateralism. We have been working to strengthen and improve the system of global governance with the UN at its core.

Since the outbreak of COVID-19, the WHO has taken an objective, scientific and just position, and played an important role in coordinating and promoting international cooperation. This has won extensive recognition from the international community.

Going forward, China will continue, as always, to support the WHO, including supporting its leadership in the current battle against COVID-19.

China will also work actively to strengthen cooperation on public health matters with countries along the Belt and Road routes and to join hands with them to build a "Silk Road of Public Health".

Fourth, we should promote inclusive cooperation in order to build an open world economy.

There may be difficulties and headwinds, but there is no reason for us to stop cooperating in an open spirit or to seek development through cooperation. Advocates of "decoupling" and a "technology blockade" will only find themselves in self-imposed isolation, restriction and backsliding.

China will remain committed to reform and opening up, and enhance coordination in macro-economic policy with other countries. We will begin to focus on what we should do after the pandemic. This includes taking all necessary measures to ensure the stability of global industrial and supply chains, to promote trade and investment liberalization and facilitation, and to build an open world economy.

Ladies and Gentlemen:

China and the UK are important partners in this battle against the virus. In the matter of one month, President Xi Jinping and Prime Minister Boris Johnson had two telephone conversations. This demonstrates the firm determination of our two countries to work together to meet the challenge of this public health crisis.

At the present moment, our two countries are sharing information and experience and conducting joint scientific research. We are both advocates of multilateralism. We are both supporters of the important role of the WHO in a united global response. We are both proponents of international cooperation under the framework of the G20. And we are both promoters of better global governance on public health.

At this crucial moment, it is important that China and the UK shoulder our responsibilities, stand together with each other, and resist noises and disruptions. We should add positive energy into our joint response to the pandemic and make new contributions to global public health.

I am confident that China and the UK will emerge from this test with a more mature and robust relationship, with broader and deeper cooperation, and with a stronger and enduring friendship between our peoples.

As a Chinese saying goes, "Victory is ensured when people pool their strength; success is secured when people put their heads together."

China stands ready to join hands with the international community, including the UK, to shore up confidence and address the current difficulties.

Together we will win this battle against the virus. Together we will create a better and brighter future for the world!

Thank you.

I am ready to take your questions.

Lord Green: Thank you Ambassador Liu and thank you very much to those who are with us. There will be many people who share the appeal for constructive international cooperation and engagement in this unprecedented situation. Unprecedented is a word that is becoming extremely frequently used, but we think it is unprecedented at least since the Second World War. It poses all sorts of challenges for individual countries. China was the first into it and seems to be the first out of it. I guess caution is always necessary. Britain as you know is still struggling, and all of Europe is struggling with this.

It seems to me that there are some short, medium and longer term challenges, some of which are deeply impacted by COVID-19, and some are not. It seems to me that clearly in the short term, we have the question of how to exit from lockdown strategies. This as you know is a topic that gets a lot of conversation in this country and around Europe more generally, and it's causing a lot of anxiety in the US as well, and maybe in some parts of East Asia. Japan has taken a particular route, which is almost explicitly allowing the possibility of a second wave of the virus. So different strategies are all agonising with the difficulty of getting out of the COVID-19 situation, particularly since we all recognise that it will take some while for an effective vaccination to be available against the virus. There are some short term challenges that have to do with the immediate economic impact of COVID-19, which we all wrestle with. For example, how tourism will reemerge as an important economic force; and about the retail industry, to what extent many small businesses will be shut down and so on.

Then there is the whole macroeconomic picture: country after country have released enormous support packages, fiscal and monetary. What are the medium term consequences of those? Does this mean that we will face, a little further down the track, a period of renewed austerity, as nations try to repair the balance of their finances? Does it mean higher taxes? Does it mean higher inflation? There are all sorts of questions that will be around. They'll be around for the Chinese authorities, I think, as the Chinese economy rebounds. They are clearly going to be around in the British context, and in a broad European context. The US will face it and it comes with a different way because it's in a special position vis à vis the dollar. And that's the kind of medium term challenge that's created by COVID-19.

I think there are some medium and longer term challenges that are not affected by COVID-19. I think that the trade order is one question. Even before the virus we were all struggling with the fact that the WTO was losing its ability to effectively arbitrate disputes because of the absence of appellate judges. I noticed that, on the 30th March, right in the thick of the pandemic, the EU and China and a number of other nations agreed on the multi-party interim appeal arbitration arrangement. There is a question in my mind about how the UK can get itself involved in that. But I think we should all recognise this is an important step in shoring up the work of the WTO. You talked about the reasons we all recognise about the WHO. I think the WHO is one important international organization, whereas the WTO is an equally important international institution that is part of a functioning multilateral order, and we all have some concerns about that. Let's face it, in both cases, America has chosen to take a less constructive view at least temporarily. And I think it's the common interest to re-establish a conviction about the importance of that international multilateral order.

And then finally, I think there is the longer-term question which is in no way going away, and that is about bio-diversity, environmental degradation, climate change. In the short term, we have seen how the decline in economic activity has improved levels of pollution in cities around the world, and has led to a reduction in carbon dioxide emissions, but in no way was it anything other than temporary. I believe that the continuing demographic pressure, the continuing pressure of urbanisation, the continuing pressure of economic development means that we are going to continue to have to grapple with this fundamental longer term challenge and COVID-19 in no way affects that. It's made it more difficult in the short term, of course by forcing China to postpone the Kunming COP15 bio-diversity conference, and forcing the UK to postpone the Glasgow COP26 which was due in November. I hope that those postponements are only for a relatively short period of time, because of all the common agendas you, Ambassador, have quite rightly referred to, this one is perhaps the most important of all. It's the most profound and the longest term. We should not allow COVID-19, and the tragedies and difficulties of the present circumstances, to take our eyes off that ball.

So there's a lot going on; We live in extraordinary times. There are plenty of challenges posed by COVID-19.

There are also challenges that inevitably affect international relationships. The big question of China and America, which we Europeans look at with hope and prayer, but this relationship will only develop on a constructive basis. And I think that there's therefore plenty of need for us to continue to have the sort of dialogues with what this occasion represents. One is here at "Asia House", we have an extremely important role in providing a platform for these dialogues, both about shorter term issues from micro to macro economics, and about the medium term issues of the trade order, and about the longer term issues of climate change cooperation and its impact on economic development.

Let me stop there. I wonder if any of what I've just said resonates with you, Ambassador?

Liu Xiaoming: Yes, Lord Green. You've touched upon many areas. I would say that I quite agree with you on many of these areas, and your points.

You talk about the challenges in each country. I think each country is different from the other. The UK is different from Germany, Italy, or France. We follow the situation very closely. But despite the differences, I think there's a commonality between countries in fighting against this virus. I talked, in my presentation, about the China-UK collaboration. I think that also applies to China's collaboration with other countries. When we're faced with these common threats, countries should work together.

First, I think we should support each other. In terms of medical supplies, when China was at its critical moment, the UK government sent two shipments of the most needed medical supplies. But now you are fighting your battle, we reciprocate your support. Just as Minister Gove said, you received much more than what you donated to China. Currently, I think ventilators are badly needed. 750 ventilators have already been shipped to the UK, and there are more to come. There are other medical supplies and equipment that we are ready to supply to the UK and to the world.

The other area is the sharing of experience. China was one of the first countries to have achieved significant progress, and we'd like to share with other countries our experience on how to contain the virus, and how to treat the patients. I'm very pleased that we are maintaining constant communications between the two sides. Secretary Matt Hancock just had a telephone conversation yesterday with his counterpart Ma Xiaowei, the Chinese Health Minister. They had a very productive and in-depth discussion on collaboration between China and the UK in fighting to the virus. They shared their experience and compared notes.

The third area is international cooperation. I touched upon that in my presentation. You used the word in a very polite and very British gentlemanly expression about the "unconstructive" approach by the United States. We are very disappointed by the US decision, but we believe that the WHO plays a very important role, especially at this critical moment. We need to support the WHO in leading the international response to this virus. I'm pleased that the UK government decided to continue to support the WHO. So China and the UK share this common position.

In addition to its 20 million US dollar donation, just a few hours before our event today, the Chinese government announced that we are going to donate another 30 million U.S. dollars to the WHO. Maybe they knew that the "Asia House" and you were going to have this event, so I can share with you firsthand information. (Laughter) We especially hope it will be used to support the public health system in developing countries in Africa and in some other places.

The fourth area where China and the UK can cooperate and also the international community can enhance its collaboration is as you said macro economic policy, that is a way to ensure that the world economy will resume growth.

In China, the major industries have already resumed 99% of their former production, and the government has introduced more policy measures to support small and medium sized businesses – that is also very important. What's more, it is still our goal to support the WTO to ensure trade liberalisation and facilitation. We would also like to work with the UK.

Climate change is very important to our agenda as well. It's a pity that we have to postpone both conferences-the COP15 and the COP26. At the very beginning of this year, I regarded it as a year of China-UK collaboration on climate change. As a matter of fact, our two countries worked very closely and coordinated with each other despite the virus.

Although we have had to postpone the conferences, the preparation work is still ongoing. I keep very close communication with Secretary Sharma. He has been designated as the President for the COP26, and we have a new Minister of Environment, Huang Ruaqiu. So I tried to connect the two of them. The working teams of our two countries are still talking to each other online.

The other important issue is that when we are enhancing international collaboration on fighting against the COVID-19 virus, we should also be on guard against a political virus. Like I said in my speech, some politicians and some forces are trying to find a scapegoat and to play a blame game in order to shirk their responsibility. You know we call on governments of all countries to focus on fighting the virus, on protecting the lives of its people, rather than fighting each other, rather than undermining international collaboration. That is also very important. So we are very disappointed, and we rejcct these so-called "accusations" from some of the American politicians. We don't think this disinformation against China serves the purpose of international response to this virus.

On China-US relations, we have every reason to maintain a sound and good relationship. President Xi had several telephone conversations with President Trump. We always believe that China and the US will gain from cooperation and lose from confrontation. We also believe it is not only in the interests of China and the US to have a sound and good relationship, but it's also in the interests of the world. We would like to have a good relationship with the US, based on mutual respect, non-confrontation and mutual collaboration, and we are working towards this goal. But you need two to tango, right? You know, the Chinese leaders, or Chinese ambassadors, Chinese diplomats are spreading the words of a community with a shared future for mankind, and are trying very hard to shore up the confidence of the international community. However, at the same time, some politicians, some people are trying to spread disinformation and rumors across the world.

That is not helpful at all! So we really hope that China and the US can work together, and the international community can work together for the common goal that serves the interests of all mankind.

Adam Keswick from Jardine Matheson Holdings: Hello Ambassador. Thank you for your words, and Stephen, yours too. I thought it is very encouraging to hear everything you've said. I hope that the networks of communications that have been put in place to fight this virus can continue to promote the economy after we've tackled this, which I'm sure we will. Ambassador, your views of what China will be doing, all of which I took a lot of comfort from. But more specifically, I feel that the eyes of the world will be watching the upcoming NPC meeting whenever that takes place. But presuming it will be sometime later in May, it would be very interesting to get your views on what specific messages, do you think, are going to come out of that meeting that the rest of the world can take further comfort from in terms of battling the virus, and also a return to some form of economic normality. Just be interested to have your views on that.

Liu Xiaoming: I think this will be very important. We call it the "Two sessions". It has been postponed. It will set policies and guidelines, not only for the development of China for this year. I think it will draw up the plan, or what we call the 14th Five-Year Plan. So, the significance of the two sessions will extend beyond this year. Of course, COVID-19 will be high on the agenda. And I wouldn't speculate on what other items will be on the agenda. But as I said in my speech that COVID-19 not only poses challenges to China, but also creates opportunities for development. I think both delegates of the National People's Congress and deputies of the People's Political Consultative Conference will focus on the new areas, the new points of growth for the future development. So, I would recommend that you follow these two sessions very closely.

Emma Roberts from BHP: Ambassador, it is very good to hear your summary of China's economy as it's moving out of the crisis and BHP obviously has very a strong relationship with its Chinese customers where its commodities are concerned. So far we've seen this demand remain rather stable even during the peak of the crisis within China. BHP has been able to work with its customers to continue that supply. However, I think there's certainly some concerns and there's been some recent press reports about whether that demand from China may ease off towards the later part of the year. Perhaps China is experiencing a dropping off of exports from Western economies as these Western countries try to come out of their lockdown and struggle to get their economies up and running. What's your thought on China's continued emergence from its crisis and the continued risk of China's economy? Do you see a dipping in that as Western economies struggle to get back, or remain rather steady and strong?

Liu Xiaoming: I think that as China gradually resumes production, it will continue to play a role, as a powerhouse of the world economy. As 99% of the major industries have resumed, China will continue to play a role as the factory of the world. China is a huge market. So we will contribute to the restoration of global growth. The outbreak of COVID-19 really brings some opportunities for us to restructure our economy. Some areas might hold great potential, including the stay-home economy, the digital economy, AI and also the medical area. Here's an example. From March 1st to April 10th, China exported about 7.2 billion masks, 55.57 million protective gowns, 20,000 ventilators and 13 million pairs of goggles. So China is really a source of medical supplies. That is also China's contribution, not only to the global response to the virus, but also it will help build the industrial and supply chain in the future.

China is committed to building an open world economy. China has achieved success in the past 40 years because of the policy of reform and opening up. I think China will stick to this policy to continue its success. There's no reason for China to close its door or abandon the reform. So reform will be ongoing and China will be open wider to the world. The 127th China Import and Export Fair will be held online in June. And also the third China International Import Expo will be held in November. These will be very valuable opportunities for China to engage with the outside world. I've been talking to British senior officials from the Department of International Trade, as well as business leaders in the UK, inviting them to participate in these two events. It will provide enormous opportunities for our two countries to work together to resume the momentum of economic growth.

Laura Mann from AstraZeneca: Thank you so much for your excellent remarks. AstraZeneca places very high value on partnership with China before and during COVID-19. We've been able to donate nine million masks around the world, and to the countries most in need, in partnership with the World Health Organization and World Economic Forum. I wondered, in your head, what do you see as the further opportunities to continue to strengthen the bilateral relationship between the UK and China? For example, in health care and life sciences.

Liu Xiaoming: As I said earlier, our two countries continue their dialogue at a very high level. You know, President Xi Jinping had two telephone conversations with Prime Minister Johnson in little more than one month. That was very rare. I've been here as ambassador for more than 10 years, and I've never seen our top leaders have such intensive communications in such a short period of time. On the ministerial level, we are having very intensive communications, as Director Yang Jiechi talked to Sir Mark Sedwill, and State Counsellor and Foreign Minister Wang Yi talked to Secretary Raab. And here in London, I have kept very close contacts with ministers and secretaries. We compare notes and share experiences.
And, China and the UK are working very closely on developing the vaccine. The scientists of our two countries are working very closely. Imperial College, Oxford and Cambridge are working very closely with their counterparts in China. While the Chinese medical team was here, they held online discussions with British experts and doctors. So we have had very intensive interactions with each other. In addition to supplying medical equipment, the vaccine really is the final solution to the battle. Both President Xi and Prime Minister Johnson expressed their support for the scientists of the two countries to work together in this very important area.
What is more in the international arena, China and the UK both work very closely. We're both supporters of multilateralism and full supporters of the WTO. You know, Lord Green cares about it very much. We see the UK as a partner for China on the Belt and Road Initiative. We are now working with the countries along the Road to build a "silk road for public health".
I think there is another area in which China and the UK can share experience and can work together. Climate change, As I said, China and the UK are leaders in environmental protection. We're supposed to host the COP 15 and the COP 26. They have been postponed, but not cancelled. We're still working on them. You know,

when this pandemic is over, the two countries will host these two conferences. They will set the agenda and direction for climate change and for environmental protection. So, there are enormous opportunities between our two countries.

And trade between us. I think there's still a great future for the trade between our two countries. Last year, a new record was set in bilateral trade -an increase of more than 7%, despite the downturn of global growth of the trade. The UK is now China's third largest trading partner within the EU. China is the third largest export market for the UK. Chinese investment in the UK is also increasing. In the past five years, the total Chinese investment has been bigger than the previous 30 years combined. Now, the UK is the number one destination in Europe for Chinese investment. Chinese businesses here are very active. A few days ago, I participated in an online donation event held by the China Chamber of Commerce in the UK. They donated ventilators, face masks, goggles and protective gowns to the NHS. And that shows their global vision and sense of social responsibility. We encourage all these interactions between China and the UK.

David Sayer from KPMG: Thank you. I'm about to say, I enjoy this remarkable technology and for that I want to address a question. You've said to me in the past that every challenge has an opportunity. And I do think, this remarkable technology allows us to have a much more direct and immediate dialogue with Chinese firms. I've been talking to clients in the UK that I can bring my Chinese partners into a virtual meeting, far more easily and far more acceptably than it's been in the past and I think that's one of the changes we'll be seeing. Virtual dialogue is becoming, and has proved it's workable. It's becoming utterly acceptable. And in the past having a dialogue with Chinese firms has always involved 20 hours on planes and the rest. I think one of the things coming out of this is the potential to accelerate dialogue between the UK and China across so many dimensions. And I just wonder the ways in which we can celebrate the facilitation of that, and whether the Embassy can play a role.

Liu Xiaoming: Yes, I'm very pleased that you have been one of the beneficiaries of this new technology. Once you have Huawei participating in your 5G development, the speed and quality of these online meetings will be even better. I know that Prime Minister Johnson has a very ambitious plan to have full 5G coverage in the

UK by 2025. I think Huawei will be a big help on this. We do hope that not only will the leaders of our two countries talk to each other, but also business leaders. I held several online meetings. As a matter of fact, this "Asia House" is really one of those webinars I have attended, and soon I will have another one with the CBI. And then another one with the CBBC. I already had one with the British Chamber of Commerce in China. We had this real time discussion. I think we benefit greatly from this technology. We should stay committed to free trade, to building our business friendly environment. The UK is well known for supporting a free and open economy. That's very important. That's why the UK can become No. 1 destination for Chinese investment. I held a meeting with many Chinese business leaders. I asked them, "Why are you here, compared with other European countries? Why do you invest your money here?" Take Jingye. I just participated in Jingye's acquisition of British Steel. They told me they found the UK very open and transparent, and the political leaders, business leaders, local leaders and local community welcome Chinese business with open arms. That's the secret of the UK's success. So, I do hope that this trend will continue. It is really not only for the benefit of China-UK collaboration. It is also for the benefit of the people of the UK.

James Landale from BBC: You placed great emphasis on international cooperation. Will China, as a result, cooperate with any independent international investigation into the origins of this pandemic? Will China provide any investigators with full access to all the relevant data, locations and witnesses?

Liu Xiaoming: China has been open, transparent and responsible from the very beginning. We have invited the WHO experts to China. They visited not only Wuhan but also other places and cities. They came up with a very extensive and comprehensive report about their study in China.
I hear quite a lot of speculation and disinformation to the effect that the Chinese are covering up and hiding something. This is not true. I do not know if you have read the WHO report. Some people already leapt to judgement beforehand. Each time they hear American politicians accusing and criticizing China for hiding or covering up, they just turn to them. But when Chinese spokesman spoke about the fact, I read very little coverage here in the Western media. They already have prejudice and bias against China. That's the problem.

I would advise the media including the British media to be balanced and objective. I'm not calling on you to be friendly to China, but just to be balanced. While you are reporting that the US Secretary of State is so-called "criticizing" but actually "stigmatizing" China, you should also report the counter argument given by China. You should also report the WHO's comment. When the media harbours this bias, they only report something they would like to hear. They don't report the other side of the story. That's the problem.

The Chinese government has been transparent and open, and has responded very quickly. When Americans complain that one month after the outbreak China had not shared information and has not reported to the WHO and international organizations, that's not true. The virus was first reported on 27th December by Dr. Zhang Jixian. She reported much earlier than Dr. Li Wenliang. We recognize Dr. Li as a hero and he gave his life fighting this virus. But he did not report to the authorities and he shared the story three days after Dr. Zhang Jixian made a report to the local health authorities. Then the government adopted very strict and swift actions, notified the WHO four days later, and shared information with Americans seven days later. So that's how Americans could have taken action to bring their nationals back and to close the border. If you check the timeline on what China was doing, you will find we have been transparent and straightforward with all the information.

You talk about having an independent investigation. It's up to the WHO. We support the WHO. We believe we should play by international norms and international rules, not by some other countries' rules. Some other countries have even sued China in their local courts. It's absurd. I've twice been posted to Washington D.C. This is not the first time that some politicians want to play the world police. This is not the era of "gunboat diplomacy". This is not the era when China was still a semi-colonial and semi-feudal society. This is the third decade of the 21st century. Those people cannot understand it. They think they still live in the old days when they could bully China and the world. If the WHO does not act their way, they cut off their support and criticize the WHO for being "China-centric". That's simply not right. So we are calling for international cooperation. That's the only weapon and the only way out to win this battle against the virus. Not by scape-goating, not by playing games, not by politicizing the virus, not by spreading a political virus. We have to guard against this while fighting this invisible enemy.

China is not an enemy of the United States. China is a friend of the United States, a partner for the United States in fighting against the virus. If they regard China as an enemy, they are choosing the wrong target. Despite these politicians spreading disinformation about China, China has provided 1. 8 billion face masks to the U.S. That means six face masks per person in the United States. We still try to lend a helping hand to the American people when they need us.

Iolo ap Dafydd from CGTN: You mentioned some of China's priorities after this pandemic. Where specifically do you think does China want to prioritize?

Liu Xiaoming: First we need to resume production. We must strike a balance between fighting against the virus and ensuring the gradual resumption of production so that social order and normal life will return to their regular track.

That is a top priority. But we also have to guard against the recurrence of the virus, because the risk now is more about imported cases. The government has adopted some measures to take care of the imported cases and we also need collaboration from other countries to achieve our goal. We have to be careful to ensure that the hard-won progress will not be reversed by suddenly lifting restrictions. In Wuhan, the ban on outbound traffic has been lifted, but there are still some restrictions in certain sectors. Schools have not fully resumed. There are certain requirements. If you meet the requirements, you can gradually resume in those sectors.

And also, we are engaging actively with the rest of the world. On diplomatic engagement, we have important agendas in front of us like climate change. I'm working now with Secretary Sharma and other senior officials on how we can engage with each other to pick up the momentum where we left off before the outbreak. We are also working very hard with the Department of International Trade on the free trade agreement between China and the UK after Brexit. I'm talking to the Ministers and the Secretary of State. So, we have a very busy agenda ahead of us. Most of them are online now. We want to make sure once this is all over, we can pick up the momentum.

Lord Green: Ambassador Liu, it has been a remarkable discussion. I've enjoyed it enormously. Your final remarks are extremely good ones, to end on that powerful reminder that there is a huge range of issues on which we have every opportunity to cooperate effectively, and that we need to keep the momentum up. And remember, there will be a time after COVID-19, lots of lessons to be learned about it, lots of shorter term issues about repairing macro economic damages. There will also be fundamental longer term issues on which we have so much in common and where we have so many opportunities to work together. So I really appreciate, on behalf of "Asia House", your taking the time to be with us. And I look forward to many future engagements. You mentioned that you are in your 11th year here. That means you know this country extremely well. And I have always enjoyed your comments on this country, because you have great insights into it and into the dynamics of the relationship. There are lots of, tremendous, opportunities for us in the midst of this crisis. And we need to never lose sight of that.

So, thank you for joining. And thank you to all of our guests. Thank you to our corporate members and all of our guests for joining us on what I think is an extremely valuable session. Thank you.

Liu Xiaoming: Thank you. See you next time.

▲ 2019年6月24日，出席英国"亚洲之家"对话会

▲ 2019年7月3日，在中国驻英国大使馆就香港发生暴力冲击立法会事件举行中外记者会

▲ 2019年8月15日，在中国驻英国大使馆就香港街头暴力激进活动举行中外记者会

▲ 2019年11月18日，在中国驻英国大使馆就香港局势举行中外记者会

▲ 2020年2月6日，在中国驻英国大使馆就抗击新冠肺炎疫情举行中外记者会

▲ 2020年7月30日，在中国驻英国大使馆就中英关系举行线上中外记者会

▼ 2020年10月13日，在国际能源信息论坛大会发表主旨演讲并回答提问

▲ 2020 年 10 月 28 日，与英国议会跨党派国际环保小组座谈

▼ 2023 年 4 月 17 日，接受俄罗斯塔斯社副总编尤莉亚·沙里夫林娜专访

▲ 2023 年 5 月 26 日，接受中央广播电视总台《鲁健访谈》栏目主持人鲁健专访

与英国议员对话

Q&A with UK Parliament

2020年10月13日，我应邀出席英国议会跨党派中国小组气候变化问题在线座谈会，发表题为《共建美好地球家园》的主旨演讲并回答议员提问。英国议会跨党派中国小组主席格雷厄姆，议会下院环境监察委员会主席邓恩，外交发展部COP26区域大使布里斯托，议会上、下两院议员，内阁办、外交发展部、环境部主管官员，保守党环保机构、英中贸协、英中协会代表等30余人参加。

10月28日，我出席英国议会跨党派国际环保小组"保护自然：通向昆明之路"线上座谈会，发表题为《谱写生态文明新篇章》的主旨演讲并回答与会人员提问。英国议会跨党派国际环保小组主席加德纳，联合国《生物多样性公约》秘书处执行秘书穆雷玛，南非环境、森林及渔业部长克里西，加蓬森林、海洋、环境和气候变化部长怀特，英国外交发展国务大臣戈登·史密斯，全球环境基金首席执行官罗德里格斯以及一些国家的议会议员出席。

共建美好地球家园
—— 与英国议会跨党派中国小组谈气候变化问题并回答议员提问

（2020年10月13日，中国驻英国使馆/英国议会）

刘晓明： 很高兴再次与英国议会跨党派中国小组各位议员座谈。我们今天座谈的主题是中英气候变化合作。2021年将是气候变化合作之年，中英将分别主办《生物多样性公约》第15次缔约方会议（COP15）和《联合国气候变化框架公约》第26次缔约方会议（COP26），这将是中英关系的大事，也将对全球气变合作和环境治理产生重要影响。

当前，新冠肺炎疫情在全球蔓延，气候变化问题持续升温。我认为，人类社会正面临与气候变化紧密相关的五大挑战：

一是全球变暖挑战。目前全球平均温度已比工业化前高出1摄氏度以上，全球海平面上升速度达到每年5毫米。未来，一些地区可能不再适宜居住。

二是生态环境挑战。人类工业化进程创造了前所未有的物质财富，也产生了严重环境污染，生物多样性面临严峻挑战。

三是新冠肺炎疫情叠加挑战。疫情客观上削弱了各国对应对气候变化问题的关注。COP15和COP26不得不推迟举行。

四是应对能力不平衡挑战。与发达国家相比，发展中国家受到气候变化冲击影响更大。国际社会消除南北发展不平衡、凝聚应对气候变化合力依然任重道远。

五是毁约退群挑战。个别国家悍然退出《巴黎协定》，这种单边霸凌行径使全球气变合作和治理遭受严重挫折。

不久前，习近平主席在出席联合国成立75周年高级别活动中宣布，中国将提高国家自主贡献力度，采取更加有力的政策和措施，二氧化碳排放力争于2030年前达到峰值，努力争取2060年前实现碳中和。这是中国基于国内可持续发展内在要求和构建人类命运共同体的责任担当，彰显了中国积极应对气候变化的坚定决心。国际社会对此予以高度评价。约翰逊首相称，习主席宣布的目标是一件了不起的事情，是向世界发出的强有力信号。中英是应对气候变化和环境治理的重要伙伴，双方合作大有可为。

一是共同做气变治理的领军者。中国积极落实应对气候变化国家战略，切实履行《巴黎协定》国际义务。2005年至2019年，中国单位GDP碳排放下降48.1%，非化石能源占比达15.3%，新能源汽车保有量占全球一半以上。英国确立了到2050年实现"净零排放"的目标。中英可以充分利用主办COP15和COP26两次会议之机，为全球气变治理发挥重要引领作用。习近平主席和约翰逊首相就两国加强COP15和COP26相互协调、相互支持达成重要共识。中国生态环境部部长黄润秋与夏尔马大臣，我本人与夏尔马大臣、布里斯托爵士等保持密切沟通。双方还在工作层建立了联合工作组。下一步，双方要加强沟通协调，调动政府、议会、商界、媒体、学界等各界人士积极性，确保两次大会办得精彩、取得成功。

二是共同做绿色发展的推动者。疫情形势下，中国政府统筹推进疫情防控与经济社会发展，推广绿色生产和生活方式，加速完善气候投融资体系。英国在清洁能源、低碳技术等方面独具特色。中英应加强在新能源、低碳城市等领域合作，实现生态环境保护和经济高质量发展双赢。中国在核能等清洁能源领域技术成熟，运营管理经验丰富。欣克利角C核电站是中、英、法在清洁能源领域合作的重要旗舰项目，建成后可满足英国7%的电力需求，每年可以减排900万吨二氧化碳。双方应共同努力确保该项目顺利成功。我们还应鼓励两国产业界在可再生能源、绿色金融、绿色"一带一路"等领域加强合作，助力两国绿色复产，带动全球绿色复苏。

三是共同做绿色创新的开拓者。中英都在积极推动绿色科技、能源、金融创新发展。两国签署了《中英清洁能源合作伙伴关系实施工作计划2019—2020》，共同制定了"一带一路"绿色投资原则，绿色合作潜力巨大。吉利、比亚迪等中资企业积极投资英国，成为两国绿色交通合作的典范。

四是共同做多边主义的捍卫者。中英双方应坚定维护多边主义，按照公平、共同但有区别的责任和各自能力原则，尽最大努力落实国家自主贡献，共同推动《巴黎协定》全面、平衡、有效实施，帮助发展中国家提升应对气变能力，深化应对气变国际合作，完善气候治理体系，共同引领全球气变治理方向和进程。

女士们、先生们，应对气候变化、保护生物多样性是中英合作的重要领域，也是中英两国作为具有全球影响的大国应肩负的使命。习近平在联合国生物多样性峰会上指出，"我们要站在对人类文明负责的高度，尊重自然、顺应自然、保护自然，探索人与自然和谐共生之路，促进经济发展与生态保护协调统一，共建繁荣、清洁、美丽的世界"。英国议会在英国应对气候变化进程中发挥着重要作用。我衷心期望各位议员继续发挥积极作用，支持中英两国政府、两国企业开展绿色合作，为办好COP15和COP26献计献策，为构建人类命运共同体、共建美好地球家园贡献力量！
谢谢！
现在我愿回答各位议员的提问。

议会跨党派中国小组主席格雷厄姆： 在新冠肺炎疫情形势下，明年COP15大会能否如期举行？

刘晓明： 现距大会召开还有7个多月，我们对COP15如期举行充满信心。目前中国国内民众已恢复正常生活，经济复工复产取得重要成果。我们将继续做好国内疫情防控工作，也会密切关注全球疫情发展。正如习近平主席在联合国生物多样性峰会上所说，欢迎大家明年聚首美丽的春城昆明，共商全球生物多样性大计，共建万物和谐的美丽世界。

议会上院议员卢卡斯勋爵： 英中在新能源特别是新能源汽车领域如何进一步开展合作？

刘晓明： 在新能源领域，中国非常愿意与英国开展互利合作。截至2019年底，中国新能源汽车保有量达381万辆，占全球一半以上，增量连续两年超过100万辆，均居全球领先地位。无论是中国比亚迪公司制造的电动大巴，还是吉利公司投资伦敦出租车公司后在英生产的全电动出租车，都为英国减少碳排放做出了贡献。此外，中国是可再生能源领域最大投资国，积极发展太阳能和风能。我认为，中英在相关领域蕴含巨大合作机遇，合作前景十分广阔。

议会上院议员卢卡斯勋爵： 你如何看待英中在核能领域的合作前景？

刘晓明： 中国核能技术成熟，运营管理经验丰富，中方愿继续与英方加强核能合作。截至2019年底，中国运行核电机组达到47台，总装机容量为4875万千瓦，仅次于美国和法国，位列全球第三。欣克利角C核电站是中、英、法在核能领域重要旗舰项目，将帮助英国实现2050年"净零排放"目标。目前这一项目面临一些杂音。我期待中英双方排除干扰，继续共同推进这一重要项目。

议会跨党派中国小组副主席克利夫顿-布朗爵士： 英国已淘汰所有煤炭发电厂。中国煤电发展是否会影响2060年实现碳中和的目标？中国将在何时淘汰煤电？

刘晓明： 中国是世界上最大的发展中国家，经济社会发展任务十分艰巨，发展不平衡、不充分等挑战仍然突出。对中国部分省区而言，煤炭仍是主要能源，逐步减少煤电需要一个过程。我曾在中国西部省份甘肃省担任省长助理，当地经济发展对煤炭仍有相当依赖。中国正严控煤炭消费总量，在工业领域提升能效环保标准，积极推进钢铁、建材、化工等高耗煤行业节能减排改造；在民生领域逐步推行天然气、电力、洁净型煤及可再生能源等清洁能源替代民用散煤，取得显著进展。中国高度重视煤电技术创新，已建成全球最大的清洁煤电供应体系，煤电超低排放机组超8亿千瓦，排放标准世界领先，为全球各国煤炭清洁利用做出了示范。着眼2060年前实现碳中和目标，中国将采取有力政策和措施，进一步推进绿色创新和能源转型，逐步减少化石能源消费，促进绿色高质量发展。

议会上院议员麦康纳尔勋爵： 人们很关注"一带一路"建设问题，中国是否会减少并最终停止对巴基斯坦等沿线国家的煤炭项目投融资？

刘晓明： "一带一路"不仅是经济繁荣之路，也是绿色发展之路。中国在"一带一路"建设实践中始终秉持绿色发展理念，推动基础设施绿色低碳化建设和运营管理，在投资贸易中强调生态文明理念，加强生态环境治理、生物多样性保护和应对气候变化等领域合作。2019年，中国与42个国家的140余家中外方伙伴一道，共同发起成立了"一带一路"绿色发展国际联盟。中国还实施"一带一路"应对气候变化南南合作计划，自2012年起每年气候南南合作资金支出达7200万美元。中国企业在承建和设计"一带一路"项目时，充分考虑生态因素，有效保护生物多样性。例如，中国企业在巴基斯坦承建卡拉公路时，在公路沿线植树近30万棵，植草500多万平方米，在建设基础设施的同时，也为当地环境绿化做出贡献。中国将坚持开放、绿色、可持续理念，与共建国家一道建设绿色"丝绸之路"，与包括英国在内的发达国家积极开展绿色领域第三方市场合作，为应对气候变化国际合作汇聚更多力量。

议会上院议员麦康纳尔勋爵： 英中企业和机构在参与推动COP15和COP26方面能发挥什么作用？中方对此有何考虑？

刘晓明： 我认为，各国企业和民间组织是促进全球生态环境保护、绿色和谐发展的重要有生力量。中方一贯鼓励利益相关方参与应对气候变化和生物多样性多边议程。明年COP15也将开展平行会议，举办大量边会和展览，充分鼓励和推动地方和社会各领域参与大会。中方还将按惯例在COP26会场设立"中国角"，为中国地方政府、科研院校、非政府组织等参与气候多边进程、建言绿色低碳发展提供平台。今年2月，我会见了伦敦金融城市长拉塞尔，就中英金融界和工商界加强绿色金融、气候变化合作，积极参与COP15和COP26等交换意见。中英两国企业及社会各界可加强交流，发挥各自优势，共同推动COP15和COP26两场大会取得成功，为全球可持续发展做出贡献。

Making Our Planet A Better Home for All
—— A Keynote Speech and Q&A at the APPCG Webinar on China-UK Cooperation on Tackling Climate Change

(13rd October 2020, Chinese Embassy / UK Parliament)

Liu Xiaoming: It is a real delight to join you again at the APPCG webinar. Today we will focus on China-UK cooperation on climate change.

The year 2021 will be an important year for joint global response to climate change. China and the UK will host the COP15 and the COP26 respectively. These are not only important events in China-UK relations but are also of great significance to global cooperation and governance on climate change and environmental protection.

Against the background of the raging COVID-19 pandemic, tackling climate change has become an increasingly urgent task. Mankind faces five major challenges where climate change is concerned.

The first challenge is global warming.

The global average temperature is now more than one degree Celsius above pre-industrial levels. The rise in global sea level has averaged 5 millimeters per year in recent years. In the future, some places may no longer be suitable for human habitation.

The second challenge is the deterioration of the eco-environment.

While creating unprecedented wealth, industrialization has caused serious pollution and posed severe challenges to biodiversity.

The third challenge is COVID-19.

This pandemic has drawn attention of many countries away from climate change. The COP15 and the COP26 have to be postponed.

The fourth challenge is the imbalance in response capacity.

Compared with developed countries, the impact of climate change on developing countries is more severe.

It remains a daunting task for the international community to redress the imbalance of development between the North and the South and to get everyone on board in tackling climate change.

The fifth challenge is the withdrawal from international treaties and organisations.

A certain country withdrew from the Paris Agreement. Such a unilateral and bullying move has led to severe setbacks in global cooperation and governance on climate change.

Last month, at a high-level UN meeting in commemoration of the 75th anniversary of the founding of the UN, President Xi Jinping announced that China will
- scale up its nationally determined contributions,
- adopt even more forceful policies and measures,
- and strive to reach a peak in carbon dioxide emissions by 2030 and achieve carbon neutrality by 2060.

This attests to China's audacity in taking up responsibilities in line with the requirements of sustainable domestic development and the goal of building a community with a shared future for mankind. It is a display of China's firm resolve to make an active response to climate change.

This announcement has been highly commended by the international community. In the words of Prime Minister Boris Johnson, this is "fantastic" and "a powerful signal to the world".

China and the UK are important partners in climate change response and environmental governance. There is enormous potential for closer cooperation between our two countries.

First, China and the UK can join hands and be the champions of global governance on climate change.

China has taken vigorous efforts to implement its National Climate Change Strategy and to fulfill its international obligations under the Paris Agreement.
- From 2005 to 2019, China's carbon emissions per unit GDP dropped by 48.1%.
- The proportion of non-fossil fuels in total energy consumption increased to 15.3%.
- And China has more than half of the world's "new energy" vehicles.

The UK has set the target of net-zero emissions by 2050.

Hosting the COP15 and the COP26 respectively will enable China and the UK to play a leading role in promoting global governance on climate change.

President Xi Jinping and Prime Minister Boris Johnson have reached an important political consensus on stepping up coordination and mutual support in hosting the COP15 and the COP26 respectively.

There have been close communications between the Minister of Ecology and

Environment of China Huang Runqiu and Secretary Alok Sharma.

I myself have remained in touch with Secretary Sharma and Sir Laurie Bristow, the UK Government's COP26 Regional Ambassador.

On an operational level, a China-UK joint working group has been set up.

Going forward, our two sides should enhance communication and coordination, and fully engage the governments, legislatures, business community, media and academia, so as to make these two conferences successful.

Second, China and the UK can join hands and be the promoters of green development.

Against the ravaging epidemic, the Chinese Government has adopted a coordinated approach to economic and social development. We have lost no time in promoting green production and a green way of life, and improving the system of climate finance and investment.

The UK has unique strengths in clean energy and low-carbon technology.

It is important that China and the UK enhance cooperation in "new energy" and low-carbon cities. These will enable us to achieve win-win results in both ecological conservation and high-quality economic growth.

China has mature technology and rich experience in the operation and management of clean energy, such as nuclear energy. The Hinkley Point C nuclear power station is a flagship project of China-UK cooperation on clean energy. Upon completion, it will meet 7% of the UK's total demand for electricity and help to eliminate 9 million tons of CO_2 emissions every year. This project is completely in the common interests of both sides. We should work together to make it a success.

Our two countries should also encourage closer cooperation between our industries in renewable energy, green finance and the green Belt and Road. This will help to boost green recovery in both our two countries and the rest of the world.

Third, China and the UK can join hands and be the pioneers in green innovation.

Both China and the UK are pursuing innovative development in green technology, energy and financial services.

In clean energy, our two countries have signed the Clean Energy Partnership Work Plan for 2019-2020 to step up cooperation on the relevant technologies.

In green finance, China and the UK have signed up to the Green Investment Principles for the Belt and Road Development. There will be huge potential for cooperation in this aspect.

In green transport, the Chinese companies Geely and BYD have actively invested in the UK, becoming shining examples of China-UK cooperation on green transport.

Fourth, China and the UK can join hands and be the defenders of multilateralism.

It is important that China and the UK stand up for multilateralism. Under the principle of equity and common but differentiated responsibilities and respective capabilities, China and the UK should make the utmost efforts to:

- implement nationally determined contributions,
- contribute to the comprehensive, balanced and effective implementation of the Paris Agreement,
- help developing countries to scale up capacity building,
- deepen international cooperation,
- improve the system of governance,
- and chart the course for global governance on climate change.

Ladies and Gentlemen:

Tackling climate change and protecting biodiversity are important areas of China-UK cooperation. They are also our mission as major global players.

As President Xi Jinping said at the UN high-level meeting,

"We need to take up our lofty responsibility for the entire human civilization, and we need to respect Nature, follow its laws and protect it. We need to find a way for man and Nature to live in harmony, balance and coordinate economic development and ecological protection, and work together to build a prosperous, clean and beautiful world."

The UK Parliament plays an important part in the UK's response to climate change. It is my sincere hope that you will continue to play a positive role and support green cooperation between our governments and businesses. I also look forward to your thoughts and ideas on hosting a successful COP15 and COP26.

Let's work together to make greater contribution to building a community with a shared future for mankind and making our planet a better home for all!

Thank you!

Now I am ready to take your questions.

Richard Graham: One of our speakers raised the question about whether the COP15 conference in Kunming will be able to go ahead on the currently planned timing given the current situation of COVID-19. How confident are you that it will be able to go ahead as planned?

Ambassador Liu: I'm very confident about that. We are still seven months away from the conference, and in China, life has returned to normal and production and social work also have resumed. Of course, we are following the pandemic very closely, both at home and around the world. As President Xi Jinping said at the UN Summit on Biodiversity, "I want to welcome you to Kunming, the beautiful "City of Eternal Spring", next year, to discuss and draw up plans together for protecting global biodiversity, and work in concert to build a beautiful world of harmony among all beings on the planet."

Lord Lucas: What are your suggestions on further China-UK cooperation in "new energy", in particular "new energy" vehicles?

Liu Xiaoming: On the electric vehicle we'll be more than happy to carry out mutually-beneficial cooperation with the UK. By the end of 2019, China owned 3.81 million "new energy" vehicles, which accounted for more than half of the world's total. The annual increment has been over one million units for two years in a row, making China a world leader in this aspect. Both the electric buses produced by BYD and the all-electric cabs produced by Geely after investing in the London Taxi Company have contributed to carbon emission reduction here in this country. China is also the largest investor in renewable energy. We have made vigorous efforts to develop solar and wind power. I believe there are enormous opportunities and huge potential for China and the UK to work together in the relevant areas.

Lord Lucas: How do you see the prospects of China-UK cooperation in nuclear power?

Liu Xiaoming: China has mature technologies, rich operation and management experience in nuclear power. China stands ready to enhance cooperation with the UK in this area. As of the end of 2019, China had the world's third largest installed capacity, trailing only the United States and France. We had 47 nuclear power units with a total capacity of 48.75 million kilowatts. The Hinkley Point C project is an important flagship project in nuclear power involving China, France and the UK. It will help the UK to realize its net-zero emission target by 2050. Though there are some contrary noises, it is my hope that our two sides will resist these disruptions and work together to promote this important project.

Sir Geoffrey Clifton-Brown: The UK has phased out all its coal-fired power stations. In order to meet the 2060 target, when will China phase out all of its coal-fired power stations?

Liu Xiaoming: In China, we are phasing out coal-fired power stations gradually. But we can't give you a date on that because China is still a developing country. We have enormous challenges facing us in terms of development. China is a large country and its development is imbalanced and inadequate. After my ambassadorship in Egypt, I was seconded as an assistant governor of Gansu province, one of the western provinces in China, which is very much dependent on coal energy. So, we have to address the imbalance of economic growth. On the other side, we also have to gradually scale down the consumption of coal to meet our targets on CO_2 emission. So it will take time, but the commitment to achieving carbon neutrality by 2060 is still there. Once we set a target, the policies will follow through. There will be a gradual scale-down of fossil fuel consumption through the green energy technologies. We have built the world's largest clean coal supply system. We have more than 800 million kilowatts of coal-fired ultra-low emission units. We lead the world in emission standards. China has set an example for the world in the clean application of coal. We encourage green consumption, green innovation and green development. When we have all these factors combined, we are confident that the fossil fuel consumption will be reduced gradually so as to promote green and high-quality development.

Lord McConnell: I have one question on Belt and Road Initiative projects. Do you think the BRI projects could reduce or indeed eliminate financing projects on coal energy in various BRI countries, like Pakistan and so on?

Liu Xiaoming: The Belt and Road Initiative is not only a road to economic prosperity but also a road to green development. China has always adhered to the green concept in the BRI development, promoting green and low-carbon infrastructure and operation management, emphasizing ecological conservation in investment and trade, and strengthening cooperation in the fields of ecological and environmental governance, biodiversity protection and climate change.

In 2019, China jointly initiated the BRI International Green Development Coalition with more than 140 partners in 42 countries. We have implemented the Belt and Road South-South Cooperation Initiative on Climate Change. Since 2012, the annual expenditure on South-South climate cooperation has reached 72 million U. S. dollars. We attach great importance to green development and biodiversity with regard to the BRI, both in terms of the project design and the project implementation. For instance, you mentioned Pakistan. When Chinese companies built the Karachi-Lahore Highway in Pakistan, they planted nearly 300, 000 trees and more than 5 million square meters of grassland along the road. Along with new road infrastructure, they also contributed to the local environment.

China will adhere to the concept of open, green and sustainable development, and work with its BRI partners to build a green "Silk Road". We have actively carried out third-party market cooperation with developed countries including the United Kingdom on a green development, pooling more efforts in international cooperation on climate change.

Lord McConnell: I wonder, in relation to both of the summits planned for next year, if there are concrete plans in place to engage with global multinationals, more than just a sponsorship level? And what are the preparations for that?

Liu Xiaoming: We believe the private sector is an important force in environmental protection and green development. We encourage the private sector and businesses, academia, and the media to participate in both the COP15 and the COP26. In the COP15, there will be a series of fringe events involving businesses and local governments from all over the world. I had a very good conversation with the Lord Mayor of London, discussing how the businesses of our two countries can work together on green finance to support the two conferences. For the COP26, in addition to sending the Chinese government delegation, we're going to set up the China Pavilion, which would involve Chinese local governments, NGOs and other institutions. I told our business people that I hope they will shoulder their responsibilities, seize the opportunities and strengthen cooperation with their British partners. I hope there will be more collaboration between our businesses on existing projects and on finding new projects for green development so as to promote global sustainable development.

谱写生态文明新篇章
——出席英国议会跨党派国际环保小组座谈会

（2020年10月28日，中国驻英国使馆/英国议会）

刘晓明： 很高兴出席英国议会跨党派国际环保小组"保护自然：通向昆明之路"线上座谈会。2021年，中英两国将分别举办《生物多样性公约》第15次缔约方会议（COP15）和《联合国气候变化框架公约》第26次缔约方会议（COP26）。这既是中英两国的大事，也是全球环境治理的大事。因此，2021年可谓全球环境治理"大年"。

再过整整200天，COP15将在中国"春城"昆明召开。今天，我们在"云端"共聚一堂，为此次大会"预热"，具有重要意义。当前，新冠肺炎疫情仍在全球蔓延，给人类经济社会发展带来严重冲击。在此背景下，保护生物多样性更显突出、更为重要，主要体现在以下三方面：

一是保护生物多样性是人类社会当务之急。全球物种灭绝速度不断加快，生物多样性丧失和生态系统退化对人类生存和发展构成重大风险。

二是保护生物多样性是建设生态文明的内在要求。生态兴则文明兴。生物多样性是人与自然和谐共生的集中体现。加强保护生物多样性，有利于推动经济和生态协调发展，形成共建良好生态、共享美好生活的良性循环。

三是保护生物多样性要求践行多边主义。只有发扬多边主义精神，各尽所能，走合作共赢之路，才能加强生物多样性保护国际合作，促进可持续发展。

不久前，习近平主席在联合国生物多样性峰会上指出，"我们要站在对人类文明负责的高度，尊重自然、顺应自然、保护自然，探索人与自然和谐共生之路，促进经济发展与生态保护协调统一，共建繁荣、清洁、美丽的世界"。明年COP15将以"生态文明：共建地球生命共同体"为主题，制定"2020年后全球生物多样性框架"，为扭转全球生物多样性丧失趋势迈出历史性一步，将在全球保护生物多样性进程中留下浓墨重彩的篇章。中国主办COP15充分体现了三个决心：

第一，推进生态文明建设的决心。中国积极做生态文明的倡导者和践行者，坚持绿水青山就是金山银山，坚持良好生态环境是最普惠的民生福祉，坚持共谋全球生态文明建设。中国将"生态文明"写入宪法，提出创新、协调、绿色、开放、共享的发展理念，将生物多样性纳入经济社会发展和生态保护修复规划，努力建设人与自然和谐共生的现代化。这与《生物多样性公约》确定的保护生物多样性、持续利用其组成部分、公平合理分享由利用遗传资源而产生的惠益的三大目标，以及"人与自然和谐共生"的2050年愿景高度契合。COP15是联合国首次以"生态文明"为主题召开的全球性会议，将发出共建地球生命共同体的强有力信号，进一步推动全球生态文明建设。

第二，保护生物多样性的决心。中国采取积极有力政策行动保护生物多样性，坚持山水林田湖草生命共同体，协同推进生物多样性治理。我们加快国家生物多样性保护立法步伐，划定生态保护红线，建立国家公园体系，实施生物多样性保护重大工程，提高社会参与和公众意识。过去10年，中国森林资源增长面积超过7000万公顷，居全球首位。中国长时间、大规模治理沙化、荒漠化，有效保护修复湿地，生物遗传资源收集保藏量位居世界前列。中国90%的陆地生态系统类型和85%的重点野生动物种群得到有效保护。COP15将成为中国与各国分享生物多样性保护实践和经验的重要平台，进一步形成保护生物多样性的全球合力。

第三，参与和引领全球生物多样性治理的决心。中国是《生物多样性公约》重要参与者和推动者，率先签署和批准公约，严格履行公约义务，积极促进与其他国际环境条约协同增效，已提前完成设立自然保护区等相关目标。中国与合作伙伴发起成立"一带一路"绿色发展国际联盟，积极加强生物多样性和生态系统保护。中国还在南南合作框架下积极帮助发展中国家提高环境管理能力。COP15将制定"2020年后全球生物多样性框架"，对未来10年乃至更长时间全球生物多样性治理做出规划。中国将在COP15大会上与各方共同努力，共同推进2020年后全球生物多样性治理进程。

2021年是全球生物多样性治理的关键节点，中英是全球环境治理的重要伙伴，在保护生物多样性和应对气候变化领域合作潜力巨大，应该相互支持、相互配合，共同确保COP15和COP26取得成功。

一是加强战略引领，全力做好COP15和COP26对接合作。习近平主席在联合国成立75周年高级别活动中宣布，中国将提高国家自主贡献力度，采取更加有力的政策和措施，二氧化碳排放力争于2030年前达到峰值，努力争取2060年前实现碳中和。习近平主席和约翰逊首相就两国加强COP15和COP26相互协调、相互支持达成重要共识。中国生态环境部部长黄润秋刚才在视频致辞中强调了中英加强两场大会合作的重要意义。下一步，我们将两场大会加强政策和议题对接合作，包括积极推广"基于自然的解决方案"，作为应对气候变化和保护生物多样性的协同解决方案，促进两次大会相得益彰、协同增效。

二是深化绿色合作，引领全球可持续发展。中国制订并实施了《中国生物多样性保护战略与行动计划》（2011—2030年），积极探索生物多样性保护与绿色发展、改善民生协同推进，倡导低碳、循环、可持续的生产生活方式。英国也发布了《未来25年环境保护计划》，倡导可持续发展，注重恢复陆地和海洋生物多样性。中英可加强对话交流，加强务实合作，挖掘绿色合作潜力，深化在应对气变、保护生物多样性、低碳经济、绿色金融、绿色科技、能源转型等领域的合作，在共建绿色"一带一路"方面加强三方合作，推动落实联合国2030年可持续发展目标，为全球可持续发展注入新动力。

三是坚持多边主义，凝聚全球生物多样性治理合力。中英应坚定维护多边主义，按照"共同但有区别的责任"原则，坚持公平公正惠益分享，照顾发展中国家资金、技术、能力建设方面关切，推动构建更加公平合理、各尽其责的多边环境治理体系。中方愿与包括英方在内的各方一道，遵循公开、透明、平衡、缔约方驱动等原则，推动COP15达成兼具雄心和务实平衡的"2020年后全球生物多样性框架"，为未来生物多样性保护绘制一幅宏伟且可实现的蓝图，为全球保护生物多样性开辟更广阔的前景。

昆明是中国历史文化名城，四季如春，风景如画。习近平主席在联合国生物多样性峰会上发出邀请，欢迎大家明年聚首美丽的春城昆明，共商全球生物多样性保护大计，共建万物和谐的美丽世界。作为COP15东道国和候任主席国，中方将全力做好COP15各项筹备工作，努力把COP15办成一届具有里程碑意义的全球环境治理盛会。我赞赏加德纳主席和英国议会跨党派国际环保小组关心和支持中国举办COP15，也期望更多的英国议员以及支持环境事业的各国人士，共同为办好COP15和COP26两场大会、深化中英和全球环境治理合作建言献策。让我们携起手来，共同谱写生态文明新篇章，共同构建地球生命共同体！

现在我愿回答各位嘉宾的提问。

加拿大前议员斯特斯基： 能否请刘大使进一步介绍中国的生态保护红线制度？

刘晓明： 关于中国的生态保护红线制度，我愿介绍三点情况：

第一，生态保护红线是被提到国家层面的"生命线"。这是中国国土空间规划和管理的重要制度创新，对维系生态安全格局、维护生态系统功能、保障经济社会可持续发展具有重要作用。中国计划到2020年底，生态保护红线划定面积约占陆域国土的25%。

第二，生态保护红线在国土空间规划中逐级划定落实。我们将生态功能极重要和极脆弱区域划入生态保护红线，覆盖以国家公园为主体的各类自然保护地等，通过严格管理，减少人为活动对生态环境的扰动。截至2018年底，中国各类自然保护地总数量已达1.18万个，自然保护地面积超过172.8万平方公里，占国土陆域面积

18%以上，提前实现了COP10通过的到2020年达到17%的目标。

第三，生态保护红线内的生态资源得到合理利用。保护红线是中国保护生物多样性、调整经济结构、规划产业发展、推进新型城镇化不可逾越的红线，但并不意味着对所有区域都实行"绝对保护"、不能利用，它既不是"无人区"，也不是发展的"真空区"。中国政府鼓励各地合理利用生态保护红线内的优质生态资源，探索实现生态产品价值的机制。把绿水青山转化为金山银山，实现生态优势向经济优势的转化。

此外，中国根据公约精神于2010年制订并实施了《中国生物多样性保护战略与行动计划》（2011—2030年），提出中国未来20年生物多样性保护总体目标、战略任务和优先行动。自2015年起，通过实施生物多样性保护重大工程，对全国野生动植物资源进行调查观测，调查记录超过210万条，不断跟踪评估《中国生物多样性保护战略与行动计划》（2011—2030年）执行进展情况。我们愿就生态保护红线制度与各方加强交流，促进各自国家行动计划的实施。

肯尼亚议会议员切普科沃尼： 中国发起的"一带一路"倡议将如何助力沿线国家实现清洁、绿色、可持续的发展？

刘晓明： "一带一路"不仅是经济繁荣之路，也是绿色发展之路。在"一带一路"建设实践中，中国始终秉持绿色发展理念，注重与联合国2030年可持续发展议程对接，推动基础设施绿色低碳化建设和运营管理，在投资贸易中强调生态文明理念，加强生态环境治理、生物多样性保护和应对气候变化等领域合作。未来"一带一路"建设将着重在以下三方面加强绿色合作：

一是建立绿色机制。2019年，"一带一路"绿色发展国际联盟成立，下设"生物多样性和生态系统"等10个专题伙伴关系，目前已有40多个国家的150余家中外合作伙伴。中国实施"绿色丝路使者计划"，与发展中国家共同加强环保能力建设，先后为120多个国家培训环保官员、专家和技术人员2000多人次。中国政府还成立"一带一路"环境技术交流与转移中心，促进先进生态环保技术的联合研发和推广应用。

二是促进绿色发展。中国企业在承建和设计"一带一路"项目时，在促进当地经济发展的同时，充分考虑环保因素。例如，中国企业在巴基斯坦承建卡拉奇—拉合尔公路时，在公路沿线植树近30万棵，植草500多万平方米，在建设基础设施的同时，也为当地环境绿化做出贡献。同样在巴基斯坦，在建设胡布燃煤电站时，使用了先进的清洁煤电技术，整个项目造价约有10%用于污染防控，其排放完全符合标准。

三是加强绿色金融合作。全球已有30多家大型金融机构签署了《"一带一路"绿色投资原则》（GIP）。GIP内容包括充分了解环境、社会和治理风险；充分披露环境信息；充分运用绿色金融工具；采用绿色供应链管理；等等。中国鼓励金融机构支持绿色"一带一路"建设，2019年中国工商银行发行了首只"一带一路"银行间常态化合作机制绿色债券，深入推进"一带一路"绿色金融合作。中国将坚持开放、绿色、可持续理念，愿与包括英国在内的发达国家积极开展绿色领域第三方市场合作；通过"一带一路"绿色发展国际联盟等平台，助力共建国家实现绿色、清洁、可持续发展。

南非议会议员弗罗里克： 中国如何看待《联合国海洋法公约》在海洋生态环境保护中的作用？

刘晓明： 海洋是地球生态系统中不可或缺的组成部分，保护海洋生物多样性对中国的可持续发展十分重要。中国作为《联合国海洋法公约》的签署国，始终致力于遵守包括《联合国海洋法公约》在内的国际法。2019年中国与法国达成的《中法生物多样性保护和气候变化北京倡议》，明确呼吁动员所有国家根据《联合国海洋法公约》制定一项具有法律约束力的国际文书，以养护和可持续利用国家管辖外生物多样性。目前，中国已批准建立国家级海洋公园超过40个，建立各级海洋自然/特别保护区（海洋公园）270余处，海洋保护区数量和面积不断扩大，保护对象类型日益丰富。

中国将与各国共同做好海洋生物多样性保护工作，共同打造海洋生物多样性保护屏障，为保护好海洋这个生机盎然的蓝色世界做出更多贡献。

英国议会上院议员兰德尔勋爵： 在疫情背景下，如何提高公众参与保护生物多样性的意识和积极性？

刘晓明： 保护生物多样性不只是政府的事情，社会各界都应广泛参与进来。提高公众参与意识是《中国生物多样性保护战略与行动计划》（2011—2030年）中的八大战略任务之一。我们建立生物多样性保护公众参与机制，开展多种形式的生物多样性保护宣传教育活动，引导公众积极参与生物多样性保护，加强学校的生物多样性科普教育。明年COP15也将开展平行会议，举办大量边会和展览，充分鼓励和推动社会各界参与大会。中方还将按惯例在COP26会场设立"中国角"，为中国地方政府、科研院校、非政府组织等参与气候多边进程、建言绿色低碳发展提供平台。中方愿与英方一道，鼓励更多企业、民间组织等社会各界参与进来，为COP15和COP26成功举办、促进全球保护生物多样性做出贡献。

墨西哥议会议员加西亚： 如何看待明年COP15和COP26之间的关系？如何才能更广泛地采用"基于自然的解决方案"？

刘晓明： 习近平主席在联合国生物多样性峰会上指出，人与自然是命运共同体。无论是保护生物多样性，还是应对气候变化，都是全球环境治理的重要方面。生物多样性保护可以帮助人类更好地减缓和适应气候变化，同时减缓和适应气候变化又能减少生物多样性受到的威胁，二者是相互协同的。COP15和COP26两场大会可以在三方面协同增效：

一是共同建设生态文明。气候变化和生物多样性都关乎人类生存和发展。我们应以两场大会为契机，站在对人类文明负责的高度，尊重自然、顺应自然、保护自然，探索人与自然和谐共生之路，促进经济发展与生态保护协调统一。

二是共同促进绿色发展。气候变化和生物多样性都与新冠肺炎疫情后经济复苏密切相关。我们要按照联合国《2030年可持续发展议程》所指明的方向，坚持绿色、包容、可持续发展。通过举办两场大会，我们可从保护自然中寻找绿色发展机遇，实现生态环境保护和经济高质量发展双赢，培育疫情后经济复苏活力。

三是共同维护多边主义。《生物多样性公约》《联合国气候变化框架公约》及《巴黎协定》等国际条约是全球环境治理的法律基础，也是多边合作的重要成果，得到各方广泛支持和参与。我们应以两场大会为契机，坚定捍卫以联合国为核心的国际体系，维护国际规则尊严和权威，凝聚全球环境治理合力。

中英都重视"基于自然的解决方案"（NBS），这也是英方举办COP26的重要领域之一。中英应积极推广NBS，将其作为应对气候变化、生物多样性丧失的协同解决方案，促进协同增效，促进全球绿色、低碳、可持续发展。

中国与新西兰共同牵头了2019年联合国气候行动峰会的NBS领域工作，在峰会上发布了《基于自然的气候解决方案政策主张》等成果文件，组建了"NBS之友小组"后续合作平台。我们还结合实践，提出了"划定生态保护红线，减缓和适应气候变化"这一NBS行动倡议，为丰富NBS贡献了中国智慧。

下一步，我们愿与英方加强有关NBS的交流与合作，共同推动各方提高对自然价值的认识，推动政府、金融机构、企业和所有其他利益相关方在保护生物多样性和应对气候变化的进程中优先考虑NBS，制订富有雄心的计划并采取切实行动，让NBS在支持生态系统保护及应对气候变化方面发挥更大作用。

A Keynote Speech and Q&A with the APPG on International Conservation of the UK Parliament

(28th October, 2020, Chinese Embassy / UK Parliament)

Liu Xiaoming: It is a real delight to join you at the "International Legislators' Summit – Protecting Nature: The Road to Kunming" hosted by the APPG on International Conservation.

In 2021, China and the UK will host the COP15 and the COP26 respectively. These are two big events not only for China and the UK but also for global governance of the environment. Therefore, 2021 can well be called "a big year" for global governance on the environment.

Exactly 200 days from now, the COP15 will be held in Kunming, known in China as the "City of Eternal Spring". It is highly significant and meaningful that we gather online today to "warm up" for this conference.

As we speak, COVID-19 is still ravaging the world, dealing a severe blow to economic growth and the social progress of mankind. Against this backdrop, protecting biodiversity becomes an increasingly prominent and important task. This is reflected in the following three aspects:

First, protecting biodiversity is the top priority of mankind.

As the mass extinction of wildlife accelerates, the loss of biodiversity and the degradation of the ecosystem pose major risks to the survival and development of mankind.

Second, protecting biodiversity is the inherent requirement of ecological conservation.

A sound ecosystem is essential to the prosperity of civilization. Biodiversity reflects the harmonious coexistence of man and nature. Protecting biodiversity will help strike a balance between economic growth and ecological conservation. This will in turn form a virtuous cycle between the conservation of nature and a better life for mankind.

Third, protecting biodiversity requires countries of the world to uphold multilateralism.

Only in the spirit of multilateralism and only when every country does its best and works for mutual benefit can countries of the world enhance cooperation on protecting biodiversity and promote sustainable development.

有问必答
No Question Unanswered

At the UN Summit on Biodiversity last month, President Xi Jinping said,
"We need to take up our lofty responsibility for the entire human civilization, and we need to respect nature, follow its laws and protect it. We need to find a way for man and nature to live in harmony, balance and coordinate economic development and ecological protection, and work together to build a prosperous, clean and beautiful world."

At the COP15, the parties will focus on the theme of "Ecological Civilization - Building a Shared Future for All Life on Earth" and strive to reach agreement on the Post-2020 Global Biodiversity Framework. This conference provides a platform for the parties to take a historic step towards reversing the loss of biodiversity and write a splendid chapter of joint global efforts to protect biodiversity.

By hosting the COP15, China will display three determinations:

First, the determination to promote ecological conservation.

China has made vigorous efforts to advocate and practice the concept of ecological conservation. We believe that clear water and green mountains are worth more than mountains of gold and silver, and that a sound ecosystem is in the interests of everyone. And we have championed international cooperation on ecological conservation in the world.

- China has written ecological conservation into its Constitution.
- It follows the concept of innovative, coordinated, green, open and shared development.
- It has made biodiversity protection part of its plans for economic and social development and ecological protection and rehabilitation.
- And it has worked vigorously to achieve a modernization that ensures harmony between man and nature.

These efforts of China are in line with the three objectives of the Convention on Biological Diversity, namely:

- The conservation of biodiversity;
- The sustainable use of the components of biodiversity;
- and the fair and equitable sharing of the benefits arising from the use of genetic resources.

They are also in line with the vision for 2050, namely "Living in Harmony with Nature", which was outlined in the Strategic Plan for Biodiversity.

The COP15 will be the first global conference of the United Nations that focuses on "ecological conservation". It will send a powerful message about building a shared future for all life on Earth and bringing global ecological conservation one step forward.

Second, the determination to protect biodiversity.

China has adopted vigorous and effective policies and measures in this aspect.

China is taking a holistic approach to the conservation of mountains, rivers, forests, farmlands, lakes and grasslands and making coordinated efforts to advance biodiversity governance.

We have stepped up national legislation for preserving biodiversity, and we are drawing red lines for protecting ecosystems. We have set up a network of national parks, carried out major biodiversity conservation projects and increased public participation and awareness.

Over the past 10 years, China has increased forest coverage by more than 70 million hectares—more than anywhere else in the world.

We have also made long-term, large-scale efforts to combat soil erosion and desertification, and we have taken effective action in wetland protection and restoration.

As a result of these efforts, China now has one of the world's largest banks of genetic resources.

In China, 90 percent of terrestrial ecosystem types and 85 percent of key wild animal populations are under effective protection.

The COP15 will serve as an important platform for China to share its practice and experience in biodiversity protection with the rest of the world and for the parties to pull together in biodiversity protection.

Third, the determination to take part and assume the lead in global biodiversity governance.

China is an important contracting party to and defender of the Convention on Biological Diversity (CBD).

- It was one of the first to sign and ratify the CBD.
- It has fulfilled its obligations under the CBD and helped to create synergy between the CBD and other international conventions on the environment.
- It has attained the goal of setting up nature reserves ahead of schedule.

Together with its partners, China has initiated the Belt and Road Initiative International Green Development Coalition to step up protection of biodiversity and the ecosystem. Under the framework of South-South cooperation, China has also made vigorous efforts to help other developing countries build up their capacity in managing the environment.

At the COP15, the Post-2020 Global Biodiversity Framework will be formulated, which will chart the course for global governance on biodiversity in the coming ten years and beyond.

China stands ready to work with all the parties at the COP15 to promote the cause of post-2020 global governance on biodiversity.

Ladies and Gentlemen:

The year 2021 will be critical for global governance on biodiversity. China and the UK are important partners in global governance on environment. There is enormous potential for China and the UK to cooperate and take action on protecting biodiversity and climate change. It is important that we support and coordinate with each other to make the COP15 and the COP26 a great success.

First, China and the UK should follow the strategic guidance of our leaders and step up coordination and cooperation on hosting the COP15 and the COP26.

Last month, at a high-level UN meeting in commemoration of the 75th anniversary of the founding of the UN, President Xi Jinping announced that China will

- scale up its nationally determined contributions,
- adopt even more forceful policies and measures,
- and strive to reach a peak in carbon dioxide emissions by 2030 and achieve carbon neutrality by 2060.

President Xi Jinping and Prime Minister Boris Johnson have reached important agreements on enhancing coordination and mutual support on the COP15 and the COP26.

In the video message just now, the Chinese Minister of Ecology and Environment Huang Runqiu emphasized the importance of China-UK cooperation.

Going forward, China and the UK should step up coordination and cooperation with regard to the policies and agenda of the two conferences. We should promote Nature-Based Solutions and derive from them a coordinated settlement for problems of climate change and biodiversity. And we should encourage the two conferences to support each other and succeed together.

Second, China and the UK should deepen green cooperation and take the lead in global sustainable development.

China has issued and vigorously implemented its National Biodiversity Conservation

Strategy and Action Plan (2011-2030). It has been exploring ways to coordinate biodiversity protection with green development and a better life for the people. And it has been championing low-carbon, circular and sustainable ways of life and production.

The UK has issued the 25-Year Environment Plan to advocate sustainable development and restore biodiversity on land and in the ocean.

China and the UK can enhance dialogue, exchanges and business cooperation. We can tap the potential for green cooperation in areas such as climate change, biodiversity protection, low-carbon economy, green finance, green technology and energy transition. We can also step up tripartite cooperation in building the green Belt and Road.

Together, we can advance the implementation of the UN 2030 Agenda for Sustainable Development and provide new impetus for global sustainable growth.

Third, China and the UK should uphold multilateralism and help to build synergy among the parties for better governance of biodiversity.

Both China and the UK should uphold the principle of common but differentiated responsibilities, ensure the fair and equitable sharing of benefits, and accommodate developing countries' concerns over funding, technology and capacity building. We need to build a fair and reasonable multilateral system of environmental governance where the parties shoulder their due responsibilities.

China stands ready to work with all participating parties, including the UK, to conclude an ambitious and pragmatic Post-2020 Global Biodiversity Framework at the COP15 through an open, transparent and parties-driven process. Together we can draw up a blueprint that is both grand and feasible, and we can open up broader prospects for global biodiversity protection in the future.

The city of Kunming is known for its long history, splendid culture, pleasant weather and beautiful landscape.

At the UN Summit on Biodiversity, President Xi Jinping said, "I want to welcome you to Kunming, the beautiful "City of Eternal Spring", next year, to discuss and draw up plans together for protecting global biodiversity and work in concert to build a beautiful world of harmony among all beings on the planet."

As the host and incoming president of the COP15, China will exert every effort to get everything ready for the conference and make it a milestone in global governance on the environment.

I appreciate the enthusiasm and support of Chairman Gardiner and the APPG on International Conservation. I look forward to more ideas and suggestions from British parliamentarians and the people of the world who support environmental actions on how to make the COP15 and the COP26 successful. I also want to listen to your thoughts on deepening China-UK cooperation on global governance of the environment.

Let's join hands to write a new chapter on ecological conservation and build a shared future for all life on Earth!

Thank you!

Now, I would like to take your questions.

Canadian Former MP Stetsky: Could Ambassador Liu shed further light on China's ecological protection red line system?

Liu Xiaoming: Regarding China's ecological protection red line system, I would like to elaborate on three points:

Firstly, the ecological protection red line is regarded as the "lifeline" at the national level. This is an important institutional innovation in the planning and management of China's territorial space. It plays a crucial role in maintaining the ecological security pattern, safeguarding the functions of ecosystems, and ensuring sustainable economic and social development. China has planned that by the end of 2020 the ecological protection red line should cover approximately 25% of its territorial land area.

Secondly, the red line is defined according to the different level of protection needed. It is drawn around ecologically vital and fragile areas. This covers various types of nature reserves primarily composed of national parks. Strict management reduces the human impact upon the ecological environment. By the end of 2018, the total number of various types of nature reserves in China had reached 11,800 and the total area exceeded 1.728 million square kilometers, accounting for over 18% of the territorial land area, surpassing the goal of 17% set by COP10 for 2020 ahead of schedule.

Thirdly, ecological resources within the red line are utilized rationally. The red line in China serves as a boundary that cannot be crossed in protecting biodiversity, adjusting economic structures, planning industrial development, and promoting new urbanization. However, it does not mean absolute preservation and the non-utilization of every space within the line. The red line is not creating a "no-go zone" nor a "developmental vacuum". The Chinese government encourages the rational utilization of high-quality ecological resources within the red line and explores mechanisms to realize the value of ecological products, transforming green mountains and clear waters into "mountains of gold and silver", achieving the conversion of ecological advantages into economic advantages.

In addition, China has formulated and implemented the "China Biodiversity Conservation Strategy and Action Plan" (2011-2030) in 2010 in accordance with the spirit of the relevant convention. This action plan outlines China's overall goals, strategic tasks and priority actions for biodiversity conservation in the next 20 years. Since 2015, through the implementation of major biodiversity conservation projects, a nation-wide investigation and observation of wild animals and plants has been conducted, with records exceeding 2.1 million, continuously tracking and evaluating the progress of the implementation of the "China Biodiversity Conservation Strategy and Action Plan" (2011-2030). We are willing to enhance communication with all parties on the ecological protection red line system and promote the implementation of respective national action plans.

Kenyan MP Chepkovoni: How will China's Belt and Road Initiative help countries along the route achieve clean, green, and sustainable development?

Liu Xiaoming: The Belt and Road is not only a road to economic prosperity but also a road to green development. In practice, China has always adhered to the concept of green development, emphasized alignment with the UN 2030 Agenda for Sustainable Development, promoted the green and low-carbon construction and operation management of infrastructure, highlighted ecological civilization concepts in investment and trade, and strengthened cooperation in ecological environment governance, biodiversity conservation, and climate change response. In the future, the Belt and Road Initiative will focus on strengthening green cooperation in three aspects:

Firstly, establishing green mechanisms. In 2019, the BRI Green Development International Alliance was established, with ten thematic partnerships including "Biodiversity and Ecosystems" and more than 150 Chinese and foreign cooperative partners from over 40 countries. China has implemented the Green Silk Road

Ambassador Program, jointly enhancing environmental protection capacity-building with developing countries, and training over 2,000 environmental officials, experts, and technicians from more than 120 countries. The Chinese government has also established the Belt and Road Environmental Technology Exchange and Transfer Center to promote joint research and development and the application of advanced ecological environmental protection technologies.

Secondly, promoting green development. Chinese companies consider environmental factors fully when undertaking and designing Belt and Road projects. For example, while building the Karachi-Lahore Motorway in Pakistan, Chinese companies planted nearly 300,000 trees and grassed over 5 million square meters of area along the highway, contributing to local environmental greening as well as infrastructure. Similarly, in Pakistan, when constructing the Hub coal-fired power station, advanced clean coal-fired technology was used, with approximately 10% of the total project budget allocated for pollution control, and the emissions were fully compliant with standards.

Thirdly, strengthening cooperation on green finance. Over 30 large financial institutions globally have signed the "Green Investment Principles of the Belt and Road Initiative" (GIP). The GIP includes fully understanding environmental, social, and governance risks; fully disclosing environmental information; fully utilizing green financial instruments; and adopting green supply chain management. China encourages financial institutions to support the green development of BRI. In 2019, Industrial and Commercial Bank of China issued the first BRI inter-bank cooperation mechanism green bond, further promoting cooperation on green finance under the BRI. China will adhere to open, green, and sustainable concepts, actively carry out third-party market cooperation on green development with developed countries including the UK. Through platforms such as the BRI Green Development International Alliance, China will help partner countries achieve green, clean, and sustainable development.

South African MP Frolick: How does China see the role of the United Nations Convention on the Law of the Sea in marine ecological environment protection?

Liu Xiaoming: The ocean is an indispensable part of the Earth's ecosystem, and protecting marine biodiversity is crucial for China's sustainable development. As a signatory to the United Nations Convention on the Law of the Sea, China has always been committed to complying with international law. This includes the United Nations Convention on the Law of the Sea. The "Sino-French Beijing Initiative on Biodiversity Conservation and Climate Change" reached between China and France in 2019 explicitly calls for mobilizing all countries to establish a legally binding international instrument under the United Nations Convention on the Law of the Sea so as to conserve and sustainably utilize biodiversity beyond national jurisdiction. Currently, China has approved the establishment of over 40 national-level marine parks, and established over 270 marine natural/special protected areas (marine parks) at all levels, with the number and area of marine protected areas continuously expanding and the types of protected objects becoming increasingly diverse. China will work together with all countries to carry out marine biodiversity protection and jointly build a protective barrier for marine biodiversity in order to make more contributions to protecting these vibrant blue resources.

British Lord Randall: How can public awareness and enthusiasm for biodiversity protection be increased in the context of the pandemic?

Liu Xiaoming: Biodiversity protection is not solely the responsibility of the government; all sectors of society should participate extensively. Enhancing public participation awareness is one of the eight strategic tasks outlined in the "China Biodiversity Conservation Strategy and Action Plan (2011-2030)". We have established mechanisms for public participation in biodiversity conservation, conducted various forms of biodiversity conservation publicity and education activities, guided the public to actively participate in biodiversity conservation, and strengthened biodiversity popular science education in schools. At next year's COP15, there will be parallel meetings and numerous side events and exhibitions to fully encourage and promote social participation in the conference. At the COP26 venue, China will, following customary practice, set up a "China Pavilion" -- a platform for Chinese local governments, research institutions, non-governmental organizations, and others to participate in the multilateral climate process and contribute to green and low-carbon development. China is willing to work with the UK to encourage more enterprises, non-governmental organizations, and other sectors of society to participate in the COP15 and the COP26, contributing to the success of the conferences and promoting global biodiversity protection.

Mexican MP García: How do you see the relationship between the COP15 and the COP26 next year? How can "Nature-Based Solutions" be more widely adopted?

Liu Xiaoming: President Xi Jinping pointed out at the UN Biodiversity Summit that humanity and nature are a community of shared future. Both biodiversity protection and climate change response are important aspects of global environmental governance. Biodiversity protection can help mankind to better mitigate and adapt to climate change, and mitigating and adapting to climate change can also reduce the threat to biodiversity. The two are mutually reinforcing. The COP15 and the COP26 can synergize in three aspects:

Firstly, jointly building an ecological civilization. Both climate change and biodiversity are related to human survival and development. We should take the two conferences as an opportunity, stand at the height of responsibility for human civilization, respect nature, follow its laws and protect resources, explore the road to harmonious coexistence between man and nature, and promote coordination between economic development and ecological protection.

Secondly, jointly promoting green development. Both climate change and biodiversity are closely related to post-pandemic economic recovery. We should adhere to the directions indicated by the UN "2030 Agenda for Sustainable Development", and persist in green, inclusive, and sustainable development. By holding the two conferences, we can find green development opportunities from nature protection, realize win-win results in ecological environmental protection and high-quality economic development, and foster vitality for the post-pandemic economic recovery.

Thirdly, jointly upholding multilateralism. International treaties such as the Convention on Biological Diversity, and the United Nations Framework Convention on Climate Change and its Paris Agreement are the legal basis for global environmental governance and important achievements of multilateral cooperation. These enjoy extensive support and participation from all parties. We should take the two conferences as an opportunity to firmly uphold the international system centered on the United Nations, safeguard the dignity and authority of international rules, and unite global environmental governance efforts.

Both China and the UK attach importance to "Nature-Based Solutions" (NBS), which is also one of the important areas for the UK to host COP26. China and the UK should actively promote NBS, take it as a synergistic solution to climate change and biodiversity loss, promote efficiency through synergy, and promote global green, low-carbon, and sustainable development.

China and New Zealand jointly led the work on NBS at the 2019 UN Climate Action Summit, and released documents such as the "Policy Advocacy for Nature-Based Climate Solutions", and established a follow-up cooperation platform, the "NBS Friends Group". We have also proposed the NBS action initiative of "Delineating Ecological Protection Red Lines, Mitigating and Adapting to Climate Change". These contribute Chinese wisdom to NBS enrichment.

Going forward, we are willing to strengthen exchanges and cooperation with the UK on the NBS, jointly promote various parties' understanding of the value of nature, encourage governments, financial institutions, enterprises, and all other stakeholders to prioritize the NBS in the process of biodiversity protection and climate change response, formulate ambitious plans, and take practical actions, allowing the NBS to play a greater role in supporting ecosystem protection and climate change response.

与专家学者和政府官员对话

Q&A With Scholars and Officials

2019年6月24日,我出席英国"亚洲之家"对话会,与"亚洲之家"主席格林勋爵就习近平外交思想、中国内外政策及有关热点问题进行交流,并回答现场听众提问。此次系"亚洲之家"首次举行该机构主席与驻英使节对话会,英国政、商、学、媒体界代表以及新加坡、巴基斯坦、黎巴嫩、比利时、爱尔兰、美国、澳大利亚、菲律宾、加拿大等国驻英使节和外交官140余人出席。

2020年7月15日,驻英国使馆与英国智库货币金融机构官方论坛、欧洲改革中心联合举行"'后疫情时代'中欧关系"在线座谈会,我发表了题为《"四个坚持"至关重要》的主旨演讲,并回答听众提问。英国货币金融机构官方论坛主席马什、顾问委员会主席德赛,欧洲改革中心主任格兰特,英中贸协主席古沛勤爵士以及两家智库会员,来自英国和欧洲、北美、大洋洲、拉美等地区的经济、金融、学术界人士等共约100人参加。英国广播公司(BBC)、天空新闻台、路透社、《每日电讯报》、《金融时报》、《卫报》、《独立报》、中国国际电视台等中英两国媒体,以及美联社、彭博社、美国全国广播公司、法新社、保加利亚电视台等14家中外媒体参加。BBC、天空新闻台对座谈会进行了现场直播,并在当天重要时段滚动报道。

英国货币金融机构官方论坛成立于2010年,是英国知名经济金融论坛组织,主要为全球各国央行、外汇储备管理部门和主权财富基金等提供政策咨询服务。欧洲改革中心是英国知名智库,成立于1996年,重点研究欧洲社会、政治和经济问题,并为欧洲各国政府、欧盟机构和商界人士提供政策咨询服务。

10月13日,我应邀出席国际能源信息论坛大会,发表题为《风雨过后见彩虹》的主旨演讲并回答主持人提问。石油输出国组织秘书长巴尔金多,沙特王子、能源大臣阿卜杜勒,阿联酋国务部长苏尔坦,阿联酋能源及工业部长马兹鲁伊，尼日利亚石油资源部长西尔瓦，印度石油、天然气和钢铁部长普拉丹，美国前助理国防部长傅立民，美国前众议员库辛尼奇，能源信息论坛大会主席穆尔、总裁辛德勒，以及来自英国、欧洲、北美、亚洲等地区的经济界、学术界、能源界人士共2000多人参加。

中国是世界和平的建设者
——出席英国"亚洲之家"对话会

（2019年6月24日，英国"亚洲之家"）

2019年6月24日，我出席英国"亚洲之家"对话会，与"亚洲之家"主席格林勋爵就习近平外交思想、中国内外政策及有关热点问题展开交流，并回答现场听众提问。

格林勋爵： 今天，"亚洲之家"很荣幸邀请中国驻英国大使刘晓明这位重量级嘉宾，与大家讨论中国这个极其重要的话题。中国过去几十年的高速发展，使世界经济重心从西方转向东方，改变了世界格局。当前，英国处于脱欧的关键期，正重塑与世界的关系，重点就是在亚洲拓展伙伴关系。英国如何在中美之间保持平衡是各界非常关注的话题。我们期待听到刘大使对当今国际形势以及中国如何与世界互动等重大问题的看法。

刘晓明： 很高兴再次做客"亚洲之家"，就中英关系和中国外交政策等议题与"亚洲之家"主席格林勋爵及各位会员进行对话。"亚洲之家"每次邀请我出席活动的时机都选得非常好。去年5月，我在这里就中美经贸问题发表演讲，恰逢中美达成协议。此后一年，形势可谓波谲云诡、瞬息万变。今天，中美经贸紧张局势又曙光初现，习近平主席与特朗普总统即将在二十国集团（G20）峰会期间举行会晤，广受关注。

环顾当今世界，我们生活在一个快速变化的时代，世界正处于百年未有之大变局。在这样的背景下，中国的发展成为国际上的热议话题，有人认为是机遇，有人认为是挑战，也有人认为是威胁。那么，中国的发展对世界到底意味着什么？我认为，习近平外交思想是新时代中国对外工作的根本遵循和行动指南，构建人类命运共同体是习近平外交思想的核心理念，中国坚持走和平发展道路，推动构建新型国际关系、构建人类命运共同体；中国坚持开放合作，推动"一带一路"建设，与世界各国分享中国发展机遇；中国不是要挑战或取代谁、不会走"国强必霸"的老路，永远做世界和平的建设者、全球发展的贡献者、国际秩序的维护者。

当前，单边主义日益抬头，保护主义甚嚣尘上。在这样的形势下，中英作为国际上有重要影响的国家，应当加强合作，发出支持多边主义、倡导自由贸易、携手应对气候变化等全球性挑战的时代强音，共同为人类社会发展进步做出贡献。上周，第十次中英经济财金对话在英成功举行，取得69项丰硕成果。我认为，此次对话传递出的一个重要信息就是，中英合作互利共赢，不仅造福两国，也惠及世界。展望未来，中国愿继续将英国作为推动构建新型国际关系、构建人类命运共同体的伙伴，为创造更加美好的世界贡献力量。

格林勋爵： 我曾多次到访中国，目睹了中国改革发展取得的巨大成就。但中国未来发展面临东西部发展不均衡、人口老龄化、水资源紧缺等现实挑战。你对此怎么看？中国将如何解决这些问题？

刘晓明： 2018年是中国改革开放40周年。40多年来，中国经济体量从世界第十跃升至第二，成功使7亿人摆脱贫困，中国人民生活水平大幅提高，人均寿命显著延长，人们的获得感、幸福感、安全感不断提升。但中国仍是一个发展中国家，人均国民生产总值与西方发达国家相距甚远。观察中国，应该看到中国的"多面"，既看到北京、上海、深圳这样可比肩欧洲的国际化大都市，也要看到相对不发达的西部省区。你刚才提到水资源问题，我有切身体会。10多年前，我曾在中国西部省份甘肃省担任省长助理，那里不少民众饮水都很困难，只能净化雨水供人、畜饮用。

对于当前中国社会的主要矛盾，中共十九大做出了准确论断，那就是人民日益增长的美好生活需要和不平衡不充分的发展之间的矛盾。展望未来，我们还有很多工作要做，肩上的担子很重。中国发展崛起不是要在国际上挑战谁，而是要解决自身发展面临的诸多挑战，不断改善民生，到2020年实现贫困人口全面脱贫目标，让发展更平衡、更充分。

格林勋爵： 我对当前全球贸易形势十分担忧，美国总统特朗普频频采取加征关税等单边主义、保护主义举措，对世贸组织和全球贸易秩序产生巨大冲击。你怎样看待全球贸易形势？中国将如何应对？

刘晓明： 关于贸易问题，我与你有同样的关切，对单边主义、保护主义逆流感到担忧。中国认为，世贸组织仍是多边贸易体制的核心。当然，这套体制并不完美，需要进行必要改革，使全球贸易更加规范、更加便利、更加开放。我们身处一个彼此利益密不可分的

"地球村",如果所有国家都基于自身利益任性自定贸易规则,或将自身利益凌驾于其他国家之上,追求所谓"本国第一",这将不可避免地导致"贸易战",对全球经济增长造成负面影响。

因此,中国支持世贸组织发挥应有作用,支持对世贸组织进行必要改革。同时,世贸组织改革要以各方共识为基础。尽管这将花费更多时间,但各方付出的代价也会小得多。中国反对"赢者通吃""零和博弈",认为只有互利合作才能实现共赢发展。

格林勋爵： 你提到的"共赢发展"是否指中国提出的构建人类命运共同体？我理解中国提出这一倡议的初衷,但在当前中美博弈的背景下,人类命运共同体能成为现实吗？

刘晓明： 我对此持乐观态度,因为各国开展互利合作是有基础的。习近平主席提出构建人类命运共同体的主张,得到了国际社会积极响应,并被写入了联合国、G20等文件。

贸易战没有赢家,中美两国都将因此蒙受损失。我曾看到一项调查,称如贸易战持续,美国将成最大"输家";最近我还注意到,很多美国企业家都对政府加征关税表示不满。中国不想看到"双输"局面,希望人们最终回归"理性",而不要在付出代价之后才意识到贸易战的负面影响。

格林勋爵： 你刚才提到世界正经历大变局。我也认为,各方力量对比发生很大变化,特别是发展中国家纷纷崛起。在这样的形势下,你认为欧洲将在世界舞台上扮演什么角色？目前,英国脱欧尚无结果,不少欧洲国家遭受民粹主义冲击。中国怎样看待欧洲的作用？

刘晓明： 中国主张世界多极化发展，认为这有利于实现世界持久和平与稳定。中国重视欧洲的作用，在战略上将欧洲视为世界重要一极。同时，在经贸上，欧洲是中国的最大贸易伙伴。中国致力于与欧盟及各欧洲国家发展关系、开展务实合作，不仅与英国、法国、德国、意大利等大国保持良好关系，与中东欧国家的"16+1"合作也有声有色。今年以来，习近平主席、李克强总理相继成功访欧，与欧洲领导人共同重申中欧发展关系的重要意义，足见中国对欧洲的高度重视。

关于脱欧问题，我们正密切关注相关进展，认为这是英欧之间的事情，相信双方有智慧、有能力妥善处理好有关问题。中方希望英欧能达成双方都满意的协议，愿推动中欧、中英关系并行发展。

格林勋爵： 我注意到，英国国内在处理对华关系上有不同意见；此外，欧方一直对"16+1"合作心存疑虑。你怎么看这些问题？

刘晓明： 我听到一种观点，认为英国须在中美之间选边站队，因此有人对发展对华关系有不同看法。我想指出的是，英国社会主流意见是将中国发展看作机遇，而非挑战，更非威胁，大都支持推进中英关系"黄金时代"。

欧方确实对中国与中东欧国家开展"16+1"合作有些误解。事实上，"16+1"合作取得积极成果对中国与欧盟都有利。中东欧很多国家发展低于欧盟平均水平，面临阻碍进一步发展的共性问题，因此他们拥有与中国加强合作的强烈意愿。中国一直与欧方保持密切沟通交流，希望通过增信释疑让大家认识到，中国致力于走出一条与以往不同的大国崛起之路，中国发展将给欧洲和世界带来更多机遇。

格林勋爵： 印度和日本都是亚洲的重要国家，但两国对华关系都有"微妙"之处。比如印度对"一带一路"倡议持保留态度，中日之间则存在重大历史遗留问题。你怎样看待中印、中日关系？

刘晓明： 中国十分重视与印度、日本这两个重要邻国的关系。没有良好的中印关系和中日关系，就不会有亚洲的持久和平、稳定与繁荣。对中印关系而言，一些西方媒体热衷唱衰中印关系，不断炒作两国之间的分歧。然而，中印关系中的共同利益远大于分歧。两国同为"金砖国家"，在一系列问题上拥有广泛共同利益。近年来，习近平主席与莫迪总理在不同场合多次会面，建立起良好的个人友谊和工作关系，也体现出中国领导人对发展中印关系的高度重视。

对中日关系而言，两国之间确实有"苦涩的过去"。中国人民有理由关注日本政府对待历史的态度，因为我们不想让历史"重演"。中国愿与日本改善关系，习近平主席即将赴日本出席二十国集团大阪峰会，我们希望这将为推动中日关系改善发展注入强劲动力。

"亚洲之家"首席执行官劳伦斯： 华为问题是当前英国舆论关注的焦点。你怎样看华为在英国的发展前景？

刘晓明： 首先我想指出的是，华为是一家优秀的企业，不仅在5G通信领域领先全球，也为英国经济社会发展做出了巨大贡献。上个月，我在回国述职期间到深圳参访了华为公司，在华为大学与公司高管及员工进行交流。我发现，华为公司上下都对与英国开展务实合作充满期待。

过去5年，华为在英国创造7500多个就业岗位，采购和投资达到20亿英镑，未来还计划投资30亿英镑。更重要的是，华为非常重视网络安全问题，在英国主动投资建立网络安全认证中心，聘用清一色英国团队实施监管，定期评估风险，不断改进技术。世界上不存在没有任何风险的设备，但华为愿与英国政、商、学界开展合作，提高设备的安全性和可靠性。事实上，英方评估认为，华为设备的安全风险是"可控的"。

我曾听到一种说法，称如禁止使用华为设备，英国5G建设将延迟一至两年。更令我感到担忧的是，英国素以开放包容的市场环境著称，一旦华为被禁，恐将对外释放极为负面的信号，特别是对中国企业在英投资经营产生极大冲击，这才是我最不愿看到的。英国的国名是"大不列颠"，之所以称其为"大"，就在于英国的独立性和自主性。我们希望英国政府自主做出符合自身长远利益并且有利于中英合作大局的决定，而不是听命于谁的指令、屈从于谁的压力。

考文垂大学教授莫里森： 几年前我曾在刘大使演讲现场听到，在全球供应链中，中国生产价值1美元的商品只能获得5美分利润，因此有很大的增长空间。请问中国如今在全球供应链中获利增长了多少？你怎么看待这种进步？

刘晓明： 如你所知，中国不可能永远停留在全球供应链"低端"。这些年，中国人民辛勤奋斗，积极发展中高端产业，确实取得了一些进步。然而，中国更重视做大"共同利益的蛋糕"，让各方都更多获益，而非仅让自己"分得更大份的蛋糕"，造成大家争夺有限的资源，这是中国人开展对外合作的哲学。

作为职业外交官，我曾长期从事对美工作。当前中美经贸关系让我想起30多年前我在美国常驻时，一位美国领导人的话，他说，美方重视对华贸易逆差，但解决办法不是减少中国对美出口，而是增加美国对华出口。我赞同这种主张，希望今天的美国当政者也能遵从同样的逻辑。美国对华加征关税不仅扰乱全球供应链，最终"埋单"的只能是美国企业和普通美国消费者。

英国亚能咨询公司主席理查德： 近期香港问题引发英国社会广泛关注，刘大使接受英国广播公司（BBC）采访时表示，《中英联合声明》已"不再有意义"。中国政府是否还在香港坚持"一国两制"政策？

刘晓明： 感谢你看了我的采访，但你的引述并不准确。《中英联合声明》的使命是确保香港政权顺利交接。1997年香港回归中国后，《中英联合声明》就已完成了历史使命。我注意到一些英国媒体质疑中国中央政府关于"一国两制"的承诺。我要强调的是，"一国两制"不是对英国的承诺,而是中国中央政府对包括香港居民在内的全体中国人民的承诺,这已经充分反映在《基本法》之中。当前,香港特区政府处理"修例"相关工作,恰恰是践行"一国两制"的生动体现。一些外国媒体和势力将香港"修例"说成是破坏"一国两制",借用一句英国谚语,这完全是"Bark up the wrong tree"(风马牛不相及)。英国政府高官近期还发表了一些不负责任的言论,这是在干涉香港事务和中国内政。如果英方真心希望香港保持长期繁荣稳定,就不要干预香港特区政府依法施政。

英中贸协主席沙逊勋爵： 刘大使提到上周举行的英中经济财金对话取得69项重要成果,这将有力促进英中务实合作,让英国商界倍感振奋。关于世贸组织改革问题,请问最终实现改革的可能性有多大？英中如何就此展开合作？

刘晓明： 世贸组织改革是一项复杂的系统工程,主要目的是反映当前世界经济的新现实,特别是充分考虑发展中国家的主要关切,推动全球贸易自由化和便利化,完善贸易争端解决机制,推动建设包容和开放的世界经济。

不久前,中方发布了《中国关于世贸组织改革的建议文件》,详细阐述了"中国方案",建议大家仔细研读。中英两国在世贸组织改革问题上拥有共同利益,我们愿与英方共同努力,将世贸组织和多边贸易体制建设得更加完善。

格林勋爵： 感谢刘大使的精彩发言。中国与世界关系问题已成为当今时代最重大的战略性命题之一，刘大使深入解读了习近平外交思想的精神实质，生动阐述了中国对外政策的关键内容。刘大使是"亚洲之家"的常客，但今天是"亚洲之家"首次邀请驻英使节以对话会形式举办活动，我们期待与刘大使的对话继续下去，为英国各界走近亚洲、认识中国、读懂中国打造更好的平台。

谢谢大家！

China Is A Builder of World Peace
——A Dialogue with "Asia House" in the UK

On 24th June 2019, I attended the "Asia House" dialogue in the UK and held discussions with Lord Green, Chairman of the "Asian House, " on Xi Jinping's diplomatic thoughts, China's domestic and foreign policies, and related hot topics, answering questions from the audience.

Lord Green: Today, "Asia House" is honored to invite Chinese Ambassador to the UK, Liu Xiaoming, as a heavyweight guest to discuss this extremely important topic, China. China's rapid development in the past few decades has changed the global landscape. The world economic center has shifted from the West to the East. Currently, the UK is at a crucial period of Brexit and is reshaping its relationship with the world, with a focus on expanding partnerships in Asia. How to keep a balance between China and the US is a topic of great concern to all sectors here in the UK. We look forward to hearing Ambassador Liu's views on the current international situation and how China interacts with the world on major issues.

Liu Xiaoming: I am delighted to be here at "Asia House" once again for a dialogue with Lord Green, Chairman of "Asia House, " and other members on topics such as China-UK relations and Chinese foreign policy. The timing of every invitation from the "Asian House" has been excellent. Last May, I delivered a speech here on China-US economic and trade issues, coinciding with the agreement reached between China and the US. Since then, the situation has been full of uncertainties and fast changing. Today, the tension in China-US economic and trade relations is showing signs of improvement, and President Xi Jinping and President Trump are about to hold a meeting at the G20 summit. This is attracting widespread attention.

Looking at the world today, we are living in a rapidly changing era, and the world is undergoing a great transformation unseen in a century. In this context, China's development has become a topic of global discussion. Some people see it as an opportunity, some as a challenge, and others as a threat. So what does China's development mean to the world? Let me refer to Xi Jinping Thought on Diplomacy. This is the fundamental principle and guideline for our actions, and building a community of shared future for mankind is its core tenet.

China adheres to the path of peaceful development and promotes the building of a new type of international relations and a community with a shared future for mankind; China adheres to opening up and cooperation, promotes the Belt and Road Initiative, and shares China's development opportunities with countries around the world; China does not seek to challenge or replace anyone, and will not go down the old path that "a strong country must be a hegemon." China will always be a builder of world peace, a contributor to global development, and a defender of the international order.

Currently, unilateralism is on the rise, and protectionism is rampant. In such a situation, China and the UK, as influential countries in the international community, should strengthen their cooperation and make a strong statement in support of multilateralism, advocating free trade, and jointly addressing global challenges such as climate change, making contributions to the development and progress of human society. Last week, the 10th China-UK Economic and Financial Dialogue was successfully held in the UK, achieving 69 fruitful outcomes. I believe that an important message conveyed through this dialogue is that China-UK cooperation is mutually beneficial; it not only benefits both countries but also the world. Looking ahead, China is willing to continue to regard the UK as a partner in promoting the building of a new type of international relations and a community with a shared future. China will contribute to creating a better world.

Lord Green: I have visited China several times and witnessed the tremendous achievements of China's reform and development. However, China's future development faces challenges such as the imbalances between the eastern and the western regions, an aging population, and water shortages. Ambassador Liu, what are your views on these issues? How will China address these problems?

Liu Xiaoming: 2018 marked the 40th anniversary of China's reform and opening up. In over 40 years, China's economy has risen from the tenth in the world to the second, successfully lifting 700 million people out of poverty. People's living standards in China have greatly improved, with significant increases in life expectancy and a continuous improvement in people's sense of gain, happiness, and security. However, China is still a developing country. Our per capita GDP is still far behind that of developed Western countries. When observing China, one should see its "multifaceted" nature. There are metropolises like Beijing, Shanghai, and Shenzhen, which can rival European cities, as well as relatively underdeveloped western provinces. You mentioned the water resource issue earlier, and I can personally relate to it. Over ten years ago, I served as assistant governor of Gansu Province, one of the poorest provinces in China, where many people had difficulty accessing clean drinking water and had to rely on purified rainwater for themselves and their livestock.

Regarding the main contradictions in Chinese society today, the 19th National Congress of the Communist Party of China accurately identified the contradiction between the growing demand for a better life and imbalanced and inadequate development. Looking ahead, we still have a lot of work to do, and the burden on our shoulders is heavy. China's rise and development are not about challenging other countries internationally, but about solving the many challenges it faces in its own development, continuously improving people's livelihoods, and achieving the goal of lifting everyone out of poverty by 2020, making development more balanced and comprehensive.

Lord Green: I am deeply concerned about the current global trade situation, with US President Trump frequently taking unilateral and protectionist measures such as imposing tariffs, which has had a huge impact on the World Trade Organization (WTO) and the global trade order. Ambassador Liu, how do you see the global trade situation, and how will China respond?

Liu Xiaoming: I share your concerns about trade issues, as I am also concerned about the wave of unilateralism and protectionism. China believes that the WTO is still at the core of the multilateral trading system. Of course, this system is not perfect and needs necessary reforms to make global trade more standardized, convenient, and open. We live in an interconnected "global village, " and if all countries base their trade rules purely on their own interests, or prioritize their own interests over others in a so-called "me-first" approach, this will inevitably lead to a "trade war" and have a negative impact on global economic growth.

Therefore, China supports the WTO in playing its due role, as well as supporting necessary reforms to the WTO. However, WTO reforms should be based on consensus among all parties. Although this will take more time, the costs will be much smaller for all parties. China opposes the "winner takes all" or "zero-sum game" approach and believes that only mutually beneficial cooperation can lead to win-win development.

Lord Green: Does the concept of "win-win development" that you mentioned refer to China's proposal to build a community with a shared future for mankind? I understand the original intention of China's proposal, but against the current backdrop of the China-US competition, can the community with a shared future for mankind become a reality?

Liu Xiaoming: I am optimistic about this because cooperation based on mutual benefit between countries is fundamentally possible. President Xi Jinping's proposal to build a community with a shared future for mankind has received positive responses from the international community and has been incorporated into United Nations and G20 documents.
There are no "winners" in a trade war, and both China and the US will suffer losses. I have seen a survey that suggests that if the trade war continues, the US will be the biggest "loser." Recently, I have also noticed that many American entrepreneurs are dissatisfied with the government's imposition of tariffs. China does not want to see a "lose-lose" situation and hopes that people will eventually return to "rationality" and recognize the negative impact of a trade war without having to pay a price for it.

Lord Green: As you just mentioned, the world is undergoing a major transformation. The balance of power is changing significantly, especially with the rise of developing countries. In such a situation, what role do you think Europe will play on the world stage? Currently, there is no result on Brexit, and many European countries are facing challenges from populism. How does China see the role of Europe?

Liu Xiaoming: China advocates for the development of a multipolar world, believing that this is beneficial to achieving lasting peace and stability in the world. China attaches importance to the role of Europe, considering it to be an important pole in the world strategically. In terms of trade, Europe is China's largest trading partner. China is committed to developing relations and conducting pragmatic cooperation with the European Union and individual European countries, maintaining good relations with major countries such as the UK, France, Germany, Italy, as well as actively cooperating with the "16+1" cooperation involving Central and Eastern European countries. This year, President Xi Jinping and Premier Li Keqiang paid successful visits to Europe where the two sides jointly reaffirmed the importance of China-Europe relations. This demonstrates the importance China attaches to Europe. Regarding the issue of Brexit, we are following closely the progress here and believe that it is a matter between the UK and the EU. We believe that both sides have the wisdom and capability to handle related issues properly. China hopes that the UK and the EU can reach an agreement that satisfies both parties and is willing to promote the parallel development of China-Europe and China-UK relations.

Lord Green: I have noticed that there are different opinions within the UK on dealing with relations with China. In addition, the Europeans have been sceptical about the "16+1" cooperation. How do you view these issues?

Liu Xiaoming: I have heard the view that the UK must choose sides between China and the US, hence the different opinions on developing relations with China. I want to point out that mainstream opinion in the UK sees China's development as an opportunity rather than a challenge or a threat, and most people support the advancement of the "Golden Era" of China-UK relations.

There are indeed some misunderstandings in Europe about the "16+1" cooperation between China and Central and Eastern European countries. In fact, the "16+1" cooperation has achieved positive results and is mutually beneficial for both China and the EU. In terms of the level of development, many countries in Central and Eastern Europe fall below the EU average and face common problems that hinder their further growth. Therefore, they have a strong desire to enhance cooperation with China. China has maintained close communication and exchanges with Europe, hoping to address any doubts or misunderstandings through increased trust and clarification. We want everyone to understand that China is committed to taking a different path from that followed by previous big powers in their rise. China's development will bring more opportunities to Europe and the world.

Lord Green: India and Japan are important countries in Asia, but both countries have delicate relations with China. For example, India has reservations about the Belt and Road Initiative, and there are significant unresolved historical legacies between China and Japan. How do you view China's relations with India and Japan?

Liu Xiaoming: China attaches great importance to its relations with India and Japan, which are important neighboring countries. Without good relations between China and India and between China and Japan, there will be no lasting peace, stability, and prosperity in Asia. Regarding China-India relations, some Western media outlets are keen on playing down the significance of the positive aspects to this and continue to hype up the differences between the two countries. However, our common interests are much greater than the differences. Both countries are members of the BRICS and have extensive common interests on various issues. In recent years, President Xi Jinping and Prime Minister Modi have met several times on different occasions, establishing a good personal friendship and working relationship, which reflects the high importance China's leaders attach to the development of China-India relations.

Regarding China-Japan relations, there are indeed "bitter memories". The Chinese people have every reason to be concerned about Japan's attitude towards history because we do not want history to "repeat itself." China is willing to improve relations with Japan, and President Xi Jinping will soon visit Japan to attend the G20 summit. We hope that this will inject strong impetus into the improvement and development of China-Japan relations.

Michael Lawrence, CEO of "Asia House": The Huawei issue is currently a focus of attention in the UK. What is your view on Huawei's development prospects in the UK?

Liu Xiaoming: First of all, I would like to point out that Huawei is an excellent company, not only leading the world in the field of 5G communications but also making significant contributions to economic and social development in the UK. Last month, during my return to China, I visited Huawei in Shenzhen and interacted with company executives and employees at Huawei University. I found that Huawei is looking forward to pragmatic cooperation with the UK.

Over the past 5 years, Huawei has created more than 7,500 jobs in the UK, with purchases and investments amounting to 2 billion pounds, and plans to invest a further 3 billion pounds in the future. More importantly, Huawei attaches great importance to cybersecurity issues, proactively investing in establishing a cybersecurity certification center in the UK, employing an all-British supervision team, regularly assessing risks, and continuously improving technology. There is no equipment without any risk in the world, but Huawei is willing to cooperate with the UK government, business, and academic circles to improve the security and reliability of their equipment. In fact, the UK side assesses that the security risks of Huawei equipment are "manageable."

I have heard it commented that if Huawei equipment is banned, the UK's 5G construction will be delayed by one to two years. What worries me more is that the UK is known for its open and inclusive market environment. If Huawei is banned, it may send a very negative signal, especially impacting Chinese companies' investment and operations in the UK. That is what I least want to see. The name of this country is "Great Britain," and its "greatness" lies in its independence. We hope that the UK government will make decisions in its own long-term interests and conducive to the overall China-UK cooperation, rather than following the instructions or succumbing to the pressure of others.

Professor Morrison, Coventry University: I attended Ambassador Liu's speech a few years ago and heard at that time that in the global supply chain, China only earned 5 cents in profit for every $1 worth of goods it produced. Hence there is a great potential for growth. How much has China's profit in the global supply chain increased now? How do you see such progress?

Liu Xiaoming: As you know, China cannot stay at the "low end" of the global supply chain forever. In recent years, the Chinese people have worked diligently and actively developed medium and high-end industries. We have indeed made some progress. However, China attaches more importance to enlarging the "cake of common interests", allowing all parties to benefit more rather than just taking a larger share of the "cake" for itself and leaving everyone competing for limited resources. This is the philosophy that China adopts when conducting cooperation with other countries.

As a career diplomat, I have been superintending China-US ties for a long time. The current China-US economic and trade relationship reminds me of a statement made by a US leader over 30 years ago when I was posted to Washington D. C. He said that the US was concerned about the trade deficit with China, but the solution was not to reduce China's exports to the US, but to increase US exports to China. I agree with this view, and I hope that today's US leaders will follow the same logic. The imposition of tariffs by the US on China not only disrupts the global supply chain but will ultimately lead to losses for US companies and ordinary American consumers.

James Richards, Chairman of Asiability: The recent Hong Kong issue has aroused widespread concern in British society. Ambassador Liu, in an interview with the BBC, stated that the "Sino-British Joint Declaration" is "no longer meaningful." Does the Chinese government still adhere to the "One Country, Two Systems" policy in Hong Kong?

Liu Xiaoming: Thank you for watching my interview, but your quote is not accurate. The mission of the "Sino-British Joint Declaration" was to ensure the smooth transfer of government in Hong Kong. After Hong Kong's return to China in 1997, the "Sino-British Joint Declaration" completed its historical mission. I have noticed that some British media question the Chinese central government's commitment to "One Country, Two Systems." I want to emphasize that "One Country, Two Systems" is not a promise to the UK. It is a commitment by the Chinese central government to all Chinese people, including Hong Kong residents, and this is fully reflected in the "Basic Law." Currently, the Hong Kong SAR government's handling of the "amendment"-related work is precisely a vivid embodiment of the practice of "One Country, Two Systems." Some foreign media and forces describe the Hong Kong "amendment" as undermining "One Country, Two Systems" . To use a British expression, this is completely "barking up the wrong tree." Some senior British government officials have also made some irresponsible remarks recently, which is interference in Hong Kong affairs and in China's internal affairs. If the British side sincerely hopes that Hong kong will enjoy long-term prosperity and stability, it should not interfere with the lawful governance of the Hong Kong SAR government.

Lord Sassoon, Chairman of the China-Britain Business Council: Ambassador Liu mentioned the 69 important outcomes achieved in last week's UK-China Economic and Financial Dialogue.This will strongly promote practical cooperation between the UK and China and greatly inspire the UK business community. Regarding WTO reform, what is the possibility of achieving it in the end? How can China and the UK cooperate on this issue?

Liu Xiaoming: WTO reform is a complex systematic project aimed at reflecting the new realities of the world economy, particularly taking into account the major concerns of developing countries, promoting global trade liberalization and facilitation, improving the dispute settlement mechanism, and promoting the construction of an inclusive and open world economy.

Not long ago, China released a "Proposal on WTO Reform," which detailed the "China Solution". I suggest that everyone take a closer look at it. China and the UK have shared interests in WTO reform, and we are willing to work with the UK to improve the WTO and the multilateral trading system.

Lord Green: Thank you, Ambassador Liu, for your wonderful speech. China's relations with the world have become one of the most significant strategic issues of our time. Ambassador Liu has provided an in-depth interpretation of the spirit and essence of Xi Jinping's diplomatic thoughts and vividly expounded on the key aspects of China's foreign policy. Ambassador Liu is a frequent guest at "Asia House," but this is the first time that "Asia House" has invited the ambassador to a dialogue. We look forward to continuing our dialogue with Ambassador Liu and creating a better platform for the UK to get closer to Asia, understand China, and comprehend China.

Thank you, everyone!

"四个坚持"至关重要
——与英国智库座谈"'后疫情时代'中欧关系"

（2020年7月15日，中国驻英国使馆/货币金融机构官方论坛）

刘晓明： 很高兴通过视频连线方式与大家座谈。我们今天座谈的主题是"'后疫情时代'中欧关系"。

今年是中国和欧盟建交45周年。近半个世纪以来，中欧关系日趋全面、成熟和稳定，给双方人民带来实实在在的好处，也为世界和平与繁荣做出积极贡献。不久前，习近平主席会见欧洲理事会主席米歇尔和欧盟委员会主席冯德莱恩，李克强总理同两位欧盟领导人共同主持第二十二次中国—欧盟领导人会晤，为"后疫情时代"的中欧关系指明方向。

当前，新冠肺炎疫情仍在全球肆虐，深刻改变国际格局和全球治理体系。这场百年未遇的疫情凸显国际社会面临四大赤字：

一是健康赤字。疫情已波及210多个国家和地区，影响70多亿人口，近1300万人感染，56万多人病亡。这场疫情成为"二战"以来最严重的全球公共卫生突发事件，对人类生命安全和健康构成严峻挑战，需要中欧与国际社会携手应对。

二是发展赤字。疫情导致世界经济陷入严重衰退。经合组织预计，欧洲可能是今年受到经济冲击最严重的地区。疫情阻碍跨境人员流动、影响各国经贸往来，冲击全球产业链。国际货币基金组织和世界银行分别预测今年全球经济将萎缩4.9%和5.2%。如何复苏和提振经济是各国面临的共同艰巨任务。

三是和平赤字。在疫情背景下，世界和平和安全面临严峻挑战。地区冲突和局部战争持续不断，恐怖主义猖獗，人道主义危机严重，不少国家民众特别是儿童饱受战火摧残。这些都严重威胁着世界和平与稳定。

四是治理赤字。此次疫情暴露出全球公共卫生治理体系的不足和短板，亟须完善提升。疫情下，贸易保护主义、单边主义和逆全球化抬头，个别国家将疫情政治化，把病毒标签化，损害国际团结和抗疫合作，全球治理体系和多边机制面临严峻考验。

此次疫情使国际社会深刻认识到，人类是一个休戚与共、紧密相连的命运共同体。"甩锅""诿责"解决不了问题，更挽救不了生命，团结合作才是战胜疫情的唯一正确选择。中欧作为世界两大力量、两大市场、两大文明，更应携手合作，共同为全球抗疫、恢复经济、完善治理、破解赤字贡献力量。

一是共守人类健康安全。中国高度重视同包括欧洲在内的国际社会开展抗疫合作。不久前，习近平主席在世界卫生大会上呼吁构建人类卫生健康共同体，宣布今后两年内中国将提供20亿美元国际援助、中国新冠疫苗研发完成并投入使用后将作为全球公共产品等重要举措。中方积极参与欧盟发起的应对新冠肺炎疫情国际认捐大会和英国主办的全球疫苗峰会视频会议。中欧要继续加强抗疫经验交流，深化疫苗和药物研发合作，加大对公共卫生体系薄弱地区的支持，积极探讨开展中欧非三方抗疫合作，筑牢守卫人类健康的坚固防线，共同构建人类卫生健康共同体。

二是共护世界和平稳定。中国与欧盟面积占世界1/10，人口占世界1/4，在联合国安理会拥有2个常任理事国席位，在维护世界和平稳定中应当发挥关键作用。中欧应加强战略对话，就重大国际和地区问题加强协调沟通。中欧应继续支持以和平手段，通过对话协商解决各类热点问题和地区冲突；坚守国际防扩散体制，维护全球战略稳定；支持打击一切形式恐怖主义，标本兼治，遏制极端思潮的蔓延。

三是共促国际发展繁荣。越是面临疫情挑战，越是要坚持开放合作。中欧作为两大经济体应该发挥世界经济"双引擎"作用，共同拉动世界经济复苏，推动有序复工复产，维护全球产业链供应链开放、稳定、安全。双方应加强宏观经济政策协调，维护开放型世界经济。今年上半年，中欧班列开行数量大幅增长，累计开行5122列，同比增长36%，成为确保中欧贸易畅通的重要通道。中欧还应拓展互联互通、绿色发展、生态环保、数字经济、人工智能等新领域的互利合作，保持相互市场开放，争取年内完成中欧投资协定谈判，达成一项全面、平衡、高水平的投资协定。

四是共建全球治理体系。今年是联合国成立75周年。中欧都坚决维护多边主义，都支持国际关系民主化，都主张维护以联合国为核心的国际体系、以国际法为基础的国际秩序、以世贸组织为基石的多边贸易体制，支持世卫组织在国际抗疫合作中发挥领导作用。中欧在维护全球公共卫生安全，应对气候变化，发展清洁能源、清洁交通、绿色科技，保护生物多样性方面有共同利益，在推进世界贸易组织改革、共同维护自由贸易等方面有广泛共识，完全可以加强沟通协作，进一步维护多边主义，完善全球治理。

女士们、先生们，中欧建交45年来，互利共赢始终是中欧关系的主旋律。面对疫情带来的新挑战，中欧关系也面临一些新问题。一些人对中国的猜忌和疑虑增多，称中国是"制度性对手"，还有人视中国为"潜在敌对国家"，扬言对华关系不会回到从前。如何看待疫情后的中欧关系，如何维护好中欧关系发展大局是我们面临的共同课题。我认为，做到"四个坚持"至关重要。

第一，坚持相互尊重，反对干涉内政。相互尊重主权和领土完整、互不干涉内政、平等互利，是《联合国宪章》确立的基本原则，也是国际关系基本准则。中欧关系45年的发展经验表明，只要这些原则得到遵守，中欧关系就能向前发展，反之就遭受挫折，甚至倒退。中国从不干涉别国内政，也坚决反对别国干涉中国内政。最近，中国全国人大常委会针对香港在维护国家安全方面存在的巨大风险，审议通过香港国安法，目的是防范、制止和惩治分裂国家、颠覆国家政权、恐怖活动、勾结外国或者境外势力危害国家安全四类罪行。香港国安法弥补了香港的国家安全漏洞，针对的是极少数严重危害国家安全的行为和活动，不影响香港的高度自治，不改变香港的独立司法权和终审权，有利于保障香港居民的权利和自由，有利于保护外国投资者在港正当权益。因此，香港国安法受到香港居民普遍欢迎，近300万市民签名支持。国际上，70多个国家表态支持香港国安法，其中包括一些欧洲国家。然而，一些欧洲政要却对该法说三道四，干涉香港事务和中国内政。我想强调的是，香港是中国的香港，香港事务是中国内政，任何外国无权干涉。我们希望欧盟方面客观、理性、公正看待香港国安法，切实遵守国际法和国际关系基本准则，停止插手香港事务和中国内政。

第二，坚持互为伙伴，摒弃"冷战思维"。中欧已建立全面战略伙伴关系，积极建设和平、增长、改革、文明四大伙伴关系。中国始终走和平发展道路，致力于与包括欧洲国家在内的世界各国和平相处、互利合作、共同发展，始终把欧洲作为平等的伙伴而不是对手。中欧之间不存在地缘政治矛盾，更没有根本利益冲突。中欧合作远大于竞争，共识远多于分歧。

那些把中国看成是"制度性对手"，甚至是"潜在敌对国家"的人，是找错了对象，看错了方向。中国最关心的是提高本国人民福祉，最重视的是实现中华民族复兴，最期待的是世界和平稳定。中欧应通过平等对话增进互信，通过互利合作实现共赢，通过建设性沟通妥善处理分歧。中欧关系应是相互成就的正循环，而不是你输我赢的淘汰赛。

第三，坚持互为机遇，反对"零和博弈"。中国的发展对欧洲是机遇而不是挑战，更不是威胁。中欧作为世界两大市场，经济总量占全球1/3，双方互为第二大贸易伙伴，经济互补性强。疫情下，"宅经济"、"云办公"、智能制造、生命健康、公共卫生等领域呈现出巨大发展活力和潜力，为中欧合作提供了新机遇、新空间。随着中国进一步深化改革、扩大开放，中欧合作面临更加广阔的前景。我相信，中欧互利合作将不仅给双方人民带来更多福祉，而且将为我们这个充满不确定性的世界提供更多稳定性和可预期性。

第四，坚持互学互鉴，共促文明进步。中欧作为东西方文化的重要发祥地，都有灿烂和悠久的文化传统。中欧历史背景、社会制度、发展阶段存在差异，这些差异不应是相互交往的障碍，而应是互学互鉴的动力。中国主张"和而不同"，强调"己所不欲，勿施于人"。中国的发展不照搬外国模式，也从不要求别人复制中国的模式。欧盟也强调"多元一体",促进平等、包容和多元。中欧应相互尊重、相互欣赏、相互借鉴、相互成就。中欧作为推进人类进步的两大文明,应共同努力,把世界的多样性和各国的差异性转化为发展活力和动力,共同促进人类文明之花竞相开放。

女士们、先生们,中国古人讲:"万物并育而不相害,道并行而不相悖。"这不仅是人与人相处之道,也是国与国共处之道。人类社会发展的历史证明,开放才能进步,包容才能交融,合作才能共赢。让我们携起手来,不断为中欧合作贡献正能量,共同为中欧关系在疫情后实现更高水平发展开创新未来!

现在,我愿回答大家的提问。

货币金融机构官方论坛主席马什(主持人): 有人认为,中国应把欧洲团结到自己这一边,促使欧洲与美国保持距离。刘大使,你对此有何看法?

刘晓明: 外界对中国立场存在不少误解。中国无意在美欧之间打入楔子,我们知道美欧是盟友。中国愿同所有国家做朋友,包括与美国保持良好关系。我曾两次在美国常驻,45年外交生涯有一半时间从事对美工作。我们始终认为,一个良好的中美关系有利于世界和平与稳定,但中美保持良好关系应建立在相互尊重和平等相待基础上。西方人讲,"探戈需要两个人跳";中国人常说,"一个巴掌拍不响"。我们希望与美国不冲突不对抗、相互尊重、合作共赢,构建以协调、合作、稳定为基调的中美关系。关于中欧关系,我刚才在演讲中已经讲过,我们始终把欧洲作为平等的伙伴而不是对手,我们应该视彼此为机遇。中欧互为第二大贸易伙伴,双方之间有很多共同利益把我们紧密联系在一起。

马什主席： 我再问一个与电信相关的问题，这与英国有关，对欧洲国家也可能有影响。昨天英国政府决定不再与华为合作。英国政府知道过去几年华为对英国5G建设的贡献，以及该决定造成的经济损失，但还是这样做了。刘大使，你认为英国宣布的这一决定将对中英合作产生什么具体影响？

刘晓明： 我认为，这个决定损害了两国之间的互信。众所周知，相互信任、相互尊重是建立任何关系的基础，人与人之间的关系如此，两国之间的关系也是如此。昨天我在推特上说："英国对华为的决定是令人失望的，是错误的。"今天，我要加上一句，这个决定不仅令人失望，"更令人寒心"。华为是一家好公司，他们在英国经营20年，不仅对英国投资了30多亿英镑，还为当地解决了2.6万个就业岗位，创造了大量税收，为英国电信业和经济社会发展做出了巨大贡献。令人寒心的是，华为的贡献被某些英国政客和媒体歪曲成"伤害"英国。而事实恰恰相反，华为才真正受到伤害，其他中国企业也正密切关注英国如何对待华为。当相互信任遭到破坏时，中资企业将很难在这里进行更多投资。因此，这个问题不需要政府来回答，我认为工商界都会得出自己的结论。中英之间的信任、两国政府之间的信任以及中资企业对投资英国的信任，都受到严重损害。

马什主席： 英中关系"黄金时代"是将延续下去，还是会某种程度上失去光泽？

刘晓明： "黄金时代"意味着中英双方要共同付出努力。"黄金时代"是2015年习近平主席对英国国事访问时，由英国领导人倡议提出的。我们认为"黄金时代"体现了中英关系的发展水平、符合两国利益，因此赞同这一倡议，与英方共同打造"黄金时代"。今年是中英关系"黄金时代"5周年，本应是值得庆祝的年份。现在中英之间发生了很多事情，但责任不在中方。

货币金融机构官方论坛会员博格斯： 当前各国似乎更加注重双边关系，这无助于多边贸易和多边合作。我们应如何在多边主义与双边关系之间重新找回平衡？

刘晓明： 中方一贯坚持多边主义。今年是联合国成立75周年，很多人不知道，中国是第一个在《联合国宪章》上签字的国家。中国坚定维护以联合国为核心的国际体系，认真履行应该承担的国际义务。中国从来不寻求"本国优先"，也没有退出任何国际条约。中国已签署了500多个多边条约，参加了100多个政府间国际组织。中国支持世界卫生组织在全球抗疫合作中发挥领导作用，向世卫组织提供了捐款。与欧洲国家一样，中国不赞成美国退出世卫组织。中国支持以世界贸易组织为基石的多边贸易体系，尽管这一体系并不完美，但仍是无法代替的。

高盛公司多永： 中欧如何在应对气候变化等领域加强合作？

刘晓明： 中国积极参与、推动并签署了《巴黎协定》，将继续认真履行《巴黎协定》。今年本应是中英环境保护合作之年，中英分别计划举办《生物多样性公约》第15次缔约方会议（COP15）和《联合国气候变化框架公约》第26次缔约方会议（COP26）。受疫情影响，两个会议都被推迟了，但双方仍就两次会议保持密切沟通。最近我与英国外交部COP26区域大使布里斯托爵士进行了很好的会谈。我们希望通过双方共同努力，使两次会议都取得成功。中英可将气候变化打造为双方合作的新亮点，共同在全球气候变化问题上发挥引领作用。

德国英国商会哈特曼： 中欧对双方贸易投资合作期待不同，中国在增加对欧洲的投资，也希望吸引欧洲国家投资，但欧盟正在出台政策加强对中国投资的审查。你如何看待双方在投资问题上的不同诉求？

刘晓明： 中欧贸易与投资合作机遇巨大。但重要的是，中欧双方如何看待对方，是将彼此视为伙伴和机遇，还是视为"系统性竞争对手"或"潜在敌对国家"？英国如何看待华为，实际上不仅是对待一家中国民营企业的问题，而是关乎英国如何看待中国的问题。显然，英国对华为的决定受到"对华鹰派"和"反华势力"的压力。这些人把中国视为"敌对"或"潜在敌对国家"，他们不信任中国，所以不信任中国企业。中方不希望把经济问题与政治问题混为一谈，反对将经济问题政治化。但现在英国将经济问题政治化了，加入了美国制裁中国企业的行列。当一个国家把中国视为"潜在敌对国家"的时候，试问，我们怎么能与其正常做生意？

马什主席： 请问，刘大使讲的意思是，外界不信任中国，中国难道没有任何责任吗？还是为了赢得更多信任，中国本可以做得更好？面对外界的不信任，中国该怎么做？

刘晓明： 那么，好，我们就以华为为例谈信任问题。有人不信任华为，说其存在安全风险。华为主动斥资建立"网络安全评估中心"，该中心完全由英国人管理运营，华为没有派任何人。英方运营团队评估得出的结论是，华为产品安全风险是可控的。这也是今年初英国政府决定允许华为参与英国5G网络建设的原因，尽管英方为华为设定了35%的市场份额上限。华为还采取措施不断改进技术，以增强产品的安全性能，努力确保英国5G网络设施更安全、更具韧性。华为已竭尽所能，我看不到对华为还应有什么抱怨的地方。

摩根士丹利公司莫戈达姆： 我提两个问题：第一，你提到欧洲和中国都支持WTO，但目前WTO面临僵局，你如何看待WTO改革问题？第二，你刚才提到中国和欧盟之间的贸易规模很大，但其中很大一部分是商品贸易，服务贸易还不够多。你对如何扩大中欧服务贸易有何看法？

刘晓明： 关于WTO，中国支持以WTO为基石的多边贸易体系，支持对WTO进行必要改革。同时，中欧在有关问题上存在分歧，特别是中国仍然是一个发展中国家，希望欧洲正确看待中国作为发展中国家的定位。中国"复关"和"入世"谈判历时15年，尽管付出了代价，但我们全面履行入世承诺，矢志不渝融入国际秩序和多边机制。关于服务贸易，欧洲包括英国在内有自己的优势，中国有广阔的市场，中欧经济互补性很强。我们欢迎更多欧洲企业对华拓展服务贸易合作。今年初，中国《外商投资法》正式实施，中国在开放服务业方面出台了很多新政策，外商投资服务业的许多限制被取消，外商投资负面清单进一步缩短，我们还取消了合格境外机构投资者（QFII）和人民币合格境外机构投资者（RQFII）投资额度限制，包括欧洲国家在内的外国银行和保险公司在中国将面临更大商机。

非洲发展银行卡巴佐： 新冠肺炎疫情将使非洲遭受25年来最严重的经济衰退，中国是否愿意在非洲面对这场前所未有的危机时提供帮助，包括减免有关债务？

刘晓明： 中国始终视非洲为好兄弟、好伙伴、好朋友。我曾两次常驻非洲，对非洲怀有深厚感情。中国积极支持非洲国家抗击疫情，克服经济困难。在今年5月举行的第73届世界卫生大会上，习近平主席宣布中国将同二十国集团成员一道落实"暂缓最贫困国家债务偿付倡议"。在不久前举行的中非团结抗疫特别峰会上，中方还宣布将在中非合作论坛框架下免除有关非洲国家截至2020年底到期对华无息贷款债务。此外，中国还派出多支医疗队帮助非洲国家抗击疫情，分享抗疫经验，提供个人防护装备和急需物资。最近我在使馆还同英国智库列格坦研究所共同主办非洲抗疫视频座谈会，就加强中、英、非三方抗疫合作深入交流。

马什主席： 在减免债务方面，中国是否会加入"巴黎俱乐部"？

刘晓明： 中国不是巴黎俱乐部的成员。中国已就债务减免问题加入多个多边安排。中国在通过双边渠道减免对外债务方面做了更多工作，因为这样做更有效、更直接。中国开展有关对外合作始终坚持平等、开放、透明，遵循市场规律和通行的国际规则，注重债务和发展的可持续性问题。

货币金融机构官方论坛专家努格： 我想更多了解中国外交政策和处理国际关系方式的变化。过去30年，中国外交一直保持耐心，但现在似乎正在失去耐心，是什么让中国决定采取更加急迫的方式应对外部问题？

刘晓明： 中国外交政策没有改变。中国是热爱和平的国家，和平深植在中华民族的基因里，中国致力于维护世界和平与稳定。改革开放40多年来，中国发展得益于和平的外部环境，我们坚信中国进一步发展仍然需要和平的国际环境。为什么要改变这一状况呢？实际上，不是中国变了，而是有些国家对华政策发生了很大变化，中国必须做出应对。在中美关系上，中方愿与美国发展良好关系，不希望两国关系恶化，但美国却执意向中方施压、妖魔化中国。在此次新冠肺炎疫情中，美国政客频频污称"中国病毒"。究竟是谁变了？人们应该有客观判断。在台湾问题上，美国大打"台湾牌"，扩大对台军售，企图助台湾扩大国际空间。是美国想要改变现状，中国必须做出回应。在香港问题上，香港回归23年来，"一国两制"取得巨大成功。但去年香港发生"修例风波"，反中乱港分子鼓吹"港独""自决"，公开挥舞英国、美国国旗，甚至邀请美军登陆香港、"解放香港"。面对这样严峻的形势，我们有充分理由采取必要果断措施，坚定维护"一国两制"。

英中贸协主席古沛勤爵士： 中国与欧洲在相互了解上似乎存在巨大鸿沟。中国很了解欧洲，但欧洲包括英国似乎对中国历史、中国共产党缺乏基本了解，尤其是欧洲决策者们似乎存在很大的对华"认知赤字"。请问刘大使，我们应该如何增加英国和欧洲的对华认知？

刘晓明： 你这个问题提得很好。或许我下次演讲时可以再加上第五个赤字，即"认知赤字"。我同意你的看法。中欧之间、中国与西方国家之间确实需要加深了解。一些西方政客指责中国时总是说"中国受到国际社会广泛批评"。我对此指出，他们仅代表了西方国家的一小部分，更谈不上代表整个国际社会。以香港国安法为例，国际上有70多个国家支持中国，但反对的只有支持中国的国家数量的1/3。我认为，解决"认知赤字"的有效办法是加强接触交流。我们需要更多的相互"挂钩"而非相互"脱钩"。我们鼓励中国和欧洲年轻人多交往、多沟通。现在有更多的中国留学生愿意到英国来学习。我希望英国能够继续保持开放，张开双臂欢迎中国留学生来英学习。

野村证券安德鲁： 我非常尊重中国反对干涉内政的立场。但现实情况是，在一个全球化的世界中，一个国家内部发生的事情会影响到其他国家。比如对环境问题、生物多样性问题，英中都有共同关切。我们应如何理解不干涉问题？

刘晓明： 我认为中国人和英国人都有足够的智慧来区分什么是干涉内政，什么是善意的建议。当外界关注中国环境问题时，我们欢迎有助于中国加强环境保护、改善环境质量的建设性建议。我们当然能够分清哪些是真心帮助中国的建议，哪些是企图蓄意改变中国政治和社会制度、把西方意志和模式强加给中国的言行。正如中方多次重申的，我们不照搬外国模式，也不输出中国模式，但我们坚决反对任何国家干涉中国内政。

蒙特罗斯商务咨询公司麦克雷： 刘大使，你讲到英国在华为问题上的决定将会损害双方互信。或许中国可以采取一些具体措施重建信任，比如中方是否愿意让世卫组织专家调查武汉实验室？能否明确承认在南海航行自由原则？在台湾问题上中国是否继续坚持和平统一？

刘晓明： 关于抗疫问题，中国一直秉持公开、透明、负责任的态度，开展国际抗疫合作。中国是第一个向世卫组织报告疫情的国家，是第一个同国际社会分享病毒基因测序的国家。我们没有任何隐瞒，反而是有的国家借疫情对中国污名化。现在世卫组织已派遣专家赴华，与中国专家一起就新冠病毒溯源工作进行科学规划。但我们应该明确两点：一是病毒溯源工作应该以科学为基础，而不是政治操弄；二是评估要包括所有国家，而不仅仅是中国。

关于南海航行自由，中方一贯尊重和支持各国依据国际法在南海享有的航行自由。中国60%的石油供应经过南海，我们比任何国家都关心这一地区的和平稳定。我们正同域内国家共同落实《南海各方行为宣言》（DOC），继续推动"南海行为准则"（COC）磋商。现在南海形势总体平稳，中方坚决反对个别域外国家派遣军舰到南海挑战中国领土主权，破坏地区稳定。

关于台湾问题，中国致力于和平统一，这一原则立场没有变。我推荐你读一读不久前我在《中国日报》发表的有关文章。我们愿再次重申，台湾是中国领土不可分割的一部分，中国一贯坚持和平统一政策。中国政府不承诺放弃使用武力，针对的是外部势力干涉和极少数"台独"分裂分子及其分裂活动，绝非针对广大台湾同胞。中国必须统一，也必然统一，这一进程是任何人、任何势力都无法阻挡的。

货币金融机构官方论坛顾问委员会主席德赛： 中国经济已在疫后迅速复苏，中国是否计划在近期内加强人民币作为国际储备货币的地位？

刘晓明： 中国一直稳步推进人民币国际化。过去10年，我们在促进人民币贸易和投资方面做了很多努力。越来越多国家将人民币作为贸易和投资货币，人民币作为国际储备货币的作用也在增强。我很高兴看到伦敦在人民币国际化进程中发挥了重要作用。伦敦目前是全球最大的人民币离岸外汇交易中心、第二大人民币离岸清算中心，香港则是全球最大的人民币离岸清算中心、第二大人民币离岸外汇交易中心。这两个城市在推动人民币国际化方面可以发挥互补优势。

西班牙对外银行里克尔梅： 我想听听你对中国与拉美国家，特别是与墨西哥关系的看法。墨西哥与美国关系密切，这是否会对中国与墨西哥的关系造成影响？

有问必答

刘晓明： 中国愿深化与拉美国家的关系。中国与拉美国家之间建立了中拉论坛等合作机制。中墨关系发展良好，我们不会为墨西哥与美国保持良好关系而感到担忧，同时我们希望美国不要干扰中国与拉美国家发展友好关系。

货币金融机构官方论坛首席执行官奥查德： 你刚刚谈到了中欧关系。随着英国脱欧，英国在中国处理对欧关系和对美关系中将处于什么位置？

刘晓明： 这取决于英国采取什么样的对华政策。我总是对英国朋友讲，第一，我们并不要求英国在中美之间选边站队，而是希望英国站在正确的一边。第二，英国只有拥有独立的外交政策，"不列颠"才能成为真正的"大不列颠"，才不会被中国和世界看作美国的"跟班"。看看英国如何对待华为，人们自然可以得出结论，无须多言。再看看美国领导人在英国政府做出决定后的表现，人们都会清楚英国为什么会做出这样的决定。所以，当英国想要打造"全球化英国"的时候，应该认真思考究竟要扮演一个什么样的角色，要在国际舞台占有一个什么样的位置。我们当然希望与英国和欧盟都保持良好关系，这一点毋庸置疑。

马什主席： 感谢刘大使，期待今后有机会与你继续深入交流。

刘晓明： 谢谢，再见。

Pulling Together in Four Aspects
—— A Keynote Speech and Q&A at the Webinar with UK Think Tanks On Post-Pandemic China-Europe Relations

On 15th July 2020, I held a webinar with the Official Monetary and Financial Institutions Forum (OMFIF) and the Centre for European Reform (CER) on China-Europe relations after the pandemic. I delivered a keynote speech entitled "Join Hands to Contribute Positive Energy and Create a Better Future for China-Europe Relationship". Around 100 people attended the event, including David Marsh, the Chairman of the OMFIF, Meghnad Desai, the Chairman of the OMFIF Advisory Board, Charles Grant, the Director of the CER, Sir Sherard Cowper-Coles, the Chairman of the China-Britain Business Council, members from the two think tanks, and representatives from the economic, financial and academic sectors of the UK, Europe, North America, Australia and South America, and journalists from 14 media agencies took part in the conference, including BBC, Sky News, Reuters, *The Daily Telegraph*, *Financial Times*, *The Guardian*, *The Independent*, CGTN, The Associated Press, Bloomberg, NBC, Agence France-Presse and Bulgarska Televizija. BBC and Sky News broadcast my keynote speech and part of the Q&A session live and run the coverage in their prime time programs. The transcript of the webinar is as follows:

Liu Xiaoming:
It is a real delight to join you on-line to talk about China-Europe relations after the pandemic.
This year marks the 45th anniversary of China-EU diplomatic relations. In the past 45 years, China's relationship with Europe has become increasingly comprehensive, mature and steady. This relationship has delivered tangible benefits to the people of both sides and contributed a positive impetus to world peace and prosperity.
Last month, the 22nd China-EU Summit was held on-line. President Xi Jinping held a meeting with President of the European Council Charles Michel and President of the European Commission Ursula von der Leyen, and Premier Li Keqiang co-chaired the summit with the two presidents. These meetings charted the course for the

relationship between China and Europe after the pandemic.

As COVID-19 continues to ravage the world, the international landscape and the system of global governance face profound changes. This most serious pandemic in a century has revealed four global deficits.

First, the health deficit.

COVID-19 has spread to more than 210 countries and regions, affecting more than 7 billion people, infecting over 13 million people and claiming over 560,000 lives. It has been the gravest global public health emergency after the Second World War. It poses severe challenge to the safety and health of mankind, and requires the joint response of the international community, including China and Europe.

Second, the development deficit.

This pandemic has resulted in a severe recession in the world economy. According to the OECD forecast, the European economy would be the hardest hit this year. International travel and trade has been disrupted by restrictions and the global industrial chain is under severe strain. The IMF and the World Bank predicted respectively a 4.9% and a 5.2% contraction in the world economy this year. How we should achieve economic recovery and continued growth is a daunting task for all countries.

Third, the peace deficit.

The pandemic has aggravated the severe challenges arising from incessant regional conflicts and wars, raging terrorism, and grave humanitarian crisis. People in many countries, especially children, are still suffering. World peace, security and stability are under grave threat.

Fourth, the governance deficit.

The pandemic has revealed the weak links in the global public health governance system which is in urgent need of improvement. Surging protectionism, unilateralism and anti-globalisation, and the politically motivated blame game are eroding international solidarity and undercutting the joint response to the pandemic. They also pose grave challenges to the global governance system and multilateral mechanisms. COVID-19 reminds the world that mankind belongs to a community with a shared future. Scapegoating and shirking responsibilities are unhelpful for solving problems or saving lives. Solidarity and cooperation are the only right way forward in this fight against the virus.

Both China and Europe are major global players, with big markets and great

civilisations. It is important that the two sides join hands to contribute
- to the global response to COVID-19,
- to world economic recovery,
- to improving global governance,
- and to overturning deficits.

First, China and Europe should work together to safeguard the health and safety of mankind.

China attaches great importance to cooperation with the international community, including Europe, on fighting the pandemic.

At the 73rd World Health Assembly last May, President Xi Jinping called for the building of a global community of health for all. He also announced that in the coming two years, China will provide 2 billion US dollars in international aid; when China is successful in developing a vaccine and has put it to use, the country will share it for the global public good.

China also took an active part in the Coronavirus Global Response Pledging Conference initiated by the EU and the Global Vaccine Summit hosted by the UK.

Going forward, China and the EU should:
- continue to share experience in epidemic-containment,
- enhance cooperation on the R&D of vaccine and medicines,
- strengthen support to regions with weak public health systems,
- and actively explore tripartite cooperation between China, the EU and Africa on epidemic response.

Together China and the EU could help to strengthen global defence against threats to public health, and contribute to building a global community of health for all.

Second, China and Europe should work together to uphold world peace and stability.

China and the EU have, between them, one tenth of the world's land area, one quarter of the world's population and two permanent members of the UN Security Council. There is every reason that China and the EU should play a key role in safeguarding world peace and stability.

China and Europe should enhance strategic dialogue to step up coordination and communication on major international and regional issues. This includes:

- supporting the settlement of all hotspot issues and regional conflicts through peaceful dialogue and consultation;

- upholding a global non-proliferation regime so as to safeguard global strategic stability.
- supporting measures aimed at cracking down upon terrorism of all forms and addressing both the symptoms and root causes of terrorism, with a view to containing the spread of extremist ideas.

Third, China and Europe should work together to promote development and prosperity in the world.

In face of the challenges from COVID-19, it is all the more important to stay committed to open cooperation.

As two major economies, China and the EU should be the "dual engines" of the world economy that:

- drive economic recovery,
- bring economic activities back on track in an orderly manner,
- and safeguard the open, stable and secure global industrial and supply chains.

To achieve these goals, China and the EU should enhance coordination on macro-economic policies and uphold an open world economy.

In the first half of this year, the China Railway Express offered an important passage for unimpeded trade between China and Europe, with 5,122 trains shuttling between China and Europe, increasing by 36% year-on-year.

New areas such as connectivity, green development, ecological conservation, environmental protection, the digital economy and artificial intelligence will create fresh opportunities for the mutually-beneficial cooperation between China and Europe.

The two sides should stay open to each other and strive to complete negotiations on the China-EU Investment Agreement with a view to reaching a comprehensive, balanced and high-standard agreement.

Fourth, China and Europe should work together to improve the system of global governance.

China and the EU are both committed to multilateralism.

- Both support greater democracy in international relations.
- Both safeguard the international system with the UN at its core, the international order based on international law, and the multilateral trade system with the WTO as its cornerstone.
- Both support the WHO in playing a leadership role in global response to COVID-19.

The two sides share common interests in:

- safeguarding global public health,
- tackling climate change,
- developing clean energy, clean transport and green technology,
- and preserving bio-diversity.

The two sides share broad consensus on advancing reforms in the WTO and upholding free trade.

In this year that marks the 75th anniversary of the founding of the United Nations, China and Europe should work together to enhance communication and coordination, safeguard multilateralism and improve global governance.

Ladies and Gentlemen:

In the 45 years of China-EU diplomatic relations, win-win cooperation has been the main theme. In face of the new challenges brought by the pandemic, this relationship has some new problems to solve.

By this I mean the misgivings and doubts of some politicians in Europe who:
- see China as a "systemic rival",
- regard China as a "potentially hostile state",
- and believe there will be no going back to "business as usual" with China.

So now, China and Europe have the same questions before them:
- What kind of relationship do they want post-pandemic?
- What should they do to preserve the overall interests of China-Europe relations?

In my opinion, China and Europe should pull together in the following four aspects:

First, respect each other and reject interference in other countries' internal affairs.

Mutual respect for sovereignty and territorial integrity, non-interference in other countries' internal affairs, equality and mutual benefit are the basic principles enshrined in the UN Charter and the basic norms governing international relations.

The experience of the past 45 years since China and the EU established diplomatic relations has told us that when these principles have been upheld, the China-Europe relationship will make progress; otherwise, this relationship will suffer setbacks or even retrogression.

China has never interfered in other countries' internal affairs, and we strongly oppose interference in China's internal affairs by other countries.

Last month, the Standing Committee of China's National People's Congress adopted the National Security Law for the Hong Kong SAR to deal with the enormous risk Hong Kong faces in safeguarding national security.

This Law is aimed at preventing, suppressing and punishing four types of criminal activities. They are secession, subversion, terrorist activities and collusion with a foreign country or with external elements to endanger national security:

- The Law plugs the legal loophole in terms of national security in Hong Kong.
- It targets very few actions and activities that gravely jeopardize national security.
- It will not affect the high degree of autonomy of Hong Kong.
- It will not alter Hong Kong's independent judicial power, including the power of final adjudication.
- It will provide better safeguards for the rights and freedoms of Hong Kong residents.
- And it will ensure better protection of the legitimate rights and interests of foreign investors in the city.

It is not surprising that the National Security Law for Hong Kong SAR has been warmly welcomed by Hong Kong residents. Nearly three million Hong Kong citizens have signed the petition in support of the Law. More than 70 countries in the world, including some European countries, have voiced their support.

However, some European politicians have made irresponsible remarks regarding this Law. They are interfering in Hong Kong affairs, which are internal affairs of China.

I want to emphasize that Hong Kong is part of China; Hong Kong affairs are China's internal affairs and brook no external interference.

It is my hope that the EU side will:

- view the National Security Law for the Hong Kong SAR from an objective, reasonable and fair perspective,
- take concrete steps to observe international law and the basic norms governing international relations,
- and stop interfering in Hong Kong affairs, which are the internal affairs of China.

Second, China and Europe should see each other as partners and abandon the "Cold War" mentality.

China and the EU have established a comprehensive strategic partnership. The two sides are building a partnership for peace, growth, reform and civilization.

China will always pursue peaceful development. It is committed to peaceful co-existence, mutually-beneficial cooperation and common development with all countries, including European countries. It has always seen Europe as an equal partner rather than a rival.

Between China and Europe, there is no geopolitical discord or conflict in fundamental interests; there is more cooperation than rivalry, more consensus than differences.

Those who see China as a "systemic rival" or a "potentially hostile state" have got it all wrong: they have chosen the wrong target and they are heading in the wrong direction.

What China cares most about is improving the well-being of the Chinese people. China's priority is to realize national rejuvenation. And in the pursuit of this purpose, China aspires for a peaceful and stable world.

China and Europe should:
- deepen mutual trust through an equal-footed dialogue,
- achieve win-win results through cooperation,
- and deal with differences appropriately through constructive communication.

It is important that China and Europe facilitate each other's success in a positive cycle, rather than engaging in a knockout match where one side's gain is built on the other's loss.

Third, China and Europe should seize the opportunities to be found in each other's development and reject zero-sum game.

China's development creates opportunities rather than challenges, much less threats, to Europe.

China and the EU, as two major markets of the world, account for one third of the world's total economy. The two sides are each other's second largest trading partner. And the two economies are highly complementary.

During the outbreak of COVID-19, enormous vitality and growth potential emerged from the "stay-home economy", "cloud office", intelligent manufacturing, life and health industries, and public health. These areas have created new opportunities and new space for China-Europe cooperation.

As China deepens reform and opens its market wider to the world, China-Europe cooperation will face more promising prospects.

I am confident that the mutually-beneficial cooperation between China and Europe will not only deliver more benefits to the peoples of the two sides but also provide greater stability and certainty for a world that is full of uncertainty.

Fourth, China and Europe should learn from each other and promote the progress of different civilizations side-by-side.

Both China and Europe, as important birthplaces of Oriental and Western cultures respectively, have splendid and time-honoured cultures.

The two sides differ in their history, social system and developmental stages. However, these differences should not become obstacles for exchanges between the two. Instead, they can provide driving forces for mutual learning.

The Chinese people believe that there is harmony without uniformity. We also believe that you should not do unto others what you do not want others to do unto you. China does not copy the developmental model of other countries. And China does not export its model to other countries.

The EU regards "united in diversity" as its motto. It values equality, inclusivity and diversity.

It is important that China and Europe respect, appreciate, learn from and support each other. As two major civilizations that have contributed greatly to human progress, China and Europe should work together to translate the diversity and differences in our world into vitality and impetus for further progress. This will enable different flowers of diverse human civilizations to come into full blossom.

Ladies and Gentlemen:

As an old Chinese saying goes,

"All living creatures grow together without harming each other;

All roads run parallel without interfering with one another. "

This should form the guideline for developing relations between not only individuals but also countries.

History tells us that openness brings progress, inclusivity leads to integration, and cooperation delivers win-win outcomes.

I hope we can join hands to contribute more positive energy to China-Europe cooperation so that after the pandemic, the relationship between China and Europe will make further progress at a higher level and embrace a better, brighter and more promising future.

Thank you!

Now I would like to take your questions.

David Marsh from the OMFIF: Thank you, Mr. Ambassador. It seems that you've missed an opportunity to bring Europe together on China's side, and to promote a kind of distance with the United States. Why haven't you taken that opportunity?

Liu Xiaoming: I think there's a lot of misunderstanding of China's position. We are not trying to drive a wedge between the United States and Europe. I know they are allies, and we simply want to be friends with everybody. We want to have good relations with the United States. I've been posted twice in Washington D.C. Half of the 45 years of my diplomatic career was dedicated to China-US relations. We want to have good relations with the United States. We always believe that there will be no world peace or prosperity without a sound, stable relationship between China and the United States, but this relationship has to be based on mutual trust and equality. You need two to tango and you need two hands to clap. So we want to have a good relationship devoid of conflict, devoid of confrontation, but instead with mutual respect and win-win cooperation based on coordination, cooperation and stability. That is what we are working for.

On China-Europe relations, as I said in my presentation, which I don't need to repeat, we want to see Europe and EU as partners of China, not rivals. We see each other as opportunities, and I am very pleased that we are one another's second largest trading partners. And there is enormous common ground, common interests to tie our two sides together.

David Marsh: Could I just ask one simple question please, which relates to the UK but may also have some bearing on the European countries, which is the question of telecommunications. We've had the decision yesterday by the British government that we won't go ahead with Huawei in the UK, even though we know what that company has done on the 5G network within a few years, and it will be bringing costs to the UK. What do you think will be the concrete results in terms of China-UK collaboration from that decision, which was announced yesterday?

Liu Xiaoming: I think it first of all undermined the trust between the two countries. You know, mutual trust and mutual respect are really the basis for a relationship, not only between individuals but also between two countries. Yesterday I tweeted, "Disappointing and wrong decision by the UK on Huawei". I would even say it's not only disappointing, it's disheartening. You know, it's a good company. They've been here for 20 years. They not only invested £3 billion in this country but also created 26, 000 jobs, paid their taxes and contributed greatly to the telecom industry of this country and to the local community. What they have done for this country is described by British media and some politicians as "hurting the country". It's very disheartening.

The way you treat Huawei will be observed very closely by other Chinese businesses. When mutual trust is undermined, it'll be difficult for the businesses to make more investments here.

So you don't need the government to say anything. I think that businesses can reach their own conclusions. So I think the trust is seriously damaged between the countries and between the governments and the businesses.

David Marsh: Will the Golden Era between Britain and China be upheld or become somewhat more tarnished?

Liu Xiaoming: The Golden Era really needs the both sides to make efforts. The Golden Era was proposed by the UK side. When President Xi Jinping was here in 2015, the UK leader proposed that we should build the Golden Era. We think this Golden Era is a reflection of the level of China-UK relationship. It is in the interests of the two countries. So we embraced this idea, we endorsed it and we agreed to this idea. So we work together to build this Golden Era. This is the fifth year of the Golden Era. I had thought we could celebrate the fifth anniversary of the Golden Era. But, you know, so many things happened. It's not because of China.

Mark Burgess from the OMFIF: We seem to have slipped into a bilateral world which I don't think helps with global trade, which we all benefit from. How do we get that balance between multilateral and bilateral back on track?

Liu Xiaoming: China is very committed to multilateralism. This year, as I said, is the 75th anniversary of the founding of the United Nations. Not many people know that China was the first country who put its signature on the UN Charter. China has been committed to the international system with the UN at the core. China has fulfilled its international obligation. China never says China comes first, and China never withdraws from any international treaties. We've signed about five hundred international treaties, and joined one hundred international organizations. We also support the WHO in playing a leading role in global response to COVID-19. And we have increased our donations to the WHO. We disagree with the United States' withdrawal from the WHO. We also support the WTO as the body superintending international trade, even though that system is not perfect. To date you cannot find a replacement.

Martine Doyon from Goldman Sachs: The question I have for you is what are the prospects and the practical steps for cooperation between China and Europe on climate change?

Liu Xiaoming: China is very committed to the Paris Agreement on climate change. This year was supposed to be the year of environmental cooperation for China and the UK. As you know, China was due to host the COP15 and UK is the host for the COP26. But because of the pandemic, we postponed these two conferences. China is working very closely with the UK online now. I just had a conversation with UK's COP26 Regional Ambassador Sir Laurie Bristow, and we want to work together to make it a new highlight, not just for China-UK relations. I think China and the UK can provide leadership on climate change, and we both want to work together to make the two conferences a great success.

Ika Hartmann from the British Chamber of Commerce in Germany: Because the EU has introduced new instruments to screen Chinese investments and enforced antitrust measures to create critical conditions for closer cooperation, it seems to me that now we've been talking in two different ways. How can you connect the two things? The EU wants to trade with China, the EU wants to keep you as strong partner. And obviously China wants to do the same, but your level of taste is just investment from Europe in China, and what we request from China in Europe is different. We don't match each other's thoughts and accountability.

Liu Xiaoming: I can say there are enormous opportunities for trade and investment collaboration with China. But the important thing is how the two sides see each other. Will they see each other as opportunities, as partners, or will they see each other as a systemic rival or a potentially hostile state? Now, look at Huawei, and the way the UK treats Huawei. It is really not about a private company. The big picture is about China. How you look at Huawei really symbolizes how you look at and treat China. You know, during the debate, we should listen to people from across the spectrum. But the decision on Huawei was made in face of pressure from these "China hawks" and "China bashers". You know, they all regard China as a hostile or a potentially hostile country. They don't trust China, so they don't trust a Chinese company. We do not want to see this economic relationship politicized. But on the other side, who has politicised our economic relations, joined the United States to sanction a Chinese company and taken China as a threat and a hostile country? How can you conduct normal business when the other side treats you as a potentially hostile country?

David Marsh: Are you saying China is generally blameless for the fact that we don't trust you? Or are you saying that there could have been things that China could have done better in order to produce more trust? You see the great difficulty from the other side for not trusting you, what could you do?

Liu Xiaoming: We have to analyze the matter case by case. Huawei has done everything they can. You know, you don't trust Huawei. You said Huawei had security problems. Then Huawei set up its own centre to analyze the security risk. And the center is managed by British people, not people from Huawei. It was British technicians who assessed the risks. Then they came to the conclusion that they believe the risk was manageable and controllable. So that's why the UK government made their decision earlier this year. Even though they gave Huawei a 35% market cap, they still think the risk is manageable. Huawei is also trying to improve their technology so as to strengthen security. And when we say security risk, it is not necessarily from a country. It may be from a group or an organization. So they want to make the UK 5G network infrastructure more secure and more resilient. They've done their best. I do not see that Huawei has anything we should complain about.

Reza Moghadam from Morgan Stanley: I have two very quick questions. First, Ambassador, you mentioned the support for the WTO both in Europe and China. But of course there is an impasse there at the moment. So my question to you is: What's China's view on WTO reform? Second, you mentioned at the outset that the very large volume of trade between China and the EU. Of course, a lot of that is in goods, but what is missing in that relationship is services. I wonder if the Ambassador has any thoughts on how to increase the volume of services trade between the EU and China. Thank you very much.

Liu Xiaoming: On the WTO, China is forthcoming in terms of engaging with the WTO, but still we have some disagreements with the European countries on how China should be treated. We still believe China is a developing country. It took China

15 years to return to the GATT and to be able to join the WTO through negotiations. It hasn't been easy. Still China has fulfilled, three years ahead of schedule, the commitment made when it joined the WTO. China is still ready to make further progress on that.

On services trade, Europe, including the UK, has its strengths and advantages. I think that's why I said, there's complementarity between China and Europe in the economy. We would like to have more European service businesses in China. If you have been following closely, China's New Foreign Investment Law came into effect at the beginning of this year. There are a lot of new policies regarding the service sector. China's service sector will be opened up wider, and many restrictions on the service sector have been lifted. More foreign banks and insurance companies are able to have more business opportunities in China. The cap has been brought down and the list of negativity has been shortened. We have also lifted the restrictions on the Qualified Foreign Institutional Investor (QFII) and the RMB Qualified Foreign Institutional Investor (RQFII).

Joel Kibazo from the African Development Bank: My question to you is that Africa is going to experience the deepest recession in 25 years. Will China, which holds a third of Africa's total external debt, be prepared to help as we go forward into what is really an unprecedented crisis?

Liu Xiaoming: Yes. China sees Africa as a good brother and good partner. I've been posted twice to Africa. I have a very strong feeling for African countries. We attach great importance to our relations with African countries. During the 73rd World Health Assembly in May, President Xi Jinping announced that China will work with the other G20 members on implementing the Debt Service Suspension Initiative for Poorest Countries. At a recent China-Africa summit on COVID-19 response, China again announced that it will exempt the interest-free debt due by the end of 2020 for African countries within the framework of the Forum on China-Africa Cooperation. In addition, China has sent many medical teams to help them fight COVID-19. We have provided them with PPEs and other most needed supplies. We have also shared experience with them. Even at the Chinese Embassy here, I worked with a British think tank to do that.

David Marsh: In terms of the writing off of debts, is it possible that China would join the Paris Club, in order to give a more formal way of rescheduling or writing off debts to the poorest countries? Is that something that China could do?

Liu Xiaoming: China has joined many multilateral arrangements on debt reduction and exemption. I think we've done more on the bilateral basis between African countries and China. We think that is more effective and more direct.

John Nugee from the OMFIF: I want to understand more on the observed change of China's international policy, its approach to international relations. What stood out for me in the last 30 years is that patience has been the watchword for China. Now we observe a change. Why has China decided to adopt a more urgent approach to many issues facing the world?

Liu Xiaoming: I would say China has not changed. You know, China is a peace loving country and peace is in the DNA of the Chinese nation. China strives very hard for world peace and stability. China benefits from a peaceful environment for the past 40 years since we opened up and implemented reform. Why should we rock the boat and why should we change course? We believe that China will continue to benefit from this peaceful environment. But I think it is the other side that has changed tremendously. China has to make a response to that. Take China-US relationship for example. We want to have a good relationship with the US. We have no reason to have a bad relationship. But it is the United States, who imposes sanctions and demonizes China. Look at this pandemic. Their President, their Secretary of State, keep on using the expression "China virus". Who has changed? I think people have to be objective with regard to change.

On Taiwan, the United States has tried to play this "Taiwan card". They increase their arms sales to Taiwan. They want to give international recognition to Taiwan. They rock the boat and we have to make response.

On Hong Kong, 23 years after the handover, "One Country, Two Systems" has been a great success. But last year, you know, there was turbulence. There was a movement for "Hong Kong independence", "self determination". They even waved the Union Jack and US flags, calling for the United States to land in Hong Kong to liberate Hong Kong. We have a reason to be worried about that and take necessary and firm measures to safeguard "One Country, Two Systems".

Sherard Cowper-Coles from HSBC: Very good to see you, Ambassador. I wanted to ask you about the disparity in understanding between Europe and China. China seems to know a lot about Europe. But there is a great gap in understanding in the UK and across Europe more generally of China and China's history, and the Chinese Communist Party. So I want to ask you, what more should we be doing to try and increase knowledge of China in Europe, particularly among those who make policy or form opinions, because there's a big deficit in understanding?

Liu Xiaoming: Thank you for sharing your question. I assume next time when I prepare my speech, I would put in a fifth deficit, namely, the understanding deficit. I quite agree with you that there's a big gap in understanding between China and Europe, mostly Western countries. So each time when some Western politicians criticize China, they always say China is widely criticized. I would say they only represent a small number of Western countries and they are not the world. Taking the National Security Law for example, more than 70 countries have shown support for this Law. And how many countries have stood against China? It's just one third of the number of countries that supported China. So I think the effective way is to engage actively with each other. I think we should not decouple from each other. That is a very bad idea. I think we need more coupling. We encourage China and Europe to nurture across-the-board engagement among the young people, the students. More Chinese students intend to study here in this country. I hope the UK will continue to be open and welcome Chinese students with open arms.

Kern Andrew from Nomura: Thank you very much, Ambassador, for your speech. I wanted to ask you about the question of interfering in the internal affairs of other nations. I understand very well the Chinese perspective and view on this and respect it. However, is it a realistic view to take in a globalised world where what happens in one country affects another? Taking for example environmental issues which you mentioned, and where China and Britain need to work together because of the upcoming conferences. What happens within China, which is a centre of biodiversity, is really very important and Britain has a real interest. China has a great interest in what happens in other countries. And when we interact, we have to speak to each other about what happens in each other's country.

Liu Xiaoming: I think both Chinese and British people are smart, clever enough to discern what are interferences in others' internal affairs, and what are suggestions and advice given with good intention. When you have complaints about environmental issues in China, we know that you want to improve China's environmental system, you want to make China's environment better. This is certainly welcomed. We can certainly identify what is advice given with a good intention and what is interference aimed at changing China's political and social system, and imposing upon China Western ideas and a Western model. As I said, we have no interest in exporting our models, but we are also strongly against foreign countries, no matter who they are, interfering in our internal affairs.

Michael Maclay from Montrose Associates: Ambassador, regarding the Huawei decision and the current bitterness and absence of trust you describe, maybe there are some specific things that China could do that would help to rebuild trust. First, for example, when the WHO team comes to China, will they be given access to the Wuhan laboratory? Secondly, might China explicitly acknowledge the principle of freedom of navigation in the South and East China Sea? And thirdly, would it still help to use the expression of "peaceful unification"?

Liu Xiaoming: On the WHO, China has been very transparent and responsible. From the very beginning, China was the first country to report a case and the first country to share the genetic sequence. We have nothing to hide and I think it is other countries that are trying to stigmatize China. WTO experts are in China right now and China is working with them. I believe the two sides will share a productive and effective cooperation. We support the WHO in playing a leading role but we have to remember two things. Firstly, research into the origin of the virus should be based on science, not on politics. Secondly, all countries should be subject to review, not only China.
On freedom of navigation, China is a country which is fully committed to the freedom of navigation. 60% of China's oil supply comes through the South China Sea. We have every reason to want to ensure peace, stability in this region and we are working very hard with the neighbouring countries, working on the DOC and the COC. And the situation would be very peaceful, were it not for some foreign naval vessels that come

here from time to time to threaten China, to infringe upon China's sovereignty.
On Taiwan, China is committed to peaceful reunification. There is no change to this principled position. I suggest you read my article on this question recently carried by *China Daily* newspaper. I wish to reaffirm that Taiwan is an inalienable part of Chinese territory. China has consistently adhered to the policy of peaceful reunification. By making no commitment to giving up the use of force, the Chinese Government is targeting external interference, and a handful of separatists who advocate "Taiwan independence" and their separatist activities. This is not aimed at our compatriots in Taiwan. China must be reunified and will be reunified. This will not be stopped by anyone or any force.

Meghnad Desai from the OMFIF: China's economy has recovered quickly following the pandemic. Does China have any plan to strengthen the status of the RMB as a possible reserve currency in the near future?

Liu Xiaoming: China is very committed to internationalization of the RMB. In the past decade, we have made many efforts in order to facilitate trade and investment. More and more countries take the RMB as not only a currency for conducting trade or investment, but also use it as a reserve currency. So I'm very pleased to see that London is now playing a leading role in the internationalization of the RMB. London now is the second largest offshore RMB clearing center, and the largest offshore RMB trading center. Hong Kong is the largest offshore RMB clearing centre, and the second largest offshore RMB trading center. I think the two cities have enormous opportunities for cooperation.

Pablo Riquelme Turrent from the BBVA: Thank you, Ambassador. I would like to hear your opinion about the future relationship with Latin America, and especially with Mexico, being so close to the United States and having this partnership with the United States and Canada. I wonder if it's going to change going forward? Is it a friendly relationship? How do you see it develop?

Liu Xiaoming: We would like to strengthen our relationship with Latin American countries. There's a mechanism between China and Latin American countries, a summit held from time to time. The relationship between China and Mexico is very strong. We are not concerned about Mexico's good relations with the United States. But we hope that the United States will not interrupt China's good relations with the Latin American countries.

John Orchard from the OMFIF: Thank you very much, Ambassador, for talking to us today. You talked at the beginning about China-Europe relations. As the UK has left the European Union, does it remain part of your Europe strategy, or is it practically part of your American strategy or something else?

Liu Xiaoming: It's up to the UK. I always argue with my British colleagues: We are not asking you to take sides between China and the United States; I'm just asking you to take the right side of the argument. That's my first point.
The second point is, I would argue that Britain can only be Great Britain when the UK has an independent foreign policy, rather than to be viewed in China or the rest of the world as just a junior partner of the United States. Look at what happened to Huawei. I do not need to elaborate the obvious. Even yesterday, President Trump said he personally pinpointed Huawei and he made great success. And look at what their Ambassador is tweeting and look at what their Secretary of State is saying after the decision was made by the UK Government. So everybody understands what the reason is behind the UK decision. When the UK wants to build a global Britain, to still exert a global influence, they really have to think deepiy about what kind of a role they are going to play, and what kind of a position they're going to take. We want to have good relations with the EU and with the UK. There's no doubt about that.

David Marsh: Ambassador, I'd like to thank you for being so frank and open with us. I do hope this won't be the last time that we have this very good conversation.

Liu Xiaoming: Thank you.

风雨过后见彩虹
——在国际能源信息论坛大会发表主旨演讲并回答提问

（2020年10月13日，中国驻英国使馆／国际能源信息论坛大会）

刘晓明： 很高兴出席此次国际能源信息论坛大会。在当前形势下，召开本届大会可谓恰逢其时。大会的主题是"能源大重启：新冠疫情、气候变化及后续"。围绕这一主题，我愿就全球气候变化与能源形势、中国引领全球气变治理和能源转型以及如何加强相关领域合作谈几点看法。

新冠肺炎疫情是百年来最严重的全球传染病大流行，给诸多行业都带来巨大冲击。在疫情背景下，气候变化与能源转型发展面临什么样的形势？我认为，主要有三个动向：

第一，气候变化与能源转型关系越来越密切。应对气候变化、推动能源转型发展，关乎人类赖以生存的地球家园，关乎人类的前途命运。极端天气频发、海平面上升、生态环境恶化、发展中国家应对能力不足、个别国家退出《巴黎协定》等气候变化挑战，都与能源行业息息相关。

第二，疫情倒逼能源转型加快发展。疫情让世界经济和能源需求按下"暂停键"，促使各国深入思考能源转型方向和路径。加强全球抗疫合作、恢复经济社会秩序与活力是当务之急。实现疫后经济绿色复苏成为国际社会共识，未来能源行业结构将日趋多元化，能源转型发展将面临更大压力。

第三，疫情启示我们要探索人与自然和谐共生之路。疫情告诉我们，人类不能再忽视大自然一次又一次的警告，不能只讲索取不讲投入，不能只讲发展不讲保护，不能只讲利用不讲修复。人与自然是命运共同体，人类要从保护自然中寻找发展机遇。只有顺应全球绿色低碳发展潮流，才能为能源行业"重启"注入动力。

在不久前举行的联合国成立75周年高级别活动上，习近平主席宣布，中国将提高国家自主贡献力度，采取更加有力的政策和措施，二氧化碳排放力争于2030年前达到峰值，努力争取2060年前实现碳中和。这是中国基于国内可持续发展内在要求和构建人类命运共同体的责任担当，是对自身气候环境政策做出的重大宣示，是向国际社会展示中国积极参与全球气变治理，引领全球绿色发展，推动全球能源转型的坚定决心。

中国将继续为推进全球气变治理做出更大贡献。中国拥有14亿多人口，是世界上最大的发展中国家，发展不平衡、不充分问题仍很突出。但中国作为负责任大国，在应对气候变化上始终"言必信，行必果"。中国全面深入落实气候变化《巴黎协定》，在节能减排等领域成绩斐然。中国2018年单位GDP碳排放强度比2005年累计降低45.8%，相当于减少二氧化碳排放52.6亿吨。2019年中国单位GDP能耗较上年降低2.6%，较2012年累计降低25.6%。中国始终坚持多边主义，积极参与全球气变治理，我们实施"一带一路"应对气候变化南南合作计划，自2012年起每年气候南南合作资金支出达7200万美元；通过"一带一路"绿色发展国际联盟等平台，为应对气候变化国际合作汇聚更多力量。

中国将继续为推动全球绿色发展做出更大贡献。中国积极倡导创新、协调、绿色、开放、共享的新发展理念，贯彻落实"绿水青山就是金山银山"重要理念，抓住新一轮科技革命和产业变革的历史性机遇，积极引领疫后世界经济"绿色复苏"。中国"十四五"规划将进一步指明绿色、循环、低碳经济的发展方向，中国统筹推进疫情防控与经济社会发展，探索以生态优先、绿色发展为导向的高质量发展新路，加速完善气候投融资体系，推广绿色生产方式和生活方式。在疫后经济恢复中，中国将培育壮大节能环保产业、清洁生产产业，促进产业和社会电气化、数字化与智能化，推动能源、交通、工业等多领域转型，继续引领全球经济走绿色和可持续发展之路。

中国将继续为促进全球能源转型做出更大贡献。中国始终坚持提高能源供给质量和效率、加快能源技术创新、推进能源市场化改革。过去10年，中国是全球可再生能源领域的最大投资国。中国已建成全球最大清洁煤电体系，深水钻探、页岩气勘探开发等技术实现重大突破，核能、风能、太阳能等新能源应用蓬勃发展，"互联网+"智慧能源等一大批能源新模式加快培育。中国积极参与国际能源合作，持续深化能源领域对外开放，海外油气、核电合作不断拓展。中国正推动落实全球能源互联网，积极开展"一带一路"能源通道建设，参与全球能源技术合作，建立双边合作机制58项，参与多边合作机制33项，在全球能源转型发展与合作中发挥中国作用、贡献中国方案。

女士们、先生们，人类社会发展史就是一部不断克服困难、战胜挑战的历史。展望未来，中国将继续应对气候变化、促进能源转型，这不仅将为全球可持续发展贡献力量，也将给包括英国在内的各国带来更多合作机遇。

一是共商全球气变和环境治理的机遇。明年是全球气变治理进程中的重要年份。不久前，习近平主席在联合国生物多样性峰会上发表讲话，指出明年在昆明举办的《生物多样性公约》第15次缔约方会议（COP15）上，中国将同各方共商全球生物多样性保护大计，共建万物和谐的美丽家园。明年英国将在格拉斯哥举办《联合国气候变化框架公约》第26次缔约方会议（COP26）。各国能源界和产业界可以参与两个大会为契机，在清洁能源、绿色金融等领域加强交流对接，充分发挥互补优势，打造更多务实合作成果。

二是共享能源开放与合作的机遇。中国致力于建设开放型世界经济，正推动形成以国内大循环为主体、国内国际双循环相互促进的新发展格局，能源开放合作是其中的重要领域。中国仍是世界上最重要、最具活力的能源消费市场和进口市场，欢迎各国企业来华投资兴业。今年11月将举办第三届进口博览会，期待包括英国在内的各国能源企业踊跃参展。欣克利角C核电项目是中、英、法合作的旗舰项目，建成后可满足英国7%的电力需求，每年可以减排900万吨二氧化碳。中英双方可以此为契机，不断深化民用核能等领域合作。

三是共促能源转型与创新的机遇。新一轮科技革命和产业革命方兴未艾，中国正积极推动绿色科技、能源、金融创新发展。中国以科技创新驱动能源事业高质量发展，以能源技术创新促进产业升级。智能电网、电动汽车、大规模储能、智慧用能等新技术新业态层出不穷，将给各国能源企业在华投资兴业带来广阔商机。

四是共建绿色"一带一路"的机遇。"一带一路"已成为规模最大的国际合作平台，绿色是"一带一路"建设的鲜明底色。中国和英国共同发布了《"一带一路"绿色投资原则》。能源企业可通过"一带一路"平台，在环保产业、节能减排、基础设施、绿色金融、金融科技等领域开拓双方、三方或多方合作的新模式，把能源转型发展更好融入全球生态环境保护和可持续发展事业之中。

女士们、先生们，西方有句谚语："Every cloud has a silver lining."（每朵乌云都镶着银边。）中国也有一句谚语，"风雨过后见彩虹"。当前人类正面对疫情蔓延的"至暗时刻"，但人类也展现出团结、勇气、决心、关爱的强大力量。中国愿与国际社会一道，坚定信心，共克时艰，共同应对气候变化挑战，共同促进能源转型发展，共同建设美好地球家园！

最后，预祝本届国际能源信息论坛大会圆满成功！

现在我愿回答主持人的提问。

主持人： 中国2060年碳中和目标对中国石油、天然气、煤炭等化石能源和可再生能源需求有何影响？

刘晓明： 中国将提高国家自主贡献力度，采取更加有力的政策和措施，二氧化碳排放力争于2030年前达到峰值，努力争取2060年前实现碳中和。中国提出2060年前实现碳中和，是一个非常有力度的积极目标，获得国际社会广泛认可。中国能源消费和经济转型、二氧化碳和温室气体减排的速度和力度，要比发达国家实现转型的速度和力度大得多。

在化石能源领域，2019年中国煤炭消费量占能源消费总量的57.7%，降至历史新低，天然气消费比重提升至7.8%。中国仍处在经济快速发展时期，许多行业和地区发展仍然依赖化石燃料。2060年碳中和目标传递了一个非常明确的信号，对于能源、交通、工业、建筑、农业无疑都具有很强的转型含义。中国将进一步发展和完善碳排放权交易市场，利用市场机制促进二氧化碳减排和企业技术创新，引领社会投资向低碳绿色产业倾斜。

在可再生能源领域，2019年中国非化石能源消费比重提升至15.3%。新能源带来的新产业蓬勃发展。截至2019年底，中国新能源汽车保有量达381万辆，约占全球总数的1/2。着眼2060年碳中和目标，中国将继续加快能源结构向清洁低碳方向转型，提高可再生能源消费比例，大力发展风能、太阳能、核能等新能源。

主持人： 如何看待疫情后中国经济快速恢复和带来的强劲能源需求？

刘晓明： 中国统筹疫情防控的同时有序推进复工复产，不断深化改革开放，经济显示出强大韧性和潜力，呈现强劲复苏势头。中国2020年第二季度GDP增速止跌回升，增长3.2%，成为世界上第一个恢复增长的主要经济体。

中国能源行业在疫情期间保证供应，为抗疫做出了重要贡献。今年上半年，中国能源消费总量同比下降0.2%，降幅较第一季度2.9%明显收窄，煤炭、石油、天然气等能源需求恢复增长。电力基建、油气管道等建设继续推进。清洁能源发电比重继续提高，上半年清洁能源发电量占全部发电量比重27.6%，比去年增长了

0.1个百分点。

中国支持"绿色复苏"理念,主张在绿色复苏进程中持续应对气候变化的长期挑战和风险。正如不久前习近平主席在联合国生物多样性峰会上的讲话中所指出的,新冠肺炎疫情对全球经济社会发展造成全面冲击,我们要着眼长远,保持定力,坚持绿色、包容、可持续发展,培育疫情后经济高质量复苏活力;要以自然之道,养万物之生,从保护自然中寻找发展机遇,实现生态环境保护和经济高质量发展双赢。

在疫情防控常态化的背景下,中方将兼顾近期任务和长期目标,统筹推进经济社会发展和应对气候变化工作。在创新、协调、绿色、开放、共享的新发展理念指导下,继续实施积极应对气候变化国家战略,持续推进国内节能和能效提升,大力推动绿色产业发展,加快补齐环境基础设施短板。

主持人: 中国为什么提高了减排目标?

刘晓明: 中国重视生态文明建设,切实履行气候变化、生物多样性等环境相关条约义务,在节能减排等领域取得巨大成就。碳中和目标是中国基于国内可持续发展内在要求和构建人类命运共同体的责任担当,对自身气候环境做出的重大宣示,展现了中国的三个"坚定决心":一是应对气候变化、走绿色低碳发展道路的坚定决心。碳中和目标为中国的中长期气候行动规划了清晰路径。中国将以绿色、低碳、可持续作为当前经济恢复、未来高质量发展的指导思想,加强应对气候变化、推进生态文明建设的战略定力绝不动摇。

二是支持多边主义的坚定决心。当前，全球气候多边进程持续受单边主义冲击，新冠肺炎疫情更为各国应对气候变化带来新挑战。中国的积极宣示为多边主义注入正能量，有力提振了国际社会应对气候变化合作的信心，是中方构建人类命运共同体理念的又一次生动体现。

三是支持《巴黎协定》履约、推进全球气候治理的坚定决心。2020年通报更新"国家自主贡献"是《巴黎协定》步入实施的重要节点。中国的宣示顺应全球加强气候行动潮流，体现了中国坚定支持《巴黎协定》履约、推进全球气候治理、与各方共建清洁美丽世界的负责任大国担当。

主持人： 中国将如何结合碳中和目标，推进建设绿色"一带一路"？"一带一路"将如何继续拓展海外伙伴关系？

刘晓明： "一带一路"不仅是经济繁荣之路，也是绿色发展之路。正如不久前习近平主席在联合国生物多样性峰会上的讲话中所指出的，生态兴则文明兴，我们要站在对人类文明负责的高度，尊重自然、顺应自然、保护自然，探索人与自然和谐共生之路，促进经济发展与生态保护协调统一。

在"一带一路"建设实践中，中国始终秉持绿色发展理念，注重与联合国《2030年可持续发展议程》对接，推动基础设施绿色低碳化建设和运营管理，在投资贸易中强调生态文明理念，加强生态环境治理、生物多样性保护和应对气候变化等领域合作。结合碳中和等减排目标，未来绿色"一带一路"可在以下三方面增进合作：

一是建立绿色机制。2019年，中国政府与42个国家的140余家中外方伙伴一道，共同发起成立了"一带一路"绿色发展国际联盟。中国将推动发展诸如现代循环农业、生物质能产业、节能环保产业、新兴信息产业、新能源产业等生态产业，构建"一带一路"绿色项目库。中国政府还成立"一带一路"环境技术交流与转移中心，促进先进生态环保技术的联合研发和推广应用。

二是加强生态环境保护。生物多样性关系人类福祉，是人类赖以生存和发展的重要基础。中国企业在承建和设计"一带一路"项目时，在促进当地经济发展的同时，充分考虑生态因素，有效保护生物多样性。例如，中国企业在巴基斯坦承建卡拉公路时，在公路沿线植树近30万棵，植草500多万平方米，在建设基础设施的同时，也为当地环境绿化做出贡献。

三是增进绿色金融合作。全球已有30多家大型金融机构签署了《"一带一路"绿色投资原则》，内容包括充分了解环境、社会和治理风险；充分披露环境信息；充分运用绿色金融工具；采用绿色供应链管理；等等。

中国将坚持开放、绿色、可持续理念，与共建国家一道建设绿色"丝绸之路"。我们实施"一带一路"应对气候变化南南合作计划，自2012年起每年气候南南合作资金支出达7200万美元；与包括英国在内的发达国家积极开展绿色"一带一路"第三方市场合作；通过"一带一路"绿色发展国际联盟等平台，为应对气候变化国际合作汇聚更多力量。

Rainbow Appears after the Storm
—— A Keynote Speech and Q&A at the Energy Intelligence Forum

On 13rd October 2020, I attended the Energy Intelligence Forum where he delivered a keynote speech entitled "Address Climate Change and Advance Energy Transition to Make Our Planet a Better Home for All" and answered questions raised by the moderator of the event.
The following is the transcript of the speech and Q&A.

Liu Xiaoming: It is a real delight to join you at the Energy Intelligence Forum.
Taking up the theme of "The Big Energy Reset: COVID, Climate, Consequences", today's Forum could not be more timely. Let me take this opportunity to share with you my views on the theme of the forum. I will focus on three questions:
• How do we assess the current situation in energy and climate change?
• What will China do?
• How can we strengthen cooperation to address climate change and promote energy transition?
COVID-19 has been the most challenging pandemic in the past century. It has dealt a severe blow to many trades and industries. Against this backdrop, what is the situation like with regard to climate change and energy transition? In my opinion, there are three major trends:
First, the connection between climate change and energy transition is increasingly close.
Addressing climate change and promoting energy transition matter a great deal to the planet Earth upon which mankind relies on for survival. In other words, how these issues are addressed holds the key to our future.
Today, we are faced with many climate change challenges, from frequent extreme weather events to the rising sea level, from the deterioration of the eco-environment and the inadequate response from developing countries to the withdrawal of a particular country from the Paris Agreement. All these challenges can be traced back to the energy industry.

Second, COVID-19 is accelerating the energy transition.

COVID-19 has pressed the "pause" button on the world economy and on energy demand, prompting countries of the world to reflect on the direction and routes the of energy transition.

The most urgent task of the day is enhancing global cooperation on fighting COVID-19, restoring the economic and social order and injecting fresh vitality. Pursuing green economic recovery has become the consensus of the international community in the post-pandemic world. The structure of the energy industry will become more diversified and this will put further pressure on energy companies to seek development through transition.

Third, COVID-19 has highlighted the need for harmonious coexistence between man and nature.

The pandemic sounded the alarm. Mankind must stop ignoring the repeated warnings from nature, stop taking without giving back, stop development at the expense of conservation, and stop utilization without rehabilitation.

Man and nature share a common future. So it is in conservation that we must explore opportunities for development. Only by following the trend of green and low-carbon development can we find the driving force to "restart" the energy industry.

Last month, at a high-level UN meeting in commemoration of the 75th anniversary of the founding of that organization, President Xi Jinping announced that China will:

- scale up its nationally determined contribution,
- adopt even more forceful policies and measures,
- and strive to peak carbon dioxide emissions before 2030 and achieve carbon neutrality before 2060.

This attests to the audacity of China in taking up responsibilities in line with the requirements of sustainable domestic development and the goal of building a community with a shared future for mankind.

It is a major policy announcement on climate change.

It is also a display of China's strong resolve to play an active part in global governance on climate change, to take the lead in global green development and to promote global energy transition.

China will make a greater contribution to advancing global governance on climate change.

With a population of 1. 4 billion, China is the world's largest developing country. It is faced with outstanding issues of imbalance and inadequacy in its development.

However, as a responsible global player, China always honors its promises on tackling climate change.

China has implemented the Paris Agreement and achieved remarkable outcomes in energy conservation and emissions reduction.

- From 2005 to 2018, China reduced its carbon intensity by 45.8%, cutting CO2 emissions by 5.26 billion tons.
- In 2019, China's energy consumption per unit GDP was down by 2.6% from the level of the previous year and by 25.6% from the level of 2012.

Committed as it is to multilateralism, China has been playing an active part in global governance on climate change.

- China has implemented the South-South Cooperation Initiative on Climate Change under the framework of the Belt and Road. Starting from 2012, China has spent $72 million on South-South cooperation in the field of climate change every year.
- China has also worked on pooling international efforts for cooperation on climate change via platforms such as the BRI International Green Development Coalition.

China will make a greater contribution to promoting green development in the world.

China advocates a new development concept, namely one that is innovative, coordinated, green, open and shared development. We are committed to the belief that "clear water and green mountains are mountains of gold and silver". We are seizing the historic opportunities of the new round of scientific and technological revolution and industrial transformation, and playing an active and leading role in the "green economic recovery" in the post-pandemic world.

China's 14th Five Year Plan will map out routes towards building a green, circular and low-carbon economy. This includes:

- a coordinated approach to epidemic response and economic and social development.
- a new path of high-quality development which gives priority to ecological conservation and is led by green technologies.
- an improved system of investment and financing for tackling climate change.
- and promotion of green production and green way of life.

In pursuing post-pandemic economic recovery, China will:

- foster and strengthen energy conservation, environmental protection and clean production industries,

- increase the industrial and domestic use of electronic, digital and smart technologies,
- promote transformation in multiple areas, including energy and transportation,
- and continue to be a global leader in green and sustainable growth.

China will make greater contribution to promoting global energy transition.

China has been committed to improving the quality and efficiency of energy supply, accelerating innovation in energy technology, and advancing market-based reform in the area of energy.

In the past decade, China has become the world's largest investor in renewable energy. We have:

- built the largest network of clean coal power generation,
- made important breakthroughs in deepwater drilling and shale gas exploration and development,
- encouraged the thriving application of new energy, including nuclear, wind and solar energy,
- and fostered "internet plus" and smart energy and other new business models.

China has also taken an active part in international energy cooperation.

- China is opening its energy sector wider to the world and keeps expanding cooperation with other countries in oil, gas and nuclear energy.
- China is implementing the Global Energy Internet, playing an active part in the development of energy routes along the Belt and Road, and participating in global cooperation on energy technology.
- China has established 58 bilateral mechanisms and participated in 33 multilateral mechanisms for cooperation.

In a word, China has played its part and contributed its solution to global development and cooperation in energy transition.

Ladies and Gentlemen:

The history of mankind is a history of difficulties overcome and challenges tackled. Going forward, China will continue to address climate change and promote energy transition. This will not only contribute to sustainable growth in the world. It will also create more opportunities for cooperation with other countries, including the UK.

First, opportunities for global governance on climate change and environment

Next year will be an important one for global governance on climate change.

In his speech at the UN Summit on Biodiversity last month, President Xi Jinping said that at the COP15 to be held in Kunming next year, China and the other participating parties would discuss and draw up plans together for protecting global biodiversity, and turn Earth into a beautiful homeland for all creatures to live in harmony.

Next year the UK will host the COP26 in Glasgow.

These two conferences will create opportunities for the energy and industrial communities of the world to enhance cooperation and foster greater synergy in areas such as clean energy and green finance. By combining their complementary strengths, the participating parties will be able to deliver concrete outcomes.

Second, there are opportunities for greater openness and cooperation in the energy sector

China is committed to building an open world economy. Its current "dual circulation" model emphasizes domestic demand and encourages mutual complementarities between domestic and international demand. In this new development model, open cooperation in energy is an integral part.

China remains the world's most important and vigorous market for energy consumption and import. China will continue to be open to investment from all over the world. In November, China will host the third International Import Expo, the CIIE, where we hope to see energy businesses from all countries, including the UK.

The Hinkley Point C nuclear power station is a flagship project of China-UK-France cooperation. Upon completion, it will meet 7% of the UK's total demand for electricity and help to eliminate 9 million tons of CO_2 emissions every year. It points to further opportunities for China and the UK to deepen cooperation in the civil application of nuclear energy.

Third, there are opportunities in energy transition and innovation

As the new round of scientific and technological revolution and industrial transformation unfolds, China is making vigorous efforts to promote innovation in green technology, and the energy and financial services.

Scientific innovation drives the high-quality development of the energy industry, and new energy technologies will lead to the upgrading of the entire sector.

The development of new technologies and new business models in China, such as the smart grid, electric vehicles, large-capacity power storage and smart energy, will create enormous opportunities for energy businesses from all countries.

Fourth, there are opportunities for building a green Belt and Road

The Belt and Road Initiative, or the BRI, has become the world's largest platform for international cooperation. The colour green is the salient background of the BRI development roadmap.

China and the UK have jointly issued the Green Investment Principles for the Belt and Road.

Via the BRI platform, energy companies can expand bipartisan, tripartite and multi-party cooperation in the areas of environmental protection, energy conservation, emissions reduction, infrastructure development, green finance and FinTech.

Through such cooperation, energy transition will be better integrated into the global efforts in the fields of ecological conservation, environment protection and sustainable development.

Ladies and Gentlemen:

A Western saying goes, "Every cloud has a silver lining". A similar Chinese saying goes, "Rainbow appears after the storm".

In the "darkest hour" of the raging pandemic, mankind has displayed strength through solidarity, courage, determination and love.

China stands ready to work with the international community to shore up confidence and tide over the hard times. Together we can address climate change and advance energy transition to make our planet a better home for all.

In conclusion, I wish the Energy Intelligence Forum great success!

Thank you!

Now I would like to take your questions.

Moderator: What does 2060 carbon neutrality mean for energy demand in China? Where does this leave fossil fuels—oil, gas, and coal—and renewables?

Liu Xiaoming: China will scale up its nationally determined contributions, adopt even more forceful policies and measures, strive to reach a peak in CO_2 emissions before 2030, and achieve carbon neutrality before 2060. Achieving carbon neutrality by 2060 is a very forceful and positive target. It has been widely recognized by the international community. The energy and economic transition and the reduction of CO_2 and greenhouse gas emissions in China are occurring much faster and with greater intensity than in the developed countries.

As to fossil fuels, China's coal consumption accounted for 57.7% of its total energy consumption in 2019, dropping to a record low. Natural gas has taken a larger share of 7.8% in the energy mix. However, China is still at a stage of rapid economic development, and many industries and regions continue to rely on fossil fuels. The 2060 carbon neutrality target is sending a very clear signal, undoubtedly pushing for transition and upgrading in sectors like energy, transportation, manufacturing, construction and agriculture. China will further develop and improve the carbon emission trading market to allow market-based incentives to do the job of promoting CO_2 emission reduction and corporate technological innovation and channeling investment toward low-carbon, green industries.

As to renewables, the proportion of non-fossil fuels in China's total energy consumption increased to 15.3% in 2019. New industries attendant upon the development of new energy are booming. By the end of 2019, the number of "new energy" vehicles (NEVs) in China reached 3.81 million, accounting for roughly one-half of the global total. Focusing on the 2060 carbon neutrality target, China will continue to promote clean and low-carbon components in its energy structure, increase the proportion of renewables in total energy consumption, and vigorously promote the application of new energy sources including wind, solar, and nuclear energy.

Moderator: How do you view China's remarkable economic recovery after the coronavirus outbreak and its strong energy demand growth?

Liu Xiaoming: While coordinating epidemic prevention and control efforts, China has been taking measures to restart the economy in an orderly manner and to continue deepening the reform and opening up. The Chinese economy has shown remarkable resilience and huge potential. The momentum for recovery is strong. GDP increased by 3.2% in the second quarter of 2020, bringing the economic contraction to an end. China became the world's first major economy to resume growth.

China's energy industry has made important contribution to the victory over COVID-19 by ensuring supply throughout. In the first half of the year, China's total energy consumption fell by 0.2% compared with the same period last year, which came down significantly from the 2.9% decline in the first quarter. Demand for coal, oil and natural gas rebounded. The construction of energy infrastructure, including electricity facilities and oil and gas pipelines, resumed. The proportion of electricity generated by clean energy has increased, accounting for 27.6% of the total in the first half of the year and rising by 0.1% over the same period last year.

China supports the concept of green recovery. Tackling the challenges and risks of climate change is a long-term, ongoing endeavour that can only be made in the process of green recovery. In his recent speech at the United Nations Summit on Biodiversity, President Xi Jinping said that:

"Globally, the coronavirus has wreaked havoc on every aspect of economic and social development. We need to have our eyes fixed on the long run, have determination and stay the course for green, inclusive and sustainable development."

"Recognizing that 'our solutions lie in Nature', we could strive to find development opportunities while preserving Nature, and achieve win-win in both ecological conservation and high-quality economic development."

Pandemic control has become the "new normal". China will take into account both short-term tasks and long-term goals, and coordinate economic and social development with addressing climate change. Under the guidance of the new development concept, namely "innovative, coordinated, green, open and shared development", China will continue to take vigorous measures to implement the national climate change strategy, to enhance energy conservation and efficiency, to promote the development of green industries and strengthen the weak links in environmental infrastructure as quickly as possible.

Moderator: Why has China stepped up its goals on emission reduction?

Liu Xiaoming: China attaches great importance to advancing ecological civilization. We take our obligations under environment-related treaties seriously, including those on climate change and biodiversity. China has made great achievements in the fields of energy saving and emission reduction. The goal of carbon neutrality is a major policy announcement concerning climate and the environment. It is based on the inherent requirements of domestic sustainable development in China and the responsibility of building a community with a shared future for mankind. It demonstrates China's three "firm determinations":

The first determination is to tackle climate change and firmly adopt the path of green and low-carbon development. The goal of carbon neutrality points to a clear path for China's mid-to-long-term climate action. China will take green, low-carbon and sustainable development as the guideline for its current economic recovery and future high-quality development. China will never waver in its strategic determination to strengthen response to climate change and advance ecological conservation.

The second determination is to firmly support multilateralism. Currently, the global multilateral climate process still faces challenges from unilateralism. COVID-19 has posed new challenges to the countries of the world in their response to climate change. By stepping up its goals on emission reduction, China is injecting positive impetus into multilateralism and boosting international confidence in tackling climate change. This is another vivid manifestation of China's commitment to building a community with a shared future for mankind.

The third determination is to resolutely support the implementation of the Paris Agreement and to strongly promote global climate governance. The submission of updated NDCs in 2020 is an important juncture for the implementation of the Paris Agreement. China's announcement is in line with the global trend of strengthening climate action. It reflects China's firm support for implementing the Paris Agreement, promoting global climate governance and working with all parties to build a clean and beautiful world.

Moderator: After President Xi's speech on carbon neutrality, can we expect the BRI to become greener with the latest commitments? Where does China see growth for its overseas partnerships?

Liu Xiaoming: The BRI is not only a road to economic prosperity but also a road to green development. As President Xi Jinping pointed out in his speech at the United Nations Summit on Biodiversity,
"A sound ecosystem is essential for the prosperity of civilization. We need to take up our lofty responsibility for the entire human civilization, and we need to respect nature, follow its laws and protect it. We need to find a way to ensure harmonious coexistence between man and Nature, a way to balance and coordinate economic development and ecological protection."

China has always adhered to the green concept in BRI development, focusing on its integration with the UN 2030 Agenda for Sustainable Development, promoting green and low-carbon infrastructure and operation management, emphasizing ecological conservation in investment and trade, and strengthening cooperation in the fields of ecological environment governance, biodiversity protection and climate change. In line with the carbon neutrality and other emission reduction targets, we could promote a greener BRI cooperation in three aspects:

The first is to establish a green mechanism. In 2019, China jointly initiated the BRI International Green Development Coalition with more than 140 partners in 42 countries. China will promote the development of conservation industries such as modern recycling agriculture and industries based on bioenergy, energy conservation, environmental protection, information technology and new energy industries with a view to setting up a BRI green project pool. The Chinese government has also established Belt and Road Environmental Technology and Transfer Centre to promote the joint R&D and application of advanced eco-friendly technologies.

The second is to strengthen ecological conservation. Biodiversity impacts upon human well-being and is an important foundation for human survival and development. In designing and constructing BRI projects, Chinese enterprises fully considered biodiversity and conservation needs as well as economic development. For example, when Chinese companies built Karachi-Lahore Highway in Pakistan, they planted nearly 300, 000 trees and more than 5 million square meters of grassland along the road. Along with new road infrastructure, they also contributed to the local environment.

The third is to enhance cooperation in green finance. More than 30 large financial institutions around the world have signed the "Green Investment Principles for the Belt and Road", which includes a full understanding of the environmental, social and governance (ESG) risks; full disclosure of environmental information; making full use of green financial tools; adopting green supply chain management, etc.

China will adhere to the concept of open, green and sustainable development, and work with BRI partners to build a green "silk road".

We have implemented the Belt and Road South-South Cooperation Initiative on Climate Change. Since 2012, the annual expenditure for South-South climate cooperation has reached 72 million U. S. dollars.

We have actively carried out third-party market cooperation with developed countries including the United Kingdom on building a green Belt and Road.

We will pool more efforts in international cooperation on climate change via platforms such as Belt and Road International Alliance for Green Development.

俄罗斯塔斯社专访

Interview with TASS

2023年3月26日至4月18日，我开展新一轮"穿梭外交"，先后访问瑞士、英国、比利时（欧盟总部）、德国、法国、俄罗斯。访问俄罗斯期间，我于4月17日接受塔斯社副总编尤莉亚·沙里夫林娜的专访，回答了有关朝鲜半岛局势、中俄关系、中美关系、亚洲地区形势、中国国防政策、乌克兰危机、台湾问题等提问。塔斯社用俄文发表专访实录全文，并分别用英文和中文发表专访详细新闻稿。以下是专访俄文实录中译文和英文详细新闻稿。

朝鲜半岛问题必须标本兼治
——接受俄罗斯塔斯社专访
（2023年4月17日，俄罗斯塔斯社总部）

沙里夫林娜： 你认为在当前紧张局势下，朝韩之间是否有可能发生军事冲突？

刘晓明： 很高兴在访问莫斯科期间接受你的专访。莫斯科是我此次出访的最后一站。我已经访问了6个国家，共24天。第一站是瑞士，参加了"采尔马特东北亚安全问题圆桌会议"。在那里，我会见了瑞士外交部国务秘书。然后我去了英国、布鲁塞尔欧盟总部、德国、法国，与政府高官会谈。现在来到了莫斯科，这是我的最后一站，也是压轴之站。

我此访是在朝鲜半岛局势出现新的紧张背景下进行的。半岛局势再度紧张，事出有因。一方面，我们听到西方国家——包括欧美国家——抱怨朝鲜自去年以来进行了一系列导弹发射，但另一方面，我们看到韩国和美国进行了五年来最大规模的军事演习。朝鲜半岛紧张局势持续升级，这是我们关切的问题。我此访的目的就是与欧洲和俄罗斯同行分享中方对朝鲜半岛局势的看法，共同寻找推动半岛问题政治解决的办法。

首先，需要让欧洲和俄罗斯同时清楚地了解中方如何看待当前朝鲜半岛的局势。美国总是指责朝鲜制造紧张局势，但应当看到另一方面。我们从美国进行了最大规模的军事演习，看到了导致局势紧张的原因。其次，朝鲜半岛局势不稳定的一个很重要的原因，也就是半岛问题的根源，恰恰是美国没有对朝鲜的安全关切给予应有的重视。他们不断施加压力，遏制朝鲜的发展，军事上威胁，政治上施压，经济上制裁。因此，对朝鲜半岛问题必须标本兼治。一方面，我们需要各方保持克制和理智，相向而行，缓和紧张局势。另一方面，我们必须解决这个问题的根源，即半岛和平机制的缺失。

今年是朝鲜半岛停战协议签署70周年，但迄今为止，半岛仍未建立任何和平机制。由于缺乏和平机制，紧张局势持续升级，危害半岛的和平与稳定。

按照我们的设想，我们需要在兼顾各方关切的情况下，逐步推进半岛无核化和建立和平机制。

朝韩是血浓于水的同胞兄弟，是半岛真正的主人。中国历来支持朝韩改善关系、推进和解合作。希望朝韩继续秉持民族大义，排除外部干扰，通过对话加强理解、增进互信。

沙里夫林娜： 你如何看待中美关系的现状？华盛顿对于北京是竞争对手、敌人还是商业合作伙伴？

刘晓明： 我们始终认为，一个健康稳定的中美关系，不仅有利于两国人民，也有利于全世界的和平与繁荣。中国国家主席习近平指出，中美能否处理好彼此关系，攸关世界前途命运。中美关系不是一道是否搞好的选择题，而是一道如何搞好的必答题。

不幸的是，美国将中国视为其主要对手和最大的地缘政治挑战。美国对华认知和定位出现了严重偏差，他们制定了投资、结盟、竞争的对华战略。我们始终按照习近平主席提出的相互尊重、和平共处、合作共赢的原则致力于推动中美关系健康稳定发展。但与此同时，如果我们的国家主权、国家尊严和领土完整受到侵犯，我们将坚决捍卫我国主权、安全和发展利益。

沙里夫林娜： 北京在军事层面如何应对和防范华盛顿影响亚洲地区稳定的图谋？

刘晓明： 美国已公开声称要"塑造中国的周边战略环境"。他们提出所谓"印太战略"，表面上标榜自由开放，实际上是在拼凑小集团、小圈子，目的是围堵中国，遏制中国的发展。在东北亚，美国、韩国和日本持续进行大规模军事演习，导致朝鲜半岛局势紧张。东南亚也正在举行美菲联合军事演习，有12000名美军参加。美国一再违反一个中国原则，"以台制华"，造成台海局势紧张。他们还不断在南海制造事端。

美国和英国还向无核武器国家澳大利亚转让核潜艇，构成严重核扩散风险，使得这个地区的和平与稳定受到严重威胁。事实证明，美国是地区和平与稳定的最大麻烦制造者和最大破坏者。

面对复杂多变的地区形势和不太平的周边环境，我们需要共商共建共享的发展之犁，同样需要捍卫自主发展成果的和平之剑。中国坚定不移走和平发展道路，坚定奉行防御性国防政策，始终以实际行动维护世界和平、促进共同发展，推动构建人类命运共同体。但是，为捍卫主权和领土完整及来之不易的发展成果，我们需要加强国防，需要建设一支世界一流军队，这对于区域及全球安全而言十分必要。

沙里夫林娜： 中国国家主席习近平此前要求中国人民解放军加强练兵备战，上述表态表明了什么？

刘晓明： 非常感谢你关注习近平主席的讲话。就在6天前，习近平主席到中国人民解放军南部战区海军视察调研，他强调要贯彻新时代党的强军思想，贯彻新时代军事战略方针，深化练兵备战，加快转型建设，全面提高部队现代化水平，坚决完成党和人民赋予的各项任务。

中国坚持走和平发展道路，奉行防御性的国防政策，始终是世界和平的建设者、全球发展的贡献者、国际秩序的维护者。翻开历史，可以看到中国人民是爱好和平的人民。新中国成立70多年来，中国从未主动挑起过一场战争，从未侵占过别人一寸土地。中国军力的增长完全是世界和平力量的增长。中国军队积极参加联合国维和、亚丁湾护航、人道主义救援等行动，努力为世界提供更多的公共安全产品。中国和中国军队维护世界和平与繁荣的积极贡献有目共睹，赢得了国际社会广泛赞誉。

当前，全球局势面临多重挑战，中国军队加强练兵备战，做好军事斗争准备，是确保本国、区域及全球安全的必要保障。中国还没有实现国家统一，中国发展军力旨在维护国家主权和领土完整，捍卫国家安全和发展利益。中国无论发展到什么程度，永远不称霸、永远不搞扩张，将继续努力为建设持久和平、普遍安全、共同繁荣、开放包容、清洁美丽的美好世界做出应有贡献。

沙里夫林娜： 美国警告对俄武器供应等同踩美"红线"，中方对上述警告是否担心？所谓对俄供武当前是否存在？

刘晓明： 中国在军品出口问题上始终秉持慎重和负责任的态度。与美国等西方国家在乌克兰危机中拱火浇油形成鲜明对照，我们提供的是和平解决方案。我想强调，中国不是乌克兰危机的制造者，也不是危机的当事方，更没有向冲突的任何一方提供武器。美国没有资格对中国发号施令，我们也从不接受美国对中俄关系指手画脚甚至胁迫施压。

沙里夫林娜： 不久前"中国气球"出现在美领空，你对此有何评论？它们的用途是什么？

刘晓明： 近期中美关系中所谓的无人飞艇事件，实际上是美国制造的一场政治闹剧。一艘中国用于气象和其他科研的民用无人飞艇，受超强西风带影响，加之自身控制能力有限，偏离了预定轨道进入美国上空。这原本是一起因不可抗力导致的偶发、意外事件，连美国国防部也说对美地面和人员构不成任何威胁。中方本着负责任的态度，第一时间向美方和国际社会介绍了情况，要求美方以理性、冷静和专业态度与中方一道妥善处理。但美方无视基本事实，悍然出动战机，用导弹将其击落。这种行为匪夷所思，近乎歇斯底里，是百分百的滥用武力，明显违反惯例和有关国际公约，这不能证明美国的强大，而恰恰说明它的虚弱。

我们就此向美方提出强烈抗议，要求美方拿出诚意，改弦更张，正视并解决事件给中美关系造成的损害。如果美方一意孤行，我们将奉陪到底。一切后果由美方承担。

沙里夫林娜： 如何评价台湾周边局势？能说今年不会发生冲突吗？

刘晓明： 台海局势紧张的根源在于岛内"台独"势力与外国势力勾结，不断挑战一个中国原则。

近期，他们进行了一系列破坏一个中国原则、危害台海稳定的活动，包括佩洛西窜访台湾和蔡英文窜访美国。

台湾自古以来就是中国不可分割的一部分，从来没有也永远不会成为一个国家——这是台湾问题的基本事实。两岸和平统一是中国人民的共同心愿，是实现中华民族伟大复兴的重要组成部分。我们愿以最大的诚意、尽最大的努力来实现和平统一。邓小平先生最早提出用"一国两制"解决台湾问题，随着时间的推移我们用"一国两制"解决了香港和澳门回归问题。实践证明"一国两制"在港澳地区是行之有效的。因此，我们有信心这个构想在台湾也会取得成功。

"一国"就是"一个中国"。"一国"是"一国两制"的前提，是基础中的基础。我们努力在"一国两制"下实现和平统一，同时保留采取一切必要措施维护我国主权和领土完整，包括我们从来没有承诺不使用武力。如果我们做了这个承诺，和平统一就根本不可能了。

我们这一立场不是针对广大台湾同胞，而是针对极少数"台独"分裂分子和企图分裂我国的外部势力。

你问，今年台海会不会发生军事冲突。我认为，与其预测台海会发生什么，不如向世界各国强调坚持一个中国原则。

一个中国原则是台海稳定与和平的"定海神针"。只要遵守这一原则，台海地区的和平与稳定就有保障，两岸就能实现和平发展。否则，台海将无宁日。我们已经看到，正是佩洛西窜台和台湾当局领导人窜美造成了台海局势的紧张不定。

沙里夫林娜： 还有外交手段可以解决这个问题吗？北京是否认为有可能对台湾发动特别军事行动？

刘晓明： 在世界大国中，中国是唯一尚未实现国家统一的国家，实现祖国统一是全体中国人民的共同愿望，也是中国宪法的明确规定。"和平统一、一国两制"这一基本方针，最符合包括台湾同胞在内的中华民族的整体利益。这是和平的方案、民主的方案、善意的方案、共赢的方案，是解决两岸制度不同的最现实、最宽容的方案。

你问，是否可以通过外交途径解决这个问题，我要强调的是，台湾问题是中国的内政，不是外交问题。如果你所说的外交手段是指和平方式，那么我认为"一国两制"正是解决这一问题的和平方案。

正如我已经说过的，我们努力实现和平统一的同时，保留采取一切必要措施维护国家主权和领土完整。这不是针对广大台湾同胞，而是针对极少数"台独"分子和境外分裂势力，因为他们的行为违反了中国宪法，违反了中国《反分裂国家法》。我们将依法制止"台独"分裂活动，捍卫国家主权和领土完整，维护台海地区和平稳定。这是我们神圣的权利。

Addressing Both Symptoms and Causes of the Korean Peninsula Issue
——An Interview with TASS Russian New's Agency

(17th April 2023,TASS Headquarters)

The following news release was distributed by TASS.
According to the Special Representative of the Chinese Government on Korean Peninsula Affairs Liu Xiaoming, "the United States has publicly declared its readiness to shape the strategic environment around China."
The United States is de facto engaged in nuclear proliferation in the Asian region, including its unlawful transfer of nuclear submarines to Australia, The Special Representative of the Chinese Government on Korean Peninsula Affairs Liu Xiaoming has told TASS in an interview.
"As far as Australia is concerned, the United States and the United Kingdom are transferring submarines to Australia. In essence, this constitutes a serious risk of nuclear proliferation and poses a serious threat to peace and stability in this region. In fact this shows that the US is the biggest troublemaker for regional peace and security," he said.
According to the Chinese official, "the United States has publicly declared its readiness to shape the strategic environment around China."
"They have put forward the Indo-Pacific strategy under the pretext of promoting freedom and openness, but in reality this is just an attempt to pull together small groups and exclusive blocs to contain China's development," Liu Xiaoming said.
"In North-East Asia, the United States, South Korea and Japan continue to hold large-scale military exercises that stir tensions on the Korean Peninsula. And in Southeast Asia, the United States is also conducting joint military exercises with the Philippines, with the participation of 12, 000 US servicemen. The United States repeatedly stokes tension in the South China Sea as well," he added.
Moreover, Liu Xiaoming continued, "the Americans are attempting to use Taiwan for containing China by playing the Taiwan card, resulting in tensions in the Taiwan Strait."
At the same time, China is "firmly committed to the path of peaceful development

and a defensive national defence policy, and, through its concrete actions, promotes world peace, common development and the building of a community with a shared future for mankind. "

"On the one hand, we need to promote development on the basis of extensive discussion, joint contribution and shared benefits, " he said. "But, on the other hand, we also need an army for peace that defends the fruits of our independent development. "

"In a nutshell, we need to strengthen national defence and create a world-class military, to defend the sovereignty, territorial integrity and the hard-won development achievements of our country, " Liu Xiaoming said. "This is also necessary for the security of our region and the entire world. "

Washington fanning Ukraine crisis, while Beijing proposes peace plan - Chinese envoy

"The Chinese side always takes a prudent and responsible approach to the export of military products, Special Representative of the Chinese Government on Korean Peninsula Affairs," Liu Xiaoming said.

The United States has been fanning the conflict in Ukraine, while China has come up with a peace plan, a senior Chinese diplomat said in an interview with TASS.

"The Chinese side always takes a prudent and responsible approach to the export of military products. Unlike the United States and other Western nations, who have been adding fuel to the fire in the Ukrainian crisis, we put forward a peace plan to resolve it, " said Liu Xiaoming, the Special Representative of the Chinese Government on Korean Peninsula Affairs.

In late February, the Chinese Foreign Ministry published a position paper on a political settlement of the crisis in Ukraine. The twelve-point document includes calls for a ceasefire, respect for the legitimate interests of all countries in the field of security, settlement of the humanitarian crisis in Ukraine, the exchange of prisoners of war between Moscow and Kiev, as well as the cancellation of unilateral sanctions imposed without a corresponding decision of the UN Security Council.

In the published document, China described dialogue and negotiations as the sole way of resolving the crisis in Ukraine and called on all parties to support Moscow and Kiev in "working in the same direction", urging a resumption of direct dialogue as soon as possible. The international community should create conditions and platforms for the resumption of talks, the document emphasized.

China cannot pledge to abstain from using force against separatists on Taiwan, says

envoy

"We strive to achieve peaceful reunification, but we reserve the right to take all necessary measures to protect our country's sovereignty and territorial integrity, " the Special Representative of the Chinese Government on Korean Peninsula Affairs Liu Xiaoming stressed.

"China reserves the right to take all necessary measures to protect its sovereignty and territorial integrity, and makes no promises to abstain from using force against separatists on Taiwan," Liu Xiaoming, the Special Representative of the Chinese Government on Korean Peninsula Affairs said in an interview with TASS.

"One country, means one China, and one country is the precondition of 'One Country, Two Systems' and the foundation upon which everything else, rests. We strive to achieve peaceful reunification under 'One Country, Two Systems', but we reserve the right to take all necessary measures to protect our country's sovereignty and territorial integrity. In particular, we have never promised not to use force. Had we made such a promise, peaceful reunification would have become absolutely impossible, " he pointed out.

"However, this position of ours is not directed against our Taiwan compatriots; it is a tiny number of 'Taiwan independence' separatists and other external forces seeking to divide our country that it is against, " the Chinese special envoy explained.

When asked about the likelihood of a military conflict around Taiwan breaking out this year, Liu noted that, in his view, "it's better to stress to all countries around the world about the importance of upholding the one-China principle. "

"The One-China principle is the anchor for stability and peace in the Taiwan Strait. As long as the principle is observed, peace and stability will be ensured in the Taiwan Strait, as well as peaceful development on both shores. Otherwise, the Taiwan Strait would plunge into instability. We can also see that it was the visit made by [former US House Speaker Nancy] Pelosi to Taiwan and the visit by the head of the Taiwan authorities to the US that gave rise to tension, " the Chinese envoy emphasized.

China not supplying weapons to Russia, Ukraine - special envoy

Liu Xiaoming also noted that the US had no right to issue orders to Beijing on its relations with Russia.

"China has never supplied weapons to Russia or Ukraine, but Beijing does not countenance blackmail and will not bow to orders issued by the US," Liu Xiaoming, the Special Representative of the Chinese Government on Korean Peninsula Affairs said in an interview with TASS.

"I would like to reiterate that China is neither the instigator of nor a party to the Ukrainian crisis and it has never supplied weapons to either of the parties to the Ukrainian conflict, " he pointed out.

The envoy also noted that the US had no right to issue orders to Beijing. " We won't accept any kind of lecturing or blackmail from the United States, " Liu added.

Chinese envoy points finger at negative US role in stoking escalation on Korean Peninsula

Liu Xiaoming criticized the United States for not having paid due attention to the DPRK's security concerns.

"Beijing is extremely concerned about the escalation of tensions on the Korean Peninsula, with the United States playing a negative role by holding joint drills with ROK," Liu Xiaoming, Beijing's Special Representative on Korean Peninsula Affairs said in an interview with TASS.

"My trip to European countries and Russia comes against the backdrop of the latest changes on the Korean Peninsula. On the one hand, we often hear Westerners - both Europeans and Americans - complain that since last year the DPRK has conducted a number of missile launches, while on the other hand, we can see that the ROK and the Americans held the largest drills over the past five years on the peninsula, " the senior Chinese diplomat lamented. "The escalation of tensions on the Korean Peninsula is ongoing, and this makes us very concerned, " he added.

Liu also criticized the United States for not having paid due attention to the DPRK's security concerns.

"First of all, I shall try to give my European and Russian counterparts a clear understanding of how China views the situation. The US always blames the DPRK for causing tensions, but there is another reason that is worth noting. We see the reason as stemming from the US conducting such major military exercises. Second, a very important cause of instability on the Korean Peninsula, and of the Korean Peninsula becoming an issue, is that the United States has not paid due attention to the DPRK's concerns in the field of security and has imposed economic sanctions, " the Chinese envoy said. "They continue to increase pressure and contain the DPRK's development; they exert political pressure and have imposed economic sanctions, " he added.

According to Liu, the goal of his tour is to share the Chinese assessment of the situation on the Korean Peninsula with his counterparts and to find a recipe for promoting a political settlement jointly with his European and Russian counterparts.

The senior Chinese diplomat said Moscow was the last stop on his 24-day foreign itinerary during which he said he had already visited Switzerland, Great Britain, Brussels, Germany and France.

Liu urged efforts to ease tensions on the Korean Peninsula. "Amid the lack of a peace mechanism, the escalation of tensions is ongoing, which threatens peace and stability on the Korean Peninsula, " he concluded.

Chinese envoy does not see sovereign future for Taiwan

"From time immemorial, Taiwan has been an integral part of China; it has never been a country and it will never become one, " Liu Xiaoming emphasized.

"Taiwan is an inseparable part of China and will never become a country," Liu Xiaoming, Beijing's Special Representative on Korean Peninsula Affairs, said in an interview with TASS.

Forces seeking independence for Taiwan have lately colluded with external forces, the senior Chinese diplomat explained. "They have conducted a number of activities that threaten stability in the Taiwan Strait and violate the One-China principle, " he said, referring to the visit of then-US House Speaker Nancy Pelosi to Taiwan as well as the visit by head of Taiwan authorities Tsai Ing-wen to the United States.

"From time immemorial, Taiwan has been an integral part of China; it has never been a country and it will never become one, " the envoy emphasized.

Liu reiterated that the peaceful reunification of the two shores of the Taiwan Strait was "the common aspiration of the Chinese people and an important component of the nation's rejuvenation. " "We will display maximum sincerity and exert utmost efforts in pursuing peaceful reunification, " he assured the TASS reporter.

He also said that Chinese compatriots on Taiwan would hopefully join together to contribute to what he said would be the great rejuvenation of the Chinese nation.

"You know that Mr. Deng Xiaoping formulated that policy with the specific aim of resolving the Taiwan question, and over time we resolved the issues of Hong Kong and Macao, and the 'One Country, Two Systems' principle proved its efficiency precisely in Hong Kong and Macao, and therefore we have confidence that this policy will be a success in Taiwan, too, " Liu concluded.

Army developing amid challenges to defence of sovereignty - China's special representative

有问必答
No Question Unanswered

Liu Xiaoming stressed that China was following a path of peaceful development and pursuing a defence policy based on defending the nation and has always made great contributions to defending global peace, promoting international development and protecting world order.

"The development of the Chinese army in the context of new challenges is aimed precisely at protecting the country's sovereignty and security interests, but, however developed China may become, Beijing will never seek hegemony or expansion, Beijing's special envoy for Korean Peninsula affairs," Liu Xiaoming, told TASS in an interview when asked for comment on Chinese President Xi Jinping's recent instructions to the Chinese People's Liberation Army (PLA) to step up training for real combat operations.

"China's work on its defence posture and efforts to strengthen the Chinese army pursue exclusively defensive aims to protect China's peaceful environment and to allow our country to make new achievements in economic development and improve the well-being of our people. In other words, any growth in China's military strength is growth in the force for global peace, " he said, adding that the Chinese army was actively involved in UN peacekeeping missions in escorting ships in the Gulf of Aden and in other humanitarian operations.

"We are exerting great efforts to provide more public goods for the world in the sphere of security, " Liu added.

"At present, the world faces multiple challenges. Under these circumstances, we need to pay attention to the fact that China has not achieved reunification of the country thus far. The development of the Chinese army is aimed precisely at protecting our sovereignty, territorial integrity, national security and development interests. Let me stress once again: No matter how developed China may become, we will never pursue hegemony or expansion. We will continue to make our contribution to building a world of lasting peace, universal security, common prosperity, openness, inclusivity, and a clean and beautiful environment. " he stressed.

Liu noted that the Chinese president recently "visited the Chinese army's Southern Theater Command and, in his speech there, pointed to the importance of implementing the Communist Party of China's thinking on strengthening the military in the new era, adhering to the military strategy of the new era, intensifying the military's training for real combat operations, accelerating the reform and upgrade of the Chinese army, and resolutely fulfilling the tasks set by the Party and the people."

Liu stressed that China follows a path of peaceful development and pursues a defence policy that is defensive in nature, and had always made great contributions to defending global peace, promoting international development and protecting the world order. He stressed the Chinese people's commitment to peace.

"In the 70-plus years since the establishment of the People's Republic of China, we never provoked a single war or took an inch of other people's land, " Liu said.

Beijing sees military operation with regard to Taiwan as legitimate option - China's envoy

When asked if Beijing considers a special military operation against Taiwan possible, Liu Xiaoming insisted that the Chinese government reserves the right to take all necessary measures to ensure the territorial integrity and sovereignty of the country.

"The question of Taiwan is not a diplomatic issue and is of no concern to outside powers, while all necessary measures are legitimate options for Beijing," China's Special Representative for Korean Peninsula Affairs, Liu Xiaoming, told TASS in an interview.

"You asked about the possibility of resolving this issue by diplomatic means, so I would like to emphasize that the Taiwan question is an internal affair of China. This is not a diplomatic issue. But if you mean a peaceful way when you say 'diplomatic method', then I think that 'One Country, Two Systems' is exactly the plan to resolve this question in a peaceful way, " he said.

When asked if Beijing considers a special military operation against Taiwan possible, Liu Xiaoming said that the Chinese government reserves the right to take all necessary measures to ensure the territorial integrity and sovereignty of the country.

"This is not directed against our compatriots in Taiwan, it is directed against a tiny number of 'Taiwan independence' separatists and other external forces, because their actions violate the Chinese constitution and contravene the Anti-Secession Law. So we will counter these actions in accordance with the law. We will take all necessary measures to protect the sovereignty and territorial integrity of our country. This is our sacred right, " he said.

The diplomat also noted that, among all world powers, China is the only country that has not yet achieved its reunification, so its reunification is the common aspiration of the entire Chinese people, as well as the clear stipulation of the Chinese constitution.

"Peaceful reunification under 'One Country, Two Systems' is a basic policy that is in the interests of the entire Chinese nation, including our Taiwan compatriots. This is a plan of peace, democracy, goodwill and mutual benefit, as well as the most realistic, most tolerant project for resolving the issue of the differing political systems on the two shores of the Taiwan Strait, " he added.

Chinese diplomat says Beijing immediately notified Washington about the balloon

Liu Xiaoming emphasized that Beijing had called on Washington "to be rational, cool-headed and professional" in order to jointly settle this situation, but that the US ignored basic facts and fired a missile to down the balloon.

A senior Chinese diplomat lambasted the recent incident with a Chinese balloon above the United States as a farce on the part of Washington, saying that Beijing notified the Americans as soon as the balloon entered their airspace.

Commenting on the incident in an interview with TASS, Liu Xiaoming, Beijing's Special Representative on Korean Peninsula Affairs said that this civilian airship was used purely for meteorological purposes and that it posed no threat to either the US population or other facilities on US soil. The balloon was brought into the US airspace by westerlies as it deviated from its designated course, Liu maintained. He insisted that the incident had been caused by "force majeure events."

"The incident with the Chinese balloon is, in fact a farce directed by the United States. The Chinese side took a very responsible approach, and it promptly passed the relevant information to the US side and the international community, " he said.

Liu emphasized that Beijing had called on Washington "to be rational, cool-headed and professional" in order to jointly settle this situation, but that the US ignored the basic facts and fired a missile to down the balloon.

"The hysteria bewildered us completely. That was 100% an abuse of military power and a gross violation of relevant international conventions and international practice. This is no proof of US greatness, but quite the opposite. We have already expressed strong protest to the US side and urged them to show sincerity, change their mistaken policies, and squarely recognize and rectify the damage caused by that incident to bilateral relations, " he maintained.

The senior Chinese diplomat warned that Beijing would not sit by and wait if the United States inflated the situation. "It is the United States who is to blame for all the consequences, " he added.

Special envoy highlights China's determination to defend national dignity from US actions

According to Liu Xiaoming, China has always believed that "healthy, stable relations between China and the US benefit not only the people of the two countries but also world peace and prosperity".

Beijing is determined to vigorously defend its sovereignty and national dignity from the actions of the United States, Liu Xiaoming, Beijing's Special Representative for Korean Peninsula Affairs said in an interview with TASS.

" President Xi Jinping outlined the main principles for building relations with the US, which include mutual respect, peaceful co-existence and win-win cooperation. We are willing to build good relations with the US based on these principles, " the Chinese special envoy noted. "However, should our sovereignty, national dignity and territorial integrity be violated, we will firmly defend our sovereignty, security and development interests, " he added.

"Unfortunately, the US views China as its primary rival and the biggest geopolitical challenge, " he went on to say. "Their perception and definition of China are seriously mistaken. They chose an erroneous strategy towards China, which is summed up in three words: invest, align and compete. "

According to Liu, China has always believed that "healthy, stable relations between China and the US benefit not only the people of the two countries but also world peace and prosperity. "

"President Xi Jinping pointed out that whether China and the US can manage their relations well bears on the future of the world. Getting the relationship right is not optional, but something we must do and must do well, " the Chinese special envoy concluded.

鲁健访谈·对话刘晓明

Interview with Lu Jian

《鲁健访谈》是中央广播电视总台高端人物访谈节目，由鲁健担任主持人，节目时长30分钟。这是央视唯一以主持人冠名的节目，旨在打造高端访谈品牌，提升国际传播影响力。据鲁健讲，自从《鲁健访谈》两年前开播以来，他一直想对我做一个专访，谈谈我的外交生涯，包括我的个人经历和家庭生活。我曾表示，我在任期间只接受关于外交工作的采访，不接受关于个人和家庭的访谈。我卸任驻英大使后，鲁健和他的团队很快联系上我，再次提出采访要求。这次我答应了。他们对采访做了大量功课，准备了一大堆问题。采访那天，我们聊了整整3个小时，可以说天南海北，无所不谈。从英国的茶道谈到英国的电视采访，从我应对英国媒体的"三套武器"谈到英国的"新闻自由"，从中英关系谈到美英关系，从西方的傲慢与偏见谈到东方的理智与情感，从"战狼外交"谈到国际话语权，从朝鲜情结谈到半岛使命，从外交生涯谈到外交官的牺牲奉献，从讲好中国故事谈到外交工作薪火相传。最后3个小时采访编辑成30分钟访谈，于2023年5月26日在央视4频道向海内外播出。

💬 《鲁健访谈·对话刘晓明》

——接受中央广播电视总台《鲁健访谈》栏目主持人鲁健专访
（2023年5月26日，北京）

鲁　健：　您尝尝这个茶，这个茶还挺好。您在英国这11年，平时喝茶多，还是喝咖啡多？

刘晓明：　都喝，总体来讲，还是喝茶喝得多。英国人对茶是情有独钟的，你别看英国不产茶，但是人均喝茶量是全世界第一。英国有一句俗语叫"当钟敲响四下，一切为茶而停止"，四下就是下午4点，喝茶雷打不动。

鲁　健：　喝茶聊天那个气氛就非常轻松了。我看您在英国期间还接受了170多场采访，其中将近30场的电视直播的采访，就是那种言辞激烈、唇枪舌剑，跟这个喝茶那是完全不一样。

刘晓明：　那肯定不一样。

鲁　健：　没茶喝对吧。

刘晓明：　给你一杯水喝就不错了。

鲁健： 其实有些时候，第一次的尝试对于每个人来讲都不容易。那您第一次在西方媒体接受访谈，是什么时候？

刘晓明： 你是指的第一次接受电视采访？

鲁健： 对，电视直播的采访。

刘晓明： 我记得很清楚，是2012年1月23日，是我们大年初一，接受杰里米·帕克斯曼——《新闻之夜》主持人的采访。帕克斯曼号称是英国最犀利、最刁钻的主持人。他来请我上这个访谈节目，说没有什么别的主题，就想跟刘大使聊聊，刘大使到英国一段时间了。我当时研究了他的背景，知道这家伙不好对付，是个"横主儿"，但是你也不能回避，所以我也接受了他的挑战。

第一次应该说多少有点紧张，但是我觉得，我身后有强大的祖国，我们中国的发展有很多的故事可以讲，所以我有足够的自信和底气，准备这场采访。

鲁健： 第一次上电视直播，即便是用自己的母语去应对，恐怕也会有忐忑不安的感觉，何况您是用英语、用对方的语言来接受采访。那您会做什么样的刻意的准备？

刘晓明： 准备是必须的。我经常讲，不打无准备之仗。不要说我们中国外交官上英国的电视台，要讲英语，就是很多被称为西方沟通大师的这些人，克林顿、布莱尔。我看过他们的回忆录，上台之前，都是进行认真彩排，把他们的助手、军师叫到一块，设想各种刁钻的问题。

鲁健： 您也有军师吗？

刘晓明： 我的军师就是我们各个处室的负责人。我们大家在一块群策群力，我们设想各种问题，各种刁钻的问题，进行"战前"的准备。

鲁健： 他们很善于挖各种各样的"坑"，那您印象最深的"坑"是哪一次？

刘晓明： 我觉得给我留下最深印象的就是第一次上BBC《新闻之夜》的直播采访，也是跟杰里米·帕克斯曼过招。第一句上来就是"你是共产党吗"，我想他的目的不是验证我的身份。因为那一段时间，在西方媒体不断出现"共产党中国"的说法。杰里米·帕克斯曼一上来就问这个问题。其实我一直在找机会，要为我们共产党正名，要为中国正名，我就抓住这个机会。我说中国是共产党领导的国家，但是你不能把中国说成是"共产党中国"，就像现在英国是保守党领导的英国，你不能说"保守党英国"一样，他马上认可这个说法。

鲁健： 对于这些他们惯于用到的套路和策略，您能够适应吗？

刘晓明： 我觉得跟他们进行博弈，你就应该做一个头脑冷静的斗牛士，而不是被轻易激怒的公牛。我不是把他看作对手，而是看作对话，通过这种对话能够跟他进行沟通，增进他们对中国的了解。我看重的是他背后的听众和读者，我是跟西方民众在对话。

我有三套"武器"。现在实际上是已经发展到高科技导弹时代，但是我把它比喻成冷兵器。第一是长矛，就是主动进攻，我必须有成套的东西，宣介我们中国的内外政策。第二，我还要准备盾牌，就是我们说要准备他挖各种"坑"，准备他扔各种手榴弹，抵挡他各种刁钻问题。第三，我还有匕首，就是说进行反击，最好的防御是进攻。

鲁健： 为什么一定要去面对这个挑战呢？其实这种挑战是有一定的风险的。

刘晓明： 对，风险跟收获总是成正比。电视直播的优势，第一，时效快，很多突发事件，媒体提出来了要采访你，你上不上？我们选择上，就可以在第一时间发出中国声音，第一时间揭穿谎言，批驳谬论。第二，我就觉得电视直播就是直观、生动、受众广、影响大。一个最典型的例子就是2020年4月份，新冠肺炎疫情发生一段时间了，当时西方充斥着谣言，特别是以美国为主的西方势力散布各种谣言，阴谋论啊，"中国病毒"啊，我就接受了《尖锐对话》主持人萨克的采访。那次谈得比较透彻，传播也广。首先是BBC（英国广播公司）现场直播，接着是在英国国内重播两次，这就三次了，然后在全球播放五次，萨克的制片人告诉我们，说刘大使这次接受采访，受众200个国家4亿观众。

鲁健： 有没有遇到过报纸拒绝发表您的文章？

刘晓明： 当然有，被拒绝过。这种情况主要是2020年以后，特别是香港黑暴事件发生之后，英国由于它的历史原因，对香港有一种特殊的情结。一些报刊编辑部的总编就明确说，我们只能登对"一国两制"提出质疑的文章。我说你这个报纸太偏了，你听不到中国方面的声音嘛。它可以登很多别的文章，甚至彭定康的文章，但是中国代表的文章它不登。

鲁健： 就拒绝给您发声的平台。

刘晓明： 对，我觉得它这个所谓的新闻自由在这个时候显得非常苍白。

鲁健： 那您从内心来讲有没有答案？就是为什么好像英国的媒体、政界有些时候确实很难放下这种傲慢与偏见？

刘晓明： 主要还是它这个"西方中心论"作怪，他们总是俯视发展中国家。他们的国力在逐渐地走下坡路，但却总是不能摆正自己的心态。我觉得也是一种缺乏自信，特别是对中国的崛起、对中国的发展不能够正确地解读，老觉得中国构成了一种挑战和威胁。

我在接受采访的时候，艾斯勒还曾经问过，就是BBC的《新闻之夜》主持人，他引用了英国著名作家吉卜林的一句话，说"东方与西方永远无法完全理解对方"。他问，"刘大使，您怎么看"。我就讲，我觉得中国对西方的情况了解得更多一些，而西方对中国的了解不够。他问，那这是什么原因呢？我说西方对中国应该少一些傲慢与偏见，多一些理智与情感。

鲁健： 2022年9月，您作为中国政府代表团的成员参加了英女王的葬礼，那现在卸任驻英大使两年之后，您现在最关注的英国政坛的变化是什么？

刘晓明： 我最关心的当然还是中英关系了。中英关系这几年确实出现了比较大的变化，英国原来把中国看作机遇，现在把中国看作挑战。

鲁健： 那您觉得到底是什么样的原因造成英国对华政策发生这样的一种非常大的改变？

刘晓明： 我觉得这几年国际上发生了很多事情，中英之间也发生了很多事情，比较大的事件就是香港。过去我们签署了《中英联合声明》，顺利解决了香港回归问题。随着香港的回归，香港成为中英关系的积极因素，但是从2019年"修例风波"以后，英国越来越深地插手香港事务。

我们一贯主张发展两国关系的准则和基础，是相互尊重，求同存异，互不干涉内政，但是英国干涉了中国内政，这必然会引起中国坚决反对。所以我说由于中英关系的基础受到了损害，必然会反映到中英关系的各个方面。

鲁健： 所以，华为5G进入英国市场也是一个例证，英国对华为5G政策也发生了180度的大转变，那您觉得英国现在对华政策是不是很大程度上也受到美国政策的影响？

刘晓明： 对，一方面确实有美国的压力，美国出于它自己的私利，调动它的盟友，打压中国的公司，围堵中国。但是英国自己内部也发生了变化，英国对中国的认知也出现了偏差，越来越不适应中国的发展，把中国的发展看作是挑战。

鲁健： 说到英美关系就有一个词，叫"特殊关系"，就是这种关系是不是也使得英国在外交上有些时候难免要跟着美国走？

刘晓明： 我觉得这个"特殊关系"呢，这是历史形成的。主要是"二战"时期，丘吉尔跟罗斯福他们使两国形成了这种盟国关系，然后两国一直保持这样密切的关系。那么到了今天，这个"特殊关系"到底怎么样，我觉得，这个让英国人自己去讲是最有说服力的。你要问一些英国人，英国人相反觉得受到美国的压力，英国人自己心里也是很不舒服的。有的人说，"特殊关系"已经名存实亡了。所以我觉得这种关系，我们不去过多地评论。我更关心的是，英美"特殊关系"不要影响中英关系，我们并不要求英国在中美之间选边站队，但是我希望英国能够站在正确的一边，站在正义的一边。

如果你完全都是yes-man（"好好先生"），都是跟着美国走，"随美起舞"，在中美发生冲突的时候，你根本不假思索盲目跟随美国，损害的是你自己的利益。

鲁健： 我们也看到这些年来一些西方的政客还有西方的媒体，不断地给中国贴标签，什么"霸凌外交""胁迫外交""战狼外交"等等，您觉得这个对于我们外交官来讲，做工作是不是会造成很大的困难和挑战？

刘晓明： 他们是想给我们制造困难，给我们贴标签，但是我觉得最后都是徒劳的。首先，这恰恰说明我们的影响越来越大，中国的外交影响越来越大，所以他们就使用各种污名化、妖魔化的手段，来贬低和削弱我们的影响。其次，我觉得他们过去总认为自己把握着话语权，不能够接受中国国际话语权在不断提升，他们对中国义正词严、理直气壮地捍卫自己主权、安全、发展利益，维护自己的形象跟尊严很不适应，所以就给你冠上"战狼外交""霸凌外交"。

鲁健： 包括您本人不是也被贴"战狼鼻祖"这样的标签和称号嘛，您本人对这样的称号是什么样的态度？

刘晓明： 我当然是拒绝这种所谓的"战狼鼻祖"，我对这个不感兴趣。我觉得我们外交官上电视也好，去发表演讲也好，我强调我是要进行对话，把辩论变成对话，把每一场对话都变成一个讲好中国故事的机会。当你面对各种谣言，你必须进行批驳，你只有揭穿谎言，才能够说明真相。

鲁健： 我看到前段时间，您是作为中国政府朝鲜半岛事务特别代表出访了欧洲多国。您也曾经担任过中国驻朝大使，而且您是志愿军的后代，那您跟朝鲜应该有非常深厚的渊源。

刘晓明： 我一岁半的时候，曾经随着我母亲去志愿军在桧仓的总部探望我的父亲，那么后来我出任了驻朝大使，现在又做朝鲜半岛事务特别代表，我对这片土地充满了感情，所以我对我现在担任的工作更有一种强烈的责任感和使命感。

鲁健： 几十年的外交生涯，我知道您的足迹遍布美洲、欧洲、亚洲、非洲，而且外交官好像这些年来应该是和家人聚少离多，这是外交官的一个工作和生活的常态吗？

刘晓明： 这应该说是一个常态，也是外交官为祖国的外交事业做出的牺牲。我们外交官呢，对过去说的"自古忠孝两难全"是深有体会的。明年我就从事外交工作50年了，将近30年时间驻外。在英国常驻期间，我母亲病危，我跟她通了话，我说这次我一定要赶回去，但是在我通话后两个小时，我的侄儿——我弟弟的孩子给我发了一个短信，说奶奶走了，我悲痛欲绝，立刻请假返回国内。我跟母亲的遗体告别，这次算是见了一面，但是母亲已经走了。
所以我也是要向我们千千万万个外交官的亲属和家人表示衷心的感谢，有他们的支持，我们才能浑身充满力量。

鲁健： 您20世纪70年代投身外交事业，马上就要满50年了，接下来在外交领域还有哪些能继续作为的呢？

刘晓明： 我去年出了两本书，《尖锐对话》和《大使讲中国故事》。这两本书提到，要讲好中国故事。我觉得这项任务还是任重道远。我想讲好中国故事，不光是领导的事，也不仅仅是外交官的事，而是每一个中国人的事。我觉得每一个中国人在国外，不论你是留学、经商、旅游，你都是中国形象的代言人，人家从你的身上就看到今天的中国，所以我愿意跟广大民众、读者分享我讲好中国故事的经验和体会。

我还需要做的工作，就是为培养年轻外交官尽一份责任，这样使我们的外交工作薪火相传，蓬勃发展。

鲁健： 现在可能也有很多的年轻人奋战在外交领域，您觉得作为外交官，最核心的本领到底是什么？比如说是他的语言能力？思辨能力？还是他的勇敢？忠诚？

刘晓明： 我觉得外交官最根本的本领就是信念。你看我在采访的时候多次提到自信、底气、担当，都是有坚定的信念。我们新中国外交队伍是周总理带出来的，他曾经对外交人员提出十六字方针："站稳立场，掌握政策，熟悉业务，严守纪律。"这十六字方针一直被继承到今天，形成了中国外交队伍的优良传统。

后记

《有问必答》终于杀青。可以说，它是《尖锐对话》的姊妹篇。《尖锐对话》出版后受到广泛好评，被《人民日报》"金台好书榜"列为"十大好书"，入选《出版业"十四五"时期发展规划》，多次在京东外交国际关系图书排行榜名列第一。《有问必答》与《尖锐对话》有相同之处，都是与西方媒体和民众对话交流，但也有不同之处。《尖锐对话》唇枪舌剑，短兵相接，很难展开讨论问题；《有问必答》则有更从容的时间、更大的舞台、更广阔的空间。

"有问必答"可以说是一种原则，可以说是一种责任，也可以说是一种境界。对记者和听众的提问，特别是敏感问题，你可以"有问不答"，也可以"有问少答"。但我坚持"有问必答"，努力化解误解和偏见。"有问必答"的英文是"Leave No Question Unanswered"，可直译为"不留下任何没有回答的问题"。这是我的原则，也是我的责任。每次记者会、每次演讲，我都让记者和听众放开提问，直到回答完最后一位举手的提问者，不留遗憾。这种答问方式不仅体现对提问者的尊重，也可以赢得对方的尊重，拉近演讲者与听众的距离，增强感染力和亲和感，努力达到不仅"听得到"，而且"听得懂"、"听得进"，进而"听而信"的境界。

虽然我们已经进入信息时代，但让世界听到中国声音仍任重道远。党的二十大报告提出，要加强国际传播能力建设，全面提升国际传播效能，形成同我国综合国力和国际地位相匹配的国际话语权。习近平总书记指出，讲好中国故事，传播好中国声音，展示真实、立体、全面的中国，是加强我国国际传播能力建设的重要任务。为此，我们要更加积极主动地讲中国故事，不仅能讲中国故事，而且会讲中国故事，讲好中国故事；不仅"有问必答"，而且"有问会答"，"有问妙答"。

在此，我要感谢北京出版集团董事长张爱军，董事、副总经理周浩，原副总经理赵安良，主题分公司总经理王曷灵、特邀译审艾玫子和责任编辑马群。他们的支持特别是编辑和出版团队的高效工作，使本书的在较短时间顺利出版。我还要感谢外交部的同事陈雯、曾嵘和冯家亮，他们参与了本书的核稿和校对，并提出宝贵意见。

2024年春分